Windows® 10
Tips and Tricks

Guy Hart-Davis

800 East 96th Street,
Indianapolis, Indiana 46240 USA

WINDOWS® 10 TIPS AND TRICKS

COPYRIGHT © 2016 BY PEARSON EDUCATION

ISBN-13: 978-0-7897-5565-0
ISBN-10: 0-7897-5565-3

Library of Congress Control Number: 2015946733

Printed in the United States of America

First Printing: November 2015

TRADEMARKS

WARNING AND DISCLAIMER

SPECIAL SALES

For information about buying this title in bulk quantities, or for special sales opportunities (which may include electronic versions; custom cover designs; and content particular to your business, training goals, marketing focus, or branding interests), please contact our corporate sales department at corpsales@pearsoned.com or (800) 382-3419.

For government sales inquiries, please contact governmentsales@pearsoned.com.

For questions about sales outside the U.S., please contact international@pearsoned.com.

EDITOR-IN-CHIEF
Greg Wiegand

ACQUISITIONS EDITOR
Michelle Newcomb

DEVELOPMENT EDITOR
Joyce Nielsen

MANAGING EDITOR
Kristy Hart

SENIOR PROJECT EDITOR
Betsy Gratner

COPY EDITOR
Cheri Clark

INDEXER
Lisa Stumpf

PROOFREADER
Leslie Joseph

TECHNICAL EDITOR
Vince Averello

EDITORIAL ASSISTANT
Cindy Teeters

COVER DESIGNER
Mark Shirar

COMPOSITOR
Nonie Ratcliff

CONTENTS AT A GLANCE

Introduction 1

1 Setting Up Windows 5

2 Navigating Windows Like a Pro 29

3 Connecting to Networks and the Internet 61

4 Connecting External Hardware 99

5 Customizing Windows to Suit Your Needs 121

6 Sorting Out Your Files, Folders, and Storage 143

7 Securing and Sharing Your Computer 181

8 Optimizing Your Computer's Performance 211

9 Installing, Running, and Managing Apps 245

10 Enjoying Music, Photos, and Videos 279

11 Browsing the Internet Safely 309

12 Communicating via Email and Skype 331

13 Updating and Troubleshooting Windows 373

14 Going Further with Advanced Moves 405

Index 437

TABLE OF CONTENTS

Introduction 1
What Does This Book Cover? 1
What Do I Need to Know to Get Started? 3

1 Setting Up Windows 5
Starting the Installation 5
Choosing Between an Upgrade and a Custom Installation 6
Choosing the Drive and Partition for a Custom Installation 7
Making the Right Choices on the Setup Screens 10
  Choosing Between Using Default Settings and Configuring
    Windows Manually 10
  Choosing Personalization and Location Settings 13
  Choosing Browser, Protection, Connectivity, and Error Reporting
    Settings 14
  Working on the Who Owns This PC? Screen 15
  Working on the Make It Yours Screen 16
  Setting a PIN and Meeting Cortana 17
  Working on the Create an Account for This PC Screen 17
  Working in the Networks Pane 20
Signing In and Out of Windows 21
Locking Windows 22
Restarting Windows 22
Putting Your Computer to Sleep or into Hibernation 22
Configuring and Using Cortana 25
  Configuring Cortana 25
  Searching with Cortana 27
Shutting Down Your Computer 28

2 Navigating Windows Like a Pro 29
Using the Start Menu 29
  Opening the Start Menu 30
  Getting Around the Start Menu 30
Tweaking Your Input Devices 31
  Adjusting the Mouse or Touchpad 32
  Choosing the Right Pen and Touch Settings 38

Configuring Pen and Touch Input 42
Configuring Your Keyboard 43
Configuring Typing Settings 44
Configuring Your Language and Keyboard Layout 46
Setting Up Speech Recognition 48

Inputting Text 50
Inputting Text with a Hardware Keyboard 50
Inputting Text with the Touch Keyboard and the Handwriting
    Panel 51
Inputting Text via Speech Recognition 54

Resizing and Arranging Windows 55
Resizing and Closing Windows with the Command Buttons 55
Using Snap and Snap Assist 56
Arranging Windows Manually 57
Resizing, Arranging, and Closing Windows with Keyboard
    Shortcuts 58
Switching Among Open Windows 58

3 Connecting to Networks and the Internet 61
Connecting to a Wired Network 62

Connecting to a Wireless Network 63
Connecting to a Wireless Network That Broadcasts Its Name ... 64
Connecting to a Hidden Wireless Network 67
Disconnecting from and Reconnecting to Wireless Networks ... 70
Whitelisting Your Device on a Wi-Fi Network 70

Managing Your Network Connections 71
Using Airplane Mode and Turning Off Wireless Devices 71
Configuring IP Settings Manually 72
Connecting Through a Proxy Server 78
Prioritizing One Network Connection over Another 81
Bridging Two or More Network Connections 82
Improving Wireless Speed and Reliability 84
Forgetting a Wireless Network 87

Connecting Through a VPN 88
Setting Up a VPN Connection 88
Connecting via the VPN 90

Mapping a Drive to a Network Folder 91

Sharing Your Computer's Internet Connection 94

Diagnosing and Repairing Network Problems 95
   Determining Whether a Problem Has Occurred 96
   Using the Troubleshoot Problems Feature 97

4 Connecting External Hardware 99
   Connecting External Drives 99
      Making the Physical Connection 99
      Formatting a Drive 100
      Configuring an External Drive for Better Performance 102
      Ejecting an External Drive 104
   Sorting Out Your Displays 104
      Connecting a Display 105
      Opening the Display Pane in Settings 105
      Choosing Essential Display Settings 106
      Choosing Advanced Display Settings 107
   Using Virtual Desktops 111
   Setting Up Your Printers 112
      Connecting a Local Printer 113
      Connecting a Network Printer 113
      Configuring Your Printer 114

5 Customizing Windows to Suit Your Needs 121
   Customizing the Start Menu 122
      Choosing Which Categories of Items to Display on the Start Menu 122
      Customizing the Start Menu Directly 124
   Customizing the Taskbar 125
      Moving and Resizing the Taskbar 126
      Configuring the Taskbar's Behavior 126
      Putting the Apps You Need Most on the Taskbar 128
      Making the Most of Taskbar Toolbars 128
      Choosing Which Icons to Display in the Notification Area 130
   Saving Time with Automatic Login—and Why You Shouldn't 133
   Making the Lock Screen Show the Information You Need 135
      Displaying the Lock Screen Pane 135
      Setting the Picture or Slideshow 135
      Adding Apps to the Lock Screen for Quick Reference 136
   Making the Recycle Bin Work the Way You Prefer 137
   Telling Windows Which Notifications You Want to Receive 139
      Opening the Notifications & Actions Pane 140
      Choosing Essential Notifications Settings 140

6 Sorting Out Your Files, Folders, and Storage 143

Navigating File Explorer Quickly and Efficiently 144

Opening a File Explorer Window 144

Putting Useful Buttons on the Quick Access Toolbar 144

Using the File Menu 146

Finding Your Way Around the Ribbon 147

Customizing How File Explorer Looks and Works 148

Changing the Layout 149

Customizing the Quick Access View 150

Choosing How to Lay Out the Items 150

Sorting and Grouping Items 151

Choosing Which Items to Show and Which to Hide 152

Adjusting Folder and Search Options 152

Finding the Files and Folders You Need 162

Using Libraries and Folders the Smart Way 163

Coming to Grips with the Default Libraries 164

Creating a New Library 165

Including Folders in Your Library 166

Setting the Library's Default Save Location and Public Save
Location 167

Configuring the Library to Work Your Way 168

Restoring Your Default Libraries 169

Managing Your Storage 170

Seeing What's Taking Up Space on Your Computer 170

Controlling Where Windows Saves Games, Apps, Music, and
Other Items 174

Creating Pooled Storage with Storage Spaces 175

Understanding Simple Spaces, Mirror Spaces, and Parity Spaces 175

Creating a Storage Space 176

Using the Storage Space 179

Changing an Existing Storage Space 180

Deleting a Storage Space 180

7 Securing and Sharing Your Computer 181

Configuring Accounts for Practicality and Security 182

Setting Your Profile Picture 182

Connecting a Local Account to a Microsoft Account 182

Securing Your Account with a Password, Picture Password,
PIN, or Windows Hello 184

Creating Accounts for Others 186

Tightening Your Computer's Security 189
   Locking Your Computer with a Startup Password 189
   Setting Your Computer to Lock Automatically 192
   Increasing Login Security with Secure Sign-In 193
   Configuring User Account Control 194
   Controlling Recent App Switching 197
   Setting Up Assigned Access 199

Configuring Sharing 200
   Sharing via a Homegroup 200
   Using Advanced Sharing 205

8 Optimizing Your Computer's Performance 211
Adding Memory If You Can 212
Turning Off Eye Candy to Boost Performance 214
Configuring the Paging File 217
Controlling Data Execution Prevention 221
Stopping Unnecessary Services 222
Turning Off Superfetch and Prefetch 227
   Turning Off Superfetch 227
   Turning Off Prefetch 227
Reducing the Number of Startup Items 229
Optimizing and Defragmenting Your Computer's Hard Drive 231
   Checking Free Space and Opening the Optimize Drives Window 231
   Analyzing and Optimizing a Drive 233
   Choosing Settings for Scheduled Optimization 234
Getting Rid of Useless Apps 235
Extending Runtime on the Battery 237
   Setting a Sensible Power Plan 237
   Using Airplane Mode and Turning Off Wi-Fi or Bluetooth 242
   Avoiding Power-Hungry Apps 242
Choosing Settings for Playing Games 242

9 Installing, Running, and Managing Apps 245
Getting the Apps You Need 245
   Getting Apps from the Store 246
   Getting and Installing Apps from Other Sources 252
Managing the Apps You're Running 261
   Closing an App That Stops Responding 261
   Going Further with Other Actions in Task Manager 262

Removing Unwanted Apps 271

Setting the Default Apps You Need 272
    Opening the Default Apps Pane in the Settings App 273
    Choosing Your Default Apps 274
    Choosing Default Apps by File Types or by Protocols 274
    Choosing Default Apps by Apps 274
    Opening a File in a Non-Default App and Changing the
       Default App 276

10   Enjoying Music, Photos, and Videos 279
   Understanding Windows Media Player and Groove Music 279

   Using Windows Media Player 280
    Setting Up Windows Media Player to Protect Your Privacy 280
    Navigating Windows Media Player 284
    Adding Your Music to Windows Media Player 286
    Playing Music with Windows Media Player 295
    Syncing Music with Your Phone or Tablet 295
    Importing Photos and Videos Using Windows Media Player 297
    Sharing Media Libraries 297

   Exploring the Groove Music App and the Groove Service 302
    Getting Started with Groove Music 302
    Adding Music to Your Groove Music Collection 304
    Playing Music with Groove Music 306
    Creating Playlists in Groove Music 306

   Watching Videos and DVDs 307

11   Browsing the Internet Safely 309
   Navigating Microsoft Edge Like a Pro 309
    Viewing Pages 312
    Working with Tabs and Windows 313
    Browsing Fast with Page Prediction 314
    Copying Text with Caret Browsing 315
    Removing Distractions with Reading Mode 315
    Browsing the Smart Way with Favorites 315
    Returning to Pages You Viewed Earlier 316
    Catching Up with Your Reading List 317

   Annotating Web Pages with Web Note 318

   Controlling Microsoft Edge with Keyboard Shortcuts 320

   Configuring Microsoft Edge for Comfort and Security 321
    Configuring General Settings 321
    Configuring Essential Advanced Settings 323

Configuring Privacy and Services Settings 325

Clearing Your Browsing Data 327

12   Communicating via Email and Skype 331

Communicating via Email 331

Setting Up Your Email Accounts 332

Navigating in the Mail App 343

Configuring Your Email Accounts and the Mail App 348

Communicating via Skype 354

Getting the Skype App 354

Completing the Initial Setup Routine 356

Navigating the Skype Screen 357

Communicating via Skype 359

Configuring Skype to Work Your Way 360

Configuring Keyboard Shortcuts on the Hotkeys Screen 369

Choosing Options on the Accessibility Screen 370

Saving Your Configuration Changes 371

13   Updating and Troubleshooting Windows 373

Making Windows Update Work Your Way 374

Configuring Windows Update 374

Applying an Update 377

Backing Up Key Files with File History 378

Enabling File History 379

Using History to Restore Files 381

Resolving Issues in Action Center 382

Reviewing Security and Maintenance Issues 384

Creating and Using System Restore Points 386

Creating System Restore Points 386

Restoring Windows to a System Restore Point 389

Undoing a System Restore Operation 393

Solving Problems with the Recovery Tools 395

Accessing the Recovery Tools 395

Resetting Your PC 396

Going Back to an Earlier Build of Windows 397

Using the Advanced Startup Tools 398

14 Going Further with Advanced Moves 405

Working with Partitions 405

Examining the Partitions on Your Computer's Drive 406

Shrinking a Partition 409

Creating a New Partition 410

Extending a Partition 413

Deleting a Partition 414

Running Multiple Operating Systems on Your Computer 416

Dual-Booting or Multi-Booting Windows with Another Operating System 416

Installing and Running Other Operating Systems with Hyper-V 419

Installing and Running Other Operating Systems with Third-Party Virtual-Machine Software 430

Making Advanced Changes by Editing the Registry 430

Opening Registry Editor and Navigating Its Interface 431

Understanding What's What in the Registry 432

Backing Up and Restoring the Registry 433

An Example: Removing an App from the Open With Submenu in File Explorer 435

Index 437

ABOUT THE AUTHOR

Guy Hart-Davis is the author of *Android Tips and Tricks* and more than 100 other computer books.

DEDICATION

I dedicate this book to my son, Edward, who builds Windows computers and tests them to destruction.

ACKNOWLEDGMENTS

My thanks go to the people whose hard work helped create this book you're reading. In particular, I'd like to thank the following people:

- Michelle Newcomb for asking me to write the book
- Joyce Nielsen for developing the outline and suggesting many improvements
- Cheri Clark for editing the manuscript with care and skill
- Betsy Gratner for coordinating the book project and keeping it moving
- Vince Averello for reviewing the manuscript for technical accuracy and contributing suggestions for improving the book
- Leslie Joseph for proofreading the book
- Lisa Stumpf for creating the index

WE WANT TO HEAR FROM YOU!

As the reader of this book, *you* are our most important critic and commentator. We value your opinion and want to know what we're doing right, what we could do better, what areas you'd like to see us publish in, and any other words of wisdom you're willing to pass our way.

We welcome your comments. You can email or write to let us know what you did or didn't like about this book—as well as what we can do to make our books better.

Please note that we cannot help you with technical problems related to the topic of this book.

When you write, please be sure to include this book's title and author as well as your name and email address. We will carefully review your comments and share them with the author and editors who worked on the book.

Email: feedback@quepublishing.com

Mail: Que Publishing
              ATTN: Reader Feedback
              800 East 96th Street
              Indianapolis, IN 46240 USA

READER SERVICES

Register your copy of *Windows 10 Tips and Tricks* at informit.com for convenient access to downloads, updates, and corrections as they become available. To start the registration process, go to informit.com/register and log in or create an account.* Enter the product ISBN, 9780789755650, and click submit. Once the process is complete, you will find any available bonus content under "Registered Products."

*Be sure to check the box that you would like to hear from us in order to receive exclusive discounts on future editions of this product.

Introduction

Windows 10 is a major upgrade to Windows, packed with powerful and time-saving new features—not to mention reintroducing the Start menu that Microsoft axed in Windows 8.

This book shows you how to get the most out of Windows 10 and your computer, whether it's a desktop, a laptop, a tablet, or one of those convertible tablets—you know, the ones to which you can attach a keyboard to create a part-time laptop.

WHAT DOES THIS BOOK COVER?

This book contains 14 chapters that cover essential Windows topics. Here are the details:

■ Chapter 1, "Setting Up Windows," shows you how to set up Windows on your computer. You learn how to choose between an upgrade to Windows 10 and a custom installation of the operating system; how to make the right choices for your needs on the setup screens; and how to perform essential moves such as

signing in and out, locking Windows, and shutting down or restarting your computer.

■ Chapter 2, "Navigating Windows Like a Pro," teaches you how to make your way around swiftly and surely in Windows. First, you come to grips with the redesigned Start menu. After that, you learn to fine-tune your input devices so that they work the way you prefer, use those devices to input text quickly and accurately, and resize and arrange your windows on the screen.

■ Chapter 3, "Connecting to Networks and the Internet," shows you how to connect your computer to a wired network or to a wireless network, how to access network folders, and how to deal with network problems. You also learn how to connect your computer to a virtual private network, or VPN, in order to establish a secure connection to a server across the Internet, and how to share your computer's Internet connection with others if necessary.

■ Chapter 4, "Connecting External Hardware," explains how to connect extra drives to your computer to give it more storage capacity, how to set up multiple monitors and virtual desktops to give yourself more work space, and how to set up printers for when you need hard-copy output.

■ Chapter 5, "Customizing Windows to Suit Your Needs," starts by digging into the ways you can customize the Start menu and the taskbar to make these essential features work the way you prefer. After that, you learn to set up automatic login if you want it, how to customize the lock screen to show the information you find most useful on it, how to make the Recycle Bin work your way, and how to take control of notifications so that Windows doesn't bombard you with useless news when you're craving quiet.

■ Chapter 6, "Sorting Out Your Files, Folders, and Storage," teaches you to use the File Explorer file-management app like a pro and customize it so that it works however suits you best. You learn to exploit the powerful file libraries—such as the Music library and the Pictures library—instead of merely creating hierarchies of folders, plus how to manage your computer's storage.

■ Chapter 7, "Securing and Sharing Your Computer," starts by showing you how to configure your user account and your unlock methods (such as a password and PIN) for your computer. The chapter then explains how to implement several security mechanisms—applying a startup password, setting your computer to lock automatically, and implementing the Secure Sign-In feature—before telling you how to share items with others via either the easy-to-use homegroup feature or Advanced Sharing.

■ Chapter 8, "Optimizing Your Computer's Performance," teaches you how to improve your computer's performance by taking steps such as adding memory, turning off unnecessary visual effects, and configuring advanced features and services. You also learn how to defragment and optimize your computer's drive, how to extend a portable computer's runtime on its battery, and how to improve performance when running games.

- Chapter 9, "Installing, Running, and Managing Apps," tackles the vital subject of apps (also called programs). You learn to install apps on your computer, manage the apps installed there, and remove apps you no longer need. You also learn how to choose your default apps for opening files.

- Chapter 10, "Enjoying Music, Photos, and Videos," shows you how to set up Windows Media Player without compromising your privacy, how to put your existing music on your computer, and how to watch videos and DVDs. This chapter also introduces you to the Groove Music app and the Groove music service.

- Chapter 11, "Browsing the Internet Safely," explains how to browse the Internet using Microsoft Edge, the new browser that is included with Windows 10. You learn how to control Microsoft Edge with the mouse or with keyboard shortcuts and how to configure it to suit your needs.

- Chapter 12, "Communicating via Email and Skype," shows you how to set up your email accounts in the Mail app and how to use Mail to send, receive, and manage email messages. You then learn to install and set up Skype, configure the most important of its many settings, and use it to communicate with your contacts across the Internet.

- Chapter 13, "Updating and Troubleshooting Windows," walks you through configuring the Windows Update feature and using it to keep Windows up-to-date. The chapter then shows you how to set up the File History tool to back up your essential files to an external drive—and how to recover them from there when you need to. You also learn to use the System Restore feature to protect and restore your computer's configuration and how to sort out serious problems by using the recovery tools.

- Chapter 14, "Going Further with Advanced Moves," explains how to split a physical drive into multiple partitions and how to manage your drive partitions; how to run multiple operating systems on your computer; and how to make changes in the Registry, the vital configuration database of Windows.

WHAT DO I NEED TO KNOW TO GET STARTED?

To get started, all you need is a basic working knowledge of your computer and Windows. If you know how to start your computer; how to use the keyboard and mouse, or other pointing device, or touchscreen; and how to launch apps and create documents, you're ready to get started with this book.

This isn't a huge book, so it can't show you screenshots of everything it covers—you'll see just the most important screens. But you'll find that the text instructions, with those screens, are pretty easy to follow.

As usual, the key information is in the main text. But this book also uses four types of special elements to present extra information and draw your attention to it: notes, tips, cautions, and sidebars.

NOTE A note provides extra information that you may find helpful for understanding a topic.

TIP A tip gives you additional information for making a decision or accomplishing a task.

CAUTION A caution warns you about a trap, pitfall, or danger you likely want to avoid.

SIDEBARS PRESENT IN-DEPTH INFORMATION

A sidebar presents in-depth extra information about a topic—like a note or a tip on steroids and with a heading.

That's more than enough introduction. Turn the page, and we'll get started.

IN THIS CHAPTER

■ Choosing between an upgrade
  and a custom installation

■ Making the right choices on the
  setup screens

■ Signing in and out, locking and
  restarting Windows, using sleep
  and hibernation, and shutting
  down

SETTING UP WINDOWS

This chapter shows you how to set up Windows 10 on your computer. You learn how to choose between an upgrade and a custom installation, if applicable; how to make the right choices for your needs on the setup screens; and how to perform essential moves such as signing in and out, locking Windows, and shutting down or restarting your computer.

STARTING THE INSTALLATION

You can start installing Windows 10 in several ways:

■ **Click the Get Windows 10 icon in the notification area of the taskbar.** This icon appears only if your computer contains a version of Windows from which you can upgrade to Windows 10.

■ **Run the DVD from your current version of Windows.** If your computer has a DVD drive and a working version of Windows, insert the Windows 10 DVD. When the

Windows 10 Setup screen appears, check the I Accept the License Terms box and click the Accept button to start the upgrade.

■ **Boot from the DVD.** If your computer has an optical drive, you can insert the DVD in the drive and boot from the DVD. How you boot from the optical drive depends on your computer, so you may have to consult the manual or the manufacturer's website. This approach is useful if your computer doesn't have Windows installed, or if Windows is installed but not working, but you can also use it even if Windows is installed and working fine.

■ **Boot from a USB drive.** You can buy Windows 10 on a USB drive for convenience. Or you can use a tool such as Rufus (free from http://rufus.akeo. ie) to create a bootable USB drive from either a Windows DVD or a Windows ISO disc image that you download from Microsoft.

CHOOSING BETWEEN AN UPGRADE AND A CUSTOM INSTALLATION

If you're installing Windows 10 on a computer that already has Windows 7 or Windows 8.1 installed, you can choose between upgrading the existing version of Windows and performing a custom installation of Windows 10. This is a massive decision, so you'll want to get it right. You make this choice by clicking either the Upgrade option or the Custom option on the Which Type of Installation Do You Want? screen of Windows Setup (see Figure 1.1).

> ☐ **NOTE** As you know, Windows 10 runs on both devices with regular screens, on which you click with a mouse or trackpad, and devices with touch-screens, which you tap (or thump, if you're my son). This book uses "click" instead of "click or tap," for concision, for clicks with the left button or regular taps on the screen, and it uses "right-click or long-press" for clicking with the right button on a mouse or performing a long press on the touchscreen.

Normally, you'll want to upgrade the existing version of Windows. Upgrading keeps all your apps and your files in place, and after the upgrade finishes, you can carry on using your computer much as before, only with the benefit of Windows 10's new features.

But if your computer's software is at all messed up, or if you want to take the new version of Windows as an opportunity to get rid of apps you no longer need and slim down your files, perform a custom installation instead. You'll then need to install the apps you want to use, and copy across the files that you want to have on the computer.

FIGURE 1.1

On the Which Type of Installation Do You Want? screen of Windows Setup, click Upgrade or Custom, as needed.

!CAUTION   Before performing a custom installation, back up any files you care about to an external drive, an online storage site, or both.

If you're installing Windows from scratch on a newly built computer or on a new hard drive, the custom installation is your only choice. But—as of this writing, anyway—the installer doesn't check that an upgrade is possible, so the Upgrade button appears to be available.

CHOOSING THE DRIVE AND PARTITION FOR A CUSTOM INSTALLATION

If you go for a custom install, the Where Do You Want to Install Windows? screen (see Figure 1.2) appears next, enabling you to choose the drive (if your computer has multiple drives) and partition on which to install Windows. From this screen, you can delete existing partitions, extend existing partitions, create new partitions, and format partitions to remove the data they contain.

> **NOTE** A partition is a logical section of a drive. You can use partitions to separate different operating systems from each other. For example, if your computer has Windows 8 installed on it, you can install Windows 10 on a separate partition without upgrading Windows 8, so you can boot the computer into either operating system. You might want to do this when evaluating Windows 10.

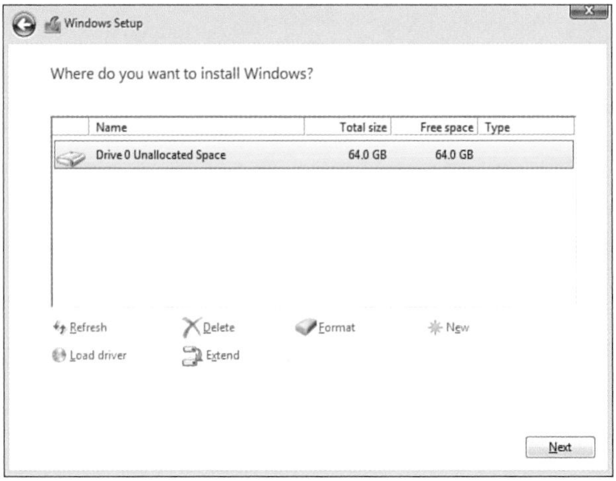

FIGURE 1.2
On the Where Do You Want to Install Windows? screen, select the drive and partition on which to install the OS.

> **CAUTION** Be very careful when working with partitions. It's all too easy to wipe out a partition that contains valuable data. Use the Total Size column and the Free Space column to verify that you're working with the correct drive and partition.

What you do on this screen depends on your computer's configuration. Here's an example starting with the blank drive on the computer shown in the screens:

1. Click the drive in the list box. In this case, it's the only item there.

2. Click the New button. The Size box and the Apply button and Cancel button appear (see Figure 1.3).

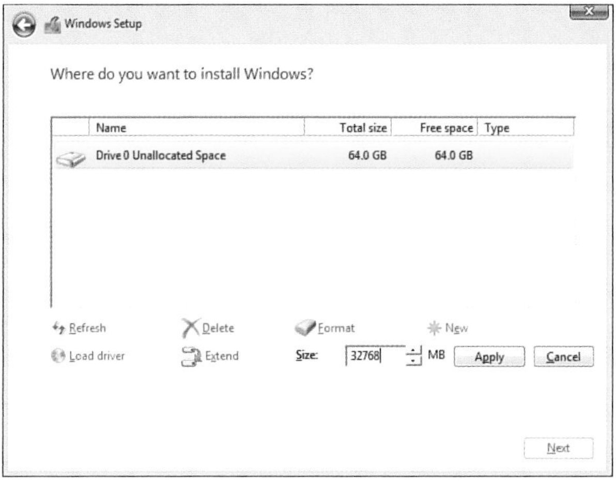

FIGURE 1.3

Enter the size for the new partition in the Size box and then click Apply.

3. Enter the size in the Size box, either by typing or by clicking the spin arrows.

4. Click Apply. The Windows Setup dialog box opens (see Figure 1.4), warning you that Windows might create additional partitions for system files.

FIGURE 1.4

The Windows Setup dialog box warns you that Windows may create extra partitions. Click OK.

5. Click OK. Windows Setup creates the partition you requested and, if needed, creates a System Reserved partition (see Figure 1.5).

After you've created the partition on which you want to install Windows, select the partition, and then click Next.

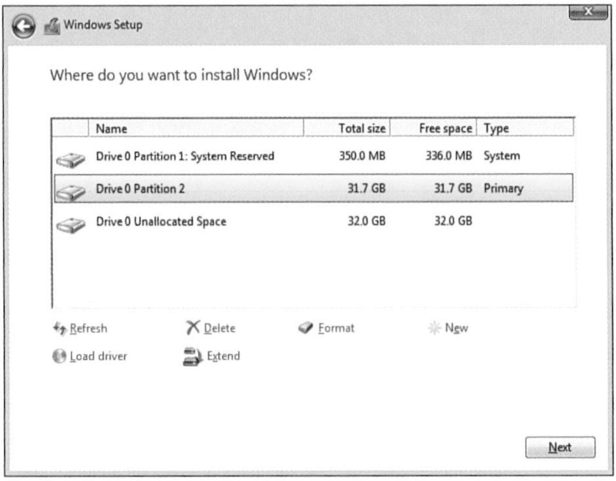

FIGURE 1.5

Windows Setup creates your partition and any system partition needed, leaving the rest of the drive as unallocated space.

MAKING THE RIGHT CHOICES ON THE SETUP SCREENS

Next, Windows Setup copies the files it needs from your install medium, and then installs them. The Installing Windows screen appears (see Figure 1.6), showing you the progress of the installation. Windows then restarts a couple of times before needing your involvement again.

CHOOSING BETWEEN USING DEFAULT SETTINGS AND CONFIGURING WINDOWS MANUALLY

The next big choice is on the Get Going Fast screen (see Figure 1.7). This screen lets you choose between configuring Windows quickly using the default settings and configuring Windows manually with custom settings. To encourage you to use the express settings, this screen has a nice big Use Express Settings button and a small Customize Settings link.

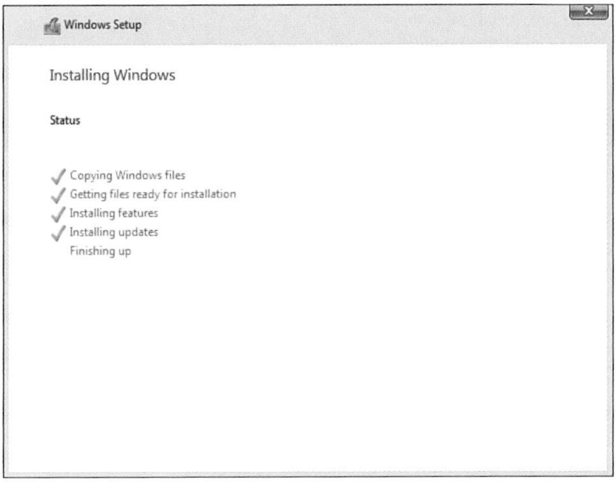

FIGURE 1.6
The Installing Windows screen appears while Windows Setup copies files and installs them.

FIGURE 1.7
On the Get Going Fast screen, you'll probably be tempted to click Use Express Settings. But it's usually better to click Customize Settings.

NOTE You can change any of the express settings afterward if you want—but it's all too easy to forget to do so. To retain as much control of your computer as you likely want, it's best to customize the settings.

On the Settings screen, click the Use Express Settings button if you want to set up Windows with the default settings. These work pretty well, but you may need to change them afterward.

! CAUTION It's easy to choose the Use Express Settings option, but this gives Microsoft a huge amount of information that you may not want to cede. It's much better to click the Customize Settings link and slog through the individual options so that you can control how much information you're giving up.

If you prefer to have full control over Windows right from the start, click the Customize Settings link. The first Customize Settings screen appears (see Figure 1.8).

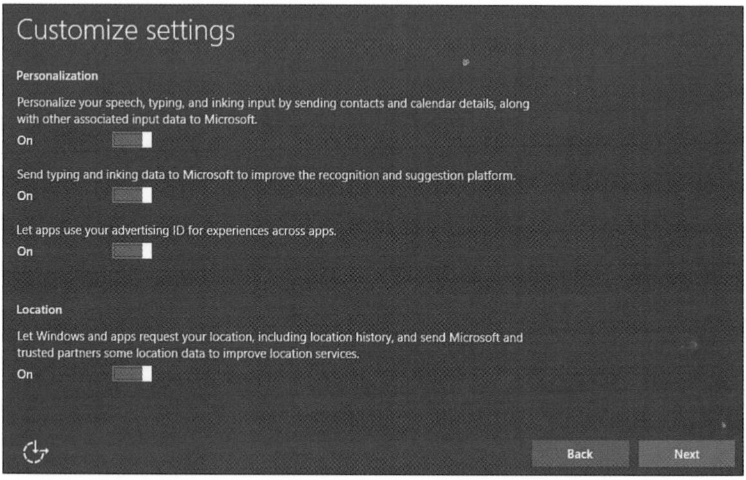

FIGURE 1.8

Choose Personalization and Location settings on the first Customize Settings screen.

📝 NOTE Three things before we start customizing settings. First, you can change any of these settings later, and I'll show you how to do so later in the book. Second, most of the settings have awkwardly long names, because Microsoft is trying to make clear what they do. Third, all the switches are set to On by default.

CHOOSING PERSONALIZATION AND LOCATION SETTINGS

In the Personalization section of the first Customize Settings screen, you can modify the following three settings.

- **Personalize Your Speech, Typing, and Inking Input by Sending Contacts and Calendar Details, Along with Other Associated Input Data to Microsoft.** Set this switch to On if you want to share your contacts, your calendar events, and other data with Microsoft to enable Windows to better recognize your speech input, typing input, and inking input. Sharing this data helps you get more accurate input results, especially for tricky items such as spoken contact names—but be sure you're comfortable sharing it.

- **Send Typing and Inking Data to Microsoft to Improve the Recognition and Suggestion Platform.** Set this switch to On if you want to share your typing and inking data anonymously with Microsoft so that it can improve recognition and suggestions. Doing this benefits Windows users over the long term.

- **Let Apps Use Your Advertising ID for Experiences Across Apps.** Your advertising ID or "advertising identifier" is a unique identifier for your Windows user account. Set this switch to On if you want apps to be able to get your advertising ID so that they can serve up targeted ads. If not, set this switch to Off.

> **TIP** You can enable or disable the advertising ID as needed after setup. Open the Settings app, click Privacy, and then set the Let Apps Use Your Advertising ID for Experiences Across Apps switch to On or Off, as needed. Setting this switch to Off resets your advertising ID, wiping out the information currently held.

In the Location section, you can modify one setting:

- **Let Windows and Apps Request Your Location, Including Location History, and Send Microsoft and Trusted Partners Some Location Data to Improve Location Services.** This is a wide-ranging setting. Set this switch to On if you want to allow Windows and apps to request your location and your location history. The main benefit of this is being able to get location-specific information automatically—for example, to get directions from wherever you've gotten lost to where you're supposed to be—without having to enter your location manually. But to get this information, you must allow both Windows and apps to access not only your current location but also your location history, which can be sensitive information. The other aspect, sending location data to help improve location services, is less controversial, and ideally you'd be able to enable it without enabling location access for Windows and apps.

> **TIP** Allowing location access tends to be much more helpful for a laptop or tablet than for a desktop that spends all its life in one location. If you're prepared to provide your location manually on occasion, I suggest setting the Let Windows and Apps Request Your Location switch to Off.

Click the Next button when you're ready to move on. The second Customize Settings screen appears, offering Browser and Protection settings and Connectivity and Error Reporting settings.

CHOOSING BROWSER, PROTECTION, CONNECTIVITY, AND ERROR REPORTING SETTINGS

In the Browser and Protection section of the second Customize Settings screen, you can modify these two settings:

- **Use SmartScreen Online Services to Help Protect Against Malicious Content and Downloads in Sites Loaded by Windows Browsers and Store Apps.** Set this switch to On if you want to use the SmartScreen feature to protect against malevolent software. This is almost always a good idea.

- **Use Page Prediction to Improve Reading, Speed Up Browsing, and Make Your Overall Experience Better in Windows Browsers. Your Browsing Data Will Be Sent to Microsoft.** Set this switch to On if you want to use Page Prediction in your browser. Page Prediction analyzes each web page you load and tries to work out which links on that page you might click; to speed up your browsing, Page Prediction preloads the pages it thinks you might want. (Preloading means that the browser downloads the pages but doesn't display them—it just caches the data.) So when you click the link for a preloaded page, the page appears more quickly, because the data is already on your computer.

> **CAUTION** If your computer uses a cellular connection for web browsing, you'll probably want to turn off Page Prediction, because it can greatly increase your data usage.

! CAUTION Page Prediction can cause your web browser to connect to web pages that you might not want to load yourself. Your browser's cache may contain data, such as images, that you didn't download yourself. The preloaded pages don't appear in your browsing history unless you choose to go to them, but to anyone (such as a government agency) who can get your browsing data from your ISP, it may appear that you visited the pages.

In the Connectivity and Error Reporting section, you can modify these two settings:

■ **Automatically Connect to Suggested Open Hotspots. Not All Networks Are Secure.** Set this switch to On if you want Windows to connect automatically to open wireless networks on Microsoft's approved list. ("Open" means the networks aren't secured with passwords or other security measures.) These are networks that Microsoft believes to be safe, but it is possible that some networks may have been compromised. You might want to set this switch to Off and manage your Wi-Fi connections manually.

⌇ NOTE The two Automatically Connect settings use a service called Wi-Fi Sense that Microsoft developed to help mobile devices running Windows online without racking up huge cellular bills. You must have Location Services turned on for Wi-Fi Sense to work.

■ **Automatically Connect to Networks Shared by Your Contacts.** Set this switch to On if you want Windows to connect automatically to networks that your contacts share. These networks aren't open—they're secured networks that your friends choose to share. Windows shares the passwords securely so that you can use the networks but not learn the passwords.

Again, click the Next button when you've made your choices. The Just a Moment screen appears while the installer implements your choices, and then the Who Owns This PC? screen appears. Continue with the next section.

WORKING ON THE WHO OWNS THIS PC? SCREEN

On the Who Owns This PC? screen (see Figure 1.9), you make an important decision by clicking either My Organization or I Own It and then clicking the Next button.

> **NOTE** The Who Owns This PC? screen does not appear for Windows 10 Home Edition, which cannot connect to domain-based networks.

FIGURE 1.9

On the Who Owns This PC? screen, click My Organization or I Own It, as appropriate.

When you click My Organization and then click the Next button, the installer walks you through the process of setting up Windows to connect to a domain-based Windows network. This is the kind of network that Windows-based companies and organizations of any size typically have.

When you click I Own It and then click the Next button, the installer leads you through setting up Windows for individual use, not connecting to a domain-based network. This is the type of setup you'll normally want for home use.

WORKING ON THE MAKE IT YOURS SCREEN

The Make It Yours screen encourages you to sign in to Windows using a Microsoft account. Normally you'll want to do this so that you can sync your apps and data across the Internet.

> **NOTE** A Microsoft account is an online account that enables you to sign in to Windows and Microsoft products and services using the same login information.

If you have a Microsoft account, enter your email address and password and then click the Sign In button.

If you don't have an account, click the Create One! link and follow the prompts to create an account.

If you have a Microsoft account but you've forgotten the password, click the Forgot My Password link and follow the prompts to get a new temporary password that enables you to reset your password.

> **NOTE** The alternative to signing in with a Microsoft account is to use a local account—an account that exists only on your computer. To use a local account, click the Skip This Step link on the Make It Yours screen and go to the section "Working on the Create an Account for This PC Screen," later in this chapter.

When you click the Sign In button, the installer displays the Please Wait screen and then the Just a Moment screen while it configures Windows. If Windows gets stuck at the Just a Moment screen, restart your computer. Normally, after booting it will reach the Who Owns This PC? screen, so you have only a couple of choices to make before you're back where you were.

SETTING A PIN AND MEETING CORTANA

Next, the Set Up a PIN screen appears, prompting you to set a PIN that you can use instead of a password for signing in. If you want to set up a PIN, click the Set a PIN button to display the Set Up a PIN dialog box, type the PIN in the New PIN box and the Confirm PIN box, and click the OK button.

After this, the Meet Cortana screen appears (see Figure 1.10), explaining the Cortana personal assistant and what information Microsoft collects in order to make Cortana work effectively. Click the Next button if you want to use Cortana; if not, click the small Not Now button in the lower-left corner of the screen.

From here, skip ahead to the section "Working in the Networks Pane."

WORKING ON THE CREATE AN ACCOUNT FOR THIS PC SCREEN

If you don't sign in to a Microsoft account on the Make It Yours screen, Windows displays the Create an Account for This PC Screen (see Figure 1.11), on which you create a local account for yourself. Follow these steps:

1. Type the user name you want in the User Name box.
2. Type a strong password (see the tip) in the Enter Password box and the Re-enter Password box.

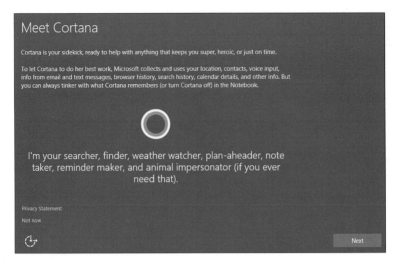

FIGURE 1.10

On the Meet Cortana screen, read the information that Microsoft will collect about you. Click the Continue button if you want to use Cortana, or click the Not Now button if you want to disable Cortana for now.

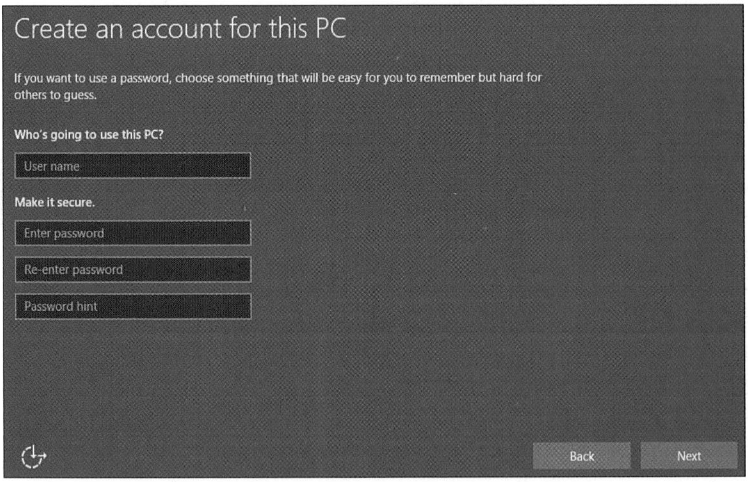

FIGURE 1.11

On the Create an Account for This PC screen, enter the user name you want and a strong password to protect your account. You can also enter a password hint.

TIP To create a strong password, include upper- and lowercase letters, numbers, and symbols (such as $, %, or &) in the password. Make the password at least 8 characters long. More than 12 characters gives you far greater protection because it is much harder to crack. Avoid any real word in any language.

NOTE The Create an Account for This PC screen encourages you to set a password for the account—but it doesn't make you set a password. However, to protect your account and your personal information, it's vital that you do set a password and that you make it a strong password.

3. Type a password hint in the Password Hint box. See the sidebar "What Sort of Password Hint Should You Create?" for advice.

Click Next when you are ready to proceed. The installer then installs your apps, displaying messages along the way. Your desktop then appears, and the Networks pane opens. Continue with the next section.

WHAT SORT OF PASSWORD HINT SHOULD YOU CREATE?

The Create an Account for This PC screen forces you to create a password hint by typing in the Password Hint box. Windows prevents you from actually entering the password here—just as well, because otherwise people do enter it—but you can enter text that makes the password completely clear to anybody who sees the hint.

The password hint is supposed to enable the user to remember the password without enabling anyone else to guess the password. That's fine in theory, but in practice it's really hard to get this balance right. So when creating a password hint, err on the side of caution lest the hint help an intruder break into your account. Windows requires only a single character, so you might want to enter a single letter or number as a cryptic hint.

WORKING IN THE NETWORKS PANE

In the Networks pane (see Figure 1.12), you can click Yes or No to choose whether to let your computer find PCs, devices, and content on the network.

FIGURE 1.12

In the Networks pane, choose whether to turn on Network Discovery for the network.

Clicking Yes in the Networks pane turns on a feature called Network Discovery that enables your computer to connect automatically to printers, TVs, and other devices on the network. Normally, it's a good idea to turn on Network Discovery for home networks and for work networks, because it makes connecting to other devices easier. You can control Network Discovery separately for each network to which your computer connects.

! CAUTION If you connect your computer to a public network, such as a Wi-Fi hotspot in a coffee shop, you must make sure that Network Discovery is off for that network. Otherwise, your computer is exposed to all the other computers and devices on that network, which compromises your security.

> **NOTE** You can easily turn Network Discovery on or off later if necessary. You can also fine-tune your Network Discovery settings, allowing some types of connections but preventing others. See Chapter 3, "Connecting to Networks and the Internet," for details.

SIGNING IN AND OUT OF WINDOWS

To use Windows, you sign in using your Microsoft account or your local account. On the login screen, click the appropriate account, type your password in the Password box, and then press Enter or click the arrow button.

To sign out, click Start, click your account name in the upper-left corner of the Start menu, and then click Sign Out on the drop-down menu (see Figure 1.13).

FIGURE 1.13

You can sign out by opening the Start menu, clicking your account name, and then clicking Sign Out.

LOCKING WINDOWS

When you want to stop using your computer but leave your apps running so that you can resume your work or play immediately when you return, lock Windows instead of signing out. To lock Windows, click Start, click your account name at the upper-left corner of the Start menu, and then click Lock.

When you return to your computer, announce your presence by pressing a key, moving the mouse, or tapping the touchscreen. Then type your password or PIN at the prompt to unlock Windows. (If you set up Windows without a password, Windows unlocks without you—or anyone else—having to provide any authentication.)

RESTARTING WINDOWS

Windows is designed to keep running for days or weeks on end, but you will need to restart it now and then. Restarting Windows can frequently resolve minor software problems that have occurred, so you may find it helpful to restart Windows every few days. Choose any of these methods to restart Windows:

- Click Start, click Power, and then click Restart.
- Right-click or long-press Start, click Shut Down or Sign Out, and then click Restart.
- On the login screen, click Shut Down (the power icon) and then click Restart on the drop-down menu.

PUTTING YOUR COMPUTER TO SLEEP OR INTO HIBERNATION

When you're not using your computer, you can put it to sleep to save power. To do so, perform one of these moves:

- Click Start, click Power, and then click Sleep.
- Right-click or long-press Start, click Shut Down or Sign Out, and then click Sleep.
- On the login screen, click Shut Down (the power icon) and then click Sleep on the drop-down menu.

> **TIP** If your computer has a dedicated Sleep button, you can press the button to put your computer to sleep. You may also be able to put a laptop to sleep by closing the lid.

UNDERSTANDING SLEEP, HIBERNATION, AND HYBRID SLEEP

Windows uses two different but related power-saving states: sleep and hibernation. As the names suggest, sleep is for the short term and hibernation for the long term. Windows also uses hybrid sleep, mostly for desktop computers.

When you put your computer to sleep, the screen goes blank and the drives and fans normally stop, but the computer retains information in its RAM. Retaining the information requires a small amount of power, so a laptop or tablet that's running on battery power will consume some of that power. Holding the data in RAM enables Windows to be running again within a few seconds of your waking the computer, so you can resume work almost immediately.

By contrast, when your computer goes into hibernation, it writes the contents of its RAM to a file on disk called the hibernation file. The hibernation file is named `hiberfil.sys` and is normally hidden to prevent users from deleting it. The computer writes the full contents of RAM, so the file needs the same amount of space on the hard drive as the computer has RAM—for example, an 8GB `hiberfil.sys` for a computer with 8GB of RAM.

When you rouse your computer from hibernation, Windows reads the contents of the hibernation file back into RAM. This takes from a few seconds to a minute or two, depending on how big the file is and how powerful the computer is.

When your computer is running on battery power, if the battery level gets critically low while the computer is asleep, Windows puts the computer into hibernation automatically.

So far, so straightforward—but Windows also uses hybrid sleep, which is a combination of sleep and hibernation. Hybrid sleep saves the contents of RAM to the hibernation file and then puts your computer into as low power a state as possible while maintaining the contents of RAM. Hybrid sleep is mainly for desktop computers as a protection against power outages: If an outage occurs, Windows can resume your session by reading the hibernation file back into RAM. If there's no outage, Windows simply resumes using the contents of RAM.

You can wake the computer more or less instantly from sleep by pressing a key on the keyboard, clicking your pointing device, or tapping the touchscreen.

> ☑ **TIP**   You may also be able to wake your computer from sleep or hibernation by pressing the power button. If the computer is a laptop, opening the lid normally wakes it.

The alternative to sleep is hibernation, which is a deeper form of sleep designed for knocking out the computer for longer periods. You can make your computer hibernate in these ways:

- Click Start, click Power, and then click Hibernate.
- Right-click or long-press Start, click Shut Down or Sign Out, and then click Hibernate.
- On the login screen, click Shut Down (the power icon) and then click Hibernate on the drop-down menu.

To wake the computer from hibernation, press a key on the keyboard, click the mouse or other pointing device, or tap the touchscreen.

ADDING THE HIBERNATE COMMAND TO THE POWER MENU

If the Hibernate command doesn't appear on the Power menu, you can add it, as long as your computer supports hibernation. Right-click or long-press Start to display the shortcut menu, and then click Power Options to display the Power Options screen in Control Panel. In the sidebar, click Choose What the Power Buttons Do to display the System Settings screen, and then check the Hibernate box in the Shutdown Settings area. If the Hibernate box is unavailable, you'll need to click the Change Settings That Are Currently Unavailable link first.

While you're on the System Settings screen, you might also want to adjust the settings in the Power and Sleep Button Settings area (on a desktop), the Power and Sleep Buttons and Lid Settings area (on a laptop or convertible), or the Power Button and Lid Settings area (on other laptops). Here, you can open the When I Press the Power Button drop-down menu and choose the action you want: Hibernate, Shut Down, Turn Off the Display, or Do Nothing. You can also open the When I Press the Sleep Button drop-down menu and choose the action you want: Hibernate, Turn Off the Display, or Do Nothing. (Some of the drop-down menus offer a different selection of options on some devices.)

For many laptops, you can also open the When I Close the Lid drop-down menu and choose Do Nothing, Sleep, Hibernate, or Shut Down, as needed. Sleep is usually the most helpful option here, but the Do Nothing setting can be useful if you're using an external display (or several) with your laptop—and it's a model that won't overheat if running with the lid closed.

When you've made your choices on the System Settings screen, click Save Changes to save the changes.

CONFIGURING AND USING CORTANA

Windows 10 includes the search assistant called Cortana, which enables you to search either using your voice or by typing terms into the Search box on the taskbar and Start menu.

As you saw earlier in this chapter, you can choose during setup whether to enable or disable Cortana. Windows enables Cortana by default, so if you accepted the default settings, or if someone else set up Windows for you, chances are that Cortana is enabled.

You can enable or disable Cortana as needed after setup. You can also configure Cortana to make it work your way.

CONFIGURING CORTANA

If you haven't yet configured Cortana, do so by following these steps:

1. Click the Search box on the taskbar to display the Cortana panel.
2. In the Great! Now What Would You Like Me to Call You? pane (shown on the left in Figure 1.14), type the name or nickname you want Cortana to use, and then click the Next button. Cortana then prompts you for permission to use your location.
3. Click the Settings button at the bottom of the pane to display the Settings pane (see the right screen in Figure 1.14).

NOTE You can display the Settings pane at any time subsequently by clicking the Settings icon (the gear icon) in the left column of the Cortana panel.

4. Set the Cortana Can Give You Suggestions, Ideas, Reminders, Alerts and More switch to On or Off, as needed.

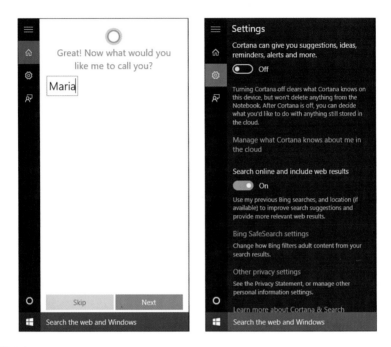

FIGURE 1.14

First, tell Cortana what to call you (left). Then, in the Settings pane, choose which Cortana features you want to use when searching.

> **! CAUTION** Like other search assistants, Cortana becomes more useful the more it knows about you. If you enable Cortana's features for giving you suggestions, ideas, reminders, and alerts, Cortana needs to know about your schedule and your actions. So when configuring Cortana, you must balance your desire for convenience against the amount of information you're willing to give to Microsoft (and maybe Microsoft's business partners).

5. Set the Search Online and Include Web Results switch to On or Off, as needed. By setting this switch to Off, you can restrict Cortana to searching only on your computer, which is sometimes useful. But if you want to be able to search both your computer and the Web, make sure this switch is set to On.

! CAUTION   When you set the Search Online and Include Web Results
switch to On, Cortana uses your previous searches on the Bing search engine, plus
your location if it is available, to try to deliver more useful search results. These
can be helpful and can save you time—but again, make sure you're happy with
the information you're giving Microsoft in exchange.

NOTE   You can click the Bing SafeSearch Settings link in the Settings
pane for Cortana to display the Search settings for your account on the Bing
search engine. Here, you can choose a SafeSearch setting to specify whether you
want to filter out adult text, images, and videos; specify your location (your city
and ZIP code) and your region (such as your country); choose whether to see
search suggestions as you type; and choose whether to play videos and panora-
mas automatically.

6. When you finish choosing settings for Cortana, click outside the pane if you
   want to close it. If you want to search, click the Search box and type your
   search terms.

SEARCHING WITH CORTANA

After configuring Cortana, you can use Cortana to search at any time. Simply click
in the Search box and start typing your search terms. Cortana displays suggestions
as you type (see Figure 1.15). You can browse the different categories of results all
together, or click either the My Stuff button to display only search results on your
computer or the Web button to display search results on the Web. Click the result
you want to view.

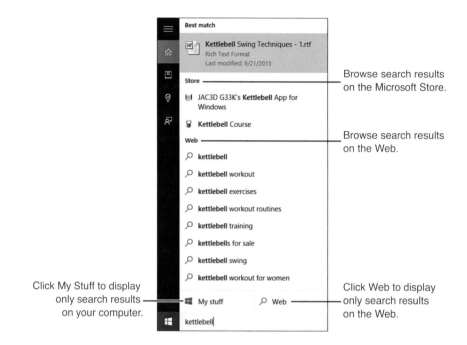

FIGURE 1.15

Cortana delivers search results on your computer, on the Microsoft Store, and on the Web.

SHUTTING DOWN YOUR COMPUTER

When you don't need to use your computer for a while, you can shut it down completely. You can shut down in any of these ways:

- Click Start, click Power, and then click Shut Down.
- Right-click or long-press Start, click Shut Down or Sign Out, and then click Shut Down.
- On the login screen, click Shut Down (the power icon) and then click Shut Down on the drop-down menu.

When you need to restart your computer, press the power button.

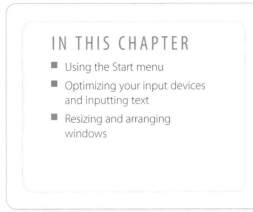

IN THIS CHAPTER

- Using the Start menu
- Optimizing your input devices and inputting text
- Resizing and arranging windows

2

NAVIGATING WINDOWS LIKE A PRO

To use Windows swiftly, you need to navigate it efficiently. This chapter starts by making sure you know your way around Windows 10's redesigned Start menu. After that, you learn to tweak your input devices so that they work the way you prefer, use those devices to input text quickly and accurately, and resize and arrange your windows on the screen.

USING THE START MENU

Windows 10 brings back the Start menu, a key feature of the Windows interface since Windows 95 in 1995, because its replacement, the Start screen in Windows 8, left many users struggling and never became popular. The Windows 10 Start menu includes elements of the Start screen, and you can expand it to fill the screen, giving you arguably the best features of both the Start menu and the Start screen.

OPENING THE START MENU

You can open the Start menu in any of these ways:

- Click the Start button at the lower-left corner of the screen.
- Press the Windows key on your keyboard.

> ☑ **TIP**   You can also press Ctrl+Esc to open the Start menu. This keyboard shortcut is mostly useful if your keyboard doesn't have a Windows key.

- Tap the Windows button on a touchscreen device.

GETTING AROUND THE START MENU

The Start menu (see Figure 2.1) contains eight main features:

- **Your user name.** Click this to display a menu containing three commands: Change Account Settings, Lock, and Sign Out.
- **Most Used.** This section of the Start menu shows the apps you have used the most.
- **Recently Added.** This section enables you to quickly locate new apps.
- **File Explorer and Settings.** Near the bottom of the menu are buttons for launching two widely used apps: File Explorer and Settings.
- **Power.** Click this item to display the Sleep, Shut Down, and Restart commands.
- **All Apps.** Click this item to display the full list of apps. You can then click an app to launch it.
- **Live Tiles.** Live tiles show small amounts of helpful information, such as the current weather, stock status, or the number of unread email messages clamoring for your attention.

> ☑ **NOTE**   You can customize the Start menu extensively so that it contains only the items you prefer. See Chapter 5, "Customizing Windows to Suit Your Needs," for details.

✅ TIP   You can drag the border of the Start menu to resize it as needed.

Most Used
Your user name | Recently Added

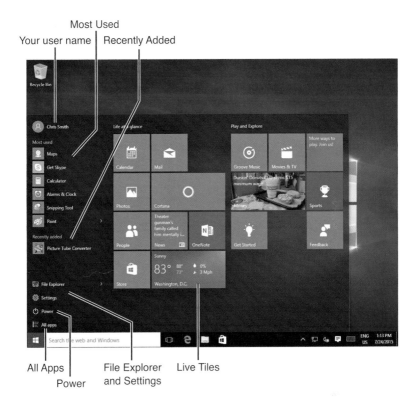

All Apps | File Explorer   Live Tiles
Power   and Settings

FIGURE 2.1

The Start menu gives you quick access to apps, information, and system features such as Power.

TWEAKING YOUR INPUT DEVICES

To create documents swiftly and efficiently, or just to chat with your friends and trounce your enemies at games, you'll need to make your computer's input devices work your way. In this section, we look at how to adjust your mouse, touchpad, or touchscreen; how to configure your keyboard; and how to change your input settings.

ADJUSTING THE MOUSE OR TOUCHPAD

To adjust your mouse or touchpad, open the Mouse & Touchpad pane in the Settings app. Follow these steps:

1. Click Start, Settings to open the Settings window.

2. Click Devices to display the Devices screen.

3. Click Mouse & Touchpad in the sidebar to display the Mouse & Touchpad pane (see Figure 2.2).

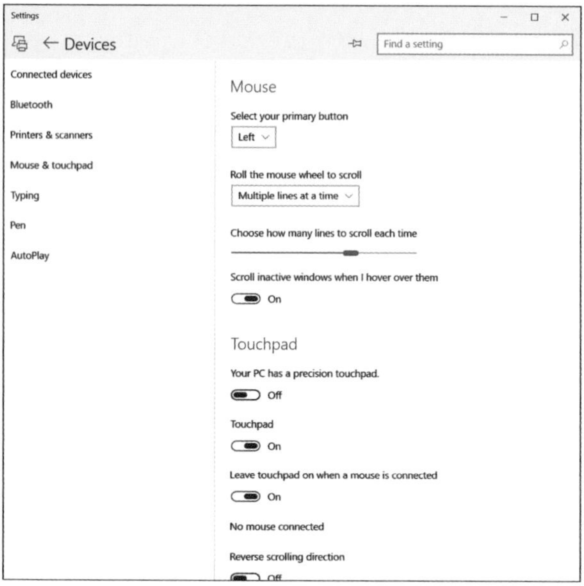

FIGURE 2.2

The Mouse & Touchpad pane in Settings enables you to configure your mouse or touchpad.

CONFIGURING YOUR MOUSE

In the Mouse section of the Mouse & Touchpad pane, you can choose the following basic settings for your mouse:

- **Select Your Primary Button.** Normally, you'll want to select Left if you use the mouse with your right hand; select Right if you use the mouse with your left hand.

- **Roll the Mouse Wheel to Scroll.** Select Multiple Lines at a Time if you want rolling the mouse wheel to scroll partway down the screen. Select One Screen at a Time if you prefer to move screen by screen.

■ **Choose How Many Lines to Scroll Each Time.** If you select Multiple Lines at a Time for the Roll the Mouse Wheel to Scroll setting, drag this slider to set the number of lines. As you drag, a number pops up above the slider. You can set any value between 1 and 100. If you select One Screen at a Time for the Roll the Mouse Wheel to Scroll setting, this setting is unavailable.

■ **Scroll Inactive Windows When I Hover over Them.** Set this switch to On if you want to be able to hover the mouse pointer over an inactive window and have the windows scroll. This behavior can be useful when you use it deliberately; if you do it by accident, it feels like a ghost in the machine, and you may prefer to set this setting to Off.

All these settings are helpful, but Windows also provides other settings to give you closer control of your mouse. To reach these settings, click Additional Mouse Options in the Related Settings area to display the Mouse Properties dialog box (see Figure 2.3).

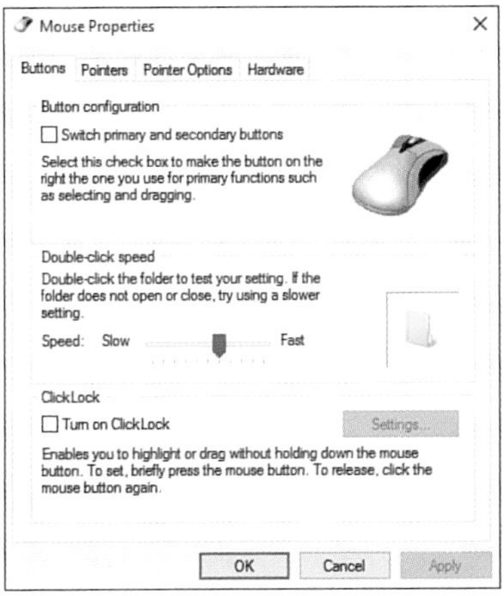

FIGURE 2.3
Choose settings in the Mouse Properties dialog box to fine-tune your mouse.

📝 **NOTE** The tabs and settings in the Mouse Properties dialog box vary depending on the mouse and its capabilities.

You can choose the following settings on the Buttons tab:

- **Switch Primary and Secondary Buttons.** Check this box to reverse the mouse's main buttons. Normally, you'd do this if you use a non-left-handed mouse with your left hand. Some left-handed mouses may also need this setting.

- **Double-Click Speed.** Drag the slider along the Slow–Fast axis to set the speed at which you have to click twice to register a double-click. Test the speed by double-clicking the folder icon, which opens or closes when you get it right.

- **Turn On ClickLock.** Check this box if you want to turn on ClickLock, which enables you to click and hold an object to lock the pointer on to it. After you've locked the object, you can release the mouse button, drag the object to where you need it, and then click again to release the lock. Normally, you'd use ClickLock if you find it awkward to drag an object while holding down the mouse button.

> **TIP** If you turn on ClickLock, click the Settings button to display the Settings for ClickLock dialog box, and then drag the slider along the Short–Long axis to set the length of time you need to hold down a click to trigger ClickLock.

On the Pointers tab (see Figure 2.4), you can choose which mouse pointers to use. Open the Scheme drop-down menu and choose the pointer scheme you want, such as Magnified (System Scheme), which has larger pointers that are easier to see on small or high-resolution screens. You can then customize the scheme by clicking a pointer in the Customize list, clicking Browse, clicking the pointer you want in the Browse dialog box, and then clicking Open. You can check the Enable Pointer Shadow box to add a shadow under the mouse pointer. Click Apply to see the pointers in action.

On the Pointer Options tab (see Figure 2.5), you can set options to control the pointer's motion, whether it snaps to default controls, and its visibility. These options are often useful; here are the details:

- **Select a Pointer Speed.** Drag this slider along the Slow–Fast axis to set the speed at which the pointer moves across the screen as you move the mouse.

> **NOTE** Windows changes the pointer speed as you drag the Select a Pointer Speed slider—you don't need to click Apply to test the change you've made.

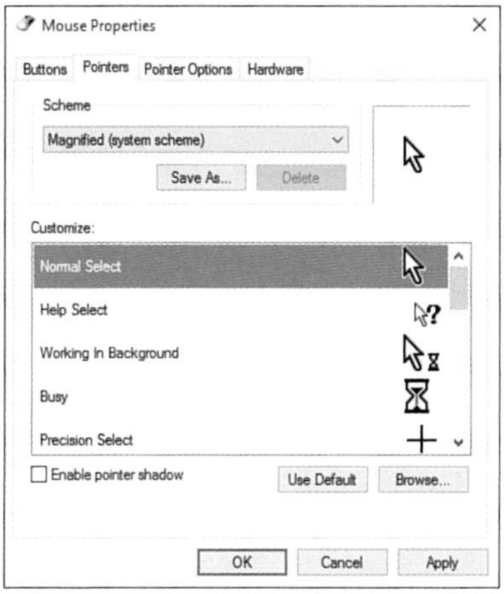

FIGURE 2.4
On the Pointers tab of the Mouse Properties dialog box, choose which mouse pointers to use. You can also enable the pointer shadow.

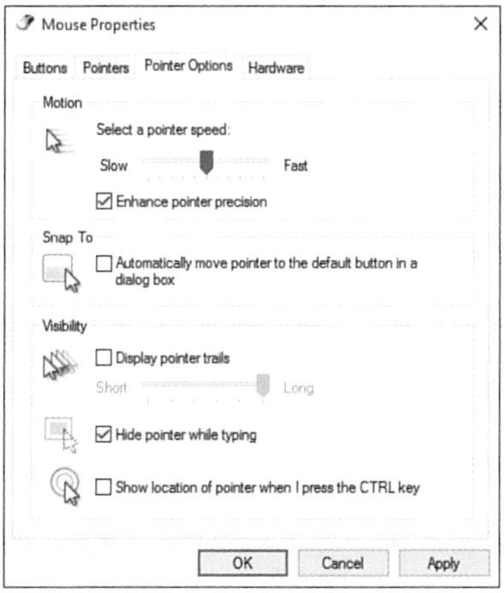

FIGURE 2.5
On the Pointer Options tab, you can make the pointer snap to the default button in dialog boxes, display pointer trails, and show the pointer location when you press Ctrl.

■ **Enhance Pointer Precision.** Check this box to make Windows automatically speed up the pointer's movement when it detects that you are making big movements and slow it down for smaller movements. This feature is helpful for general computing, especially if you have a large screen, because you can move the pointer from one extreme of the screen to another more quickly.

> ☑ **TIP** If you play shooter games on your computer, you'll probably want to turn off Enhance Pointer Precision in order to move accurately and shoot straight.

- **Automatically Move Mouse Pointer to the Default Button in a Dialog Box.** Check this box if you want Windows to snap the mouse pointer to the default button (such as the OK button) when a dialog box opens. Some people find this option helpful; others don't.

- **Display Pointer Trails.** Check this box to make a trail of pointer shadows appear behind the pointer as it moves. This option can be helpful if you have vision problems or use an assistive device to move the mouse—or you may just enjoy the visual effect. Drag the slider along the Short–Long axis to set the length of the trails.

- **Hide Pointer While Typing.** Check this box to make the pointer disappear while you are typing. Hiding the pointer is usually helpful because it makes sure the pointer isn't in the way of the text.

- **Show Location of Pointer When I Press the Ctrl Key.** Check this box to give yourself an easy way of locating the pointer if you tend to lose it on the screen. Press Ctrl to make Windows flash a contrasting circle around the pointer.

The options on the Wheel tab of the Mouse Properties dialog box enable you to control vertical scrolling and horizontal scrolling:

- **Roll the Wheel One Notch to Scroll.** This setting has the same effect as the Roll the Mouse Wheel to Scroll setting (in the Mouse & Touchpad pane in Settings). You can either select the option button called The Following Number of Lines at a Time and specify the number of lines in the box, or select the One Screen at a Time option button.

- **Tilt the Wheel to Scroll the Following Number of Characters at a Time.** In this box, set the number of characters you want to be able to scroll left or right by tilting the mouse wheel in that direction.

The Hardware tab of the Mouse Properties dialog box lets you see the device names for each mouse or other pointing device Windows has identified. You can click a device and click Properties to display the Properties dialog box for a device if you want to see more details, including the driver the device is using.

When you finish choosing settings in the Mouse Properties dialog box, click OK to close it.

TAKING CONTROL OF YOUR TOUCHPAD

In the Touchpad area of the Mouse & Touchpad pane, you can choose the following settings:

- **Your PC Has a Precision Touchpad.** If this switch appears, your computer has a precision touchpad, one that you can use to give touch gestures to Windows. Make sure this switch is set to On.

> **NOTE** The settings in the Touchpad area of the Mouse & Touchpad pane may vary depending on the computer you're using and the capabilities of its touchpad.

- **Touchpad.** Set this switch to Off if you need to disable the touchpad. For example, if you have a Surface tablet with a Microsoft Touch Keyboard, but you prefer giving commands by using the touchscreen, you may want to disable the touchpad so that you can't give commands on it by accident. Otherwise, make sure this switch is set to On.
- **Leave Touchpad On When a Mouse Is Connected.** Set this switch to Off if you want Windows to automatically disable your computer's touchpad when you connect a mouse. (Windows does this so that you don't give commands accidentally on the touchpad.) If you want to be able to use both the mouse and the touchpad, set this switch to On.
- **Reverse Scrolling Direction.** Set this switch to On if you want to reverse the scrolling direction. This is sometimes useful, but if you don't need it, leave this switch set to Off.
- **To Help Prevent the Cursor from Accidentally Moving.** In this drop-down menu, set the delay you need in order to avoid accidental cursor movements when you're typing. Your choices are No Delay (Always On), Short Delay, Medium Delay, and Long Delay. You'll need to experiment with this setting to find out what works for you.
- **Change the Cursor Speed.** Drag this slider to set the speed at which the cursor moves across the screen as you move your finger across the touchpad.
- **Allow Taps on the Touchpad.** Set this switch to On to enable yourself to click by tapping the touchpad.
- **Allow Right-Clicks on the Touchpad.** Set this switch to On to enable yourself to right-click by clicking the lower-right corner of the touchpad.

- **Allow Double-Tap and Drag.** Set this switch to On to enable yourself to double-tap on the touchpad to pick up an object and then drag it.
- **Use a Two Finger Tap for Right-Click.** Set this switch to On to enable yourself to right-click by tapping with two fingers on the touchpad.
- **Use a Two Finger Drag to Scroll.** Set this switch to On to enable yourself to scroll by dragging with two fingers on the touchpad.
- **Use a Two Finger Pinch to Zoom.** Set this switch to On to enable yourself to zoom in by placing two fingers (or your thumb and finger) on the screen and pinching outward, and to zoom out by pinching inward.
- **Choose What to Do with Three Finger Drags and Slides.** In this drop-down menu, choose Switching Apps to enable switching apps by dragging three fingers across the screen. Choose Nothing if you don't want to use this feature.

CHOOSING THE RIGHT PEN AND TOUCH SETTINGS

If your PC has a touchscreen, spend a few minutes adjusting pen and touch settings so that it works the way you prefer. First, open the Pen and Touch dialog box by following these steps:

1. Right-click or long-press Start to display the shortcut menu.
2. Click Control Panel to open a Control Panel window.
3. Click Hardware and Sound to display the Hardware and Sound pane.
4. Click Pen and Touch to display the Pen and Touch dialog box. As you can see on the left in Figure 2.6, this dialog box has three tabs: Pen Options, Flicks, and Touch.

On the Pen Options tab, you can choose the following settings:

- **Pen Actions.** In this box, you can click either the Double-Tap action or the Press and Hold action and then click Settings to display the Settings dialog box for configuring it. For example, in the Press and Hold Settings dialog box (shown on the right in Figure 2.6), you can enable or disable the feature, adjust its speed, and adjust its duration.
- **Use the Pen Button as a Right-Click Equivalent.** Check this box if you want to be able to click the pen button to give a right-click.
- **Use the Top of the Pen to Erase Ink (Where Available).** Check this box if you want to be able to erase ink by touching it with the top of the pen.

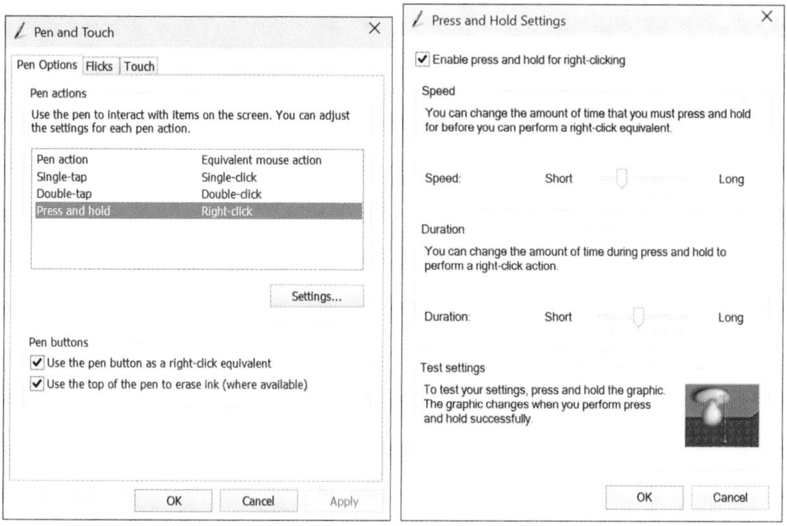

FIGURE 2.6

Choose pen actions and pen buttons on the Pen Options tab in the Pen and Touch dialog box (left). Use the Press and Hold Settings dialog box (right) to enable and customize pressing and holding to right-click.

On the Flicks tab (shown on the left in Figure 2.7), you can enable and disable flicks, choose between using navigational flicks only and using navigational flicks and editing flicks, and adjust flick sensitivity. These are the settings:

- **Use Flicks to Perform Common Actions Quickly and Easily.** Check this box to enable flicks.

- **Navigational Flicks.** Select this option button to use only navigational flicks. Table 2.1 explains the navigational flicks.

- **Navigational Flicks and Editing Flicks.** Select this option button to use both navigational flicks and editing flicks. Table 2.1 explains the standard editing flicks.

- **Customize.** Click this button to display the Customize Flicks dialog box (shown on the right in Figure 2.7), in which you can choose which action to assign to each flick. Choose the (None) option to leave a flick without an action. Click Restore Defaults to go back to the default flick actions.

> **NOTE** Some tablets do not display the Flicks tab or the Pen Options tab.

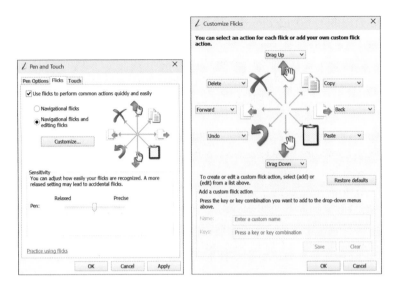

FIGURE 2.7
On the Flicks tab of the Pen and Touch dialog box (left), choose which flicks to use and adjust the sensitivity as needed. You can use the Customize Flicks dialog box (right) to customize the flick actions.

NOTE You can add a custom flick action by choosing the (Add) item in the appropriate drop-down menu in the Customize Flicks dialog box. After selecting (Add), type the name in the Name box, click in the Keys box and press the key or key combination, and then click Save.

- **Pen.** Drag this slider along the Relaxed–Precise axis to set how precisely Windows requires the flicks to be. You'll need to experiment with this setting to get it right for you and the way you use the pen.

Table 2.1   Navigational Flicks and Editing Flicks

Flick Type	Flick Direction	Effect
Navigational	Left	Move forward
Navigational	Right	Move back
Navigational	Up	Drag up
Navigational	Down	Drag down

Flick Type	Flick Direction	Effect
Editing	Diagonally up and to the left	Delete
Editing	Diagonally up and to the right	Copy
Editing	Diagonally down and to the right	Paste
Editing	Diagonally down and to the left	Undo

On the Touch tab of the Pen and Touch dialog box (shown on the left in Figure 2.8), you can configure how Windows responds to your touches. These are the settings available:

▪ **Touch Actions.** In this box, you can click either the Double-Tap action or the Press and Hold action and then click Settings to display the Settings dialog box for configuring it. For example, in the Double-Tap Settings dialog box (shown on the right in Figure 2.8), you can change the speed and the spatial tolerance.

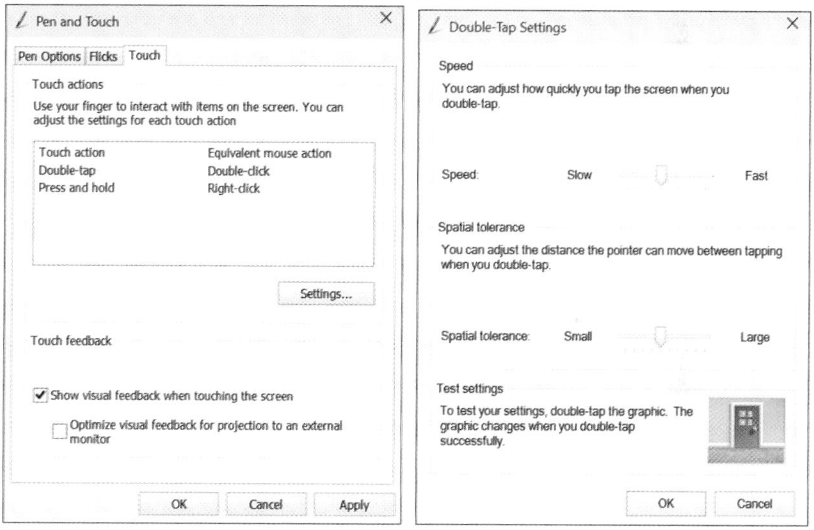

FIGURE 2.8

On the Touch tab of the Pen and Touch dialog box (left), tap Settings to configure a touch action, and then work in the Settings dialog box that opens (right).

▪ **Show Visual Feedback When Touching the Screen.** Check this box to have Windows display visual feedback when you touch the screen so that you can tell that your touches are being recognized.

■ **Optimize Visual Feedback for Projection to an External Monitor.** If you check the Show Visual Feedback When Touching the Screen check box, you can select this check box to make the feedback suitable for showing on an external monitor—for example, when you are demonstrating a technique.

Click OK when you finish making your choices in the Pen and Touch dialog box.

CONFIGURING PEN AND TOUCH INPUT

Windows enables you to configure your pen and touch displays and to calibrate a touchscreen for pen and touch input. You can also switch between right-handedness (the default) and left-handedness, in which menus appear to the right of your hand so that it doesn't obscure them.

First, open the Tablet PC Settings dialog box by following these steps:

1. Right-click or long-press Start to display the shortcut menu.

2. Click Control Panel to open a Control Panel window.

3. Click Hardware and Sound to display the Hardware and Sound pane.

4. Click Tablet PC Settings to display the Tablet PC Settings dialog box. As you can see in Figure 2.9, this dialog box has two tabs: Display and Other.

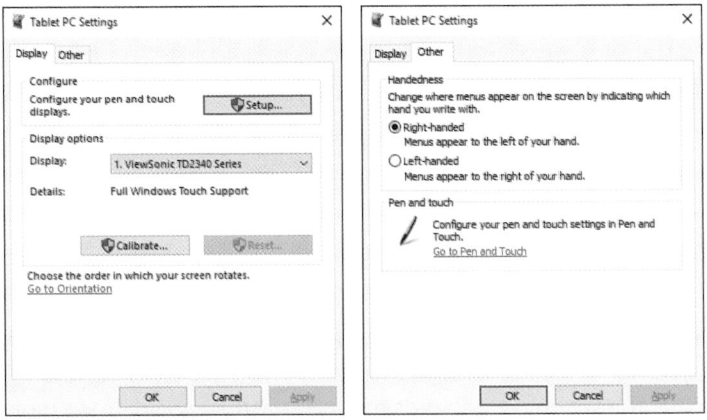

FIGURE 2.9
On the Display tab of the Tablet PC Settings dialog box (left), you can configure and calibrate your pen and touch displays. On the Other tab (right), you can change from right-handedness to left-handedness.

Start on the Display tab, where you can configure the pen and touch displays and choose display options. Follow these steps:

1. Click Setup in the Configure box, and then follow through the process for identifying your pen screens and touchscreens. In the Identify Pen or Touch Input Screens dialog box that opens, click the Pen Input button or the Touch Input button, as appropriate. Then, if Windows prompts you to identify the correct screen, touch it with your finger or the pen; if the screen is wrong, press Enter to move to the next screen, and then touch that screen if it's the right one.

2. In the Display Options box, make sure the Display drop-down menu shows the right display, such as NotebookPanel; if not, open the drop-down menu and pick the right display.

3. Also in the Display Options box, click Calibrate to launch the calibration process. In the Calibrate Pen or Touch Input Screens dialog box that opens, click the Pen Input button or the Touch Input button, as appropriate. The calibration process then prompts you to touch various points on the screen. When you finish, click Yes in the Digitizer Calibration Tool dialog box that opens prompting you to save the calibration data.

> **NOTE** If the User Account Control dialog box opens when you're calibrating a screen, make sure the program name is Digitizer Calibration Tool, and then click Yes.

After you finish with the Display tab, click the Other tab, and then click the Right-Handed option button or the Left-Handed option button in the Handedness box. Then click OK to close the Tablet PC Settings dialog box.

CONFIGURING YOUR KEYBOARD

If you use a physical keyboard with your computer, you can configure the repeat delay, the repeat rate, and the cursor blink rate. If you're fine with the default settings, you don't need to change them; but if you get doubled keystrokes, or you find that the keyboard responds more slowly than you'd like to repeated keystrokes, you may want to tweak the settings. To do so, follow these steps:

1. Right-click or long-press Start to display the shortcut menu.

2. Click Control Panel to open a Control Panel window.

3. Click the View By drop-down menu and then click Large Icons to switch to Large Icons view.

4. Click Keyboard to display the Keyboard Properties dialog box. This dialog box has two tabs, Speed and Hardware. The Speed tab is where you adjust the

settings; the Hardware tab shows you the names of the keyboard devices and enables you to view their properties.

5. On the Speed tab, drag the Repeat Delay slider along the Long–Short axis to adjust the repeat delay. This is the time Windows waits after one press of a key before registering a second press. So if you're getting unintentional double presses of letters, move the Repeat Delay slide toward the Long end.

6. Drag the Repeat Rate slider along the Slow–Fast axis to set the repeat rate. This is the speed at which a key repeats when you hold it down. You can test the repeat rate by clicking in the text box below the slider and holding down a key.

7. Drag the Cursor Blink Rate slider along the None–Fast axis to set how fast the cursor blinks. Set the slider to None if you want to prevent the cursor from blinking at all.

8. Click OK to close the Keyboard Properties dialog box.

CONFIGURING TYPING SETTINGS

Windows provides a handful of Typing settings that you can configure to control spelling, typing, and the touch keyboard on tablets and convertible PCs. To access these settings, choose Start, Settings, click Devices, and then click Typing in the sidebar.

> **NOTE** The selection of typing settings depends on your computer's hardware configuration.

In the Typing pane of the Devices screen (see Figure 2.10), you can choose two Spelling settings:

- **Autocorrect Misspelled Words.** Set this switch to On to have Windows automatically fix typos such as "teh" or "aslo."

- **Highlight Misspelled Words.** Set this switch to On to have Windows highlight misspelled words that Autocorrect can't fix.

For a computer that uses the touch keyboard, you can choose the following settings in the Typing section:

- **Show Text Suggestions as I Type.** Set this switch to On to have Windows display suggestions for completing the word you're typing. The suggestions appear on a bar above the keyboard. You can tap a suggestion to insert the word.

- **Add a Space After I Choose a Text Suggestion.** Set this switch to On to have Windows insert a space automatically after you choose a text suggestion.

- **Add a Period After I Double-Tap the Spacebar.** Set this switch to On to enable yourself to type a period by tapping the spacebar twice in quick succession.

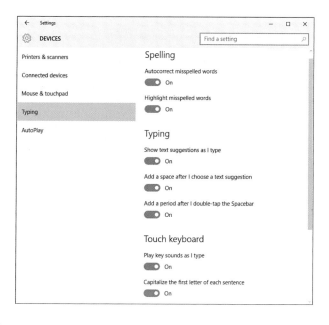

FIGURE 2.10

In the Typing pane of the Devices screen, choose settings for spelling, typing, and the touch keyboard (if you have one).

Also for a computer that uses the touch keyboard, you can choose the following settings in the Touch Keyboard section:

- **Play Key Sounds as I Type.** Set this switch to On if you want to hear a sound for each key you press. Some people find this feedback helpful; others don't.

- **Capitalize the First Letter of Each Sentence.** Set this switch to On to have Windows automatically set Shift to On when you start a new sentence or new paragraph. You can tap Shift to turn it off if you need a lowercase letter instead.

- **Use All Uppercase Letters When I Double-Tap Shift.** Set this switch to On to enable yourself to apply Caps Lock by double-tapping Shift. This is usually helpful.

■ **Add the Standard Keyboard Layout as a Touch Keyboard Option.** Set this switch to On if you want to be able to use the standard keyboard layout on the touch keyboard as well as the touch-optimized layout.

> **NOTE** The standard keyboard for the touch keyboard has a full-ish keyboard layout, including keys such as Esc, Tab, Caps Lock, and Alt (which the touch layout doesn't have). The main disadvantage of the standard keyboard is that the keys are much smaller, so you need to tap more precisely.

CONFIGURING YOUR LANGUAGE AND KEYBOARD LAYOUT

Windows enables you to enter text in many languages and using different keyboard layouts. To configure your language and keyboard layout, you work in the Region & Language pane in Settings, which you open like this:

1. Choose Start, Settings to open the Settings window.

2. Click Time & Language to display the Time & Language screen.

3. Click Region & Language in the sidebar to display the Region & Language pane (see Figure 2.11).

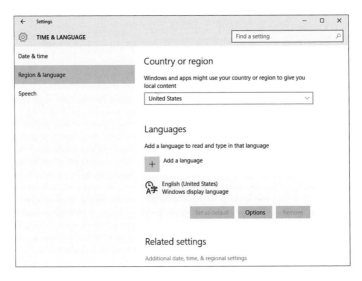

FIGURE 2.11

In the Region & Language pane, you can choose your country or region, add a language, or add a keyboard layout.

If the Country or Region drop-down menu doesn't show the right country or region, click it and choose your country or region.

If you want to add a language, click Add a Language to display the Add a Language screen, and then click the appropriate language. Windows may need to download and install a language pack for the language.

To add a keyboard layout, follow these steps:

1. Click the language for which you will use the layout. The Set as Default button, the Options button, and the Remove button appear.

2. Click Options to display the Language Options pane (see Figure 2.12).

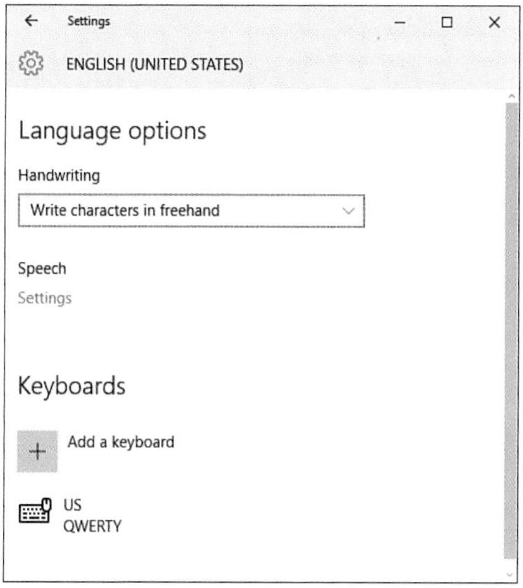

FIGURE 2.12
In the Language Options pane, you can configure handwriting or add a keyboard layout.

> **TIP** In the Language Options pane, you can also open the Handwriting drop-down menu and switch between Write Characters in Freehand and Write Each Character Separately.

3. Click Add a Keyboard to display a drop-down menu of available keyboards.

4. Click the appropriate keyboard, such as United States-Dvorak or Canadian French.

> **NOTE** To remove a keyboard, click its button in either the Language Options pane or the Region & Language pane, and then click Remove.

SETTING UP SPEECH RECOGNITION

The Windows 10 Speech Recognition feature enables you to enter text in apps by speaking. If your environment permits dictation, it can be a great way of entering text fast and accurately.

Before you can use Speech Recognition, you must set it up. Follow these steps to display the Speech Recognition screen:

1. Right-click or long-press Start to display the shortcut menu.
2. Click Control Panel to open a Control Panel window.
3. If the View By setting shows Large Icons or Small Icons, click View By and then click Category to switch to Category view.
4. Click Ease of Access to display the Ease of Access pane.
5. Click Speech Recognition to display the Speech Recognition screen.

From the Speech Recognition screen, click Start Speech Recognition. The Set Up Speech Recognition Wizard opens and walks you through the process of setting up the microphone. Here are the screens where you need to pay attention:

- **What Type of Microphone screen.** On this screen (see Figure 2.13), click Headset Microphone, Desktop Microphone, or Other, as needed.

> **NOTE** If you're using a microphone built into your computer, click Other.

- **Improve Speech Recognition Accuracy screen.** On this screen, click the Enable Document Review option button to allow Speech Recognition to scan your documents and email messages to learn the words and phrases you use frequently. This helps Speech Recognition identify what you say.

> **NOTE** If you enable document review, Speech Recognition scans only the documents and email messages that you index for searching. Speech Recognition doesn't scan anything you exclude from indexing, such as private or confidential materials.

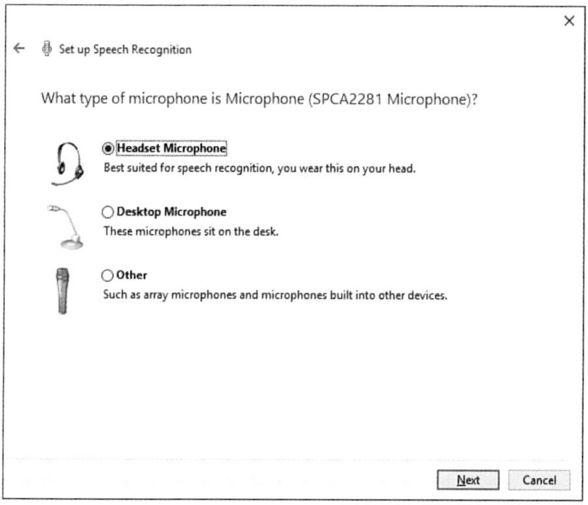

FIGURE 2.13

On the What Type of Microphone screen, specify which type of microphone you have.

■ **Choose an Activation Mode screen.** On this screen, click the Use Voice Activation Mode option button if you want to be able to restart Speech Recognition by saying, "Start listening!" Otherwise, click the Use Manual Activation Mode option button; you'll need to use the mouse or the keyboard to restart Speech Recognition.

■ **Run Speech Recognition Every Time I Start the Computer screen.** On this screen, check the Run Speech Recognition at Startup box if you want to use Speech Recognition each time. Otherwise, uncheck this box and start Speech Recognition manually when you need it.

> **TIP** Speech Recognition can be a great boon, but it is resource-hungry and can cost you battery power on a laptop or tablet. So if you use Speech Recognition only occasionally, uncheck the Run Speech Recognition at Startup box to spare your computer's processor and power supply. To turn this option off later, open Control Panel, click Ease of Access, and then click Speech Recognition. Now click Advanced Speech Options in the left pane to open the Speech Properties dialog box, uncheck the Run Speech Recognition at Startup check box in the User Settings area on the Speech Recognition tab, and click the OK button.

■ **You Can Now Control This Computer by Voice screen.** Click Start Tutorial if you want to take the tutorial, which is a good idea if you have time; if not, click Skip Tutorial.

> **✓ TIP** If you prefer to take the tutorial later, you can click Take Speech Tutorial in the Speech Recognition window at any point. You can click Train Your Computer to Better Understand You and read a set text to your computer to improve the accuracy of dictation. You can also click Open the Speech Reference Card to see a list of common commands for using Speech Recognition.

When you finish the Set Up Speech Recognition Wizard, Speech Recognition starts, and the Speech Recognition control panel appears (see Figure 2.14). You can turn on Speech Recognition by clicking the microphone button at the left end or by saying, "Start listening!" (if you chose Voice Activation mode). To turn off Speech Recognition, click the microphone button again or say, "Stop listening!"

FIGURE 2.14

Click the microphone button at the left end of the Speech Recognition control panel to turn on Speech Recognition.

INPUTTING TEXT

After configuring your input methods, you should be all set to input text in documents. In this section, we look quickly at inputting text with a hardware keyboard, with the touch keyboard and handwriting panel on a touchscreen device, and with Speech Recognition on a computer with a microphone.

INPUTTING TEXT WITH A HARDWARE KEYBOARD

To input text with a hardware keyboard, you simply press the keys as usual. The only complication is if you have configured multiple languages or keyboard layouts. If so, you can switch among them by clicking the language and keyboard readout in the notification area and then clicking the appropriate language and keyboard on the pop-up panel (see Figure 2.15).

FIGURE 2.15

To switch languages or keyboards, click the language and keyboard readout in the notification area, and then click the appropriate language and keyboard on the pop-up panel.

TIP To switch quickly to the last input method you were using, press Windows Key+Ctrl+spacebar. While you press this keyboard shortcut, Windows displays a drop-down menu onscreen so that you can see the input method to which you're switching. To switch to another input method, hold down the Windows key and press spacebar to display the drop-down menu. Press spacebar as many times as needed to select the input method you want, and then release the Windows key.

INPUTTING TEXT WITH THE TOUCH KEYBOARD AND THE HANDWRITING PANEL

Inputting text with the touch keyboard is also largely straightforward, but you'll want to use its extra features for helping you enter text quickly and comfortably.

Depending on the app you're using, the touch keyboard may appear automatically when you tap in a text area. If not, click or tap the Touch Keyboard icon (the keyboard icon) in the notification area to display the touch keyboard.

When you start typing, the suggestions bar displays possible words (see Figure 2.16). You can tap a word to insert it.

NOTE If no suggestions appear, open the Settings app, click Devices, click Typing, and then set the Show Text Suggestions as I Type switch to On.

Tap a suggestion to insert it.   Tap to undock the keyboard.

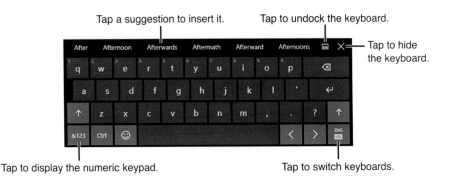

Tap to hide the keyboard.

Tap to display the numeric keypad.   Tap to switch keyboards.

FIGURE 2.16

Tap a suggestion on the suggestions bar above the touch keyboard to insert that word.

TIP To give a keyboard shortcut starting with Ctrl, tap Ctrl and then tap the appropriate letter. You don't need to tap the keys at the same time. To turn on Caps Lock, double-tap the Shift key; tap again when you're ready to turn off Caps Lock.

To type a number, tap and hold the key in the top row that shows that number, and then tap the number on the pop-up panel that appears. For example, to type 1, tap and hold the Q key, and then tap 1 on the pop-up panel. To type many numbers, touch the &123 key to display the numeric keypad.

NOTE If the touch keyboard layout you are using has a separate row of numbers above the letter keys, as on most hardware keyboards, you can simply tap the appropriate number keys to type numbers.

TIP To type a character that includes a diacritical mark, such as å or ñ, tap and hold the base character (such as *a* for å or *n* for ñ), and then tap the appropriate character on the pop-up panel.

Tap Undock to shrink the keyboard down and make it mobile (see Figure 2.17). You can then tap the Move icon (the icon that shows arrows pointing in all four directions) and drag the keyboard to where you want it on the screen.

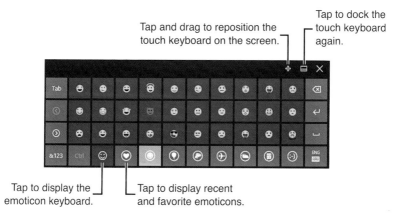

Tap and drag to reposition the touch keyboard on the screen.

Tap to dock the touch keyboard again.

Tap to display the emoticon keyboard.

Tap to display recent and favorite emoticons.

FIGURE 2.17
You can undock the touch keyboard so that you can move it around the screen.

Tap the Emoticon button to display the emoticon keyboard (also shown in Figure 2.17). You can then tap the other buttons on the bottom row to switch among the sets of emoticons. Within a set, tap > to display the next screen of emoticons, or tap < to display the previous set. When you locate the emoticon you want, tap it to insert in the document.

> ☑ **TIP** To type symbols such as ©, ®, or ÷, tap the !? button at the bottom of the emoticons keyboard, and then tap the appropriate button.

To switch among the available keyboards, tap the button in the lower-right corner of the keyboard. On the pop-up panel (see Figure 2.18), tap the keyboard you want to display:

- **Touch Keyboard.** This is the default layout, optimized for touch.
- **Split Keyboard.** The split keyboard is good for when you're holding a tablet in both hands and typing with your thumbs.
- **Handwriting Panel.** Use the handwriting panel (see Figure 2.19) when you need to enter text with a capacitive stylus, a Surface Pen (for Microsoft's Surface tablets), or your fingertip.

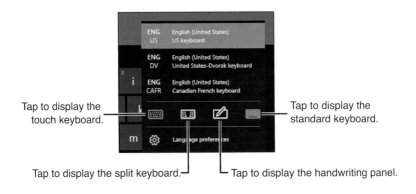

Tap to display the touch keyboard.

Tap to display the standard keyboard.

Tap to display the split keyboard.

Tap to display the handwriting panel.

FIGURE 2.18

Use the pop-up panel to switch among the available keyboards.

Tap to type a space.

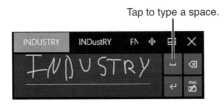

FIGURE 2.19

Use the handwriting panel to enter text with your finger, a stylus, or the Surface Pen.

> **NOTE**   If you have a hardware keyboard attached, pressing a key on the hardware keyboard makes Windows hide the touch keyboard.

INPUTTING TEXT VIA SPEECH RECOGNITION

After setting up the Speech Recognition feature as explained earlier in this chapter, you can turn on Speech Recognition and dictate text into apps.

If you've set Speech Recognition to run automatically when you start Windows, you can just say, "Start listening!" to switch on Listening mode. If not, follow these steps to launch Speech Recognition:

1. Right-click or long-press Start to display the shortcut menu.

2. Click Control Panel to open a Control Panel window.

3. Click Ease of Access to display the Ease of Access pane.

4. Click Speech Recognition to display the Speech Recognition screen.

5. Click Start Speech Recognition.

You can then open or switch to the app into which you want to dictate text, activate Speech Recognition, and then say the text you want to enter.

> **TIP** After you start Speech Recognition, you can activate it by clicking the microphone icon at the left end of the Speech Recognition control panel or pressing Ctrl+Windows Key.

RESIZING AND ARRANGING WINDOWS

You can arrange windows either manually or by using the Snap feature. When rearranging windows manually, you can use the command buttons on the title bar, use keyboard shortcuts, or simply drag the windows and their borders.

RESIZING AND CLOSING WINDOWS WITH THE COMMAND BUTTONS

The quick way to resize windows is by clicking the three command buttons that appear at the right end of the title bar for a nonmaximized window (see the top screen in Figure 2.20) or the three command buttons that appear for a maximized window (see the bottom screen in Figure 2.20):

- **Minimize.** Reduces the window to the app's button on the taskbar. To get the window back, click the app's button; if there are multiple windows, click the one you want on the drop-down menu.

- **Maximize.** Enlarges the window to take up the full screen. When you maximize a window, the Restore Down button replaces the Maximize button.

- **Restore Down.** Restores the window to the size and position it was in before you maximized it. When you restore down a window, the Maximize button replaces the Restore Down button.

- **Close.** Closes the window.

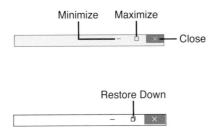

FIGURE 2.20

Click the Minimize button, Maximize button, or Close button to resize or close a window using the mouse (top). Click the Restore Down button to return a maximized window to its nonmaximized size (bottom).

USING SNAP AND SNAP ASSIST

The Snap feature enables you to arrange windows quickly and regularly on the left or right side of the screen. The Snap Assist feature helps you to quickly snap another open window to the opposite side of the screen.

To use Snap, click the title bar of the appropriate window, and then drag it to the left side or the right side of the screen. When the pointer reaches the side of the screen, Windows displays an overlay showing where the snapped window will go. If this is where you want the window, release the mouse button, and the window snaps into place.

> **TIP** Press Windows Key+Left to snap the active window to the left side of the screen, or press Windows Key+Right to snap it to the right side. When you release the Windows key, Snap Assist appears, and you can click a window's thumbnail to snap it to the other side of the screen.

Snap Assist then automatically displays thumbnails of your other open windows on the other side of the screen (see Figure 2.21). You can click a window to snap it to that side, giving yourself two windows side by side in moments.

> **TIP** Drag a window to the top of the screen to maximize it via Snap.

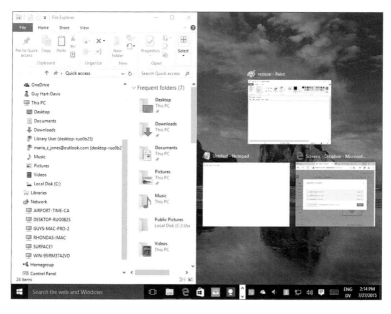

FIGURE 2.21

When you snap a window to the left or right side of the screen, the Snap Assist feature displays thumbnails of your other open windows on the opposite side of the screen so that you can click the window you want.

After snapping a window to the left side or right side of the screen, you can press Windows Key+Up to snap the window to the upper-left quadrant or upper-right quadrant. Pressing Windows Key+Up again for that window maximizes the window. Pressing Windows Key+Up for a window you haven't snapped to the side also maximizes that window.

Similarly, after snapping a window to the left side or right side of the screen, you can press Windows Key+Down to snap the window to the lower-left quadrant or lower-right quadrant. Pressing Windows Key+Down again for that window minimizes the window. Pressing Windows Key+Down for a window you haven't snapped to the side also minimizes that window.

ARRANGING WINDOWS MANUALLY

You can easily arrange windows manually. Simply grab the window by the title bar and drag it to where you want. If you need to resize the window, drag the appropriate corner or side as needed.

RESIZING, ARRANGING, AND CLOSING WINDOWS WITH KEYBOARD SHORTCUTS

If your computer has a keyboard, you can manipulate windows quickly and accurately by using keyboard shortcuts. Table 2.2 has the details.

Table 2.2   Keyboard Shortcuts for Manipulating Windows

Keyboard Shortcut	Window Action
Home	Display the top of the active window.
End	Display the bottom of the active window.
Windows Key+M	Minimize all windows.
Windows Key+Up	Maximize the active window (press twice if the window is snapped to the side).
Windows Key+Down	Restore down the active window if it is maximized. Minimize the active window if it is not maximized or snapped.
Ctrl+F4	Close the active window.
Alt+F4	Close the active app (closing all its windows).
F11	Switch the active window between full-screen and its previous, non-full-screen state.

SWITCHING AMONG OPEN WINDOWS

Windows gives you three main ways to switch among your open windows:

- **Click the window.** If you can see the window you need, simply click that window to bring it to the front.

- **Use Task view.** Click the Task View button on the taskbar or press Windows Key+Tab to switch to Task view (see Figure 2.22). You can then click the window you want to see.

> **TIP**   To switch quickly among open windows using the keyboard, hold down Alt and press Tab. On the first press, the Task view screen appears. Press Tab repeatedly to cycle through the windows in Task view from left to right; when you reach the app you want, release the Alt key. If you need to move backward (from right to left) through the open windows, hold down Shift as well as Alt.

- **Use the Taskbar.** Click the Taskbar button for the app you want. If the app has multiple windows open, click the appropriate window on the drop-down menu.

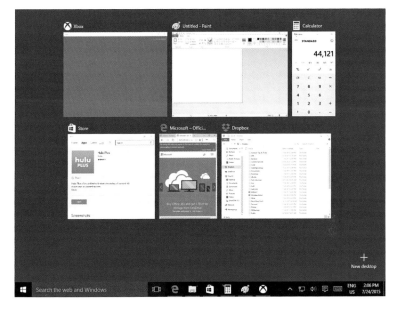

FIGURE 2.22

Task view enables you to switch quickly among your open windows.

TIP Press Windows Key+D to show the desktop, hiding all your apps. This move is most useful if you need to open an app or a document from an icon on the desktop.

IN THIS CHAPTER

- Connecting to wired networks and wireless networks
- Managing your network connections, using VPNs, and mapping network drives
- Diagnosing and repairing connection problems

3

CONNECTING TO NETWORKS AND THE INTERNET

To get the most out of your computer, you'll want to connect it to the Internet. Normally, the easiest way to do this is to connect it to a local area network that is connected to the Internet. For example, a typical home broadband connection includes a switch or router to which you can connect your computers and other devices (such as smartphones or tablets) so that they can access the Internet and also share files, printers, and other devices with each other locally. Similarly, your workplace likely has a network that enables the computers and devices to connect to servers, printers, and other shared resources, and to access the Internet.

This chapter shows you how to connect your computer to a wired network or to a wireless network, how to connect to network folders, and how to deal with network problems. You

also learn how to connect your computer to a virtual private network, or VPN, in order to establish a secure connection to a server across the Internet, and how to share your computer's Internet connection with others.

CONNECTING TO A WIRED NETWORK

To connect to a wired network, plug one end of an Ethernet cable into the Ethernet port on your computer and the other end into an Ethernet port on a switch, router, or hub.

For many networks, making the physical connection is all you need to do, because Windows tries to configure the connection automatically when it detects the cable. If the network uses DHCP (see the nearby sidebar), Windows can apply suitable settings, and your computer can start using the network.

Windows doesn't display any fly-out or dialog box when it connects successfully to a network, so you'll probably want to check that the connection is working. Usually, the easiest way is to open a web browser, such as Microsoft Edge; if it displays your home page, all is well; but if it displays an error, you will need to configure the connection.

See the section "Configuring IP Settings Manually," later in this chapter, for instructions on configuring a wired connection manually.

WHY DO YOU SOMETIMES NEED TO CONFIGURE NETWORK SETTINGS?

To connect to a network, your computer must have suitable Internet Protocol (IP) settings: the IP address, the gateway address, the network prefix length, and the addresses of the domain name system (DNS) server it should use. Typically, the computer receives these settings automatically from the network, but you can also set them manually if necessary.

Most wired and Wi-Fi networks use Dynamic Host Configuration Protocol (DHCP), a protocol in which a DHCP server or DHCP allocator automatically provides IP addresses and network configuration information to computers that connect. DHCP is an efficient way of sharing available IP addresses among computers, so it's widely used. But some networks use static IP addresses instead, assigning a particular address to each computer. For such networks, you must configure your computer's IP settings manually.

> **NOTE** The quick and easy way to disconnect from a wired network is to unplug the Ethernet cable from your computer. Alternatively, you can leave the cable connected but disable the Ethernet adapter. To do this, right-click or long-press the Network icon in the notification area and click Open Network and Sharing Center. Next, click Change Adapter Settings, and then right-click or long-press Ethernet and click Disable on the shortcut menu.

CONNECTING TO A WIRELESS NETWORK

Wired networks can be great for high speeds and reliability, but if your computer is a laptop or a tablet, you will likely find wireless networks more convenient. Windows enables you to connect to wireless networks easily and quickly.

To connect to a wireless network, you need to know its name (so that you can identify the network) and its security mechanism, such as a password.

UNDERSTANDING SSIDS AND HIDDEN NETWORKS

Each Wi-Fi network has a network name to identify it. The administrator assigns the name when setting up the network. The name contains alphanumeric characters—letters and numbers—and has a maximum length of 32 characters. The technical term for a wireless network's name is *service set identifier*, which is abbreviated to SSID.

When setting up a Wi-Fi network, the administrator can decide whether to have the router broadcast the network's name—as networks normally do—or whether to create a *hidden* network, one that doesn't broadcast its name. A hidden network is also called a *closed* network.

Creating a hidden network is one of the security measures an administrator can take for a wireless network. It is only moderately effective: Casual intruders may miss the network, but anyone with a Wi-Fi scanner will still be able to detect the network. For technical reasons, network professionals recommend *not* creating hidden networks, but many people use them nonetheless.

CONNECTING TO A WIRELESS NETWORK THAT BROADCASTS ITS NAME

Follow these steps to connect to a wireless network that broadcasts its name:

1. Click the Network icon in the notification area to display the Network fly-out.

2. If Wi-Fi is turned off (the Wi-Fi button is gray, and no networks appear), click Wi-Fi to turn Wi-Fi on. The list of available networks appears (see Figure 3.1).

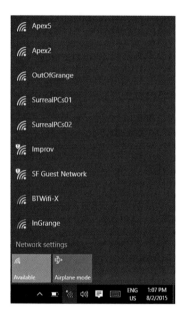

FIGURE 3.1

To start connecting to a wireless network, click the Network icon in the notification area, and then click the network name.

> **NOTE** An exclamation point in the upper-left corner of a wireless network's icon in the Network fly-out indicates that the wireless network is not secured.

3. Click the network to which you want to connect your computer. If the list of networks is long, you may need to scroll down to find the network. The connection controls appear (see Figure 3.2).

FIGURE 3.2

With the connection controls displayed in the Network fly-out, check the Connect Automatically check box if necessary and then click the Connect button.

4. Check the Connect Automatically check box if you want your computer to connect automatically to this network in the future when the network is available. You'd want to do this for your main wireless networks at home, work, and other regular locations.

5. Click Connect. Windows prompts you to enter the network security key (see Figure 3.3).

FIGURE 3.3

Type the password in the Enter the Network Security Key box and click Next.

> **NOTE** Windows doesn't prompt you for the password if you have connected to this network before and Windows has saved the password. Similarly, if the wireless network doesn't use security, there's no password to enter.

6. Type the password.

> **TIP** The password characters appear as dots for security. You can click the symbol at the right end of the Enter the Network Security Key box to reveal the characters momentarily to check that you have the password right.

7. Check the Share Network with My Contacts check box if you want Windows to share the network with your contacts via Wi-Fi Sense.

8. Click Next. Windows prompts you to decide whether to find PCs, devices, and content on the network and to connect automatically to devices like printers and TVs.

> **NOTE** Allowing Windows to find PCs, devices, and content on the network, and to connect automatically to devices, configures sharing settings for the network. See the section "Configuring Sharing" in Chapter 7 for instructions on configuring sharing manually.

9. Click Yes or No, as appropriate. Normally, you'd want to click Yes if this is your home network or a work network that you use regularly, and click No if this is a public network or a network you don't use regularly.

When Windows connects successfully to the network, it automatically determines and applies the IP settings needed for your computer to communicate through the network. The network appears at the top of the Network fly-out and *Connected* appears underneath it.

When your computer is connected to the network, check that the connection is working. If the network has an Internet connection, you can check easily by opening Microsoft Edge or another web browser and making sure that it can load web pages.

If the connection isn't working, you will need to configure it manually. See the section "Configuring IP Settings Manually," later in this chapter, for instructions.

CONNECTING TO A NETWORK USING WPS

Some Wi-Fi routers include a feature called Wi-Fi Protected Setup (WPS) to help you set up networks securely. WPS is mostly used by Wi-Fi routers designed for the home market. It is a moderately secure way of establishing a connection to a Wi-Fi network.

When Windows detects that the Wi-Fi router offers WPS, it prompts you to press the WPS button on the router as an alternative to entering the network security. When you press the button, Windows communicates with the router to get the security settings needed for the network.

To use WPS, you need physical access to the router. If you don't have this, enter the network security key as usual to connect to the network.

CONNECTING TO A HIDDEN WIRELESS NETWORK

A hidden wireless network doesn't broadcast its name, so you need to tell Windows the network name as well as the network security key. Windows enables you to connect to a hidden wireless network by using either the Network fly-out or the Manually Connect to a Wireless Network Wizard. The Manually Connect to a Wireless Network Wizard offers an extra setting, so it's worth knowing both techniques.

After you specify the details of the hidden wireless network, you can connect to it from the Network fly-out in the same way you connect to other wireless networks.

ADDING A HIDDEN WIRELESS NETWORK VIA THE NETWORK FLY-OUT

To connect to a hidden wireless network via the Network fly-out, follow these steps:

1. Click the Network icon in the notification area to display the Network fly-out.
2. Click the Hidden Network item at the bottom of the fly-out.
3. Check the Connect Automatically check box if you want your computer to connect to this network automatically.
4. Click Connect. Windows prompts you to enter the name (the SSID) for the network.
5. Click Next. Windows prompts you to enter the network security key.
6. Type the network security key.
7. Check the Share Network with My Contacts check box if you want Windows to share the network with your contacts via Wi-Fi Sense.
8. Click Next. Windows prompts you to decide whether to find PCs, devices, and content on the network and to connect automatically to devices like printers and TVs.
9. Click Yes or No, as appropriate.

ADDING A HIDDEN WIRELESS NETWORK VIA THE MANUALLY CONNECT TO A WIRELESS NETWORK WIZARD

Follow these steps to add a hidden wireless network using the Wireless Network Wizard:

1. Right-click or long-press the Network icon in the notification area to open the shortcut menu.
2. Click Open Network and Sharing Center to open the Network and Sharing Center window.

3. In the Change Your Networking Settings list, click Set Up a New Connection or Network to launch the Set Up a New Connection or Network Wizard. The Choose a Connection Option screen appears.

4. Click Manually Connect to a Wireless Network.

5. Click Next. The Manually Connect to a Wireless Network Wizard starts and displays the Enter Information for the Wireless Network You Want to Add screen (see Figure 3.4).

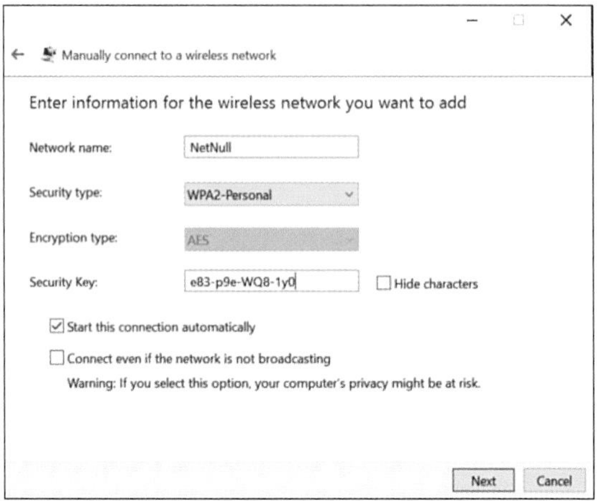

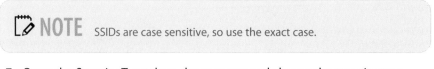

FIGURE 3.4

To connect to a hidden wireless network, enter its name and connection information in the Manually Connect to a Wireless Network Wizard.

6. Type the network's SSID in the Network Name box.

> **NOTE** SSIDs are case sensitive, so use the exact case.

7. Open the Security Type drop-down menu and choose the security type, such as WPA2-Personal.

8. If the Encryption Type drop-down menu is available, open it and choose the appropriate encryption type.

9. Check the Hide Characters check box if you need to hide the password from shoulder-surfers.

10. Type the password in the Security Key box.

11. Check the Start This Connection Automatically check box if you want Windows to connect automatically to this network. You may want to do this if this is a network you use regularly.

> **! CAUTION** Selecting the Start This Connection Automatically check box causes Windows to try to connect to the network even when it's not there—for example, when you're using your tablet somewhere else. Anybody running a network scanner can see that your computer is looking for a hidden network.

12. Check the Connect Even If the Network Is Not Broadcasting check box only if it's essential to connect your computer to this network. See the nearby Caution.

> **! CAUTION** Selecting the Connect Even If the Network Is Not Broadcasting check box makes Windows keep trying to connect to the network. Someone using a network scanner can read the probe packets that Windows sends and from them learn the network's name and the settings required. With this information, that person can set up a dummy access point, and your computer will connect to it as if it were the real one. This is why Windows says that your computer's privacy may be at risk if you use this option. Another downside to enabling this option and the previous option is that they use more battery power on a laptop or tablet.

13. Click the Next button. The Manually Connect to a Wireless Network Wizard displays the Successfully Added screen, letting you know that it has added the network.
14. Click Close to close the Wizard.

CONNECTING TO THE HIDDEN NETWORK YOU ADDED

After you've added the hidden network, it appears in the list of networks in the Network fly-out when your computer is within range of it. To connect to the hidden network, click the Network icon in the notification area, and then click the network's name on the Network fly-out, as for a non-hidden wireless network.

DISCONNECTING FROM AND RECONNECTING TO WIRELESS NETWORKS

When you're ready to stop using a wireless network, disconnect from it. Click the Network icon in the notification area to display the Network fly-out, click the network's name, and then click Disconnect.

> **TIP** If you need to connect to a different wireless network than the one your computer is currently using, you can simply connect to that network. When you do so, Windows disconnects automatically from the previous network.

To reconnect to a network you've used before, click the Network icon in the notification area to open the network fly-out, click the network's name, and then click Connect.

> **TIP** If you try to reconnect to a wireless network whose password you've previously entered and saved but you get the message "Can't connect to this network," chances are that the network's password has changed. To connect to the network, tell Windows to forget it (see the section "Forgetting a Wireless Network," later in this chapter), and then connect to the network as if it were a new network.

WHITELISTING YOUR DEVICE ON A WI-FI NETWORK

Some Wi-Fi networks use whitelists to determine which devices are allowed to connect to them. A whitelist is a list of approved MAC addresses on devices.

> **NOTE** MAC is the abbreviation for Media Access Control. A MAC address is a unique hexadecimal identifier (such as `f8:a9:d0:73;c4:dd`) burned into the network hardware of a device.

Here's how to find your computer's MAC address:

1. Choose Start, Settings to open the Settings window.
2. Choose Network & Internet to display the Network & Internet screen.
3. Click Wi-Fi in the left column if it's not already selected.

4. Click Advanced Options below the list of Wi-Fi networks. (You may need to scroll down.)

5. Look at the Physical Address readout on the Wi-Fi screen.

6. If necessary, click Copy to copy all the information shown.

! CAUTION If you're administering a wireless network, a whitelist of MAC addresses is a useful security measure for preventing unauthorized devices from connecting. But it's not foolproof, because software can *spoof* (fake) an authorized MAC address that an attacker has grabbed using a network sniffer tool.

You can then give the address to your network's administrator to add to the MAC whitelist—or, if the network is your own, add the address yourself.

MANAGING YOUR NETWORK CONNECTIONS

If your computer is a laptop or a tablet, chances are that you'll use multiple network connections rather than just one. This section shows you how to use Airplane mode to turn off communications, how to configure network settings manually when necessary, and how to connect through a proxy server. You also learn how to prioritize network connections, how to bridge multiple connections, how to improve wireless speed and reliability, and how to forget a wireless network you no longer want to use.

USING AIRPLANE MODE AND TURNING OFF WIRELESS DEVICES

When you need to shut down communications, you can switch on Airplane mode. As its name suggests, Airplane mode is mainly designed for air travel, but you can use it any other time you need it.

NOTE Switching on Airplane mode turns off all your computer's wireless communications hardware: Wi-Fi, Bluetooth, and cellular connectivity (if your computer has it). After turning on Airplane mode, you can turn individual items back on as needed. For example, you can turn Wi-Fi back on.

The quick way to turn Airplane mode on or off is to click the Network icon in the notification area and then click Airplane Mode on the Network fly-out.

Alternatively, choose Start, Settings, choose Network & Internet, click Airplane Mode in the left column, and then set the Airplane Mode switch to On or Off, as needed.

> **NOTE** After turning on Airplane mode, you can open the Network fly-out and click Wi-Fi to turn Wi-Fi on or off. Similarly, on the Airplane Mode screen, you can set the Wi-Fi switch and the Bluetooth switch in the Wireless Devices area to On or Off, as needed.

CONFIGURING IP SETTINGS MANUALLY

As discussed earlier in this chapter, Windows tries to automatically detect and apply suitable network settings when you connect to a wired network or wireless network. But if the network doesn't use DHCP, or if your computer needs a static IP address for other reasons, you can configure IP settings manually.

Normally, you'll just need to configure the essential settings, which we cover in the first subsection. But there are also more advanced settings you may need sometimes; we cover those in the second subsection.

CONFIGURING THE IP ADDRESS, GATEWAY, AND DNS SERVERS

Follow these steps to configure IP settings:

1. Click the Network icon in the notification area to open the Network fly-out.

2. Click the Network Settings link to display the appropriate pane on the Network & Internet screen in the Settings app. For a wireless network, the Wi-Fi pane appears; for a wired network, the Ethernet pane appears.

3. Click Change Adapter Options to display the Network Connections window.

> **TIP** You can also open the Network Connections window by right-clicking the Network icon in the notification area, clicking Open Network and Sharing Center, and then clicking Change Adapter Settings in the left column.

4. Right-click the entry for the adapter you want to configure, and then click Properties on the shortcut menu. For example, right-click Ethernet and click Properties to open the Ethernet Properties dialog box (see Figure 3.5).

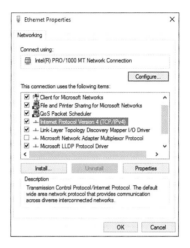

FIGURE 3.5

In the Properties dialog box for the connection, click the appropriate Internet Protocol item, and then click Properties.

5. Click the appropriate Internet Protocol item. For most networks, you'd click Internet Protocol Version 4 (TCP/IPv4).

6. Click Properties to display the Properties dialog box—for example, the Internet Protocol Version 4 (TCP/IPv4) Properties dialog box (see Figure 3.6).

7. Check the Use the Following IP Address option button. When you do this, Windows automatically selects the Use the Following DNS Server Addresses option button in the lower part of the dialog box.

8. Type the static IP address in the IP Address box.

> **NOTE** Normally, you'll be using an IPv4 address, which consists of four groups of numbers in the 0–255 range, separated by periods—for example, 192.168.1.44 or 10.0.0.250. If you're connecting to an IPv6 network, the address consists of six hexadecimal groups separated by colons—for example, fe80:0000:faa9:d0fe:fe72:c4dd. If a group consists of zeroes, you can collapse it to nothing, simply putting a pair of colons to indicate where it would be. For example, the previous address can also be written fe80::faa9:d0fe:fe72:c4dd, with the group of zeroes removed.

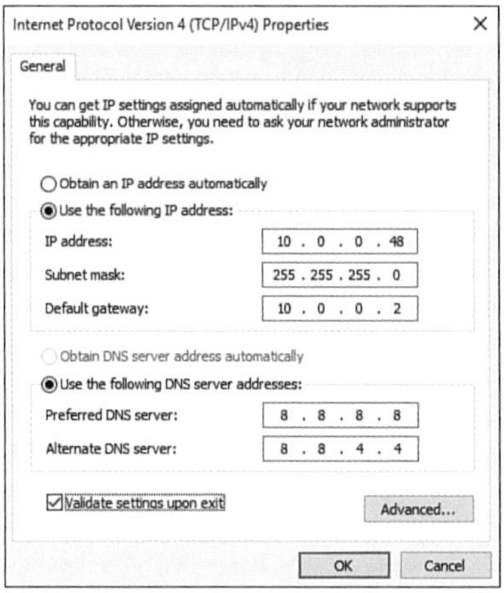

FIGURE 3.6

In the Properties dialog box for the protocol, such as the Internet Protocol Version 4 (TCP/IPv4) Properties dialog box, specify the IP settings the connection needs.

9. Type the subnet mask in the Subnet Mask box.

> **TIP** Many home networks use the subnet mask 255.255.255.0.

> **NOTE** When configuring an IPv6 connection, you specify the subnet prefix length instead of the subnet mask. The subnet prefix length is a number such as 64.

10. Type the IP address of the network router or gateway in the Default Gateway box. If you administer your network, this is the address of your router; if you're on someone else's network, ask the network's administrator for this information and for the DNS server addresses.

11. Type the IP address of the first DNS server your administrator or ISP has given you in the Preferred DNS Server box.

> **☑ TIP**   Some administrators refer to the DNS servers as "primary" and "secondary" rather than "preferred" and "alternate." If you're short of a DNS server address, you can use Google's DNS servers, `8.8.8.8` (primary) and `8.8.4.4` (secondary). For IPv6, use `2001:4860:4860::8888` (primary) and `2001:4860:4860::8844` (secondary).

12. Type the IP address of the second DNS server in the Alternate DNS Server box.
13. Check the Validate Settings upon Exit check box if you want Windows to check the configuration when you close the Internet Protocol Version 4 (TCP/IPv4) Properties dialog box. This is normally a good idea.
14. Click OK.

If you selected the Validate Settings upon Exit check box, Windows checks for obvious problems with the connection. If the settings seem valid, Windows closes the dialog box without comment. But if there's a problem, Windows displays a Microsoft TCP/IP dialog box such as that shown in Figure 3.7 to warn you of the problem. Normally, you'll want to click No, which returns you to the Internet Protocol Version 4 (TCP/IPv4) Properties dialog box so that you can fix the problem.

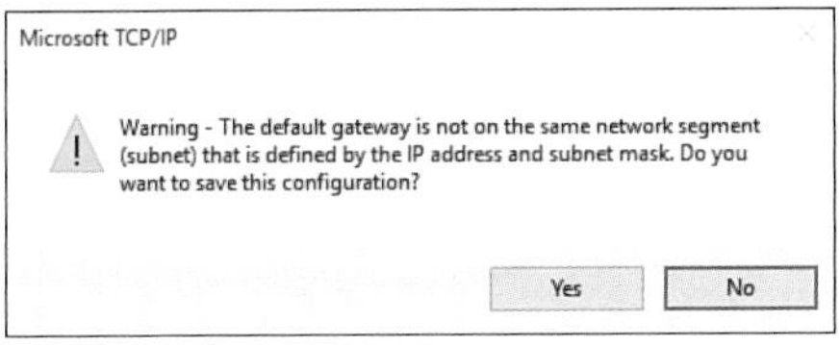

FIGURE 3.7

The Microsoft TCP/IP dialog box opens if Windows detects a problem with the IP settings you have chosen. Click No to go back and make changes to fix the problem.

When the settings are okay, you can close the Properties dialog box for the connection, the Network Connections window, and the Settings window.

CONFIGURING ADVANCED SETTINGS

For some networks, you may need to configure advanced settings in order to give your computer the connectivity it needs. For example, you may need to assign further IP addresses, configure default gateways, or specify DNS suffixes.

Click the Advanced button in the Internet Protocol Version 4 (TCP/IPv4) Properties dialog box or the Internet Protocol Version 6 (TCP/IPv6) dialog box to display the

Advanced TCP/IP Settings dialog box. For IPv4, this dialog box has three tabs: the IP Settings tab, the DNS tab, and the WINS tab. For IPv6, this dialog box has only the IP Settings tab and the DNS tab.

> **NOTE** WINS is the acronym for Windows Internet Naming System, an older method for locating computers on a network. If necessary, you can configure WINS settings for an adapter by working on the WINS tab of the Advanced TCP/IP Settings dialog box. Normally, however, you don't need to use WINS these days.

On the IP Settings tab of the Advanced TCP/IP Settings dialog box (see Figure 3.8), you can take the following actions:

■ **Add, edit, and remove IP addresses.** Use the Add, Edit, and Remove buttons below the IP Addresses box to add new IP addresses or to edit or remove existing ones. The adapter must have at least one IP address.

FIGURE 3.8

On the IP Settings tab of the Advanced TCP/IP Settings dialog box, you can add, edit, and remove IP addresses and default gateways.

■ **Add, edit, and remove default gateways.** Use the Add, Edit, and Remove buttons below the Default Gateways box to add new default gateways or to edit or remove existing ones. For each default gateway, you can either assign a specific interface metric or allow Windows to assign the metric automatically. The adapter must have at least one default gateway.

- **Choose between automatic metric and a specific interface metric for this network adapter.** Check the Automatic Metric check box at the bottom of the IP Settings tab to let Windows choose which adapter to use when multiple adapters have connections. Clear this check box and enter a value (an integer in the range 1–9999) if you want to weight this adapter against other adapters manually.

> **NOTE** The metric is an integer value in the range 1–9999 that represents the cost assigned to a specific route. Windows uses the default gateway with the lower metric. Generally, it is best to check the Automatic Metric check box and let Windows choose which default gateway to use unless you need to force Windows to favor one default gateway over another.

On the DNS tab of the Advanced TCP/IP Settings dialog box (see Figure 3.9), you can take the following actions:

- **Add, edit, and remove DNS servers.** Use the Add, Edit, and Remove buttons below the DNS Server Addresses, in Order of Use box to add new DNS servers or to edit or remove existing ones.

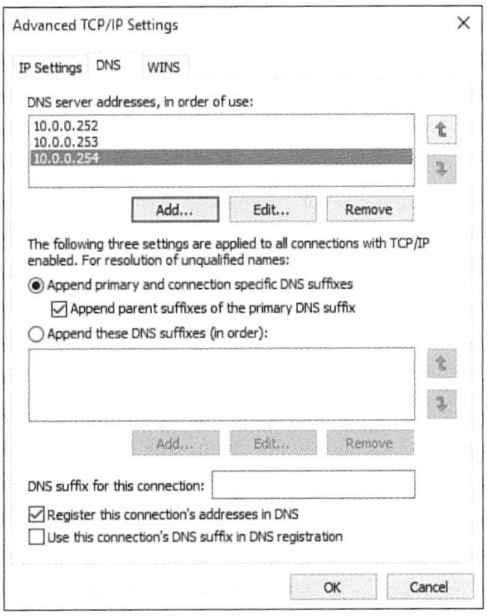

FIGURE 3.9

You can configure additional DNS settings on the DNS tab of the Advanced TCP/IP Settings dialog box.

■ **Change the order in which to use DNS servers.** Use the Move Up button and Move Down button on the right side to shuffle the DNS servers into the order in which you want Windows to use them.

■ **Specify how to resolve unqualified DNS names.** For unqualified DNS names (see the nearby note), you normally want to select the Append Primary and Connection Specific DNS Suffixes option button. You then can check the Append Parent Suffixes of the Primary DNS Suffix check box to append parent suffixes as well. (For example, with the primary DNS suffix of test.surrealpcs.com, Windows appends .surrealpcs.com and .com to queries.) Alternatively, you can check the Append These DNS Suffixes (in Order) check box and then build the list of suffixes in the list box.

> **NOTE** An unqualified DNS name is one that does not have a full address—for example, que instead of que.com. To qualify the domain fully, Windows can automatically apply DNS suffixes either from its built-in list or from a list of DNS suffixes that you supply, and in the order you specify.

■ **Specify the DNS suffix for this connection.** Type the appropriate suffix in the DNS Suffix for This Connection box.

■ **Register this connection's addresses in DNS.** Check the Register This Connection's Addresses in DNS check box if you want your computer to try to dynamically create DNS records in this DNS zone. Creating the records may help other computers to locate this computer.

■ **Use this connection's DNS suffix in DNS registration.** If you check the Register This Connection's Addresses in DNS check box, you can check the Use This Connection's DNS Suffix in DNS Registration check box to make your computer try to register its DNS suffix in this DNS zone. You don't usually need to do this, because Windows automatically registers the full computer name in the DNS zone.

CONNECTING THROUGH A PROXY SERVER

Instead of connecting to websites directly, your computer can connect through a proxy server. This is a server that fulfills network requests for your computer, either by providing data that the server has previously cached or by relaying the requests to a suitable server. For example, instead of requesting a web page directly from the web server, your computer requests it from the proxy server. The proxy server either delivers the web page from its cache, providing the data more quickly and reducing Internet use, or requests the web page from the web server and passes it along to your computer.

> **TIP** Normally, you'd connect through a proxy server in a corporate or organizational setting, where the proxy server not only caches data but also prevents access to blocked sites. You can also connect through a proxy server with the aim of disguising the location where the network requests are coming from.

Windows can use a proxy server in three ways:

- **Automatically.** Depending on the network setup, Windows may be able to detect the proxy server and automatically select settings to use the server. You can control whether Windows does this by setting the Automatically Detect Settings switch to On or Off, as needed.

- **Using a configuration script.** Windows can use the configuration script you specify to select settings for using the proxy server. You can control this feature by setting the Use Setup Script switch to On or Off, as needed.

- **Manually.** You set the details of the proxy server.

To set up a network connection to use a proxy server, follow these steps:

1. Choose Start, Settings to open the Settings window.
2. Choose Network & Internet to display the Network & Internet screen.
3. Choose Proxy in the left pane to display the Proxy pane. Figure 3.10 shows the top part of the Proxy pane.
4. Set the Automatically Detect Settings switch to On if you want Windows to detect the proxy server automatically. Otherwise, set this switch to Off.
5. Set the Use Setup Script switch to On if you need to use a script, and then enter the script's location in the Script Address box and click Save. Otherwise, set the Use Setup Script switch to Off.
6. Assuming you haven't chosen either of the automatic options, go to the Manual Proxy Setup section and set the Use a Proxy Server switch to On.
7. Type the proxy server's address in the Address box (see Figure 3.11). This can be either a hostname, such as proxy.surrealpcs.com, or an IP address, such as `10.0.0.254`.
8. Type the port number in the Port box. The port depends on how the server is configured, but ports 3128 and 8080 are widely used.

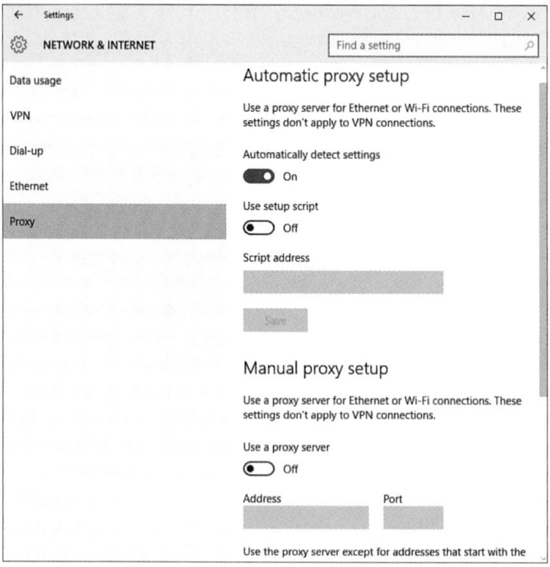

FIGURE 3.10

At the top of the Proxy pane, choose whether to use the Automatically Detect Settings feature or the Use Setup Script feature.

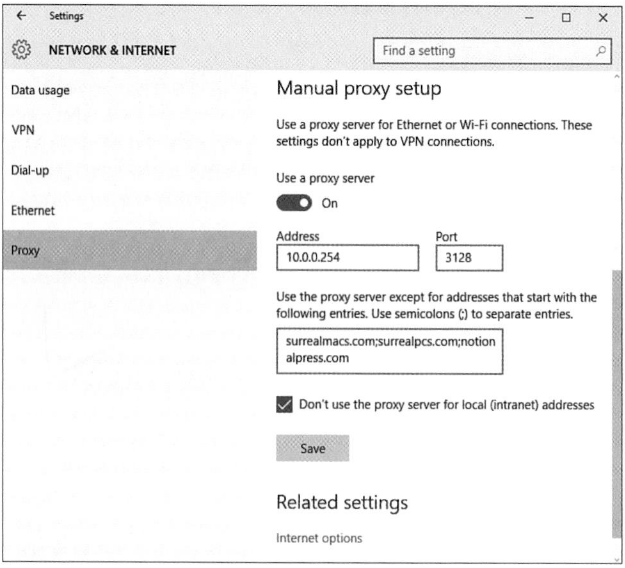

FIGURE 3.11

In the lower part of the Proxy pane, set the Use a Proxy Server switch to On, enter the address and port, and specify any exceptions.

9. Enter any proxy exceptions in the Use the Proxy Server Except for Addresses That Start with the Following Entries box, separating them with semicolons. A proxy exception is an address for which you don't want Windows to use the proxy server. You enter the first part of the address. For example, to create a proxy exception for the surrealpcs.com site, you would enter **surrealpcs.com**; to create an exception just for FTP traffic on surrealpcs.com, you would enter **ftp://surrealpcs.com**.

10. Check the Don't Use the Proxy Server for Local (Intranet) Addresses check box if you want to create an exception for all local addresses.

11. Click Save. Windows saves the proxy configuration.

USING A PROXY SERVER FOR JUST SOME APPS

When you set up a proxy server as explained in the main text of this section, Windows uses the proxy server for all apps and all traffic, except for any traffic that matches proxy exceptions you have configured. Instead, you can configure some apps individually to use a proxy server. Most web browsers and some games enable you to do this.

For example, to set the widely used Firefox browser to use a proxy server, click the Menu button to open the menu, and then click Options to open the Options dialog box. Click the Advanced button on the toolbar to display the Advanced tab, and then click Network to display the Network pane. In the Connection area, click Settings to open the Connection Settings dialog box. Select the Manual Proxy Configuration option button, enter the details in the HTTP Proxy box and the Port box, and then click OK. Click OK to close the Options dialog box as well.

PRIORITIZING ONE NETWORK CONNECTION OVER ANOTHER

If your computer has two or more network connections at any given time, you should tell Windows which connection to use first. Otherwise, you may be stuck using a slow wireless connection when a fast wired connection is available.

To set the priority for connections, follow these steps:

1. Right-click or long-press the Network icon in the notification area to open the shortcut menu.

2. Click Open Network and Sharing Center to open a Network and Sharing Center window.

3. Click Change Adapter Settings in the left column to open a Network Connections window.

4. Press Alt to display the menu bar.

5. Click the Advanced menu and then click Advanced Settings to display the Advanced Settings dialog box. The Adapters and Bindings tab appears at the front (see Figure 3.12).

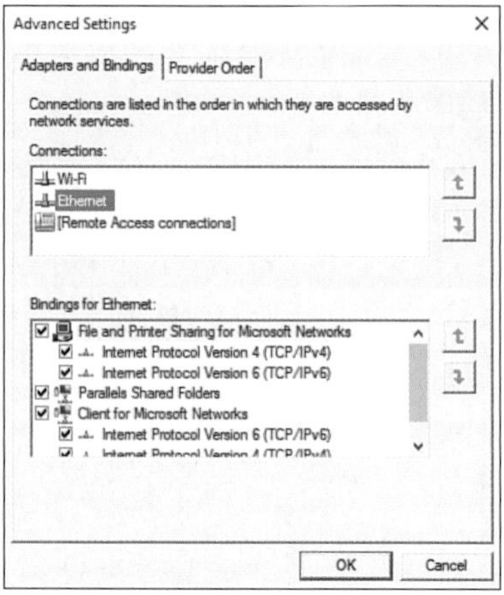

FIGURE 3.12

Set the priority for your computer's network connections by working in the Connections box on the Adapters and Bindings tab of the Advanced Settings dialog box.

6. In the Connections box, click a connection, and then click Move Up or Move Down, as appropriate.

7. When you finish, click OK to close the Advanced Settings dialog box.

BRIDGING TWO OR MORE NETWORK CONNECTIONS

If your computer connects to two separate networks, you can create a network bridge to enable the computers and devices on each of those networks to communicate with computers and devices on the other network.

> **NOTE** Bridging network connections is a relatively specialized move. Don't create a bridge unless you're certain you need to do so.

Follow these steps to bridge network connections:

1. Right-click or long-press the Network icon in the notification area to open the shortcut menu.

2. Click Open Network and Sharing Center to open a Network and Sharing Center window.

3. Click Change Adapter Settings in the left column to open a Network Connections window.

4. Click the first connection you want to bridge, and then Ctrl+click each of the other connections.

5. Right-click or long-press one of the selected connections, and then click Bridge Connections on the shortcut menu.

The Network Bridge dialog box appears while Windows sets up the bridge, and then disappears automatically when the Network Bridge item appears in the Network Connections window. You've now connected the two networks, and the computers and devices can communicate across the bridge.

> **TIP** You can create only one network bridge at a time, but you can add as many connections as necessary to that bridge.

> **! CAUTION** Use bridging only for network connections, not for a network connection and an Internet connection. Bridging an Internet connection can make your network accessible to any computer on the Internet, which exposes computers on your network to attack.

After creating a bridge, you can manipulate it as follows:

- **Add a connection to the bridge.** Right-click or long-press the connection in the Network Connections window, and then click Add to Bridge on the shortcut menu.

- **Remove a connection from the bridge.** Right-click or long-press the connection in the Network Connections window, and then click Remove from Bridge on the shortcut menu.

- **Remove the bridge.** Remove each connection from the bridge. After you remove the last connection, Windows removes the bridge automatically.

> **☑ TIP** After you remove a network bridge, you may find that one or more of the connections that formed the bridge fails to regain its previous network settings. If this happens, right-click or long-press the connection in the Network Connections window and click Disable on the shortcut menu to disable it for a moment. Right-click or long-press the connection again and click Enable on the shortcut menu to enable it again. Normally, disabling and reenabling the connection makes it reestablish its settings.

IMPROVING WIRELESS SPEED AND RELIABILITY

Wi-Fi connections can be great for convenience and flexibility but can suffer from dropped connections and slowdowns. In this section, we look briefly at what you can do to improve the speed and reliability of your wireless connections.

First, if your computer keeps dropping the connection and then having to reestablish it, try turning Wi-Fi off and back on again. The easiest way to do this is to click the Network icon in the notification area and then click the Wi-Fi button at the bottom of the Network fly-out to turn off Wi-Fi temporarily. Repeat the move to turn Wi-Fi back on. If the connection is still problematic, and it's a network that you administer, restart the wireless router.

> **☑ TIP** If turning Wi-Fi off and back on doesn't stop your computer from dropping the connection, restart Windows. Restarting is tedious if you're in a hurry, but it can clear up many lingering configuration problems.

Second, look at the connection's status to see whether there's anything obviously wrong. The Network icon in the notification area gives you a rough indication of signal strength—the more white bars, the better—but to see the details, you need to look in the Wi-Fi Status dialog box.

Follow these steps to open the Wi-Fi Status dialog box:

1. Right-click or long-press the Network icon in the notification area to open the shortcut menu.

2. Click Open Network and Sharing Center to open a Network and Sharing Center window.

3. In the Access Type section of the View Your Active Networks box, click the link for the Wi-Fi connection to display the Wi-Fi Status dialog box (see Figure 3.13).

FIGURE 3.13

Look at the Speed readout and Signal Quality readout in the Wi-Fi Status dialog box to try to identify problems with the connection.

These are the main things you can do from the Wi-Fi Status dialog box:

- **Check that the connection has Internet access.** Look at the IPv4 Connectivity readout and the IPv6 Connectivity readout. Make sure that at least one of these says *Internet* rather than *No Internet Access*.

- **Check the connection speed.** Look at the speed readout to see whether it's reasonable. (See the nearby sidebar about wireless speeds.) If it's not, you may be able to get a higher speed by disconnecting from the network and then connecting to it again.

- **Check the signal quality.** Look at the Signal Quality readout, which shows from one to five green bars—as usual, the more the merrier.

- **View more details about the wireless connection.** Click Details to display the Network Connection Details dialog box. This includes a wealth of detail, of which the following items are usually most useful: the hardware (MAC) address; whether the connection uses DHCP; the IP address and the subnet mask; and the addresses of the default gateway, the DHCP server, and the DNS server.

- **Change the wireless network's properties.** If you need to control whether Windows connects automatically to this network, click Wireless Properties to display the Wireless Network Properties dialog box. On the Connection tab, you can check or clear the Connect Automatically When This Network Is in Range check box, as needed.

> **NOTE** In the Wireless Network Properties dialog box, you can also check the Look for Other Wireless Networks While Connected to This Network check box if you want Windows to look for other networks. You can check the Connect Even If the Network Is Not Broadcasting Its Name (SSID) check box if you need to try to force a connection to the network. As mentioned earlier in this chapter, this option may expose your computer to attack via a dummy access point, so use it only if you must.

■ **Diagnose problems with the connection.** If the connection isn't working correctly, click Diagnose to launch the Windows Network Diagnostics Wizard.

WHAT WIRELESS SPEEDS SHOULD YOU BE GETTING?

What wireless speeds your computer gets depends on several things, including the capabilities both of your computer's wireless network adapter and of the wireless router, the distance between your computer and the wireless router, and how much wireless activity is taking place in the area.

Wireless networks use a plethora of confusingly numbered standards, most of which people refer to simply as "Wi-Fi." At this writing, the fastest standard is 802.11ac, which gives speeds up to 1,300 megabits per second (Mbps)—in other words, 1.3 gigabits per second (Gbps), or faster than a Gigabit Ethernet connection, which is the fastest widely used standard for wired connections. Next in speed is 802.11n with 600Mbps, followed by 802.11g and 802.11a with 54Mbps each, and last 802.11b with 11Mbps.

Each of these is the maximum theoretical speed, and in practice, the speeds your computer achieves are likely to be much lower than the maximum, especially when many computers and devices are using the same wireless router.

Many wireless devices support multiple standards, enabling you to connect to a wide variety of devices.

> ☐ **NOTE** Windows usually connects at the highest link speed possible. But if you establish the connection when your computer is relatively far from the wireless access point and the signal is correspondingly weak, you may get a low link speed that persists even when you move your computer closer to the wireless access point. If this happens, drop the connection and reconnect to try to get a higher link speed.

Third, you may need to change channels to get a decent connection. A wireless network can use any of a variety of channels, which the administrator can choose using whatever configuration utility the wireless access point provides. If many of the wireless networks in your immediate vicinity use the same channels, you may get lower throughput.

To see which network is using which channels, you can install a Wi-Fi analyzer app or Wi-Fi stumbler app such as InSSIDer or Kismet. Many are available with different features, but most show you the available networks, their relative signal strength, and the channels they are using. Armed with this information, you can set your wireless network to avoid the channels your neighbors are using.

> ☐ **TIP** A Wi-Fi analyzer app or Wi-Fi stumbler app is also useful for locating available wireless networks when you need to get online.

FORGETTING A WIRELESS NETWORK

When you no longer want to use a particular wireless network, tell your computer to forget it. Follow these steps:

1. Click the Network icon in the notification area to open the Network fly-out.

2. Click Network Settings to display the Network & Internet screen in Settings.

3. Click Manage Wi-Fi Settings (below the list of Wi-Fi networks) to display the Manage Wi-Fi Settings screen.

4. Click the appropriate network in the Manage Known Networks list. The Forget button appears.

5. Click Forget. Windows removes the network from the list and deletes the saved password and settings for it.

UNDERSTANDING WI-FI SENSE

Wi-Fi Sense is a feature that helps you connect your computer to Wi-Fi hotspots. Microsoft introduced Wi-Fi Sense on Windows Phone but now has made the feature available on desktops, laptops, and tablets as well. Wi-Fi Sense tends to be more useful on mobile devices than on desktop computers.

Wi-Fi Sense maintains a database of crowd-sourced open Wi-Fi networks and detects known networks that are nearby. Wi-Fi Sense can accept a network's terms of use for you, enabling your computer to connect to the network more easily. To do this, Wi-Fi Sense needs to use your computer's location services.

You can turn Wi-Fi Sense on or off by setting the Connect to Suggested Open Hotspots switch and the Connect to Networks Shared by My Contacts switch on the Manage Wi-Fi Settings screen to On or Off.

CONNECTING THROUGH A VPN

Virtual private networking (abbreviated to VPN) enables you to create a secure connection to a server across an insecure network. You'd typically use a virtual private network (also abbreviated to VPN) for connecting across the Internet to a work network.

TIP   Here are two more uses for VPN. First, when you connect to a Wi-Fi hotspot, you can use a VPN to secure your Internet traffic against snooping. Second, you can use a VPN when you need to make your computer appear to be in a different location than it actually is. For example, if you subscribe to a U.S.-based media service, you may not be able to access it when you travel abroad. But by connecting to a VPN server within the U.S., you can make your computer appear to be in the country, enabling you to use the service. Leading VPN services include IPVanish (www.ipvanish.com), StrongVPN (www.strongvpn.com), and CyberGhost VPN (www.cyberghostvpn.com).

SETTING UP A VPN CONNECTION

To set up a VPN connection on your computer, you'll need to know the following:

- **VPN type.** This can be PPTP, L2TP/IPSec, SSTP, or IKEv2.
- **Server address.** This can be a server name (such as vpnserv.surrealpcs.com) or an IP address (such as 209.14.241.1).

- **L2TP secret.** This is a text string used for securing some L2TP connections.
- **IPSec identifier.** This is a text string used for some IPSec connections.
- **IPSec preshared key.** This is a text string used for some IPSec connections.

Ask the VPN's administrator for this information. Ask also for your user name and password for the VPN connection. You don't need these for setting up the connection, but you'll need them when you connect.

When you've gathered this information, follow these steps to set up the VPN on your computer:

1. Choose Start, Settings to open a Settings window.
2. Choose Network & Internet to display the Network & Internet screen.
3. Choose VPN in the left pane to display the VPN pane.
4. Choose Add a VPN Connection to display the Add a VPN Connection pane (shown in Figure 3.14 with settings chosen).

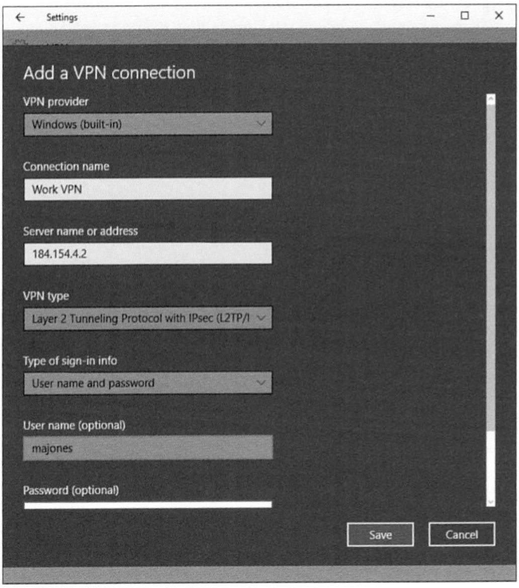

FIGURE 3.14
In the Add a VPN Connection pane, enter the details for the VPN connection and click Save.

5. Open the VPN Provider drop-down menu and choose the provider. If you're not sure what the provider is, choose Windows (Built-In).
6. Type a descriptive name for the connection in the Connection Name box. This name is to help you identify the VPN—for example, Work VPN.

7. Type the server's hostname (such as vpn1.surrealpcs.com) or IP address (such as `205.14.152.18`) in the Server Name or Address box.

8. Open the VPN Type drop-down menu and choose the VPN type, such as Layer 2 Tunneling Protocol with IPsec (L2TP/IPsec).

9. Open the Type of Sign-In Info drop-down menu and then choose User Name and Password, Smart Card, or One-Time Password, as appropriate.

10. For a VPN that uses a user name for signing in, type the user name in the User Name box.

NOTE The User Name box and Password box are marked "optional" because, instead of entering them while setting up the connection, you can enter them each time you use the connection. Entering your credentials each time is more secure but takes more time and effort.

11. For a VPN that uses a password for signing in, type the password in the Password box.

12. Check the Remember My Sign-In Info check box if you want Windows to store your sign-in information.

13. Click Save.

CONNECTING VIA THE VPN

After you've set up a VPN connection, you can connect via the VPN like this:

1. Choose Start, Settings to open a Settings window.

2. Choose Network & Internet to display the Network & Internet screen.

3. Choose VPN in the left pane to display the VPN pane.

4. Click the VPN in the VPN list to display control buttons for it (see Figure 3.15).

5. Click Connect. Windows establishes the connection, and then displays the Connected readout and the Disconnect button.

After connecting, you can work across the VPN connection in much the same way as a local network connection. Normally, the speeds will be much slower across the VPN, so you may need to be patient while transferring data.

When you're ready to stop using the VPN, click the Disconnect button in the VPN pane. If you've left the VPN pane open, you can go straight there; if you've closed it, click the Network icon in the notification area, click the VPN's name at the top of the network fly-out, click the VPN's name in the VPN pane, and then click Disconnect.

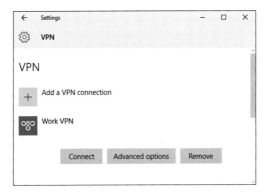

FIGURE 3.15

In the VPN pane in the Settings app, click the VPN to display its control buttons, and then click Connect.

MAPPING A DRIVE TO A NETWORK FOLDER

When you work with other people, it's often useful to share files on a network. If you need to connect to the same network folder regularly, you can map a drive to it. When you do this, Windows displays a drive, marked with your chosen letter, that you can use to connect to the network folder quickly and easily.

Follow these steps to map a drive to a network folder:

1. Open a File Explorer window. For example, click File Explorer on the Taskbar.

2. Choose Home, New, Easy Access, Map as Drive to display the Map Network Drive dialog box (see Figure 3.16).

3. Click the Drive drop-down menu and choose the drive letter you want to assign. Windows starts with Z: (if it is as yet unassigned) and walks backward from there, but you can choose any available drive letter.

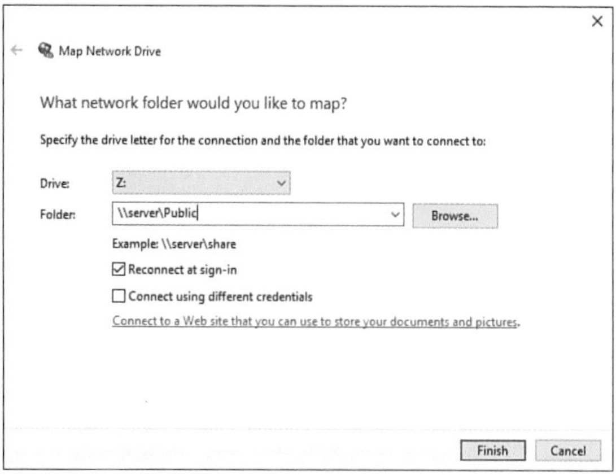

FIGURE 3.16

In the Map Network Drive dialog box, specify the drive, choose the folder, and choose options for reconnection and credentials.

WHY DOES WINDOWS SUGGEST Z: FOR THE FIRST NETWORK DRIVE?

Windows drive-naming conventions derive from DOS (disk operating system), a predecessor of Windows.

Drive A: was the first floppy disk drive, and drive B: the second floppy disk drive. Drive C: was, and remains, the first hard drive, with any subsequent hard drives receiving the next letters (drive D:, drive E:), and any optical drives picking up the next available letter (drive D:, drive E:, drive F:).

Network drives originally used to pick up the next unused letter, but more recently they've walked backward from Z: to make a distinction between local drives and network drives.

4. In the Folder box, enter the address of the folder to which you want to map the drive. You can type in the address if you know it verbatim, or paste it in if you have somewhere from which you can copy it, but usually it's easiest to click Browse, locate and select the folder in the Browse for Folder dialog box, and then click OK.

> **✓ TIP** Enter the folder address in the format `\\server_name\folder`. For example, you would enter `\\server1\Public` to connect to the folder named `Public` on the server named `server1`. The server name can also be an IP address, giving an address such as `\\10.0.0.100\Files`.

5. Check the Reconnect at Sign-In check box if you want Windows to connect automatically to this folder each time you sign in. You'd do this for a folder you connect to every day with your desktop computer at work, but normally you will be better off connecting manually on a laptop or a tablet that you use in multiple locations.

> **✓ TIP** Another way to start mapping a network drive is to use File Explorer. Browse to the computer and drive in the Network section, and then right-click or long-press the appropriate folder and click Map Network Drive. Windows displays the Map Network Drive dialog box with the server name and folder path already entered in the Folder box.

6. Check the Connect Using Different Credentials check box if you need to provide different credentials for the folder than the credentials you're using for Windows.

7. Click Finish. If you checked the Connect Using Different Credentials check box, Windows displays the Windows Security dialog box (see Figure 3.17); continue with the next steps. If not, Windows connects to the folder; skip the rest of the steps in this list.

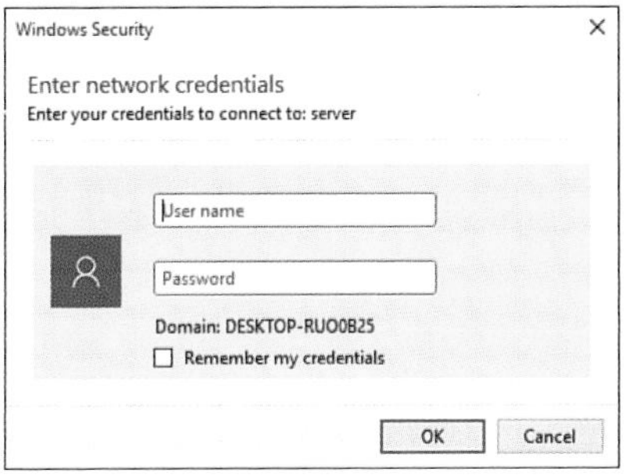

FIGURE 3.17

In the Windows Security dialog box, type your user name and password for the server, check the Remember My Credentials check box if necessary, and then click OK.

8. Type your user name for the server.

9. Type your password for the server.

10. Check the Remember My Credentials check box if you don't want to have to enter them next time.

11. Click OK. The Windows Security dialog box closes, and Windows connects to the folder.

SHARING YOUR COMPUTER'S INTERNET CONNECTION

Windows includes a feature called Internet Connection Sharing that enables you to share your computer's Internet connection with other computers and devices.

Internet Connection Sharing can work pretty well, but normally you'd want to use it only in these circumstances:

- You have a wired connection that's available only to your computer. For example, your broadband router is connected directly to your computer via USB and doesn't have an Ethernet port or wireless capabilities.

- Your computer has a cellular connection that you want to share temporarily.

!CAUTION Avoid using Internet Connection Sharing if you have a better alternative available, such as sharing the connection via your broadband router either using cables or wirelessly.

Follow these steps to set up Internet Connection Sharing:

1. Right-click or long-press the Network icon in the notification area to open the shortcut menu.

2. Click Open Network and Sharing Center to open a Network and Sharing Center window.

3. Click Change Adapter Settings in the left column to open a Network Connections window.

4. Right-click or long-press the Internet connection, and then click Properties on the shortcut menu to open the Properties dialog box for the connection.

5. Click the Sharing tab to display its contents (see Figure 3.18).

6. Check the Allow Other Network Users to Connect Through This Computer's Internet Connection check box.

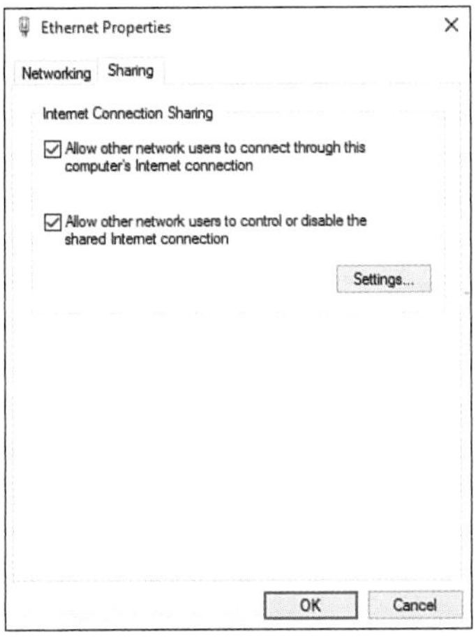

FIGURE 3.18
You can control Internet Connection Sharing on the Sharing tab of the Properties dialog box for the connection.

7. Check the Allow Other Network Users to Control or Disable the Shared Internet Connection check box only if you want others to be able to manipulate the Internet connection. You may prefer to keep control of it yourself.

8. Click OK. Windows shares the connection.

> **NOTE** When you want to stop sharing your computer's Internet connection, open the Properties dialog box, uncheck the Allow Other Network Users to Connect Through This Computer's Internet Connection check box, and click OK.

DIAGNOSING AND REPAIRING NETWORK PROBLEMS

Networks are great when they work, but they can be a source of painful headaches when they don't. To help you avoid reaching for the acetaminophen, Windows includes tools for diagnosing and repairing network problems.

DETERMINING WHETHER A PROBLEM HAS OCCURRED

When your computer loses its network connection, chances are that you'll notice soon enough—or immediately if you're using the Internet.

When you detect the problem, look first at the Network icon in the notification area. If it shows an exclamation point, as in Figure 3.19, you'll know there's a problem. If you're using a mouse, you can hold the pointer over it to display a ScreenTip showing details, such as "Unidentified network: No Internet access." On any computer, you can open the Network fly-out to see the network status readout at the top, which shows a similar message.

FIGURE 3.19

The Network icon in the notification area shows an exclamation point to alert you to problems.

From the Network fly-out, click the Network Settings link to open the Network & Internet screen in the Settings app. Here, you have various options, but the best approach is usually to click Network and Sharing Center to open a Network and Sharing Center window (see Figure 3.20).

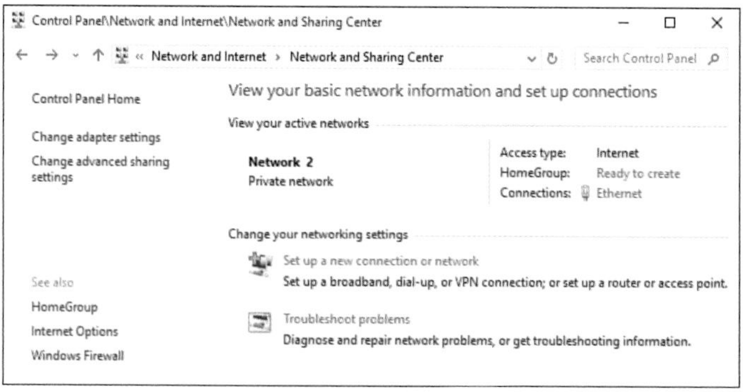

FIGURE 3.20

In the Network and Sharing Center window, click Troubleshoot Problems.

USING THE TROUBLESHOOT PROBLEMS FEATURE

Sometimes you may be able to diagnose the cause of the problem immediately. For example, if you can see that your Ethernet cable has come unplugged (or that your pet has bitten through the cable) or that your wireless router has lost power, you'll probably want to start by fixing physical problems such as these.

If the cause of the problem isn't immediately apparent, try using the Troubleshoot Problems feature to identify what's wrong.

From the Network and Sharing Center, click Troubleshoot Problems to display the Troubleshoot Problems screen (see Figure 3.21), and then click the item that seems to be the source of the problem. For example, if your Internet connection isn't working, click Internet Connections.

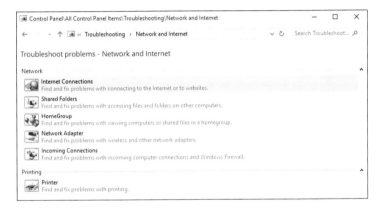

FIGURE 3.21

On the Troubleshoot Problems screen, click Internet Connections to start troubleshooting your network connection.

The Troubleshoot Problems feature displays the first screen of the troubleshooter you chose, such as the Internet Connections screen shown in Figure 3.22, and you can follow its steps. The steps vary depending on the troubleshooter and what it discovers is wrong with your computer.

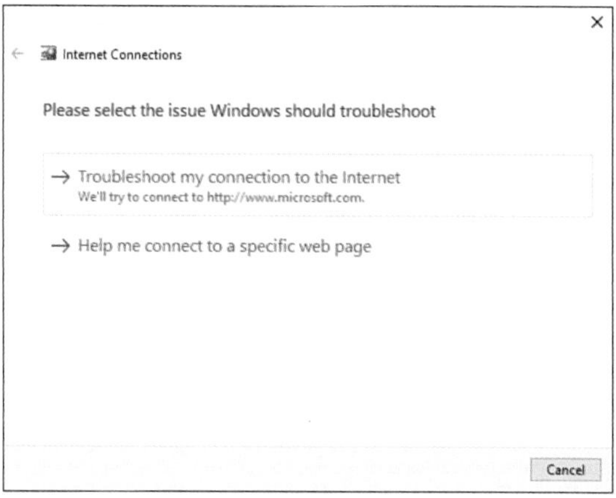

FIGURE 3.22

Follow through the screens of a troubleshooter such as Internet Connections to fix problems with your computer's configuration.

TIP By default, the Troubleshoot Problems feature applies repairs automatically when it can determine what is wrong. You can turn off automatic repairs by clicking Advanced on the opening screen of the troubleshooter and then deselecting the Apply Repairs Automatically check box.

IN THIS CHAPTER

▪ Connecting external drives
▪ Using multiple displays and virtual desktops
▪ Setting up printers

4

CONNECTING EXTERNAL HARDWARE

Even if your computer is built as a standalone unit, you'll likely need to connect external hardware to it. In this chapter, we look at how to connect extra drives to give more storage capacity, how to set up multiple monitors and virtual desktops to give you more work space, and how to set up printers for when you need hard-copy output.

CONNECTING EXTERNAL DRIVES

You can connect one or more external drives when you need extra storage capacity, when you need to back up your computer, or when you need to copy data to or from it.

MAKING THE PHYSICAL CONNECTION

These days, most external drives connect via USB, which provides a simple and effective connection. Smaller drives can be powered via the USB connection, which is great for

portable drives that you use with laptops or tablets. Larger drives, and those that need more power for greater performance, typically need their own power supply.

> **TIP** If you're buying an external drive with a USB connection, make sure it's USB 3.0 rather than USB 2.0. USB 3.0, assuming your system also has these ports, is much faster than USB 2.0, so USB 3.0 drives can transfer data far more quickly. USB 3.0 ports, which usually have an "SS" marked on their logo, also deliver more power than USB 2.0 ports, enabling you to power a larger drive from your computer rather than using a separate power supply. As you'd imagine, USB 3.0 drives are more expensive than USB 2.0 drives, but the price differential is gradually decreasing.

After you connect a drive to your computer, Windows automatically mounts the drive in your computer's file system, and you can start using it. For example, you can open a File Explorer window and copy files to the drive.

If the drive doesn't appear in File Explorer, you may need to format it, as explained in the next section.

FORMATTING A DRIVE

Here's how to format a drive you've connected to your computer:

1. Right-click or long-press Start to display the shortcut menu.

> **CAUTION** Formatting a drive deletes all the files it contains. Before formatting a drive, make sure it contains no files that you want to keep.

2. Click Disk Management to open a Disk Management window.

3. Right-click or long-press the drive to display the shortcut menu.

4. Click New Simple Volume to launch the New Simple Volume Wizard.

5. Click Next to display the Specify Volume Size screen.

6. In the Simple Volume Size in MB box, enter the size you want to make the volume. Normally, you'll want to make the volume the full size of the drive, which is the default setting.

7. Click Next to display the Assign Drive Letter or Path screen.

8. Select the Assign the Following Drive Letter option button.

9. Click Next to display the Format Partition screen (see Figure 4.1).

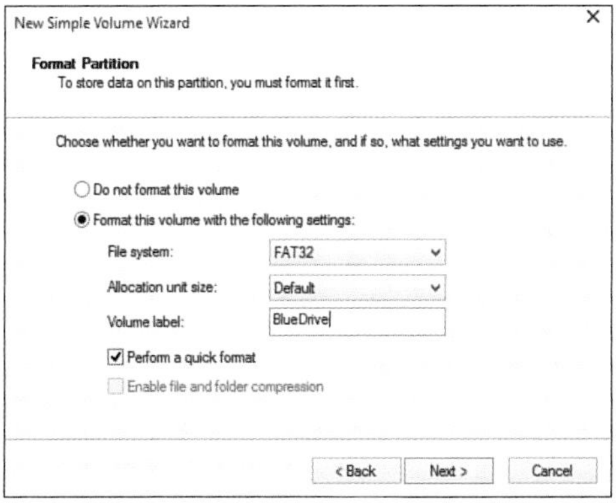

FIGURE 4.1

On the Format Partition screen, choose the file system to use for the drive and type the volume label you want to give it.

10. Select the Format This Volume with the Following Settings option button.

11. Open the File System drop-down menu and choose the file system you want to use.

> **TIP** The FAT32 file system has extremely wide compatibility, so it is usually a good choice for portable drives. But FAT32 has one limitation you must know about: The maximum file size is 4GB. If you will need to put large video files on the drive, format it as NTFS instead of FAT32.

12. Open the Allocation Unit Size drop-down menu and specify the allocation unit size if necessary. Usually you'll get good results from using Default, which allows Windows to choose the allocation unit size based on the drive's capacity.

13. In the Volume Label box, type the name you want to assign to the volume. The default name is New Volume, which you should definitely change. Make your name descriptive so that you can readily identify the drive from it.

14. Uncheck the Perform a Quick Format check box (which is checked by default) if you want to fully format the drive. Unless you're in a hurry, a full format is a good idea.

> **NOTE** If the Enable File and Folder Compression check box is available, you can check it to turn on compression for the drive. Compression enables you to fit more uncompressed files on the drive but may reduce the drive's performance a little.

15. Click Next. The Completing the New Simple Volume Wizard screen appears, summarizing the choices you've made.

16. Review the You Selected the Following Settings list. If you need to make a change, click Back.

17. Click Finish to finish creating the volume and to format it.

After you format the drive, it appears in the File Explorer window, and you can use it like any other drive.

CONFIGURING AN EXTERNAL DRIVE FOR BETTER PERFORMANCE

Windows enables you to configure an external drive for either quick removal or better performance. Normally, Windows configures USB flash drives, SD cards, and physically small memory devices for quick removal; Windows configures larger drives, such as external hard drives, for better performance.

> **NOTE** Better performance uses a technology called *write caching*, which allows Windows to tell an app that data has been written to disk before it actually has been written. Windows subsequently writes the data to disk while performing other write operations. This improves performance because the app doesn't have to wait for Windows to write the data to disk.

Follow these steps to configure an external drive for better performance (or for quick removal, if that's what you need):

1. Right-click or long-press Start to display the shortcut menu.

2. Click Device Manager to open a Device Manager window.

3. Double-click the Disk Drives heading to display its contents.

4. Double-click the external drive you want to configure. The Properties dialog box for the drive opens.

5. Click the Policies tab to display its contents (see Figure 4.2).

FIGURE 4.2

To configure an external drive for better performance, click the Better Performance option button in the Removal Policy box on the Policies tab of the Properties dialog box for the drive.

6. In the Removal Policy box, click the Better Performance option button. (If you want to configure the drive for quick removal, click the Quick Removal option button instead.)

7. Click OK to close the Properties dialog box.

> **! CAUTION** After configuring an external drive for better performance, you must use the Safely Remove Hardware and Eject Media feature to eject the drive from your computer's file system before you physically disconnect it. If not, you may lose or corrupt data. This feature is covered in the next section.

EJECTING AN EXTERNAL DRIVE

After using an external drive, you may need to eject it from Windows before physically disconnecting it from your computer.

> **NOTE** Whether you need to eject the drive depends on whether the drive is configured for better performance or for quick removal. If you are not certain that the drive is configured for quick removal, eject the drive anyway to make sure that you don't interrupt data transfer.

To eject a drive, click the Safely Remove Hardware and Eject Media icon in the notification area, the icon that shows a device and a green circle containing a white check mark. (If the Safely Remove Hardware and Eject Media icon doesn't appear in the notification area, click Show Hidden Icons, the ∧ icon, and then click Safely Remove Hardware and Eject Media.) In the drop-down menu that appears, click the Eject option for the drive you want to remove (see Figure 4.3).

FIGURE 4.3
Use the Safely Remove Hardware and Eject Media feature to eject an external drive before you physically disconnect it.

SORTING OUT YOUR DISPLAYS

To see what's happening on your computer, you need a display—or perhaps several of them. Windows enables you to use either a single display or multiple displays. This section shows you how to configure your displays.

> **NOTE** Windows also uses the word "monitor" to refer to a display.

CONNECTING A DISPLAY

Connect the display to your computer using a suitable cable, such as HDMI or DVI, and to a power source. Press the Power button to turn on the display. If the display has multiple input sources (such as HDMI, DVI, and VGA), set the display to use the source to which you connected the cable.

Windows should then recognize the display, and you can configure it as explained in the next sections.

OPENING THE DISPLAY PANE IN SETTINGS

To start configuring your displays, open the Display pane in the Settings app (see Figure 4.4). The quick way to do this is to right-click or long-press open space on the desktop and then click Display Settings on the shortcut menu. You can also choose Start, Settings and then click System; this brings up the Display pane because Display is the first item on the System screen.

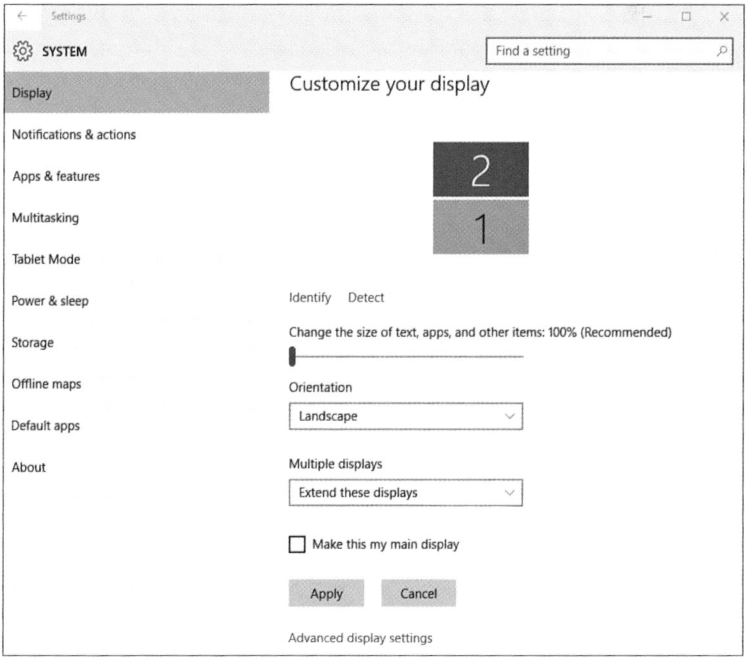

FIGURE 4.4
Use the Display pane in the Settings app to set the layout and orientation of your displays.

CHOOSING ESSENTIAL DISPLAY SETTINGS

The controls in the Display pane enable you to perform basic configuration. Here's what you can do:

- **Verify that Windows shows all your displays.** Look at the display thumbnails under the Customize Your Display heading. If all the displays are represented, you're good to go. If not, click Detect to make Windows detect the missing displays.

> **✓ TIP** If Windows can't detect a display, make sure that the display is connected to the correct ports and that it is receiving power. Restart Windows if necessary.

- **Identify your displays.** If you have connected multiple displays, click Identify to display a black box with the identifier number on each display.
- **Position your displays.** Click the thumbnails and drag them to position them in the same way that the physical displays are positioned—for example, side by side, or in a vertical arrangement (as in the example).
- **Boost the size of text, apps, and icons.** If everything appears too small on the screen, drag the Change the Size of Text, Apps, and Other Items slider to the right. Click Apply to effect the change. Windows then prompts you to sign out and back in to make sure all apps pick up the change; you can click Sign Out Later if you want to make other changes first.
- **Change the orientation of a display.** If you've rotated a display, click its thumbnail, open the Orientation drop-down menu, and then click Portrait, Landscape (Flipped), or Portrait (Flipped) instead of the default Landscape setting. Portrait orientation is rotated 90 degrees counterclockwise; Portrait (Flipped) is rotated 90 degrees clockwise; and Landscape (Flipped) is rotated 180 degrees, or upside-down in everyday terms.
- **Choose how to use multiple displays.** If you've attached multiple displays, open the Multiple Displays drop-down menu and click the appropriate setting: Duplicate These Displays, Extend These Displays, Show Only on 1, or Show Only on 2 (or Show Only on and a higher number if you have more displays).

TIP If you're using multiple displays for work, choose Extend These Displays to give yourself more desktop space. You'd typically use Duplicate These Displays when giving a presentation or a demonstration. The Show Only On commands let you turn off the other displays without disconnecting them; you may find this capability useful occasionally, but normally the whole point of connecting multiple displays is to use them.

- **Designate your main display.** Click the thumbnail for the appropriate display, and then check the Make This My Main Display check box.

NOTE The main display is the one on which the task-switcher appears when you press Alt+Tab, and Task view appears when you press Windows Key+Tab.

After choosing settings, click Apply to apply them.

CHOOSING ADVANCED DISPLAY SETTINGS

If you need to change settings that the Display pane doesn't offer, such as changing the resolution or calibrating the colors, click Advanced Display Settings at the bottom of the Display pane to show the Advanced Display Settings pane (see Figure 4.5).

In the Advanced Display Settings pane, you can identify displays, reposition them, and specify what to show on multiple displays, just as you can in the Display pane. But you can also take the following actions:

- **Change resolution.** Click the display you want to affect, click the Resolution drop-down menu, and then click the resolution you want to apply.

TIP Each LCD panel has what's called a *native resolution*, the resolution at which the pixels the computer is outputting actually align with the physical pixels that make up the screen. The native resolution gives the sharpest image. This is why Windows discourages you from changing resolution (by not putting resolution settings in the Display pane) and recommends changing the size of text, apps, and icons instead.

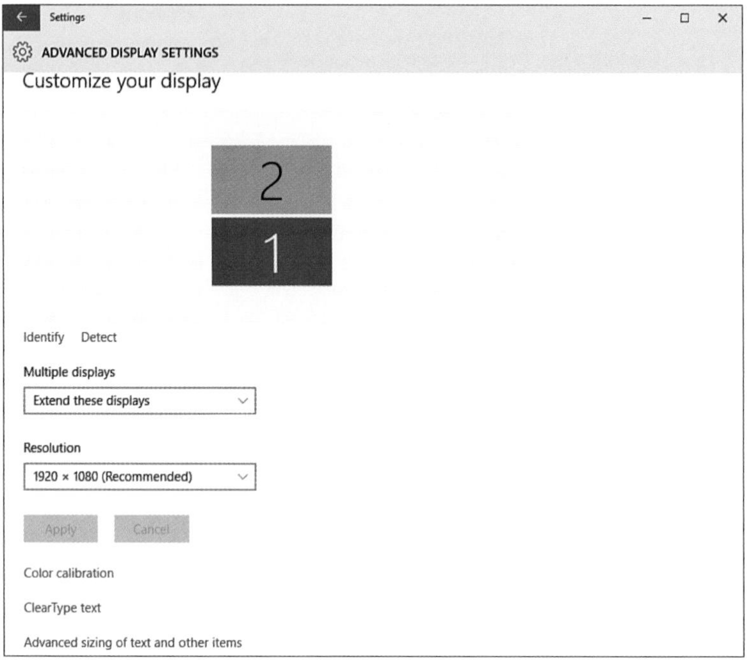

FIGURE 4.5

In the Advanced Display Settings pane, you can change display resolution and access settings such as color calibration and ClearType.

■ **Calibrate color.** Click Color Calibration to launch the Display Color Calibration Wizard, which walks you through the process of configuring the display by choosing basic settings; adjusting the gamma values (see Figure 4.6); and adjusting brightness, contrast, and color balance. You can save your new calibration and switch among calibrations as needed.

■ **Configure ClearType.** ClearType is a Microsoft technology for improving the look of text on LCD screens. To configure ClearType, click ClearType Text at the bottom of the Advanced Display Settings pane and follow through the steps of the ClearType Text Tuner Wizard. Tuning is easy—you just need to look at various blocks of text and pick the one that looks best to you.

> **NOTE** ClearType is a clever technology, but its effects don't suit everyone. If you don't like the way ClearType looks, turn it off by unchecking the Turn On ClearType check box on the first screen of the ClearType Text Tuner Wizard.

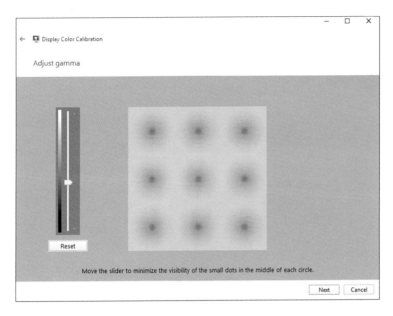

FIGURE 4.6

The Display Color Calibration Wizard walks you through adjustments such as gamma, brightness, contrast, and color balance.

- **Apply Custom Sizing to Text and Other Items.** If you need finer control over the size of onscreen items than the Change the Size of Text, Apps, and Other Items slider in the Display pane provides, click Advanced Sizing of Text and Other Items at the bottom of the Advanced Display Settings pane and then work on the Display screen in Control Panel (see Figure 4.7). In the Change Only the Text Size section, you can choose an item in the drop-down menu, choose the font size (the default size is 9 points), and then check the Bold check box if you want boldface as well. Click the Apply button to put the changes into effect.

- **Set properties for the display adapter.** Click Display Adapter Properties at the very bottom of the Advanced Display Settings pane to display the Properties dialog box for the graphics adapter. Figure 4.8 shows an example of this dialog box, but the tabs and controls in it vary depending on the adapter's capabilities and the tools that the manufacturer has provided for configuring it. The change you're most likely to want to make here is on the Monitor tab, where you can open the Screen Refresh Rate drop-down menu and then set the refresh rate you prefer.

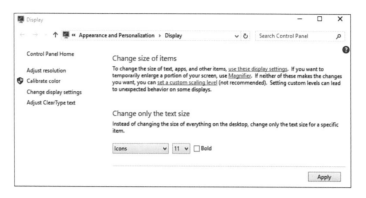

FIGURE 4.7

The Display screen in Control Panel enables you to adjust the text size for individual items, such as icons, menus, or title bars.

FIGURE 4.8

In the Properties dialog box for the monitor, you can change the screen refresh rate and other settings.

TIP The usual reason for changing the screen refresh rate is to eliminate flicker on a CRT screen (a cathode ray tube screen—one of the old-style, bulky monitors). Generally speaking, the higher the refresh rate, the less you'll notice flicker. Small CRT screens usually need a refresh rate of 60 Hertz or more; 72 Hertz is better. Large CRT screens may need 85 Hertz or more.

! CAUTION Leave the Hide Modes That This Monitor Cannot Display check box checked to avoid applying a refresh rate that might damage the monitor. On some computers, you'll find that this check box is dimmed and unavailable, which helps you to avoid the temptation of finding out whether your monitor is vulnerable.

USING VIRTUAL DESKTOPS

Windows provides virtual desktops, extra desktops that you can create and remove as needed. You can use virtual desktops to organize different groups of apps and windows. For example, you may want to keep your productivity apps on one virtual desktop and your communications apps on another.

Windows makes virtual desktops easy to use. Here are the moves you need to know:

- **Create a new desktop.** Click the Task View button on the taskbar and then click New Desktop in the lower-right corner of the screen.

☑ TIP You can also press Windows Key+Tab to open task view. You can press Windows Key+Ctrl+D to create a new desktop.

- **Switch to another desktop.** Click the Task View button on the taskbar and then click the desktop you want to use. Figure 4.9 shows Task view with three desktops.

☑ TIP You can press Windows Key+Ctrl+right arrow to display the next virtual desktop to the right of the one you're on. Press Windows Key+Ctrl+left arrow to display the next virtual desktop to the left.

- **Move an app to a different desktop.** Click the Task View button on the taskbar, and then right-click or long-press the window for the app you want to move. On the shortcut menu that opens, click or highlight Move To, and then click the appropriate desktop on the submenu that opens.

■ **Close a desktop.** Click the Task View button on the taskbar, move the mouse pointer over the thumbnail for the desktop you want to close, and then click the Close (×) button that appears. The windows open on the desktop you close move to the previous desktop.

FIGURE 4.9
Use Task view to switch among your virtual desktops.

📝 **TIP** You can close the active virtual desktop by pressing Windows Key+Ctrl+F4.

SETTING UP YOUR PRINTERS

The dream of the paperless office is now at least 30 years old and remains as elusive as ever. If you create documents on your computer, or simply receive documents from others, most likely you will need to print hard copies of some of them.

Windows enables you to print on either a local printer—one attached directly to your computer—or a network printer.

> **NOTE** Windows can locate driver software for many printers automatically. If Windows cannot locate driver software for the printer, Windows prompts you to provide the software. For example, you may have printer software that you have downloaded from the printer manufacturer's website, or software that came on a disc with the printer.

CONNECTING A LOCAL PRINTER

The most direct way to set up a printer is to connect it directly to your PC. Most modern printers have USB connections; some have Ethernet and Wi-Fi connections as well.

When you connect a printer directly to your PC, Windows detects the printer and automatically installs driver software for it (see Figure 4.10).

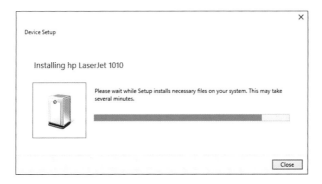

FIGURE 4.10
Windows automatically installs driver software for a printer you connect to your computer.

CONNECTING A NETWORK PRINTER

If the printer you need to use is connected to a network, you use a different means of connecting to it. Follow these steps:

1. Choose Start, Settings to open a Settings window.
2. Click Devices to display the Devices screen.
3. Click Printers & Scanners to display the Add Printers & Scanners pane.

> **NOTE** If the printer doesn't appear in the list in the Add Printers & Scanners pane, click Refresh to force Windows to search again. If this doesn't work, there may be a problem with the network connection between your system and printer.

4. Click the printer in the list. The Add Device button appears (see Figure 4.11).

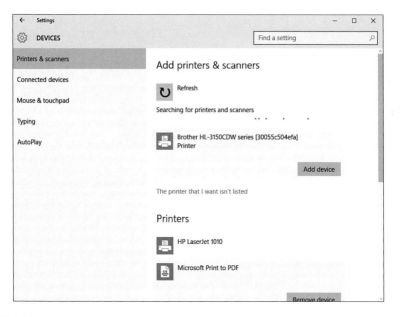

FIGURE 4.11
In the Add Printers & Scanners pane in Settings, click the printer you want to add, and then click Add Device.

5. Click Add Device. Windows automatically installs the printer. The printer then appears in the Printers list.

CONFIGURING YOUR PRINTER

When you add a printer, Windows sets it up with a default configuration. This may work well enough for you, but it's a good idea to spend a few minutes looking through the settings to see whether you need to change any to make the printer work your way.

To configure a printer, you use the Devices and Printers screen in Control Panel rather than the Settings app. Follow these steps to open the Devices and Printers screen:

1. Right-click or long-press Start to display the shortcut menu.
2. Click Control Panel to open a Control Panel window.
3. Under the Hardware and Sound heading, click View Devices and Printers. The Devices and Printers screen appears.

SETTING PRINTING PREFERENCES

On the Devices and Printers screen, right-click or long-press the printer you want to configure, and then click Printing Preferences on the shortcut menu. The Printing Preferences dialog box for the printer appears, and you can choose settings for layout and paper quality.

The selection of settings depends on the capabilities of the printer and the driver software, but the Layout tab typically contains settings such as these:

- **Orientation.** Open this drop-down menu and choose Portrait or Landscape, as needed.
- **Page Format.** Make sure the Pages per Sheet drop-down menu shows 1 unless you need to print multiple document pages on the same sheet of paper.

The Paper/Quality tab (see Figure 4.12) contains settings such as these:

- **Paper Source.** In this drop-down menu, choose a specific paper tray (such as Tray 1 or Manual Feed Tray) or choose Automatically Select to let the printer pick a tray that contains paper.
- **Media.** In this drop-down menu, choose the media type, such as Plain Paper.
- **Quality Settings.** In this box, click the Best option button, the Better option button (the default), or the Draft option button, as needed.
- **Color.** In this box, click the Black & White option button or the Color option button.

> **TIP** To change the print resolution—the number of dots per inch, or dpi, that the printer uses—click Advanced. In the Advanced Options dialog box that opens, click the Print Quality drop-down menu, and then click the dpi setting you need. The Print Quality menu for some printers offers choices such as Normal or Fine rather than dpi numbers.

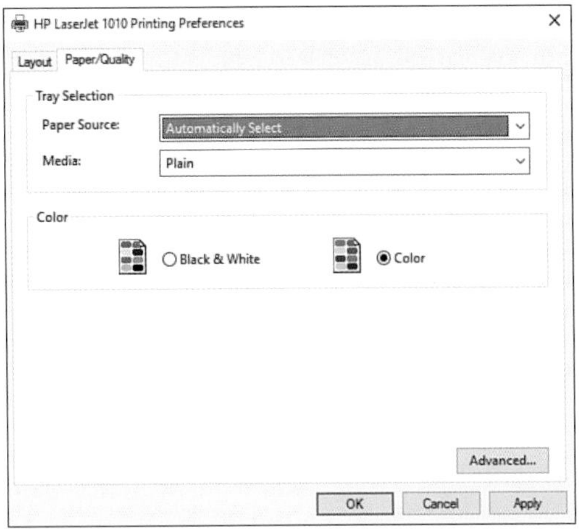

FIGURE 4.12

On the Paper/Quality tab of the Printing Preferences dialog box for the printer, choose the paper source, the paper type, and whether to print in black and white or in color.

When you finish setting printing preferences, click OK to close the Printing Preferences dialog box.

SETTING PRINTER PROPERTIES

On the Devices and Printers screen, right-click or long-press the printer you want to configure, and then click Printer Properties to display the Printer Properties dialog box for the printer.

On the General tab (see Figure 4.13), you can set general information for the printer:

- **Name.** (This is the unnamed box at the top.) Type the name under which you want the printer to appear in Windows. You may prefer a descriptive name (such as Color Laser Printer) rather than the brand and model number.

- **Location.** You can type a description of where the printer is located. Having the location visible is especially helpful when you share the printer on a network.

- **Comment.** You can type a comment to help yourself or others understand when to use the printer—for example, "Use this printer for color printing on plain paper" or "Use this printer for photos."

- **Print Test Page.** You can click this button to print a test page to make sure the printer is working correctly.

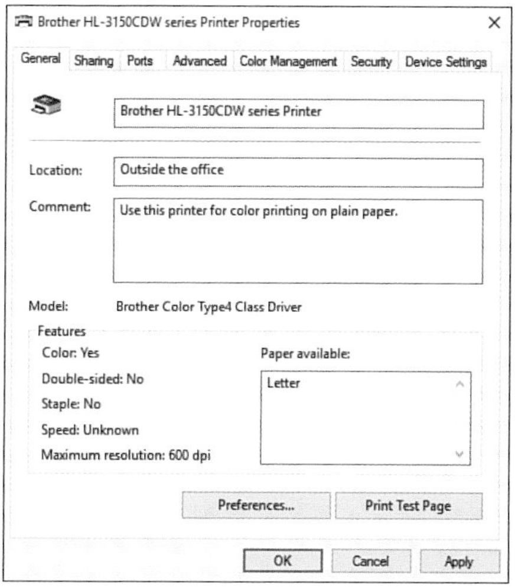

FIGURE 4.13

You can set descriptive information for the printer on the General tab of the Printer Properties dialog box.

On the Sharing tab, you can share the printer on the network by using the following options. If the options are dimmed and unavailable, click the Change Sharing Options button.

- **Share This Printer.** Check this check box to share the printer on the network.

- **Share Name.** After checking the Share This Printer check box, you can edit its default name or simply type a descriptive name.

- **Render Print Jobs on Client Computers.** Check this check box to make the computer that requests a print job do the rendering rather than having your computer do the rendering.

On the Ports tab, you can choose which ports Windows uses for printing to this printer. Normally, you won't need to adjust the settings here.

On the Advanced tab (see Figure 4.14), you can control which times the printer is available, configure spooling, and configure a handful of other settings. Here's what you need to know:

- **Always Available.** Select this option button to make the printer available all day and all night.

- **Available From.** Select this option button to limit the printer's use to the hours you specify in the two boxes—for example, from 8:00 AM to 6:00 PM.

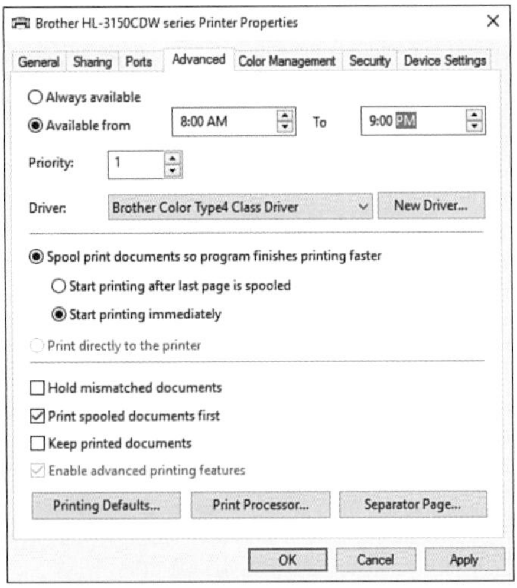

FIGURE 4.14
Use the controls on the Advanced tab of the Printer Properties dialog box to specify when the printer is available and to set advanced options.

- **Priority.** If you use multiple printers, you can set the printer's priority. Otherwise, leave it set to 1.

- **Spool Print Documents So Program Finishes Printing Faster.** Select this option button to use spooling, in which Windows saves the print jobs quickly to disk and then sends them to the printer at a speed the printer can accept. Normally, spooling is a good idea, because it enables you to resume work more quickly in the app from which you printed. If you select this option button, you can choose either the Start Printing After Last Page Is Spooled option button or the Start Printing Immediately option button; Start Printing Immediately is usually the better choice.

- **Print Directly to the Printer.** Select this option button (if it is available) to print without spooling. Normally, it's better to use spooling.

- **Hold Mismatched Documents.** Check this check box to make Windows hold in the print queue any documents not correctly configured for the printer.

- **Print Spooled Documents First.** Check this check box to make Windows print completely spooled documents before partially spooled documents that have higher priorities.

- **Keep Printed Documents.** Check this check box only if you need Windows to keep the spooled files on disk after printing the documents. Normally, you don't want to do this.

■ **Enable Advanced Printing Features.** Check this check box (which may be checked already and dimmed so that you cannot change it) to enable advanced printing features for the printer.

> ☑ **TIP** If you share your printer in an office environment, you may want to click Separator Page on the Advanced tab of the Printer Properties dialog box and choose a separator page to print at the beginning of each document. Separator pages can help you split up printed documents correctly, but they do little to prevent co-workers from peeking at each other's printed documents.

On the Color Management tab, you can click the Color Management button to configure color management for the printer.

On the Security tab, you can choose which groups and users can use the printer, manage it, and manage documents on it.

On the Device Settings tab, you can assign forms to particular paper trays and configure installable options, such as duplex units for printers that support them.

When you finish choosing settings, click the OK button to close the Printer Properties dialog box.

IN THIS CHAPTER

- Customizing the Start menu
- Customizing the taskbar
- Customizing the lock screen, the Recycle Bin, and notifications

5

CUSTOMIZING WINDOWS TO SUIT YOUR NEEDS

Windows provides a wide variety of settings you can customize to make the operating system work your way. In this chapter, we'll start by digging into the ways you can customize the Start menu, which is arguably the key component of the Windows interface. We'll then move on to customizing the taskbar, which can make a huge difference in the speed and efficiency with which you use Windows.

After that, we'll look at how you can set up automatic login, if you're certain you need it; customize the lock screen to show the information you find most useful on it; make the Recycle Bin work your way; and configure notifications to prevent Windows from bombarding you with news you don't need at times when you'd prefer peace.

CUSTOMIZING THE START MENU

You can customize the Start menu by choosing which categories of items appear on it and by pinning or removing specific items. You use the Start pane in the Settings app to specify the categories of items. To pin and remove specific items, you work directly on the Start menu.

CHOOSING WHICH CATEGORIES OF ITEMS TO DISPLAY ON THE START MENU

To choose categories of items, follow these steps to open the Start pane on the Personalization screen in the Settings app:

1. Right-click or long-press open space on the desktop to display the shortcut menu.

2. Click Personalize to display the Personalization screen in the Settings app.

3. Click Start in the left column to display the Start pane (see Figure 5.1).

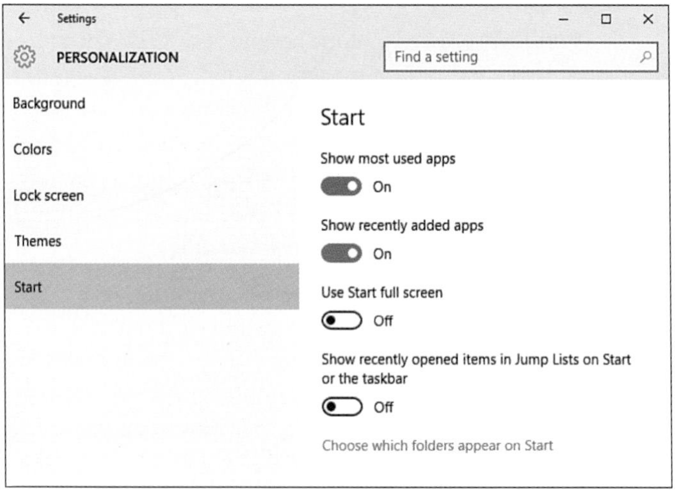

FIGURE 5.1
Use the Start pane on the Personalization screen in Settings to choose which categories of items appear on the Start menu and to control whether the Start menu appears full-screen.

In the Start pane, you can configure the following settings:

■ **Show Most Used Apps.** Set this switch to On to display the Most Used section. This section is usually helpful for giving you access to the apps you use most, but if you find the section unhelpful or indiscreet, set the switch to Off to suppress it.

■ **Show Recently Added Apps.** Set this switch to On to display the Recently Added section, which helps you find apps you've added recently. If you don't find Recently Added helpful, set the switch to Off.

■ **Use Start Full Screen.** Set this switch to On if you want the Start menu to appear full-screen when you open it.

■ **Show Recently Opened Items in Jump Lists on Start or the Taskbar.** Set this switch to On if you want Windows to display jump lists on the Start menu and on the taskbar to give you quick access to recent items. Again, this feature is usually handy, but turn it off if you don't want these items to show—for example, because other people can observe your screen.

After setting the switches in the Start pane, click Choose Which Folders Appear on Start to display the Choose Which Folders Appear on Start screen. You can then set the switch for each of the items listed in Table 5.1 to On or Off, as needed.

Table 5.1   Items on the Choose Which Folders Appear on Start Screen

Folder	Notes	Default Setting
File Explorer	File Explorer; has a drop-down menu to folders such as Desktop and Downloads	On
Settings	The Settings app	On
Documents	The Documents library	Off
Downloads	The Downloads folder	Off
Music	The Music library	Off
Pictures	The Pictures library	Off
Videos	The Videos library	Off
HomeGroup	The HomeGroup folder, which appears in the Desktop view	Off
Network	The Network folder, which appears in the Desktop view	Off
Personal Folder	The folder with your user name; it appears in the Desktop view	Off

CHOOSING COLORS FOR THE START MENU

To choose colors for the Start menu, click Colors in the left pane on the Personalization screen. You can then choose an accent color for your Windows look by setting the Automatically Pick an Accent Color from My Background switch to Off and clicking the appropriate color in the Choose Your Accent Color grid.

Set the Show Color on Start, Taskbar, and Action Center switch to On if you want Windows to use your color choice on the Start menu, the taskbar, and Action Center. Set the Make Start, Taskbar, and Action Center Transparent switch to On if you want to make these three interface items transparent so that you can see the desktop background through them.

CUSTOMIZING THE START MENU DIRECTLY

These are the moves you need to know to make the Start menu work the way you prefer:

- **Resize the Start menu.** Move the pointer over a border, and then click and drag.
- **Pin an item to the Start menu.** Right-click or long-press the item and click Pin to Start on the shortcut menu.

> **TIP**   If you want quick access to the Recycle Bin, pin the Recycle Bin to the Start menu. Right-click or long-press the Recycle Bin icon on the desktop, and then click Pin to Start. You can then remove the icon from the desktop if you want.

- **Unpin a pinned item from the Start menu.** Right-click or long-press the item and then click Unpin from Start on the shortcut menu.
- **Remove an item from the Start menu.** Right-click or long-press the item and click Don't Show in This List on the shortcut menu.

> **TIP**   You can also remove an item from the Start menu by dragging it off the menu and dropping it elsewhere.

- **Resize a tile.** Right-click or long-press the tile, click or highlight Resize on the shortcut menu, and then click Small, Medium, Wide, or Large, as needed.

Some tiles don't support all four sizes—for example, if you add the Notepad tile to the Start menu, you can only apply the Small or Medium size to the tile.

- **Turn a live tile off or on.** Right-click or long-press the tile to display the shortcut menu, and then click Turn Live Tile Off or Turn Live Tile On.
- **Move a tile.** Drag the tile to where you want it.
- **Create a new tile group.** Drag a tile down to open space at the bottom of the Start menu. When Windows displays a horizontal bar, drop the tile to create a new tile group. Move the pointer above the tile to display the Name Group bar. Click the bar, type the name for the group in the edit box that appears, and then press Enter.

NOTE The shortcut menu for the File Explorer app item on the Start menu offers several commands. Click Manage to open a Computer Management window. Click Map Network Drive to launch the Map Network Drive wizard, or click Disconnect Network Drive to launch the Disconnect Network Drives wizard. Click Properties to display the System screen in Control Panel.

TIP The shortcut menu for an app on the Start menu also contains two other handy commands. You can click Run as Administrator to run the app with administrator privileges instead of the level of privileges your account has. You can click Open File Location to open a File Explorer window showing the folder that contains the item.

CUSTOMIZING THE TASKBAR

After the Start menu, the taskbar is perhaps the second most important item in the Windows interface, giving you quick access both to the apps you're already running and to those you need to run.

You can customize the taskbar by moving and resizing it, changing its behavior, and putting the apps you need on it. You can also configure taskbar toolbars and choose which icons to display in the notification area.

MOVING AND RESIZING THE TASKBAR

The taskbar appears at the bottom of the screen by default, but you can move it to whichever side of the screen you find most helpful.

If the taskbar is locked, you need to unlock it before you can move it or resize it. To toggle locking on or off, right-click or long-press open space in the taskbar, and then click Lock the Taskbar, either placing a check mark (to lock the taskbar) or removing the check mark (to unlock it).

With the taskbar unlocked, click open space in the taskbar and drag it to the edge of the screen you want it to inhabit.

To resize the taskbar, move the pointer over the border between the taskbar and the rest of the screen. When the pointer becomes a two-headed arrow, click and drag the border.

> **TIP**   After you've gotten the taskbar to the position and size that suits you best, it's a good idea to lock the taskbar to avoid accidental changes.

CONFIGURING THE TASKBAR'S BEHAVIOR

To configure the taskbar's behavior, open the Taskbar and Start Menu Properties dialog box by right-clicking or long-pressing open space in the taskbar and then clicking Properties on the shortcut menu. You can then configure the following settings on the Taskbar tab (see Figure 5.2):

- **Lock the taskbar.** Check or uncheck this check box to toggle locking. You can also unlock the taskbar by clicking the Lock the Taskbar command on the taskbar's shortcut menu.

- **Auto-Hide the Taskbar.** Check this check box to make the taskbar hide itself automatically when the pointer is not over it. This is a good way of saving screen real estate, but having to move the pointer to the edge of the screen to produce the taskbar can slow down your work rate a little.

- **Use Small Taskbar Buttons.** Check this check box if you want to use the smaller version of taskbar buttons. This is useful if the taskbar tends to get full.

- **Taskbar Location on Screen.** In this drop-down menu, choose Bottom, Left, Right, or Top, as needed. When the taskbar is unlocked, you can also drag it to the side of the screen you want.

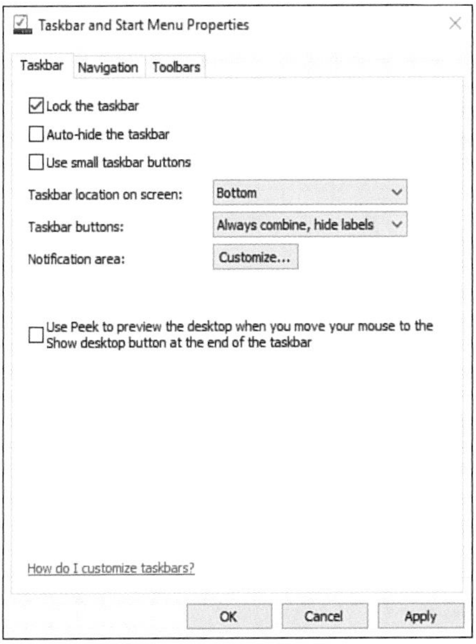

FIGURE 5.2

Use the controls on the Taskbar tab of the Taskbar and Start Menu Properties dialog box to configure the taskbar.

■ **Taskbar Buttons.** In this drop-down menu, specify how you want taskbar buttons to behave. Choose "Always Combine, Hide Labels" to make Windows combine related taskbar buttons into a single button. Choose Combine When Taskbar Is Full to keep separate taskbar buttons until Windows runs out of space for them. Choose Never Combine if you prefer to keep taskbar buttons separate and harvest by scythe.

■ **Notification Area.** Click the Customize button to open the Notifications & Actions pane on the System screen in the Settings app. We'll look at choosing settings in the Notifications & Actions pane in the section "Telling Windows Which Notifications You Want to Receive," later in this chapter.

■ **Use Peek to Preview the Desktop When You Move Your Mouse to the Show Desktop Button at the End of the Taskbar.** Check this check box if you want to enable the Peek feature, which shows previews of your open windows, when you move the pointer over the Show Desktop button on the taskbar.

NOTE The Navigation tab of the Taskbar and Start Menu Properties dialog box contains a single check box called Replace Command Prompt with Windows PowerShell in the Menu When I Right-Click the Lower-Left Corner or Press Windows Key+X. Check this check box if you want an easy way to open either a standard-user Windows PowerShell window or an administrator-level Windows PowerShell window.

The Toolbars tab of the Taskbar and Start Menu Properties dialog box enables you to display or hide taskbar toolbars. As you'll see a little later in this chapter, you can also toggle the display of taskbar toolbars from the taskbar shortcut menu, which is usually quicker.

When you finish choosing settings in the Taskbar and Start Menu Properties dialog box, click OK to close it.

PUTTING THE APPS YOU NEED MOST ON THE TASKBAR

What you'll probably want to do next is put some of the apps you use most on the taskbar so that you can launch them instantly. You can put an app on the taskbar in moments by opening the Start menu, right-clicking or long-pressing the app's icon, and then clicking Pin to Taskbar.

TIP You can rearrange the items on the taskbar by dragging them into the order you prefer.

NOTE To remove an item from the taskbar, right-click or long-press the app's taskbar icon and then click Unpin This Program from Taskbar on the shortcut menu.

MAKING THE MOST OF TASKBAR TOOLBARS

Windows includes three built-in taskbar toolbars that you can display and use if you find them helpful or hide if you don't. These are the toolbars:

- **Address.** This toolbar contains a box into which you can type an address and press Enter to go to it. You can type in a URL to go to it using Microsoft Edge (or your default browser, if you have configured another), or type in a folder path to go to that folder in a File Explorer window.

■ **Links.** The Links toolbar gives you a quick way to go to websites you've bookmarked.

■ **Desktop.** The Desktop toolbar gives you quick access to all the objects on the desktop. This can be handy if the desktop is obscured; otherwise, you may prefer to give the Show the Desktop command and simply access these items directly on the desktop.

To toggle the display of a taskbar toolbar, right-click or long-press open space in the taskbar, click or highlight Toolbars on the shortcut menu, and then click the toolbar's name on the Toolbars submenu, either placing a check mark next to the name (to display the toolbar) or removing the check mark (to hide the toolbar).

> **NOTE** Depending on the apps you have installed, your computer may have other taskbar toolbars. For example, if you install Apple's iTunes app, you'll find that the iTunes taskbar toolbar is available too.

You can also create new taskbar toolbars as needed. A taskbar toolbar displays the contents of a folder that you choose, giving you quick access to the files it contains—and to any subfolders and their files.

Follow these steps to create a new taskbar toolbar:

1. Right-click or long-press open space on the taskbar to display the shortcut menu.

2. Click or highlight Toolbars to display the Toolbars submenu.

3. Click New Toolbar. The New Toolbar – Choose a Folder dialog box opens.

4. Navigate to the folder whose contents you want the toolar to display, and then click Select Folder.

The new toolbar appears on the taskbar, and you can click it to display a drop-down menu of its contents. You can then click the item you want to open.

> **NOTE** When you no longer need a custom taskbar toolbar, turn it off using the same technique as for hiding a built-in taskbar toolbar: Right-click or long-press open space on the taskbar, click or highlight Toolbars, and then click the toolbar's name on the Toolbars submenu to remove the check mark next to it. Windows removes the taskbar toolbar from display and from the Toolbars list; if you need it again, set it once more as you did before.

WHY DID MY TASKBAR ICONS JUST DISAPPEAR?

On a tablet or other touchscreen computer, Windows can automatically hide the app icons on the taskbar when the device goes into tablet mode. Windows hides the icons to simplify the interface and give you more space to work in.

To control whether Windows hides the app icons when your computer goes into tablet mode, choose Start, Settings, click System to display the System screen, and then click Tablet Mode in the left column. In the Tablet Mode pane, set the Hide App Icons on the Taskbar in Tablet Mode switch to On or Off, as needed.

CHOOSING WHICH ICONS TO DISPLAY IN THE NOTIFICATION AREA

Next on your customization list is the notification area at the right end of the taskbar (or, if you've put the taskbar at the left or right side of the screen, at the bottom of the taskbar).

NOTE The notification area is also sometimes called the *system tray*. The selection of notification-area icons varies depending on your computer's hardware and software and on the services you use.

Right-click or long-press the notification area and click Customize Notification Icons on the shortcut menu to display the Notifications & Actions pane on the System screen in the Settings app (see Figure 5.3).

Next, click the Select Which Icons Appear on the Taskbar link to display the Select Which Icons Appear on the Taskbar screen (see Figure 5.4). Here, you can either set the Always Show All Icons in the Notification Area switch to On to make all the icons appear all the time or set this switch to Off and then set each individual switch to On or Off, as needed.

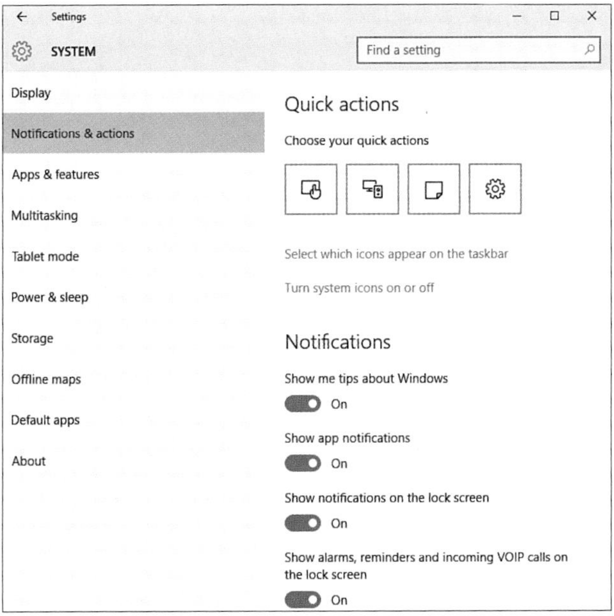

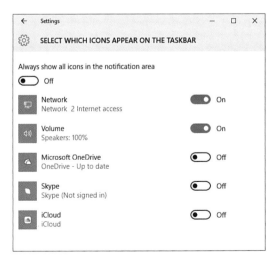

FIGURE 5.3

From the Notifications & Actions pane in the Settings app, you can choose which icons to display in the notification area.

FIGURE 5.4

The Select Which Icons Appear on the Taskbar screen enables you to set all icons to display all the time or choose which ones to display.

After making your choices on the Select Which Icons Appear on the Taskbar screen, click the Back button in the upper-left corner of the window to return to the Notifications & Actions pane. You can then click the Turn System Icons On or Off link to display the Turn System Icons On or Off screen, on which you can set the switches for the following system icons to On or Off, as needed:

■ **Clock.** The Clock icon is usually useful, because it shows the date and time and enables you to display the Date and Time fly-out, which shows the current month's calendar and gives you quick access to the Date and Time settings.

■ **Volume.** The Volume icon is useful for adjusting the volume unless your computer provides hardware volume keys, which can be faster and easier. If you right-click or long-press the Volume icon, the shortcut menu provides access to settings for playback devices, recording devices, sounds, and (on some computers) a volume mixer.

■ **Network.** The Network icon is useful if your computer connects frequently to wireless networks. If your computer stays connected to a wired network, you can probably dispense with this icon if you're short of space.

■ **Power.** On a laptop or tablet, the Power icon is useful for seeing how much power is left and verifying that the battery is charging when it should be.

> **TIP** You can right-click or long-press the Power icon to display shortcut-menu commands for adjusting screen brightness, opening Windows Mobility Center, and accessing the Power Options screen.

> **NOTE** The switches for the Power icon and the Location icon may be unavailable on a desktop computer.

■ **Input Indicator.** The Input Indicator icon is useful if you need to be able to switch among multiple input sources, such as between touchscreen input and keyboard input on a convertible computer or between different keyboard layouts on a desktop or laptop. Otherwise, you may not need it.

■ **Location.** The Location indicator can be useful on a tablet or device you use out and about. You can click Open Location Privacy Settings on the shortcut menu to go to the Location pane on the Privacy screen in the Settings app.

■ **Action Center.** The Action Center icon enables you to see at a glance whether you have notifications in Action Center (the icon appears white) or not (the icon appears dark). You can click the icon to toggle the display of Action Center.

> 🗒 **NOTE**   On a touchscreen device, you may find it easier simply to swipe Action Center open when you need to check what's new.

SAVING TIME WITH AUTOMATIC LOGIN—AND WHY YOU SHOULDN'T

Windows sets up your computer to use the lock screen by default to help prevent unauthorized people from using your computer. Normally, you'll want to continue using the lock screen, to keep others out of your account and to keep your data secure.

That said, Windows does enable you to turn off the lock screen if necessary. For example, if your computer stays in a secure room and doesn't connect to the Internet or any network, you might want to set it to log in by default to your account so that you can get right to work without even typing your password. Or if you set up a computer in a café or library situation, you might set it to log in to a default account so that anyone there can use it anytime.

> ❗**CAUTION**   Turn off the lock screen only if you're certain doing so is safe. Normally, it is not safe.

If you do decide to set up automatic login, follow these steps:

1. Click Start or press the Windows key to open the Start menu.
2. Type **netplwiz** in the Search box.
3. Click the "netplwiz: Run Command" item that appears in the search results. The User Accounts dialog box opens, with the Users tab at the front (see Figure 5.5).
4. In the Users for This Computer list, click the account you want to sign in automatically.

FIGURE 5.5

On the Users tab of the User Accounts dialog box, uncheck the Users Must Enter a User Name and Password to Use This Computer check box to set up automatic login.

5. Uncheck the Users Must Enter a User Name and Password to Use This Computer check box on the Users tab.

6. Click the OK button. The Automatically Sign In dialog box opens (see Figure 5.6), with the user name entered in the User Name box.

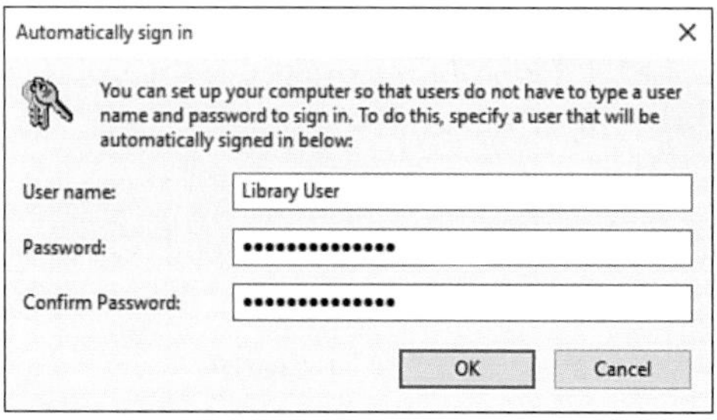

FIGURE 5.6

In the Automatically Sign In dialog box, type the password for the user account twice, and then click OK.

7. Type the account's password in the Password box and the Confirm Password box.

8. Click OK.

After setting up automatic login, test it at once and make sure it works as you expect.

MAKING THE LOCK SCREEN SHOW THE INFORMATION YOU NEED

Windows enables you to configure the lock screen with three items:

- The picture of your choice—or a slideshow
- One app showing detailed status
- Up to seven apps showing quick status

You can also configure screen timeout settings and set up a screen saver.

DISPLAYING THE LOCK SCREEN PANE

To configure the lock screen, you use the Lock Screen pane in the Settings app. Follow these steps to display the Lock Screen pane:

1. Choose Start, Settings to open the Settings window.

2. Click Personalization to display the Personalization screen.

3. Click Lock Screen in the left column to display the Lock Screen pane.

SETTING THE PICTURE OR SLIDESHOW

In the Lock Screen pane, click the Background drop-down menu and choose Picture or Slideshow, as needed.

If you choose Picture, you can click one of the default pictures in the Choose Your Picture area or click Browse and use the Open dialog box to select a picture of your own.

If you choose Slideshow, go to the Choose Albums for Your Slideshow list and click the folder you want to use. You can click Add a Folder to select a folder that isn't listed.

After you've chosen the folder, click Advanced Slideshow Settings to display the Advanced Slideshow Settings pane (see Figure 5.7). Here, you can configure the following settings:

- **Include Camera Roll Folders from This PC and OneDrive.** Set this switch to On to include the pictures in your `Camera Roll` folders on your computer and on OneDrive.

- **Only Use Pictures That Fit My Screen.** Set this switch to On if you want the slideshow to use only photos that have the right aspect ratio for your computer's screen. Experiment with this switch set to Off and see whether your pictures look okay before turning it on.

- **Play a Slideshow When Using Battery Power.** Set this switch to On if you want a slideshow to display when you are using battery power on a laptop or tablet.

- **When My PC Is Inactive, Show Lock Screen Instead of Turning Off the Screen.** Set this switch to On if you want the lock screen to appear (and your slideshow to play) when Windows would otherwise have turned off the screen.

- **Turn Off Screen After Slideshow Has Played For.** In this drop-down menu, choose Don't Turn Off if you want to keep the slideshow playing until you return. Otherwise, choose 30 Minutes, 1 Hour, or 3 Hours.

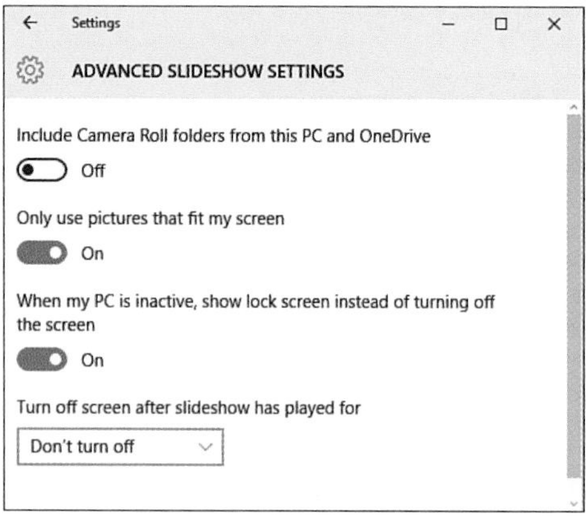

FIGURE 5.7

On the Advanced Slideshow Settings screen, choose which pictures to use for your slideshow and when to end the slideshow.

ADDING APPS TO THE LOCK SCREEN FOR QUICK REFERENCE

You can add one app showing detailed status to the lock screen and up to seven apps showing quick status.

Click the app icon in the Choose an App to Show Detailed Status area to display the drop-down menu. You can then click None or one of the apps—such as Weather, Calendar, or Xbox—as needed.

! CAUTION Remember that any information you display on the lock screen will be visible to anybody within eyeshot of your computer.

Click the first + button in the Choose Apps to Show Quick Status area to display the drop-down menu. You can then click None or one of the apps—such as Weather, People, Alarms & Clock, Calendar, Mail, Store, or Xbox—as needed.

MAKING THE RECYCLE BIN WORK THE WAY YOU PREFER

As you know, when you give the Delete command for a file on a fixed local drive, Windows doesn't actually delete the file immediately but instead puts the file in the Recycle Bin. The file stays there until one of these three things happens:

- You realize you didn't mean to delete the file, retrieve it, and wipe the sweat of averted disaster from your brow.

NOTE If the file you're deleting is larger than the Recycle Bin, Windows deletes the file immediately. This situation is rare but can happen with a giant file (such as a monster video file) or a small Recycle Bin.

- You empty the Recycle Bin manually.
- The Recycle Bin gets full and Windows deletes old files to make room for new arrivals.

NOTE Windows uses the Recycle Bin only for fixed local drives, not for removable drives or for network drives. When you give the Delete command for a file on a removable drive or a network drive, Windows deletes it immediately.

> **!CAUTION** Never rely on the Recycle Bin to save your bacon if you delete files by mistake. Back up your files regularly, and make sure your backups work.

By default, Windows keeps a separate Recycle Bin for each of your computer's fixed local drives. You can configure the Recycle Bin in three ways:

- You can change the amount of space set aside for the Recycle Bin on a drive. The default size is 10% of the drive size.
- You can stop using the Recycle Bin for a drive so that Windows deletes files immediately when you give the Delete command.
- You can choose whether to display the Delete confirmation dialog box.

To configure the Recycle Bin, follow these steps:

1. Right-click or long-press the Recycle Bin icon on the desktop to display the shortcut menu.

> **TIP** If the Recycle Bin doesn't appear on the desktop, and you want to put it back there, click Start, type **desktop icons**, and then click the Show or Hide Common Icons on the Desktop search result. In the Desktop Icon Settings dialog box, check the Recycle Bin check box, and then click OK.

2. Click Properties to display the Recycle Bin Properties dialog box (see Figure 5.8).
3. In the box at the top, click the drive you want to affect. If your computer has only one fixed local drive, it should be selected already.
4. In the Settings for Selected Location box, select the "Don't Move Files to the Recycle Bin. Remove Files Immediately When Deleted" option button if you don't want to use the Recycle Bin for this drive. Otherwise, select the Custom Size option button and type the maximum size in the Maximum Size box. You specify this in megabytes—for example, 8192 MB to devote 8 gigabytes to the Recycle Bin.

> **NOTE** If your computer has multiple fixed local drives, repeat steps 3 and 4 to configure each of them.

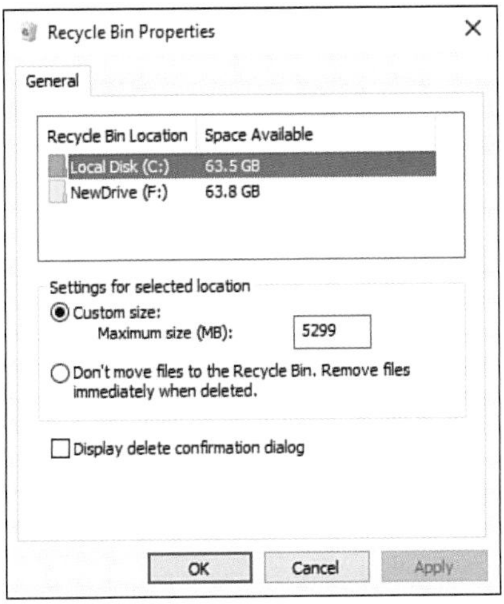

FIGURE 5.8
Open the Recycle Bin Properties dialog box when you want to configure the Recycle Bin for one or more local fixed drives.

5. If you want Windows to display a confirmation dialog box each time you give the Delete command, check the Display Delete Confirmation Dialog check box.

> **NOTE** The Display Delete Confirmation Dialog setting is for all your drives. You can't have delete confirmation for one drive but not for other drives.

6. When you finish making choices, click OK to close the Recycle Bin Properties dialog box.

TELLING WINDOWS WHICH NOTIFICATIONS YOU WANT TO RECEIVE

Like most modern-day operating systems, Windows seems convinced that it can improve your life by bombarding you with notifications. To preserve your sanity, you'll likely want to spend a while telling Windows which notifications you do want to see and—more important—which notifications to suppress.

OPENING THE NOTIFICATIONS & ACTIONS PANE

To configure notifications, first open the Notifications & Actions pane like this:

1. Choose Start, Settings to open the Settings window.

2. Click System to display the System screen.

3. Click Notifications & Actions to display the Notifications & Actions pane (shown in Figure 5.3, earlier in this chapter).

CHOOSING ESSENTIAL NOTIFICATIONS SETTINGS

In the Notifications list, you can configure the following settings:

- **Show Me Tips About Windows.** Set this switch to Off or On, as needed.

- **Show App Notifications.** Set this switch to On if you want to see notifications from the apps in the Show Notifications from These Apps list. (We'll get to this list in a moment.) Set this switch to Off if you want to turn off all notifications from apps.

- **Show Notifications on the Lock Screen.** Set this switch to On or Off, as needed.

> **! CAUTION** Remember that any notifications you set Windows to display on the lock screen will be visible to anyone who can see your computer's screen. On a laptop or tablet, it's best to err on the side of caution with lock-screen notifications.

- **Show Alarms, Reminders and Incoming VOIP Calls on the Lock Screen.** Set this switch to On if you want to see these items on the lock screen. This is usually helpful.

- **Hide Notifications While Presenting.** Set this switch to On if you want Windows to hide all notifications when you're using PowerPoint in Slide Show view. Hiding notifications while presenting is usually a good idea.

In the Show Notifications from These Apps list, set the switch for each app to On or Off, as needed, to specify which apps can give you notifications and which cannot.

TIP You can configure the length of time for which Windows displays notifications. To do so, choose Start, Settings, click Ease of Access, and then click Other Options. In the Visual Options list, click the Show Notifications For drop-down menu, and then click the length of time. Your choices range from 5 Seconds to 5 Minutes.

IN THIS CHAPTER

- Navigating and customizing File Explorer
- Using libraries and folders the smart way
- Managing your storage and using storage spaces

SORTING OUT YOUR FILES, FOLDERS, AND STORAGE

Windows 10 provides the file-management app called File Explorer to help you keep your files and folders in order. To get the most out of your computer, you will want to navigate File Explorer like a pro and customize it so that it works the way you prefer. To manage your files efficiently, you must exploit the powerful file libraries Windows provides instead of merely creating folders. And to give yourself space in which to keep your files, you will likely need to manage your storage tightly, perhaps using the Storage Spaces feature if your computer is suitable for it.

NAVIGATING FILE EXPLORER QUICKLY AND EFFICIENTLY

Chances are you'll do a lot of work in File Explorer windows, so learning to navigate quickly and efficiently in File Explorer can save you time, effort, and frustration.

OPENING A FILE EXPLORER WINDOW

You can open a File Explorer window in several ways. These are usually the most convenient ways:

■ **Taskbar.** Click the File Explorer button to open a window to your default location. To open another frequently used location, right-click or long-press the File Explorer button, and then click the location on the shortcut menu.

> **TIP** If you already have multiple File Explorer windows open, hold the pointer over the File Explorer button on the taskbar to display thumbnails of the windows, and then click the thumbnail for the window you want.

■ **Start menu.** Choose Start, File Explorer. You can click the Show Jump List button (the > button) to the right of File Explorer and then click the frequently used location you want.

■ **File Explorer.** You can open a new window by choosing File, Open New Window or by simply pressing Ctrl+N.

After you've opened a window, File Explorer should look something like Figure 6.1—but only something like it, because you can customize File Explorer extensively.

PUTTING USEFUL BUTTONS ON THE QUICK ACCESS TOOLBAR

By default, the Quick Access Toolbar appears at the left end of the title bar in File Explorer windows and contains only the Properties button and the New Folder button. You can change the buttons displayed on the Quick Access Toolbar and move it to appear below the Ribbon. Many of the figures in this chapter show the Quick Access Toolbar customized with several extra buttons for additional functionality.

File menu

Quick Access
Toolbar   Ribbon tabs

Details pane

Quick Access view

Navigation pane

FIGURE 6.1

The main components of a File Explorer window.

To customize the Quick Access Toolbar, click the drop-down button at its right end to display the Customize Quick Access Toolbar drop-down menu. You can then click a button to check it (putting it on the Quick Access Toolbar) or uncheck it (removing the button).

TIP You can control the order in which the buttons appear on the Quick Access Toolbar. Uncheck each check box to remove all the buttons, and then check the boxes in the order you want the buttons displayed.

Click the Show Below the Ribbon command on the drop-down menu if you want the Quick Access Toolbar displayed below the Ribbon rather than in the title bar. This takes up more space but puts the Quick Access Toolbar closer to the files and folders, which you may find helpful.

USING THE FILE MENU

The File menu, at the left end of the Ribbon, gives you access to essential commands and frequent places. Figure 6.2 shows the File menu open.

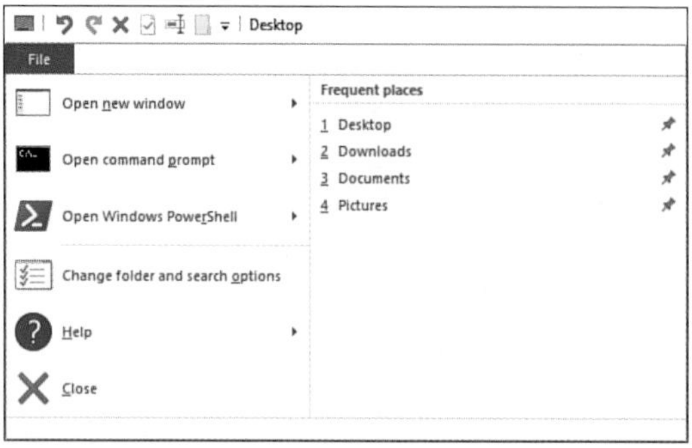

FIGURE 6.2

From the File menu, you can open a new window, a command prompt, or Windows PowerShell; change folder and search options; or go to a frequently visited place.

Here's what you can do from the File menu:

- **Open a new window.** Click the main part of the Open New Window button to open a new window in the same process. Point to the arrow button to the right of Open New Window and then click Open New Window in New Process if you want to open the new window in a separate process (see the nearby tip).

> **TIP** Opening a window in a new process gives you better protection against crashes. If errors occur in File Explorer and it crashes (or you force it to close), all windows in the affected process close. If all your File Explorer windows are running in the same process, that means all of them close. If the windows are running in separate processes, only the process that suffered the error crashes; the other processes are—or at least should be—unaffected. The disadvantage to opening windows in new processes is that doing so takes up more memory.

- **Open Command Prompt.** Click the main part of the Open Command Prompt button to open a regular command prompt, one that has the same level of permissions as your user account. If you need to give commands as an administrator, click the arrow button to the right of Open Command Prompt and then click Open Command Prompt as Administrator.

> **NOTE** If the Open Command Prompt button and the Open Windows PowerShell button are dimmed and unavailable, select another folder or location in the Navigation pane and open the File menu again.

- **Open Windows PowerShell.** Click the main part of the Open Windows PowerShell button to launch a Windows PowerShell session. If you need to issue Windows PowerShell commands as an administrator, click the arrow button to the right of Open Windows PowerShell and then click Open Windows PowerShell as Administrator.

- **Change Folder and Search Options.** Click this button to display the Folder Options dialog box. We'll cover the Folder Options dialog box in the section "Adjusting Folder and Search Options," later in this chapter. Depending on your selection in the Navigation pane, you might see Options as the button name instead of Change Folder and Search Options. Both versions display the Folder Options dialog box.

- **Help.** Click this button to open a Help window.

- **Close.** Click this button to close the File Explorer window. It's usually easier to click the Close button at the right end of the window's title bar.

- **Frequent Places.** You can click one of these places to display it in the File Explorer window.

> **TIP** You can unpin a place from the Frequent Places list by clicking the pushpin to the right of its name.

FINDING YOUR WAY AROUND THE RIBBON

To the right of the File menu, the Ribbon in File Explorer windows contains three static tabs—the Home tab, the Share tab, and the View tab—plus various context-sensitive tabs that appear only when needed. For example, the context-sensitive Library Tools tab appears only when you have selected a library.

The Home tab of the Ribbon (see Figure 6.3) contains the following five groups of controls:

- **Clipboard group.** This group contains the Pin to Quick Access button; the Copy, Cut, and Paste buttons; and the Copy Path and Paste Shortcut buttons.

FIGURE 6.3

The Home tab of the Ribbon in File Explorer windows contains commands for creating, organizing, and working with files and folder.

- **Organize group.** This group contains the Move To drop-down menu, the Copy To drop-down menu, the Delete button and Delete drop-down menu, and the Rename button.

- **New group.** This group contains the New Folder button for creating a new folder; the New Item drop-down menu for creating new items including shortcuts, contacts, text documents, and compressed (zipped folders); and the Easy Access drop-down menu, which provides ways to give yourself easy access to a particular file or folder.

- **Open group.** This group contains the Properties button and Properties drop-down menu; the Open button and Open drop-down menu; the Edit button; and the History button, which takes you to the File History feature (more on this later in this chapter).

- **Select group.** This group contains the Select All button for selecting all the items in the current location; the Select None button for deselecting all the selected items; and the Invert Selection button for inverting the selection—deselecting all selected items and selecting all deselected items.

We'll look at Pin to Quick Access, Easy Access, and File History later in this chapter.

The Share tab of the Ribbon contains the Send group and the Share With group. We'll look at how you use these controls in Chapter 7, "Securing and Sharing Your Computer."

The View tab of the Ribbon contains commands for customizing the layout and the view. We'll look at these commands in the next section.

CUSTOMIZING HOW FILE EXPLORER LOOKS AND WORKS

Until you change it, File Explorer opens with a default view that presumably pleased some testers in Microsoft's usability labs. To get quickly to the files you want, you'll likely need to customize the view. You can do this in several ways: by changing the layout in File Explorer; by sorting and grouping items; by choosing which items to show and, more important, which to hide; and by choosing folder and search options.

CHANGING THE LAYOUT

You can change the layout in File Explorer to suit your needs. Start by clicking the View tab of the Ribbon to display its contents (see Figure 6.4) and choosing settings in the Panes group.

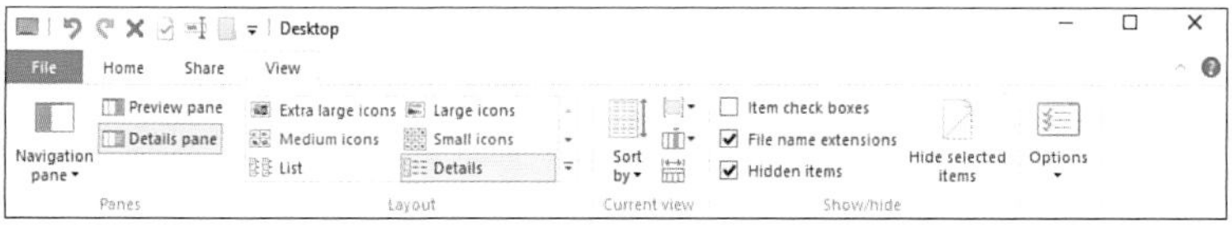

FIGURE 6.4
The View tab of the Ribbon enables you to customize the layout and look of a File Explorer window.

The Panes group contains three buttons:

■ **Navigation Pane.** Click this button to display the Navigate Pane drop-down menu. You can then click Navigation Pane to turn off the display of the Navigation pane altogether, or click one of the other three commands to enable or disable it: Expand to Open Folder, which controls whether the Navigation pane expands the folders needed to reach the current folder; Show All Folders, which controls whether the Navigation pane displays all folders automatically; or Show Libraries, which controls whether the libraries appear in the Navigation pane.

■ **Preview Pane.** Click this button to display the Preview pane on the right side of the File Explorer window instead of the Details pane.

> **NOTE** The Preview Pane button works as an option button pair with the Details Pane button: Turning Preview Pane on turns Details Pane off, and vice versa. To hide both panes, click the button for the pane that's currently displayed.

■ **Details Pane.** Click this button to display the Details pane on the right side of the File Explorer window instead of the Preview pane.

CUSTOMIZING THE QUICK ACCESS VIEW

The Quick Access view appears at the top of the Navigation pane in File Explorer windows by default. As its name suggests, the point of Quick Access is to give you rapid access to the files and folders you need, so you'll likely want to customize its contents to suit your needs.

Here's how to customize the Quick Access view:

- **Add an item.** To keep a particular file or folder in Quick Access, select it and then choose Home, Clipboard, Pin to Quick Access. Alternatively, right-click or long-press the item and then click Pin to Quick Access on the shortcut menu.

- **Remove an item.** Right-click or long-press the item and then click Unpin from Quick Access on the shortcut menu.

- **Rearrange the items.** Drag items up or down the list as needed.

- **Remove recently used files.** Choose File, Change Folder and Search Options and uncheck the Show Recently Used Files in Quick Access check box in the Privacy group on the General tab of the Folder Options dialog box. Click OK.

- **Remove frequently used folders.** Choose File, Change Folder and Search Options, and uncheck the Show Frequently Used Folders in Quick Access check box in the Privacy group on the General tab of the Folder Options dialog box. Click OK.

CHOOSING HOW TO LAY OUT THE ITEMS

You can use the controls in the Layout group of the View tab of the Ribbon to control how files and folders appear in the main part of the File Explorer window. You have the following eight layout options; if the last few don't appear, click the More button in the lower-right corner of the Layout group to display the others.

- **Extra Large Icons.** This view displays a massive icon for each file, with the filename under the icon. It's most useful for sorting through graphics, because the icon is large enough to identify most files. The icons appear in a grid pattern, at least if the window is large enough.

TIP When using Extra Large Icons view, display the Details pane rather than the Preview pane, because the icon is effectively a preview.

- **Large Icons.** This view displays a large icon for each file, with the filename under the icon. The icons appear in a grid pattern.
- **Medium Icons.** This view displays a medium-size icon for each file, with the filename under the icon. The icons appear in a grid pattern.
- **Small Icons.** This view displays a small icon for each file, to the left of the filename.
- **List.** This view displays a list of the folder names and filenames. Scroll right rather than down to see other items in the list.
- **Details.** This view displays a list of the filenames and folder names together with other columns of information such as Date, Type, and Size. You can sort the rows by clicking the column heading by which you want to sort.
- **Tiles.** This view displays a tile for each item. The tile shows a small icon, the filename, the file type, and the size.
- **Content.** This view displays a tablelike layout with one item per row. For each item, a small icon appears, followed by the filename, the type, and the size.

SORTING AND GROUPING ITEMS

You can use the controls in the Current View group on the View tab of the Ribbon to sort and group items however you find most helpful. These are the controls:

- **Sort By.** Click this drop-down menu and choose the item you want to sort by, such as Name, Date, Type, or Size. You can then click again and click Ascending to sort in ascending order (A to Z, low numbers to high, older to newer, and so on) or Descending to sort in descending order (Z to A, high numbers to low, and so forth).

> **NOTE** The selection of sortable fields depends on the view and type of folder you have chosen. Details view is usually the best view for sorting items because it gives you a wide choice of columns for sorting. You can click Choose Columns on the Sort By drop-down menu and then choose the columns and their order in the Choose Details dialog box that opens.

- **Group By.** Click this drop-down menu and choose the item by which you want to group the items, such as Date or Type. Here, too, you can click Choose Columns and use the Choose Details dialog box to choose which columns to display and the order in which to display them.

- **Add Columns.** You can click this drop-down menu and then click to check or uncheck the items on the menu to control which items appear. Again, you can click Choose Columns and select columns using the Choose Details dialog box.
- **Size All Columns to Fit.** You can click this button to resize all columns to fit their contents. How helpful this is depends on how big a screen and window you're using and how well the information fits in it.

CHOOSING WHICH ITEMS TO SHOW AND WHICH TO HIDE

The controls in the Show/Hide group on the View tab of the Ribbon enable you to control which items are visible and which are not. These are your options:

- **Item Check Boxes.** Check this check box if you want Windows to display a check box on each item as you hold the pointer over it. You can click the item (or the check box) to check the box, selecting the item. The advantage of displaying check boxes is that you can select multiple items easily without having to hold down Ctrl or Shift and without dragging. They also make it easier to select items when you are using a touchscreen.
- **File Name Extensions.** Check this check box if you want File Explorer to display filename extensions, such as the `.xlsx` file extensions on Excel workbook files or the `.txt` file extensions on text files.
- **Hidden Items.** Check this check box if you want File Explorer to display hidden files and folders.
- **Hide Selected Items.** You can click this button to apply the Hidden attribute to files or to remove the attribute from them. When the Hidden attribute is on for an item, Windows hides that item—unless you check the Hidden Items check box to display hidden items.

ADJUSTING FOLDER AND SEARCH OPTIONS

If you really want to take control of File Explorer and your computer's file system, spend a few minutes choosing folder and search options. Choose File, Change Folder and Search Options or View, Options (clicking the main part of the Options button, not the drop-down button) to display the Folder Options dialog box, and then get to work.

> **NOTE** You'll notice that the options in the Folder Options dialog box overlap with some of the options on the Ribbon, even though some of the individual names vary somewhat. When there's overlap, you can use whichever means of giving a command you find most helpful.

SELECTING THE RIGHT GENERAL OPTIONS FOR YOUR NEEDS

You'll want to explore all the options on the General tab of the Folder Options dialog box (see Figure 6.5), because they make a huge difference in your use of File Explorer.

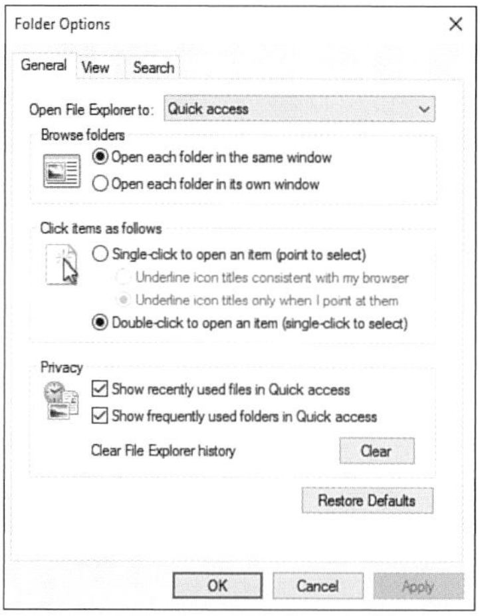

FIGURE 6.5
The General tab of the Folder Options dialog box enables you to configure a wide range of options to make File Explorer work the way you prefer.

Start by clicking the Open File Explorer To drop-down menu and choosing what each new File Explorer window you open should show. Your choices are Quick Access or This PC.

> **TIP** You can't choose a specific folder in the Open File Explorer To drop-down menu. If you need to open new File Explorer windows to a particular folder, create a shortcut to that folder and place it somewhere convenient, such as on your desktop.

In the Browse Folders box, select the Open Each Folder in the Same Window option button or the Open Each Folder in Its Own Window option button, as needed. If you need to browse deep into the file system, Open Each Folder in the Same Window is usually the better choice, because Open Each Folder in Its Own Window will leave a trail of windows cluttering the screen.

In the Click Items as Follows box, choose the effect of mouse clicks, which this list explains in reverse order for clarity:

- **Double-Click to Open an Item (Single-Click to Select).** Select this option button for normal Windows behavior: You click an item to select it, and you double-click an item to open it.

- **Single-Click to Open an Item (Point to Select).** Select this option button to turn on the alternate mode, in which you point at an item (without clicking) to select it and click an item to open it—like clicking a link in a web page to open it. This behavior can be faster than the normal Windows behavior, but you might find it takes a while to get used to. If you choose this option, you can choose when to underline icon titles—select the Underline Icon Titles Consistent with My Browser option button or the Underline Icon Titles Only When I Point at Them option button.

In the Privacy box, you can check or uncheck the following two check boxes as needed:

- **Show Recently Used Files in Quick Access.** Check this check box to make the Quick Access view display files you've used recently. This can be handy for quick access to files, but you may want to turn it off if you prefer not to have these files displayed (for example, for discretion).

- **Show Frequently Used Folders in Quick Access.** Check this check box to make the Quick Access view display folders you use frequently. As with the previous setting, having these folders displayed can be handy, but you may prefer to turn off this option.

> **TIP** You can click the Clear button in the Privacy box on the General tab of the Folder Options dialog box to clear your File Explorer history. You might want to do this to prevent private or sensitive files or folders from appearing in the Quick Access view.

CONFIGURING VIEW OPTIONS

On the View tab of the Folder Options dialog box (see Figure 6.6), you can manipulate a wide range of advanced settings. You can also apply your current view to all folders of the same type.

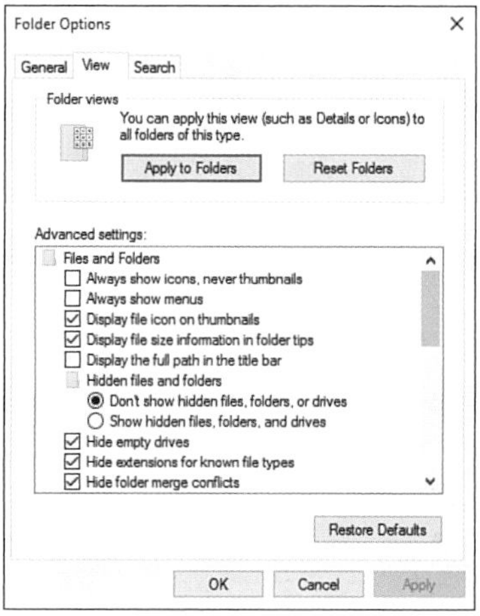

FIGURE 6.6

The View tab of the Folder Options dialog box enables you to apply your preferred view to all folders of the same type and to choose advanced settings.

To apply the current view to folders of the same type, set up the active File Explorer window with the view you prefer. For example, after navigating to a folder of the appropriate type, you might choose View, Layout, Details to switch to Details view, and then use the controls in the Current View group on the View tab of the Ribbon to customize the columns displayed. Then choose View, Options (clicking the main part of the Options button, not the drop-down arrow) to open the Folder Options dialog box, click the View tab, and then click Apply to Folders. Windows displays the Folder Views dialog box to confirm that you want all folders of this type to match the current folder's view settings; click Yes to apply the change.

> **NOTE** If you don't like the effect of the folder view you applied, click Reset Folders in the Folder Views box. Again, Windows displays the Folder Views dialog box to confirm the move; again, click Yes to effect the change.

In the Advanced Settings box, you can adjust the following settings:

- **Always Show Icons, Never Thumbnails.** Check this check box to display icons for files rather than thumbnails, small pictures of the files' contents. Displaying icons is faster than generating thumbnails, so you might want to use this setting if your computer isn't the fastest.

- **Always Show Menus.** Check this check box to make File Explorer always show menus in the interface rather than hiding them when they're not available. This setting doesn't have much effect in File Explorer windows that use the Ribbon because the Ribbon tabs and the File menu remain visible anyway. But if you check the Always Show Menus check box and click Apply and then open a Control Panel window, you'll see that the menu bar appears instead of being hidden until you press Alt.

- **Display File Icon on Thumbnails.** Check this check box to make File Explorer display an icon indicating the file type in the lower-right corner of a document thumbnail. For example, if you have created a Word document and saved a thumbnail preview for it, File Explorer shows the thumbnail with a Word icon on the lower-right corner.

> **NOTE** To save a thumbnail preview of a Word document, you check the Save Thumbnail check box in the Save As dialog box. If you want thumbnail previews for all documents, open the Properties dialog box for an open document (on Windows), click the Summary tab, and then check the Save Thumbnails for All Word Documents check box; on the Mac, open the Save preferences and check the Save Preview Picture with New Documents check box.

- **Display File Size Information in Folder Tips.** Check this check box to include the file size in the ScreenTip that appears when you hold the pointer over a folder. Calculating the file size makes your computer work a fraction harder, so if you don't find the size useful, uncheck this check box.

- **Display the Full Path in the Title Bar.** Check this check box to make File Explorer show the full path (such as C:\Users\Maria\Pictures\Best Pics) in the window's title bar instead of just the folder name (such as Best Pics).

> **☑ TIP** Displaying the full path in the title bar is especially helpful if you work with standardized folder structures. For example, say you work with projects, and each project folder contains a folder named `Documents`, a folder called `Spreadsheets`, and a folder called `Presentations`. Displaying the full path enables you to identify the windows you need more quickly. If all your folders have unique names, you probably don't need to display the full path.

- **Hidden Files and Folders.** Select the Don't Show Hidden Files, Folders, or Drives option button if you don't want to see hidden items; this is the default setting. Select the Show Hidden Files, Folders, and Drives option button when you want to see these items.

- **Hide Empty Drives.** Check this check box if you want File Explorer to hide any drives that are empty. This setting works on optical drives (so that when there's no DVD in it, the optical drive doesn't appear) and removable drives such as USB flash drives.

> **❗ CAUTION** The Hide Empty Drives feature can cause plenty of confusion, especially when you plug in a USB flash drive that happens to be empty but that you don't know is empty. For clarity, uncheck the Hide Empty Drives check box—and tuck this feature away in your mental troubleshooting toolbox for when someone complains that Windows won't recognize a USB flash drive.

- **Hide Extensions for Known File Types.** Check this check box to hide file extensions for file types that are registered in Windows. For example, after you install Microsoft Word, its various file types are registered, so Windows knows that (say) the `.docx` file extension is associated with the Word Document file type. Because the file type is registered, File Explorer windows don't show the `.docx` file extension, just the document name.

- **Hide Folder Merge Conflicts.** Check this check box if you want Windows to merge folders without warning you. A merge conflict occurs when you copy or move a folder to a destination that already contains a folder of the same name. Instead of overwriting the existing folder with the incoming folder, Windows merges the contents of each folder into a single folder. If you uncheck this check box, Windows displays the Confirm Folder Replace dialog box (see Figure 6.7) when a merge conflict occurs; you can then click Yes to merge the folders or click No to stop the operation.

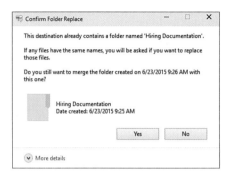

FIGURE 6.7

Uncheck the Hide Folder Merge Conflicts check box if you want to see the Confirm Folder Replace dialog box when you merge folders in File Explorer.

> **TIP** If your work (or play) includes projects that use a standard set of folders (such as a project folder containing Documents, Presentations, and Receipts subfolders), uncheck the Hide Folder Merge Conflicts check box to make sure that Windows warns you when you drag a folder to the wrong project.

> **NOTE** Even if you check the Hide Folder Merge Conflicts check box, Windows warns you about file merge conflicts—when a copy or move operation will cause one file to overwrite a file of the same name.

- **Hide Protected Operating System Files (Recommended).** Leave this check box checked (as it is by default) to hide the Windows protected operating system files. These are files marked System and Hidden to stop you from messing with them. Normally, you won't need to change the protected operating system files; if you do, uncheck this check box, and then click Yes in the Warning dialog box (see Figure 6.8) that Windows displays, acknowledging that you are aware that deleting or editing the files may make your computer stop working.

- **Launch Folder Windows in a Separate Process.** Check this check box if you want Windows to open each folder in a separate area of the computer's memory. This feature is turned off by default because it may reduce your computer's performance, but it can make Windows run more stably.

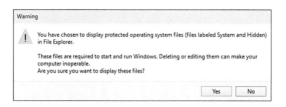

FIGURE 6.8

Click Yes in the Warning dialog box if you are determined to explore your computer's protected operating system files—or make changes to them.

> **TIP** Check the Launch Folder Windows in a Separate Process check box if your computer has plenty of RAM and normally runs well. Launching folder windows separately from each other can help you avoid crashes that freeze the desktop and force you to restart your computer. If you find that your computer slows down after you turn on this feature, turn it off again.

- **Restore Previous Folder Windows at Logon.** Check this check box if you want Windows to automatically open at login the same folders you were using when you logged out. This can be a great time-saver for picking up where you left off.

- **Show Drive Letters.** Check this check box to make Windows display drive letters (such as C: or D:) as well as drive names (such as Local Disk or DVD Drive).

- **Show Encrypted or Compressed NTFS Files in Color.** Check this check box to make File Explorer display encrypted files in green characters and compressed files in blue characters instead of black characters.

- **Show Pop-Up Description for Folder and Desktop Items.** Check this check box if you want Windows to display a ScreenTip (also called a ToolTip) containing information when you hold the pointer over an item. For example, when you hold the pointer over a file in the Recent Files list, the ScreenTip shows *Path:* and the folder path to the file.

- **Show Preview Handlers in Preview Pane.** Check this check box if you want to view previews in the Preview pane. Previews can help you identify the files you need, but because displaying previews can sap your computer's performance, you may want to turn them off.

- **Show Status Bar.** Check this check box to display the status bar at the bottom of each File Explorer window. The status bar displays information such as the number of items in the current folder or other container and the file size of the selected item. Usually, the status bar is helpful unless you need every square inch for displaying other information.
- **Use Check Boxes to Select Items.** Check this check box if you want Windows to display a check box on each item as you hold the pointer over it.
- **Use Sharing Wizard (Recommended).** Check this check box to make File Explorer use the Sharing Wizard for sharing items (such as folders). The Sharing Wizard simplifies the process of sharing, but you can uncheck this check box if you prefer to control sharing manually.
- **When Typing into List View.** Select the Select the Typed Item in the View option button if you want to be able to "type down" to select an item: You start typing its name, and File Explorer selects the matching item as soon as you've typed enough to identify it. Select the Automatically Type into the Search Box option button if you want any characters you type to go into the search box instead.

In the Navigation Pane settings at the bottom of the Advanced Settings list, you can check or uncheck the following three check boxes as needed:

- **Expand to Open Folder.** Check this check box to make File Explorer automatically expand the Navigation pane showing the path to the open folder. This setting is usually helpful.
- **Show All Folders.** Check this check box to display all the folders in the Navigation pane when you open a window. If you have a screen big enough for large File Explorer windows, or you prune the list of items in the Navigation pane to fit your window size, this setting is useful, because it saves you from having to expand items all the time to reach the ones you need.
- **Show Libraries.** Check this check box to display libraries in the Navigation pane. If you work with libraries much, you'll probably want to use this setting.

TIP You can set the three Navigation Pane settings more easily from the Ribbon: Choose View, Panes, Navigation Pane to open the Navigation Pane drop-down menu, and then click Expand to Open Folder, Show All Folders, or Show Libraries, placing or removing a check mark next to the appropriate item.

CONFIGURING SEARCH OPTIONS

On the Search tab of the Folder Options dialog box (see Figure 6.9), you can choose a few options to configure searching.

FIGURE 6.9

The Search tab of the Folder Options dialog box enables you to turn off use of the index and control how Windows searches non-indexed locations.

In the How to Search box, you can check the Don't Use the Index When Searching in File Folders for System Files (Searches Might Take Longer) check box if you're searching for a system file and can't find it. Normally, you'll want to leave this check box unchecked.

In the When Searching Non-Indexed Locations box, you can check or uncheck these three check boxes:

- **Include System Directories.** Check this check box to include system folders in searches of locations that are not in the search index that Windows keeps.

- **Include Compressed Files (ZIP, CAB, …).** Check this check box if you want to search through compressed files, which Windows normally excludes from searches. Searching through compressed files takes longer, so you'll probably want to uncheck this check box unless you keep files in compressed files.

> **NOTE** ZIP is a widely used standard for compressed files. CAB files are cabinet files, a compressed format used by Microsoft mostly for distributing Windows files.

- **Always Search File Names and Contents (This Might Take Several Minutes).** Check this check box if you need to be able to search by the contents of files as well as by their names. Searching through file contents can take a while, so normally it's best to leave this check box unchecked unless your searches aren't turning up files that you know are there.

When you finish choosing settings in the Folder Options dialog box, click OK to close it.

FINDING THE FILES AND FOLDERS YOU NEED

To find the files and folders you need, you can search in File Explorer. Follow these steps:

1. Open a File Explorer window. For example, click File Explorer on the Taskbar.

2. Navigate to the folder from which you want to start the search. The more you can narrow down the area you're searching, the fewer irrelevant results you'll need to wade through.

3. Click in the Search box below the right side of the Ribbon. The Search Tools tab appears on the Ribbon (see Figure 6.10).

Search box

FIGURE 6.10
The Search Tools tab on the Ribbon provides controls for focusing your searches and saving them for future use.

4. Type your search term or terms.

5. In the Location group, make sure the right item is selected. Normally, you'll want All Subfolders to search the current folder and all its subfolders. If you want to restrict the search to the current folder, excluding its subfolders, click Current Folder. If you need to widen the search to your computer's entire file system, click This PC.

6. In the Refine group, specify any constraints needed to refine the search. You can click Date Modified and specify a date range, such as Yesterday or This Week; click Kind and select the file type, such as Folder, Picture, or Task; click Size and specify the approximate size, such as Tiny (0–10 KB) or Huge (16–128 MB); or click Other Properties and then choose a property appropriate to the file type, such as Tags or Date Taken for a photo or video.

7. In the Options group, you can click Advanced Options to display the Advanced Options drop-down menu. You can then click Change Indexed Locations to change the locations that Windows indexes for searching. Alternatively, you can enable or disable the options on the In Non-Indexed Locations part of the Advanced Options drop-down menu: File Contents, System Files, or Zipped (Compressed) Folders. Look back to the previous section, "Configuring Search Options," for coverage of these options and their effects.

By this point, the File Explorer window should be displaying the items you need. If not, you'll need to go back and change the location, your search parameters, or both.

USING LIBRARIES AND FOLDERS THE SMART WAY

Windows enables you to use both libraries and folders to store and organize your files. To make the most of libraries and folders, you need to be clear on the difference between the two:

- **Folder.** A folder is a special kind of file that acts as a container for other files and folders (technically, subfolders). Each folder is stored at a specific point in your computer's file system.

- **Library.** A library is a kind of smart folder that presents files from different folders as if they were all stored in the same location. In fact, each file remains in the folder in which you stored it, but the library gives you an easy way to access it.

> **NOTE** Any library can be optimized for one of four categories of content—Documents, Music, Pictures, or Videos—or for General Items. The optimization controls which options File Explorer gives you for sorting files in the library. For example, if the library is optimized for documents, you can sort them by author; if it's optimized for music, you can sort by album; if it's optimized for pictures, you can sort by tags; and if it's optimized for videos, you can sort by length.

If File Explorer isn't displaying the list of libraries in the Navigation pane, choose View, Panes, Navigation Pane, Show Libraries to display them.

COMING TO GRIPS WITH THE DEFAULT LIBRARIES

Windows comes with six default libraries to take care of essential types of files such as documents, music, and pictures. Table 6.1 gives you brief details. You can create other libraries as needed; the next section shows you how to do this.

Table 6.1   The Six Default Windows Libraries

Library Name	Contains Files Such As	Optimized For
Camera Roll	Pictures from your computer's camera	Pictures
Documents	Word processing documents, spreadsheets, presentations	Documents
Music	Music in various formats	Music
Pictures	Pictures in various formats	Pictures
Saved Pictures	Pictures you have saved from sources such as web pages and email messages	Pictures
Videos	Videos in various formats	Videos

Windows stores libraries in the Libraries folder, which you can access through File Explorer. The Libraries folder doesn't actually appear on your computer's desktop unless you put it there, so you'll normally want to go through File Explorer.

> **NOTE** Windows also displays some libraries in the Quick Access view of the Navigation pane by default. You can customize the Quick Access view as needed; see the section "Customizing the Quick Access View," earlier in this chapter, for details.

Each user account on your computer has separate libraries, so your library items don't appear in other users' libraries unless you choose to share them. But Windows also provides public libraries for items that you want to share with all users. Windows keeps these public libraries in the Users\Public\ folder; each user's libraries draw in these files automatically, so they appear alongside the user's private content.

> **☑ TIP** You can include external drives in your libraries. Just add the appropriate folders as explained in the section "Including Folders in Your Library," later in this chapter. After you add folders on an external drive, Windows automatically pulls new files in those folders into the appropriate libraries, giving you easy access to them without navigating around your computer's file system.

CREATING A NEW LIBRARY

If the default libraries don't cover your needs, you can create new libraries of your own. For example, if you work with many documents, you might want to create a separate library for each document category, such as Spreadsheets, Word Processing Documents, and Presentations.

Follow these steps to create a new library:

1. Open a File Explorer window. For example, click the File Explorer icon on the Taskbar or choose Start, File Explorer.

2. In the Navigation pane, click Libraries to display the `Libraries` folder.

> **✎ NOTE** If you can't see the Libraries folder in the Navigation pane, you'll need to display this. If you can find open space in the Navigation pane, right-click or long-press there and then click Show Libraries, placing a check mark by the Show Libraries item on the menu that appears. If you can't find open space, go to the Ribbon and choose View, Panes, Navigation Pane, Show Libraries.

3. Choose Home, New, New Item, Library. File Explorer creates a new library, gives it the default name `New Library`, and selects the name so you can change it.

> **☑ TIP** You can also create a new library by right-clicking or long-pressing in open space in the main part of the window and then choosing New, Library from the shortcut menu.

4. Type the new name and press Enter to apply it.

You now have a new library, but it's not going to do anything until you tell Windows which folders to include in it. Read on.

INCLUDING FOLDERS IN YOUR LIBRARY

You can include folders in a library using several methods. Here's the method you'll probably want to use with your freshly minted library:

1. Open a File Explorer window to the `Libraries` folder. If you just created a library in the preceding section, you should be here already.

2. Click the library file you just created. When you select the library file, the Library Tools tab appears on the Ribbon.

3. Choose Library Tools, Manage, Manage, Manage Library to open the Library Locations dialog box for the library (shown in Figure 6.11 with a folder included).

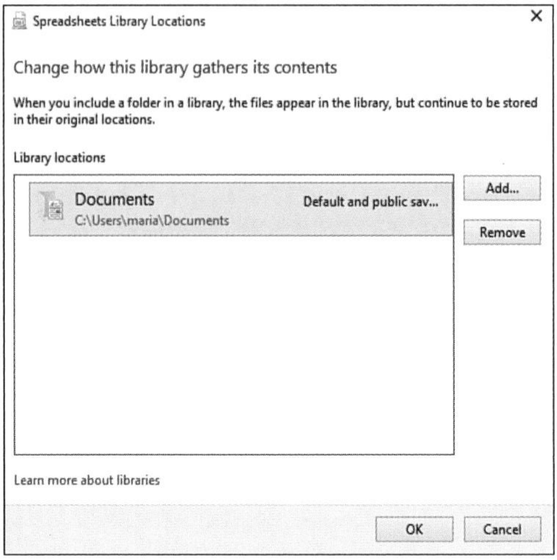

FIGURE 6.11

Use the Library Locations dialog box to specify which folders to include in your new library. The dialog box's title shows the library's name, such as Spreadsheets Library Locations.

4. To add a folder, click Add, select the file in the Include Folder in *Library* dialog box that opens, and then click Include Folder.

> **NOTE** The first folder you include in the library becomes its default save location. I'll explain the two save locations and how to change them in the next section.

5. To remove a folder, click it in the list box and then click Remove.

6. When you finish setting up the list of folders, click OK to close the Library Locations dialog box.

> **NOTE** You can't add individual files to a library directly. Instead, put the files in a folder, and add the folder to the library.

> **TIP** Another way to add a folder to a library is to open a File Explorer window, right-click or long-press the folder, click or highlight Include in Library on the shortcut menu, and then click the library on the submenu that opens. This method is great for adding individual folders to a library as needed. The submenu also contains a Create New Library command that enables you to start a new library containing the folder you picked.

SETTING THE LIBRARY'S DEFAULT SAVE LOCATION AND PUBLIC SAVE LOCATION

After you've included two or more folders in the library, you need to set its save locations. There are two save locations:

- **Default Save Location.** This is the folder in which the library saves new documents you create. The default save location enables you to save a file to the library rather than having to save the file to a folder. This is a small convenience provided that you set the appropriate folder as the default save location.

- **Public Save Location.** This is the folder in which the library saves new documents that other users create.

You can set the default save location and public save location in a couple of ways. The easiest way is to select the library in a File Explorer window, go to the Ribbon, and choose Library Tools, Manage, Manage, Set Save Location to open the Set Save Location drop-down menu (see Figure 6.12). You can then set the default save location by choosing the appropriate folder on the drop-down menu, which shows the folders you've included in the library. To set the public save location, click or highlight Set Public Save Location on the drop-down menu, and then click the appropriate folder on the submenu, which also shows the folders included in the library.

FIGURE 6.12
Use the Set Save Location drop-down menu to set the default save location and the public save location for a library.

CONFIGURING THE LIBRARY TO WORK YOUR WAY

From the Library Tools tab of the Ribbon, you can also choose the type of files for which to optimize the library: Choose Library Tools, Manage, Manage, Optimize Library For to display the Optimize Library For drop-down menu, and then click General Items, Documents, Music, Pictures, or Videos, as needed.

You can also change the library icon to give it a different look in your folders. To change the icon, choose Library Tools, Manage, Manage, Change Icon; click the icon in the Change Icon dialog box; and then click OK.

> **TIP** The Change Icon dialog box shows the icons in a file named SHELL32.dll, one of the dynamic link library files that Windows uses extensively. If none of these icons appeals to you, try browsing other .dll files to find other icons. You might start with moricons.dll, which contains various premillennial icons. Or if you have an icon file of your own, you might prefer to use that instead.

If you want the library to appear in the Navigation pane, choose Library Tools, Manage, Manage, Show in Navigation Pane.

You can also configure the library by working in its Properties dialog box. Right-click or long-press the library in a File Explorer window, and then click Properties on the shortcut menu to display the Properties dialog box (see Figure 6.13). You can then use the Library Locations list box at the top to review the folders in the library, and use the Add button and Remove button below the list box to change the list of folders; use the Set Save Location button and Set Public Save Location button to set the save locations; choose the means of optimization in the Optimize This Library For drop-down menu; and click the Change Library Icon button to change the icon.

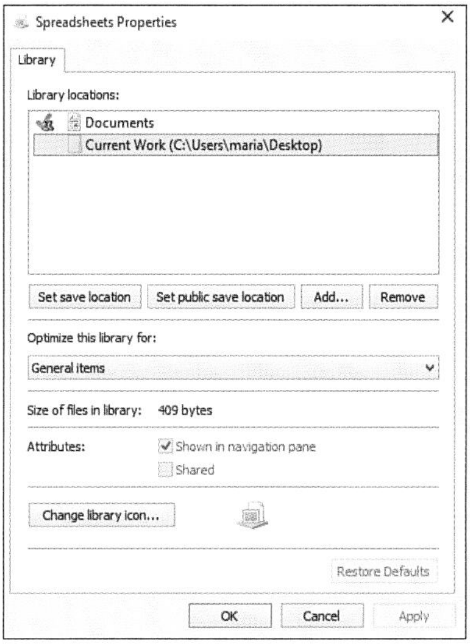

FIGURE 6.13

In the Properties dialog box for the library, click Add to start adding folders to the Library Locations list box.

> **NOTE**   The Properties dialog box for a library provides a handy one-stop place to work on the library, but it has no particular advantage over using the Library Tools tab on the Ribbon.

RESTORING YOUR DEFAULT LIBRARIES

If you delete any of your default libraries by mistake, you can restore them easily. To do so, open a File Explorer window, right-click or long-press Libraries in the Navigation pane, and then click Restore Default Libraries on the shortcut menu.

If you mess up the settings for an individual library, you can restore them to their defaults to get the library working normally again. Open a File Explorer window to the `Libraries` folder, click the library, and then choose Library Tools, Manage, Manage, Restore Settings.

MANAGING YOUR STORAGE

When you need to manage your computer's storage, use the Storage feature in the Settings app. Follow these steps to display the Storage pane:

1. Choose Start, Settings to open a Settings window.

2. Click System to display the System pane.

3. Click Storage in the left column to display the Storage screen (see Figure 6.14).

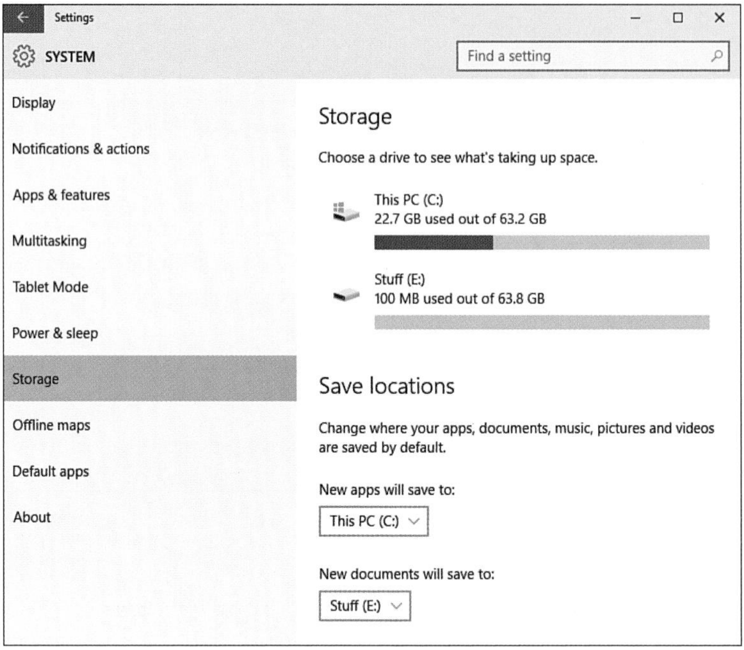

FIGURE 6.14

From the Storage pane in Settings, you can see what's taking up space on your computer and choose default locations for storing files.

SEEING WHAT'S TAKING UP SPACE ON YOUR COMPUTER

To see what's taking up space on your PC, click This PC in the Storage section. The This PC screen appears (see Figure 6.15), showing how much space the different categories of items are taking up. Click the item whose details you want to see. Windows displays the corresponding screen, which shows details of the files in the category and actions that you can perform on them.

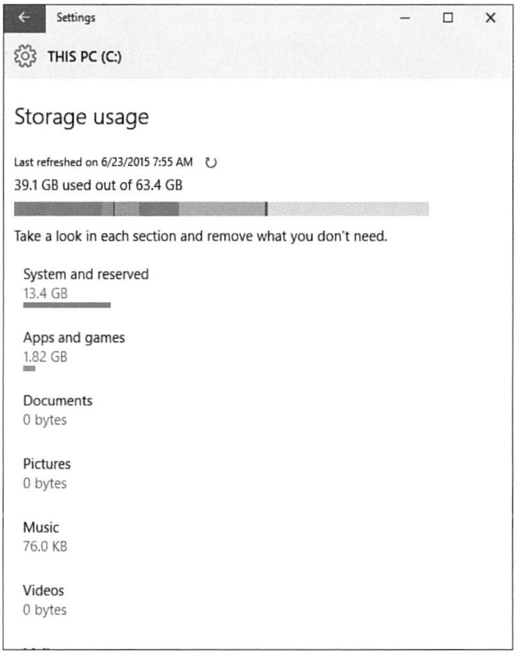

FIGURE 6.15
On the This PC screen, you can see how much space is free overall and how much space each category of items is occupying.

These are the items you'll find on the This PC screen:

- **System and Reserved.** System files are Windows files that you shouldn't change. Reserved files include backup files with which Windows can repair itself after you do change or delete something vital; the paging file, which Windows uses to supplement virtual memory; the hibernation file, which Windows uses for deep sleep; and System Restore files, which save snapshots of your computer's configuration so that you can restore it to an earlier configuration (for example, after something goes wrong). You can click Manage System Restore to display the System Protection tab of the System Properties dialog box.

> **NOTE** See Chapter 8, "Optimizing Your Computer's Performance," for instructions on configuring the paging file. See Chapter 13, "Updating and Troubleshooting Windows," for details on how to use System Restore.

- **Apps and Games.** These are apps (programs) and games, both those that come preinstalled on your computer and those you have installed yourself. On the Apps and Games screen, you can sort the apps by size, by name, or by install date; search for an app by name; and uninstall an app by clicking it and then clicking Uninstall. You can also click the Manage Optional Features link to display the Manage Optional Features window, which enables you to add or remove items such as handwriting recognition and optical character recognition.

- **Documents.** These are the files in the Documents library, such as Microsoft Office documents, spreadsheets, presentations, and databases. On the Documents screen, you can click View Documents to display the Documents library in a File Explorer window.

- **Pictures.** These are the files in the Pictures library. On the Pictures screen, you can click View Pictures to display the Pictures library in a File Explorer window.

- **Music.** These are the files in the Music library. On the Music screen, you can click View Music to display the Music library in a File Explorer window.

- **Videos.** These are the files in the Videos library. On the Videos screen, you can click View Videos to display the Videos library in a File Explorer window.

- **Mail.** This readout shows the amount of space your mail is taking up. On the Mail screen, you can click Manage Mail to open the system's default mail app.

- **OneDrive.** These are copies of files stored on OneDrive that you have downloaded to your computer so that they are available even when an Internet connection is not. On the OneDrive screen, you can click Manage OneDrive to open the Sync Your OneDrive Files to This PC dialog box, in which you can specify which files to sync.

- **Desktop.** These are files on your desktop, because many people store many files there. On the Desktop screen, you can click View Desktop to display the Desktop folder in a File Explorer window.

- **Maps.** These are files containing map data that the Map app has downloaded. On the Maps screen, you can click Manage Maps to display the Offline Maps pane in System settings. Here, you can click Delete All Maps if you want to get rid of all the downloaded maps.

- **Other Users.** This shows the amount of space that other users' files are taking. On the Other Users screen, you can click Manage Other Users to display the Accounts screen in Settings, where you can work with user accounts.

▓ **Temporary Files.** This shows the amount of space that various types of temporary files are taking up. We'll look at the details in a moment, because this is where you'll likely want to start recovering space.

▓ **Other.** This category contains the largest folders Windows has identified that don't fit into any of the other categories.

Normally, the best place to start when you need to reclaim space is the Temporary Files screen, because you can often reclaim several gigabytes of space here simply by getting rid of files you no longer need. Follow these steps:

1. Click Temporary Files on the This PC screen to display the Temporary Files screen (see Figure 6.16).

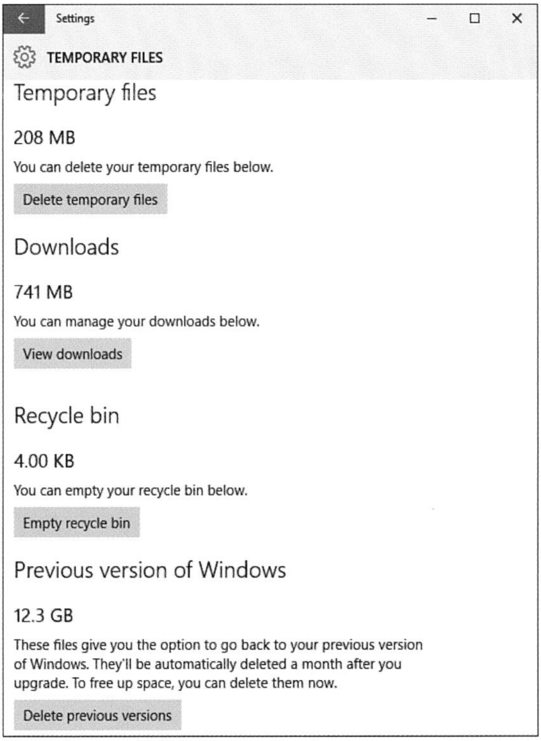

FIGURE 6.16
The Temporary Files screen is normally the best place to start recovering space on your PC.

2. In the Temporary Files area, click Delete Temporary Files, and then click Yes, I'm Sure in the confirmation dialog box that opens.

3. In the Downloads area, look at the amount of space that files in the `Downloads` folder are taking up. If there's enough space to be worth recovering, click View Downloads to display the `Downloads` folder in a File Explorer window, and then delete any files you don't need.

> **TIP** When reclaiming space from the `Downloads` folder, move any files you want to keep to other folders. If you treat your `Downloads` folder as temporary storage rather than long-term storage, you'll have a much easier time avoiding wasting space in it.

4. In the Recycle Bin area, look at the amount of space that files in the Recycle Bin are taking up. If you're confident that the Recycle Bin doesn't contain anything you'll miss, go ahead and click Empty Recycle Bin and then click Yes, I'm Sure in the confirmation dialog box; if you're not confident, first open the Recycle Bin and check through it for any files whose loss would hurt.

5. In the Previous Version of Windows area, look at the amount of space that files from your previous version of Windows are taking up. You can delete these files if you're certain that you won't want to roll Windows back to an earlier state or version.

> **CAUTION** Don't delete your Previous Version of Windows files unless you're completely sure you won't need to roll Windows back. Windows automatically deletes the files a month after an upgrade, so they won't hang around forever if you leave them be.

6. When you finish on the Temporary Files screen, click Back (the arrow at the top) to return to the This PC screen.

Back on the This PC screen, click the next item you want to clear out, such as Apps and Games, and work on the screen that appears.

CONTROLLING WHERE WINDOWS SAVES GAMES, APPS, MUSIC, AND OTHER ITEMS

The Save Locations list on the Storage screen in the Settings app enables you to control where Windows saves your apps, games, documents, music, pictures, and videos by default. Simply click the appropriate location button, such as the New

Apps Will Save To button, and then choose where to save the items. The default setting is This PC, which is usually the best choice until you start running out of space.

> **! CAUTION** Before moving items to another location, make sure it will always be available when you need those items.

CREATING POOLED STORAGE WITH STORAGE SPACES

If your computer has two or more drives, you can combine them into a single pooled drive by using the Storage Spaces feature. Storage spaces are useful for improving performance, enabling you to work with large files, and avoiding data loss.

> **NOTE** Technically, you can use storage spaces on any computer that has multiple drives. But because most tablets and laptops have only a single drive, and no means to connect another drive permanently, in practice you'd normally use storage spaces only on a desktop computer.

UNDERSTANDING SIMPLE SPACES, MIRROR SPACES, AND PARITY SPACES

Windows enables you to create three types of storage spaces, each of which works in a different way—so it's vital that you understand the differences and choose the type you need.

These are the three types of storage spaces:

- **Simple Space.** A simple space is a space that gives better performance and (usually) more storage but doesn't provide any protection against data loss or drive failure. You can create a simple space with a single drive, but normally you'll want to use two or more drives in order to give yourself space.

- **Mirror Space.** A mirror space is a space that gives better performance and also protects your files against drive failure by keeping multiple copies. You can create a two-way mirror space by using two or more drives; for a three-way mirror space, which gives greater protection and redundancy, you need at least five drives.

■ **Parity Space.** A parity space is a space that provides efficient storage and protects your files against drive failure; it does not provide better performance. You need at least three drives to protect your data against a single drive failing; to protect against two drives failing, you need at least seven drives.

WHICH STORAGE SPACE TYPE SHOULD YOU USE?

Create a simple space when you need somewhere to put large files temporarily, such as when you are rendering video, not for long-term storage.

Create a mirror space for general-purpose use, such as when you are sharing files with others on a network.

Create a parity space for storing data in the long term or for streaming music and video files.

CREATING A STORAGE SPACE

Now that you know the different types of storage spaces and have decided which type to create, follow these steps to create it:

1. Right-click or long-press Start to display the shortcut menu.

2. Click Control Panel to open a Control Panel window.

3. Click System and Security to display the System and Security pane.

4. Click the Storage Spaces heading to display the Storage Spaces pane. Figure 6.17 shows the Storage Spaces pane as you'll see it at first, before you've set up any storage spaces.

5. Click Create a New Pool and Storage Space. The Select Drives to Create a Storage Pool screen appears (see Figure 6.18).

NOTE If the User Account Control dialog box opens when you click Create a New Pool and Storage Space, verify that the program name is Storage Spaces Settings, and then click Yes.

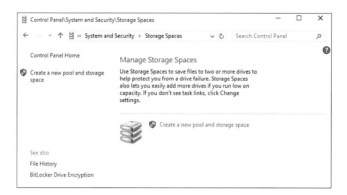

FIGURE 6.17

To start creating a storage space, click Create a New Pool and Storage Space in the Storage Spaces pane in Control Panel.

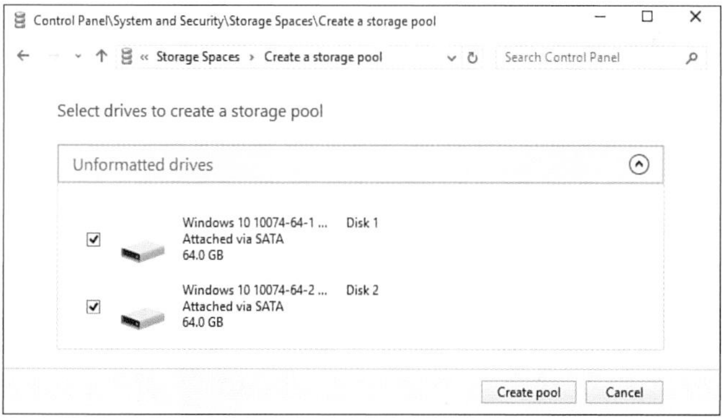

FIGURE 6.18

On the Select Drives to Create a Storage Pool screen, check the check box for each drive you want to use, and then click Create Pool.

6. Check the check box for each drive to include in the pool.

7. Click Create Pool. Windows creates the pool and then displays the Enter a Name, Resiliency Type, and Size for the Storage Space screen (see Figure 6.19).

8. Type the name for the storage space in the Name box. If you're creating a single storage space for your own use, you can call it whatever you like; but if you're creating multiple storage spaces, you'll usually be better off using a naming convention.

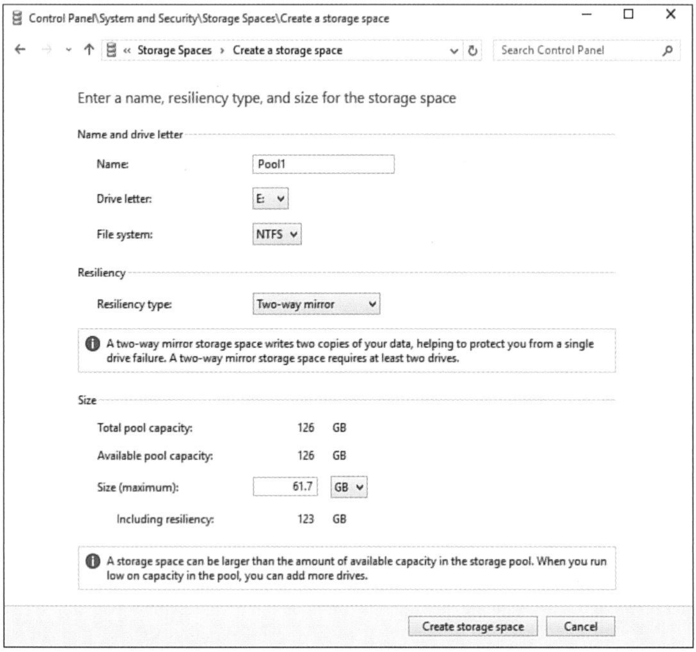

FIGURE 6.19
On this screen, name your storage space, choose its drive letter and file system, and select the resiliency type.

9. In the Drive Letter drop-down menu, choose the letter you want to assign to the drive. Windows suggests the next unused letter, such as E: if your computer has drives C: and D:.

10. In the File System drop-down menu, make sure NTFS is selected. Depending on your computer's configuration, this may be the only choice.

11. Open the Resiliency Type drop-down menu and choose the storage space type you want: Simple (No Resiliency), Two-Way Mirror, Three-Way Mirror, or Parity. As I mentioned earlier, Three-Way Mirror needs a minimum of five drives, and Parity needs a minimum of three drives; you can create a Simple or Two-Way Mirror storage space with two drives.

12. In the Size area, look at the readouts and make sure they show what you expect. Briefly, a Simple (No Resiliency) storage space gives you the full amount of space on the drives minus a small overhead for administration; a Two-Way Mirror storage space gives you half the total drive space minus some overhead; a Three-Way Mirror storage space gives you a third of the total drive space minus the overhead; and a Parity storage space with three drives gives you two-thirds of the total space minus the overhead.

> **NOTE** You can set the Size (Maximum) for the storage space to a value larger than the space provided by the drives you've chosen. Do this if you plan to add more drives to the storage space later.

13. Click Create Storage Space. Windows creates the storage space, and it appears on the Storage Spaces screen (see Figure 6.20).

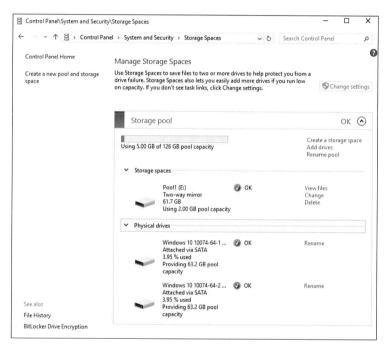

FIGURE 6.20

Your new storage space appears on the Storage Spaces screen. You can view the usage of the storage space and the physical drives, add drives, or reconfigure the storage space.

USING THE STORAGE SPACE

After creating a storage space, you can use it as you would use any other drive. The storage space appears in your computer's file system under the drive letter you specified in the Drive Letter drop-down menu, and you can create files and folders on it using File Explorer and other apps.

CHANGING AN EXISTING STORAGE SPACE

You can change an existing storage space by displaying the Manage Storage Spaces screen and clicking Change to the right of the storage space. Windows displays the Change a Storage Space screen, in which you can change the name, the drive letter, and the maximum size of the storage space. When you finish, click Change Storage Space to commit the changes.

NOTE You cannot change the type of an existing storage space. If you find you need a different type of storage space than you have created, you will need to delete the existing storage space and set up a new storage space of the right type.

DELETING A STORAGE SPACE

When you no longer need a storage space, you can delete it.

CAUTION Deleting a storage space deletes all the files it contains. Unless you have been using the storage space only for temporary files, you must copy or move the files to another location—and verify the copied or moved files—before deleting the storage space.

To delete a storage space, display the Manage Storage Spaces screen and click Delete to the right of the storage space. Windows displays the Confirm Deletion of the Storage Space screen; click Delete Storage Space if you're certain you want to proceed.

IN THIS CHAPTER

- Configuring accounts for practicality and security
- Tightening your computer's security
- Configuring sharing

7

SECURING AND SHARING YOUR COMPUTER

Even if you are the only person to use your computer, you'll need to configure your user account and your unlock methods. If you share your computer with others, you'll need to set up an account for each person.

To keep your computer safe against intruders, you can take various steps, such as applying a startup password, setting the device to lock automatically, and implementing the Secure Sign-In feature.

To share items with others, you can either use the Windows homegroup feature or configure Advanced Sharing manually.

CONFIGURING ACCOUNTS FOR PRACTICALITY AND SECURITY

In this section, we'll look at four actions you will likely need to take with user accounts:

- Setting your profile picture
- Connecting a local account to a Microsoft account
- Securing your account with a password, picture password, PIN, or Windows Hello
- Creating accounts for other people

SETTING YOUR PROFILE PICTURE

To help identify your account, you can set a profile picture for it. Follow these steps:

1. Click Start to open the Start menu, and then click your account name to display the drop-down menu.
2. Click Change Account Settings to display the Your Account pane in the Accounts screen in Settings.
3. To use an existing picture, click Browse, select a picture in the Open dialog box, and then click Choose Picture.

> **☑ TIP** You can add two other pictures by repeating step 3. The current picture appears as a large circle, with the previous pictures appearing in smaller circles to the right. You can click one of the previous pictures to make it the current picture.

4. To take a photo with your computer's camera, click Camera, and then follow the prompts to shoot a satisfactory picture.

CONNECTING A LOCAL ACCOUNT TO A MICROSOFT ACCOUNT

Windows enables you to create both local accounts and Microsoft accounts on your computer:

- **Local Account.** A *local account* is one that exists only on your computer. You use the account to sign in to Windows.

■ **Microsoft Account.** A *Microsoft account* consists of an email address and password. You use the Microsoft account both to sign in to Windows and to access apps and services online. For example, if your Microsoft account is an Outlook.com account, you use the account to access your email on Outlook.com as well as to sign in to your computer. You can also sync your settings and files automatically via the Internet.

> **☑ TIP** If you're not sure whether you're signed in using a local account or a Microsoft account, click Start, click your account name, and then click Change Account Settings on the drop-down menu. At the top of the Your Account pane in the Accounts screen in Settings, look at the readout below your name. If it shows an email address, you're using a Microsoft account, and there's a Sign In with a Local Account Instead link you can click to create a local account and sign in to it; if it shows Local Account, you're using a local account.

> **✎ NOTE** If your computer connects to a network that uses Windows domains, you'll use a domain account. This has the format *domain\username*.

If you're using a local account, you can connect it to your Microsoft account by following these steps:

1. Click Start to open the Start menu, and then click your account name to display the drop-down menu.
2. Click Change Account Settings to display the Your Account pane in the Accounts screen in Settings.
3. Click Sign In with a Microsoft Account Instead to display the Switch to a Microsoft Account on This PC dialog box.
4. Type the password for the account you're currently using, and then click Next. The Sign In to Your Microsoft Account dialog box appears.
5. Type the email address and password for your Microsoft account, and then click Next.

> **NOTE** Depending on the security arrangement for your Microsoft account, you may have to provide an alternative email address or cell phone number, receive a code sent to that address or number, and then enter the code on your computer to authorize connecting your local account to your Microsoft account.

6. When the final Switch to a Microsoft Account on This PC dialog box opens, announcing that your existing account will be changed to a Microsoft account, click Switch.

SECURING YOUR ACCOUNT WITH A PASSWORD, PICTURE PASSWORD, PIN, OR WINDOWS HELLO

To keep your computer and your data safe, you must secure your account against intrusion. Windows lets you choose which of four unlock methods to use:

- **Password.** A password is a string of characters—preferably including uppercase and lowercase letters, numbers, and symbols (such as $, ^, or @). This is the essential unlock method, and you can use it when other unlock methods fail.
- **PIN.** A PIN is a code consisting of four or more numbers. You can use the PIN as an alternative to the password—entering a PIN can be easier than entering a password, especially on a touchscreen device. You can also use the PIN to sign in to apps and services.

> **TIP** Every extra digit you add to your PIN makes it 10 times harder to crack. A 4-digit PIN is convenient but provides only modest security. Use 8 digits for stronger security; use 12 or more digits to make the PIN really hard to crack. Memorize a longer PIN by breaking it into groups of 3 or 4 digits like a phone number—but don't use your actual phone number as the PIN!

- **Windows Hello.** Windows Hello uses biometrics—measurements of your (preferably) living body—to authenticate you. Depending on the capabilities of your computer, you can set up Windows Hello to use your face, your iris, or your fingerprint as the biometric.
- **Picture Password.** A picture password is a security device for touchscreen PCs. To set up the picture password, you choose a picture and then draw a

pattern on it using circles, straight lines, and taps. To unlock your computer using the picture password, you replicate that pattern on the picture.

> **NOTE** The Password and PIN unlock methods work on any Windows device. The Windows Hello method works on any Windows device that has the hardware needed to recognize the appropriate biometric—for example, a camera to scan your face or your iris, or a fingerprint reader to capture your fingerprint.

To set up your unlock methods, you work on the Sign-In Options screen (see Figure 7.1). Follow these steps to display the Sign-In Options screen:

1. Click Start to open the Start menu, click your account name, and then click Change Account Settings on the drop-down menu. The Settings app opens, showing the Your Account pane on the Accounts screen.
2. Click Sign-In Options in the left column to display the Sign-In Options screen.

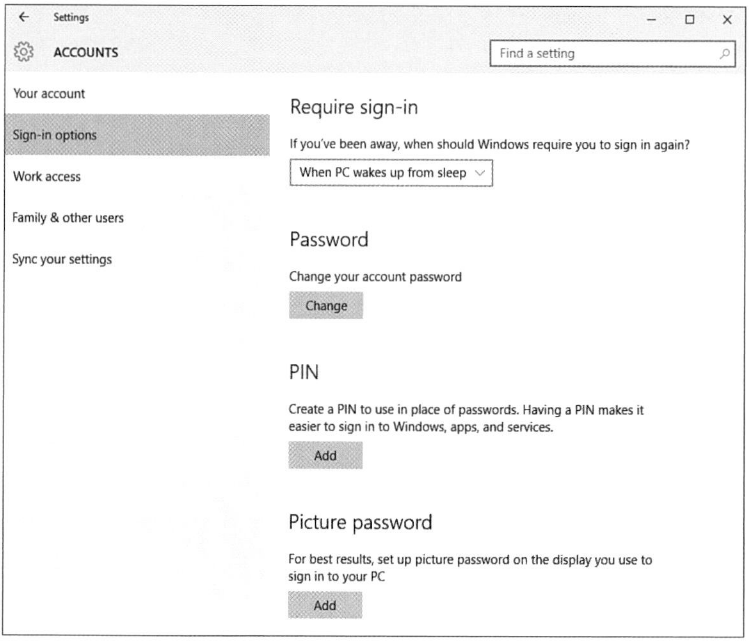

FIGURE 7.1

On the Sign-In Options screen in the Settings app, you can configure your means of unlocking Windows and signing in to apps and services.

You can now add an unlock method by clicking the Add button below its heading, or change an existing unlock method by clicking the Change button below its heading.

📝 **TIP**   Set up multiple unlock methods so that you can use whichever method is most convenient for the device you happen to be using. But make sure each unlock method is secure.

❗**CAUTION**   In the "If You've Been Away, When Should Windows Require You to Sign In Again?" drop-down menu in the Require Sign-in area, do not choose Never—this setting means that anyone who wakes your computer from sleep can start using it without having to provide any authentication. Instead, choose When PC Wakes Up from Sleep if this choice appears on your computer; if not, choose either Every Time or a specific time, such as 1 Minute.

USE A NON-ADMINISTRATOR ACCOUNT FOR EVERYDAY COMPUTING

Chances are that you've set yourself up with an administrator account so that you can manage your computer. This is fine and normal—but you can make your computer more secure by creating a second account, a standard account, for yourself. You can then use the standard account for everyday computing and keep the administrator account strictly for administration.

To be honest, most people don't bother to do this, but that's no reason why you shouldn't. Having a second account also has another benefit: If your standard account becomes corrupted or has startup items that prevent it from loading correctly, you can use your administrator account to sort out the problems.

CREATING ACCOUNTS FOR OTHERS

If other people will use your computer regularly, create an account for each of them. That way, each person can have a separate area for his own files, can keep his email private, and can customize his desktop and settings without other people changing them.

> **NOTE** Previous versions of Windows included a Guest account suitable for use by anyone who needed to use your computer only once. As of this writing, the Guest account is disabled and not functional in Windows 10. There *are* ways to enable it, but even if you do so, it is not currently usable. This situation may well change.

Windows provides different features for adding family members than for adding people who are not part of your family. You create both types of accounts from the Your Family pane in the Settings app.

> **NOTE** Windows uses Microsoft accounts to set up user accounts. When setting up the account on your computer, you provide the email address for the Microsoft account. The user can then log in by providing the password for the Microsoft account, so you do not have to set even a temporary password for the user.

OPENING THE YOUR FAMILY PANE IN THE SETTINGS APP

Follow these steps to create an account for someone else:

1. Choose Start, Settings to open a Settings window.
2. Click Accounts to display the Accounts screen.
3. Click Family & Other Users in the left pane to display the Your Family pane.

You can now create accounts as explained in the next two subsections.

> **NOTE** Windows creates each new user account as a standard account. If you want to make the new user an administrator, see the section "Changing an Existing Account to an Administrator Account," later in this chapter.

CREATING AN ACCOUNT FOR A FAMILY MEMBER

Follow these steps to create an account for a family member:

1. In the Your Family pane, click Add a Family Member. Windows displays the Add a Child or an Adult? dialog box.

2. Click the Add a Child option button or the Add an Adult option button.

3. Click in the Enter Their Email Address box and type the person's email address.

4. Click Next. The Add This Person? dialog box opens.

5. Look to make sure you've gotten the email address right, and then click Confirm. Windows adds the user account.

CREATING AN ACCOUNT FOR SOMEONE WHO ISN'T A FAMILY MEMBER

Follow these steps to create an account for someone who isn't a family member:

1. In the Your Family pane, click Add Someone Else to This PC. Windows displays the How Will This Person Sign In? dialog box.

2. Click the box and type the person's email address.

3. Click Next. The Good to Go! screen appears.

4. Click Finish. The user's new account appears in the Other Users list.

CHANGING AN EXISTING ACCOUNT TO AN ADMINISTRATOR ACCOUNT

Sometimes you may need to promote an existing user account to an administrator account so that that user can help administer the computer. To promote an account to administrator, follow these steps:

1. Click Start to open the Start menu, and then click your account name to display the drop-down menu.

2. Click Change Account Settings to display the Your Account pane in the Accounts screen in Settings.

3. Click Family & Other Users in the left pane to display the Your Family pane.

4. In the Other Users list, click the account you will promote. The Change Account Type button and Remove button appear under the account.

5. Click Change Account Type to display the Change Account Type dialog box (see Figure 7.2).

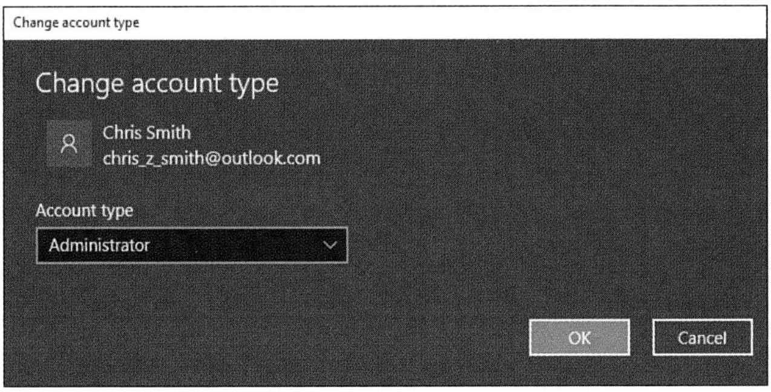

FIGURE 7.2
You can promote a standard account to an administrator account by choosing Administrator in the Account Type drop-down menu in the Change Account Type dialog box and then clicking OK.

6. Click the Account Type drop-down menu, and then click Administrator.

7. Click OK. Windows changes the account type.

> **NOTE** As you'd imagine, you can use the same technique to demote an administrator account to a standard account—for example, because you find that the user misuses the administrator powers.

TIGHTENING YOUR COMPUTER'S SECURITY

This section shows you how to tighten your computer's security by applying a startup password, setting your computer to lock automatically after a period of inactivity, and implementing the Secure Sign-In feature. You also learn how to configure User Account Control to a level that suits you, disable recent app switching, and use the Assigned Access feature to limit a particular user account to using a single app.

LOCKING YOUR COMPUTER WITH A STARTUP PASSWORD

For an extra level of security, you can set Windows to demand a startup password each time your computer starts. Figure 7.3 shows the Startup Password dialog box.

FIGURE 7.3

You can set Windows to display the Startup Password dialog box before the logon screen.

Follow these steps to set a startup password:

1. Click Start to display the Start menu.

2. Type **syskey** in the Search box. Windows displays a list of search results.

3. Click the "syskey: Run Command" result. It normally appears at the top of the list.

4. If the User Account Control dialog box appears, verify that the Program Name readout shows SAM Lock Tool and that the Verified Publisher readout shows Microsoft Windows. If so, click Yes. The Securing the Windows Account Database dialog box appears (see Figure 7.4).

FIGURE 7.4

In the Securing the Windows Account Database dialog box, click Update to display the Startup Key dialog box.

5. Click Update to display the Startup Key dialog box (see Figure 7.5).

6. Select the Password Startup option button.

7. Type a strong password in the Password box and in the Confirm box.

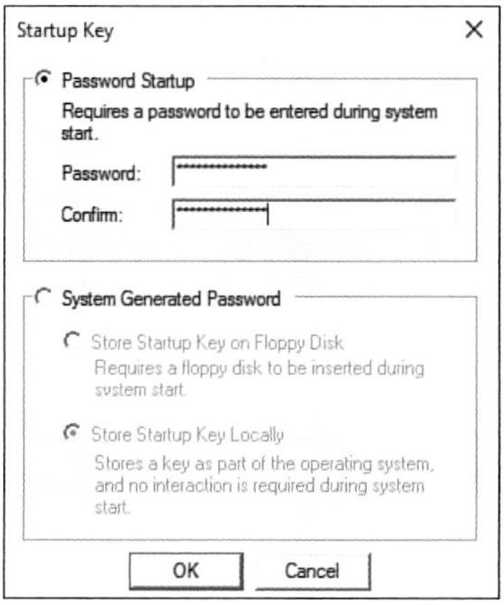

FIGURE 7.5

In the Startup Key dialog box, select the Password Startup option button, type a strong password twice, and then click OK.

> **NOTE** A strong password is one that combines uppercase and lower-case letters, numbers, and symbols; is at least 8 characters long, and preferably 12 characters or longer; and is not a real word or a combination of real words in any language.

8. Click OK. The Success dialog box appears, telling you that "the Account Database Startup Key was changed."

9. Click OK to close the Success dialog box. Both the Startup Key dialog box and the Securing the Windows Account Database dialog box also close.

> **NOTE** To remove the startup password, open the Startup Key dialog box and select the System Generated Password option button. In the System Generated Password box, select the Store Startup Key Locally option button. Click OK and then enter the startup password to prove you know it.

SETTING YOUR COMPUTER TO LOCK AUTOMATICALLY

To protect your data, you should lock your computer every time you step away from the keyboard. But because it's easy to forget, especially in a busy office situation, you should set your computer to lock itself automatically. You can do this by configuring a screensaver to kick in after a period of inactivity and specifying that Windows display the logon screen when someone interrupts the screensaver.

> **TIP** Normally, you can lock your computer by pressing Windows Key+L. You may find that administrators disable this keyboard shortcut on some computers.

Follow these steps to set your computer to lock itself automatically:

1. Right-click or long-press Start to display the shortcut menu.
2. Click Control Panel to open a Control Panel window.
3. Click Appearance and Personalization to display the Appearance and Personalization screen.
4. Click Change Screen Saver to display the Screen Saver Settings dialog box (see Figure 7.6).

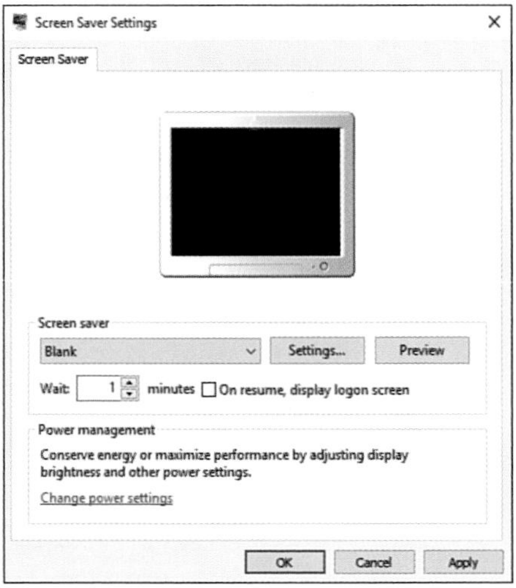

FIGURE 7.6

In the Screen Saver Settings dialog box, choose a screensaver, set a short Wait time, and check the On Resume, Display Logon Screen check box.

5. Click the Screen Saver drop-down menu and choose the screensaver you want to use. The Blank screensaver is the most eco-friendly one, not to mention the easiest on anyone who happens to have your computer screen in her line of vision.

6. Depending on the screensaver you chose, click Settings and choose settings for it. The Blank screensaver has no settings.

7. In the Wait box, set the number of minutes of inactivity you want to elapse before Windows turns on the screensaver. The smaller the number you choose here, the more secure your computer will be—but the more frequently you will have to log on after even the briefest of breaks from the keyboard.

8. Check the On Resume, Display Logon Screen check box. You must check this check box for the security to be any use—if you leave this check box unchecked, any touch to your computer's keyboard, mouse, or screen displays your work immediately.

9. Click OK to close the Screen Saver Settings dialog box.

INCREASING LOGIN SECURITY WITH SECURE SIGN-IN

To help increase your computer's security level, you can enable the Secure Sign-In feature.

> **NOTE** Secure Sign-In forces anyone logging on to the computer to press the Ctrl+Alt+Delete system command to display the sign-in screen. This extra step helps prevent users from entering their user names and passwords at a fake sign-in screen designed to harvest credentials and share them with malefactors.

To enable Secure Sign-In, follow these steps:

1. Click Start to display the Start menu.

2. Type **netplwiz** in the Search box and press Enter. Windows displays the User Accounts dialog box.

3. Click the Advanced tab to display its controls (see Figure 7.7).

4. Check the Require Users to Press Ctrl+Alt+Delete check box.

5. Click OK to close the User Accounts dialog box.

FIGURE 7.7
To turn on Secure Sign-In, check the Require Users to Press Ctrl+Alt+Delete check box on the Advanced tab of the User Accounts dialog box.

From now on, when the computer is locked, the screen displays the message Press Ctrl+Alt+Delete to Unlock. When you press the key combination, the sign-in screen appears, and you can sign in as usual.

CONFIGURING USER ACCOUNT CONTROL

User Account Control is one of the Windows security mechanisms. User Account Control attempts to detect when an app tries to make changes to your computer or when you make changes to Windows settings.

DEALING WITH USER ACCOUNT CONTROL QUERIES

When User Account Control detects an action that could result in a serious change, you see a User Account Control dialog box (see Figure 7.8) that prevents you from taking any other action on your computer until you deal with it.

> **NOTE** As you can see in Figure 7.8, User Account Control can detect the changes that User Account Control itself is trying to make—and can refuse them automatically.

FIGURE 7.8

User Account Control warns you if an app tries to make changes to your computer or if you change certain Windows settings.

When a User Account Control dialog box opens, look at three things:

- **The color of the dialog box.** The User Account Control dialog box changes the color of the bar below the title bar to give you a rough idea of the severity of the warning. A blue bar indicates the program is considered safe; a yellow bar indicates mild danger; an orange bar indicates greater danger; and a red bar indicates severe danger.

- **The Program Name readout.** This name may enable you to identify the program immediately, such as the UserAccountControlSettings program in the example; if not, you might look it up on the Internet after clicking No in the User Account Control dialog box.

- **The Verified Publisher readout.** This readout shows the publisher responsible for the digital certificate used to sign the program. In the example, the verified publisher is Microsoft Windows, indicating that UserAccountControlSettings is part of Windows.

> **NOTE** You can click Show Details in the User Account Control dialog box to display the details section. The details section shows the program location (including the app name and any command parameters used) and a Show Information About This Publisher's Certificate link that you can click to display the digital certificate used to sign the program.

If you don't respond to the User Account Control dialog box within a couple of minutes, User Account Control cancels the change that prompted the query. The User Account Control dialog box then closes automatically.

CONFIGURING USER ACCOUNT CONTROL

You can set User Account Control to any of four sensitivity levels to control—very approximately—how many User Account Control dialog boxes appear.

> **NOTE** Normally, your motivation for configuring User Account Control would be to ratchet down the feature's sensitivity after receiving a barrage of User Account Control dialog boxes. But if you haven't had such a barrage, it's a good idea to check your User Account Control settings anyway and make sure that User Account Control isn't set too low.

To configure User Account Control, follow these steps:

1. Right-click or long-press Start to display the shortcut menu.
2. Click Control Panel to open a Control Panel window.
3. Click System and Security to display the System and Security pane.
4. Under the Security and Maintenance heading, click Change User Account Control Settings to display the User Account Control Settings dialog box (see Figure 7.9).

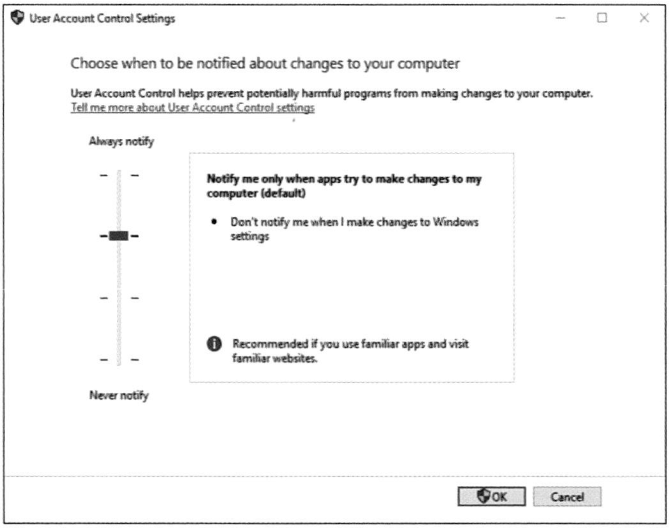

FIGURE 7.9

In the User Account Control Settings dialog box, drag the slider up or down the Never Notify–Always Notify axis to choose the types of changes for which you want to receive notifications.

5. Drag the slider on the left up or down to set the level. The box to the right of the slider shows the details for the current level, together with information explaining whether Microsoft recommends the setting (and if so, for which users) or not.

> **! CAUTION** Receiving frequent User Account Control dialog boxes can be disruptive and annoying, but never choose the lowest level of notification, because doing so risks compromising the security of your computer and your data. Even the second-lowest setting is risky, so normally you should choose either the top level or second level of notifications.

6. Click OK to close the User Account Control Settings dialog box.

7. If you chose either the top level or the second level of notifications, click Yes in the User Account Control dialog box that appears.

CONTROLLING RECENT APP SWITCHING

As you know, Windows enables you to switch quickly among your recent apps by using Task view. This feature is normally not only helpful but also a time-saver, but in some cases you may want to disable it—for example, to minimize distractions.

To disable recent app switching, follow these steps:

1. Click the Start button to display the Start menu.

2. Type **group policy** to display a list of suggestions.

3. Click the Edit Group Policy, Control Panel suggestion. Windows displays a Local Group Policy Editor window. Figure 7.10 shows the Local Group Policy Editor window expanded to the setting you need to change.

4. In the left pane, expand the User Configuration item to display its contents if necessary. You can either click the arrow to its left or (easier) double-click the item itself.

5. Still in the left pane, expand the Administrative Templates item.

6. Still in the left pane, expand the Windows Components item.

7. Click the Edge UI item to display its controls in the main part of the window.

8. Double-click the Turn Off Switching Between Recent Apps item to display the Turn Off Switching Between Recent Apps window (see Figure 7.11).

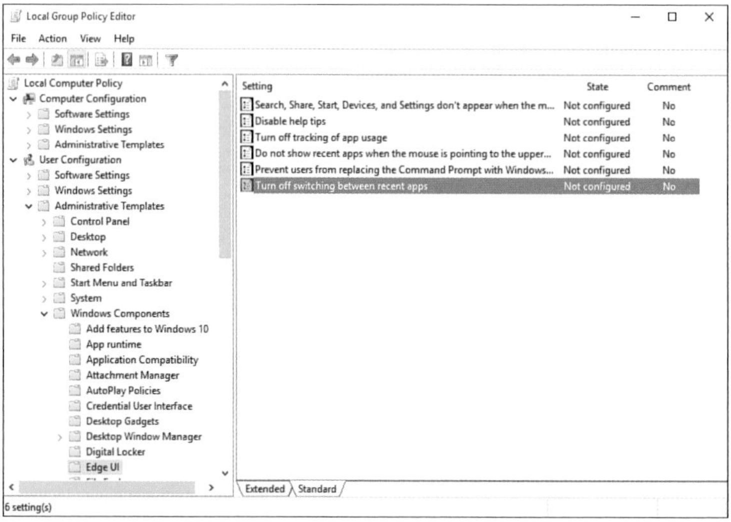

FIGURE 7.10

In some versions of Windows, you can use Local Group Policy Editor to turn off recent app switching.

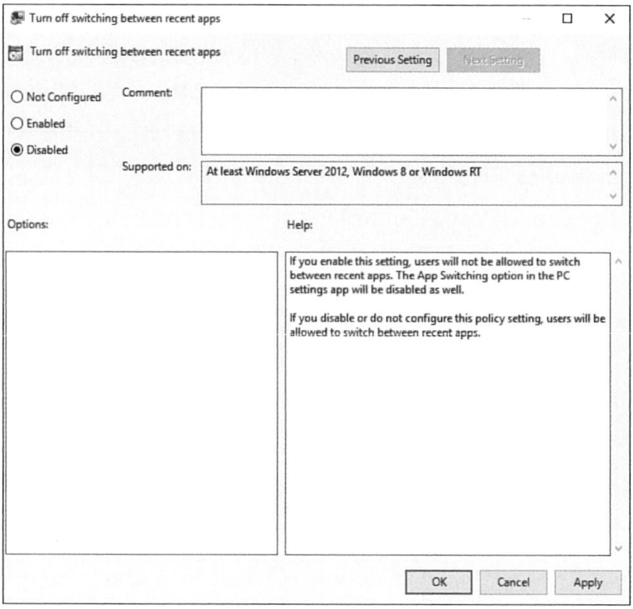

FIGURE 7.11

In the Turn Off Switching Between Recent Apps dialog box, select the Enabled option button and then click OK.

9. Click the Enabled option button to select it. (You're enabling the Turn Off Switching feature, not disabling switching.)

10. Click OK to close the Turn Off Switching Between Recent Apps dialog box. You can then close the Local Group Policy Editor window.

SETTING UP ASSIGNED ACCESS

Sometimes you may need to limit a particular user to using only one app acquired from the Windows Store. For example, you may need to allow someone to use your PC to perform a particular task, such as editing photos or videos. For when you need to do this, Windows provides the Assigned Access feature.

To set up Assigned Access, follow these steps:

1. Click Start to open the Start menu, and then click your account name to display the drop-down menu.

2. Click Change Account Settings to display the Your Account pane in the Accounts screen in Settings.

3. Click Family & Other Users in the left pane to display the Your Family pane.

4. At the bottom of the pane, click Set Up Assigned Access to display the Set Up Assigned Access screen (see Figure 7.12).

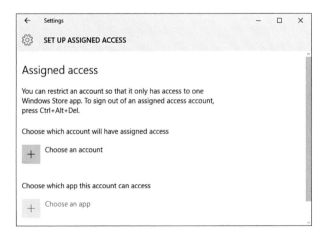

FIGURE 7.12

On the Set Up Assigned Access screen, choose the account you want to restrict, and then choose the app to which you want to restrict the account.

5. Click Choose an Account to display the Choose an Account dialog box, and then click the appropriate account.

6. Click Choose an App to display the Choose an App dialog box, and then click the app the account will use.

7. Restart your PC when Windows prompts you to do so.

CONFIGURING SHARING

Windows enables you to share folders, printers, and devices with other computers on the same network. You'll want to configure sharing carefully to ensure you do not expose your computer or your data to attack across the network.

SHARING VIA A HOMEGROUP

If you've used Windows in a work environment, you may have encountered the workgroup features that Windows provides for sharing on small networks. For sharing in home situations, Windows provides the homegroup feature, which works in a similar way.

A homegroup is simply a group of PCs on your home network. The homegroup provides features that enable you to share files (such as documents and media files) and printers more easily.

> **NOTE** You can share items on your home network without creating a homegroup. But given that a homegroup simplifies sharing, it's usually best to try using a homegroup and see whether it meets your needs.

CREATING YOUR HOMEGROUP

Windows sometimes sets up a homegroup automatically during installation; or, if you've upgraded your computer to Windows 10 from Windows 7, Windows 8, or Windows 8.1, you may already have a homegroup set up. If not, you can set up a homegroup quickly and easily.

Follow these steps to create a homegroup:

1. Right-click or long-press Start to display the shortcut menu.

2. Click Control Panel to open a Control Panel window.

3. Click Network and Internet to display the Network and Internet screen.

4. Click Homegroup to display the Homegroup screen (see Figure 7.13).

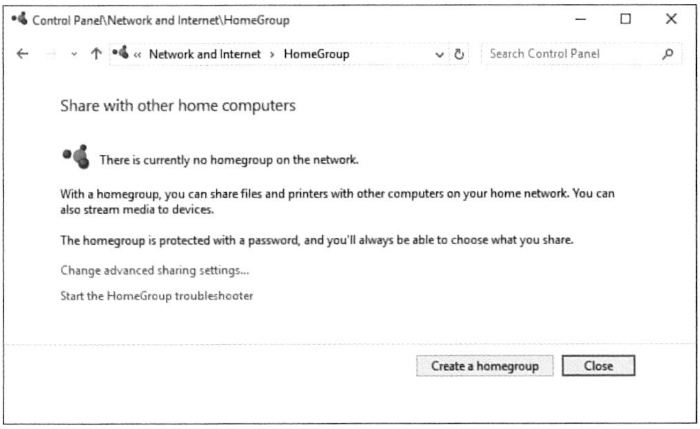

FIGURE 7.13
If the Homegroup screen in Control Panel shows the message "There is currently no homegroup on the network," click Create a Homegroup to start creating a homegroup.

5. Click Create a Homegroup to launch the Create a Homegroup Wizard.

6. Click Next to display the Share with Other Homegroup Members screen of the Create a Homegroup Wizard (see Figure 7.14).

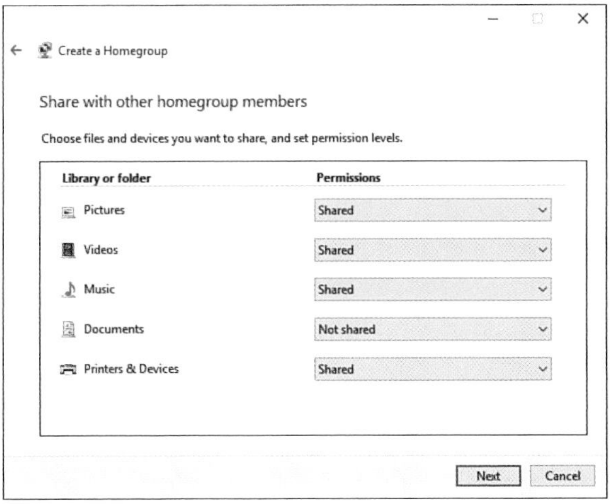

FIGURE 7.14
On the Share with Other Homegroup Members screen of the Create a Homegroup Wizard, choose which items to share.

7. Specify which items to share by setting the Permissions drop-down menu for each library or folder—`Pictures`, `Videos`, `Music`, `Documents`, and `Printers & Devices`—to Shared or Not Shared.

> **! CAUTION** Any items you share with the homegroup will also be available to any children who use the computers in the homegroup. If a library contains items that are not child-friendly, do not share the library. Instead, you can share particular folders. See the section "Changing the Items Your Computer Is Sharing with the Homegroup," later in this chapter, for instructions on sharing individual folders.

8. Click Next. Windows sets up the homegroup and then displays the Use This Password to Add Other Computers to Your Homegroup screen.

9. Write down the password somewhere handy. You may also want to click the Print Password and Instructions link and print the password.

> **TIP** Another way to save the password is to open Snipping Tool and take a screen capture of the Use This Password to Add Other Computers to Your Homegroup screen. You can also view the homegroup password at any time from the Homegroup screen in Control Panel.

10. Click Finish to close the Create a Homegroup Wizard. The homegroup appears on the Homegroup screen, showing what you're sharing and displaying controls for managing the homegroup (see Figure 7.15).

ADDING ANOTHER COMPUTER TO THE HOMEGROUP

Now that you've set up the homegroup, you can add another computer to it by following these steps on that computer:

1. Right-click or long-press Start to display the shortcut menu.
2. Click Control Panel to open a Control Panel window.
3. Click Network and Internet to display the Network and Internet screen.
4. Click Homegroup to display the Homegroup screen.

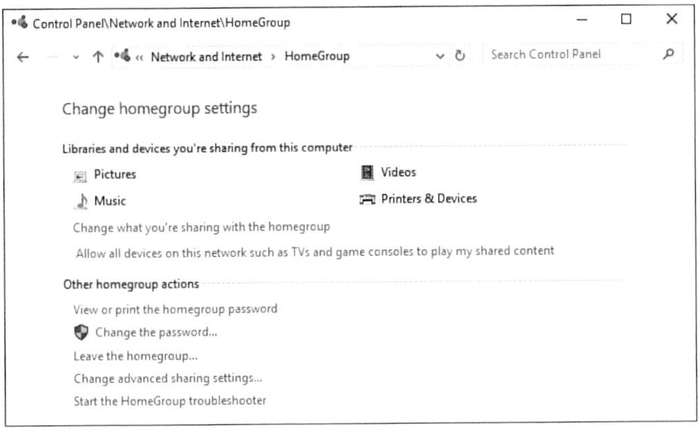

FIGURE 7.15

The homegroup appears on the Homegroup screen in Control Panel. You can see which items your computer is sharing, and you can take other actions with the homegroup.

> **NOTE** If the Homegroup screen doesn't show a homegroup you've just created on another computer, click Start the HomeGroup Troubleshooter to force Windows to search for the homegroup. Usually, Windows then locates the homegroup. Failing that, restart both computers and try again.

5. Click Join Now to launch the Join a Homegroup Wizard. This is the Create a Homegroup Wizard in drag.

6. Click Next to display the Share with Other Homegroup Members screen. Look back to Figure 7.14 to see the Create a Homegroup Wizard's version of this screen.

7. Specify which items to share by setting the Permissions drop-down menu for each library or folder—Pictures, Videos, Music, Documents, and Printers & Devices—to Shared or Not Shared.

8. Click Next. The Type the Homegroup Password screen appears.

9. Type the password and click Next. Your computer joins the homegroup, and the You Have Joined the Homegroup screen appears.

10. Click Finish. You can now start using the homegroup.

NOTE You can remove a computer from the homegroup by clicking Leave the Homegroup in the Other Homegroup Actions area of the Homegroup screen in Control Panel. The Leave the Homegroup Wizard walks you through the process of leaving. If all the computers leave the homegroup, Windows removes the homegroup.

ACCESSING FILES IN THE HOMEGROUP

Now that you have multiple computers in the homegroup, you can access files and devices in the homegroup by navigating through the Homegroup item in your computer's file system. For example, open a File Explorer window and then click Homegroup in the Navigation pane to display the computers in the homegroup. You can then double-click a computer to view the libraries and other items it is sharing.

CHANGING THE ITEMS YOUR COMPUTER IS SHARING WITH THE HOMEGROUP

You can change the items your computer is sharing with the homegroup in three ways:

- **Change the libraries you're sharing.** Open the Homegroup screen in Control Panel and then click Change What You're Sharing with the Homegroup to display the Share with Other Homegroup Members screen in the Change Homegroup Sharing Settings Wizard. For each library or folder, open the Permissions drop-down menu and choose Shared or Not Shared, as needed. Click Next and then click Finish.

- **Share individual files or folders with the entire homegroup.** Open a File Explorer window to the folder that contains the file or folder you want to share. Right-click or long-press the file or folder, click Share With on the shortcut menu, and then click Homegroup (View) to share the item so that other homegroup users can open and view it. If you want homegroup users to be able to change the item, choose Share With, Homegroup (View and Edit) on the shortcut menu instead of Homegroup (View).

CAUTION Give View and Edit access or the Read/Write permission (which is the same thing by a different name) only to people you trust with your files. Use View access or Read permission (again, these are the same thing) for most sharing.

- **Share individual files or folders with specific people.** Open a File Explorer window to the folder that contains the file or folder you want to share. Right-click or long-press the file or folder, click Share With on the shortcut menu, and then click Specific People to display the File Sharing dialog box (see Figure 7.16). Type the person's account name or email address in the box and then click Add. You can then click the Permission Level drop-down menu for the person and choose Read or Read/Write, as needed. After choosing the people and permissions, click Share.

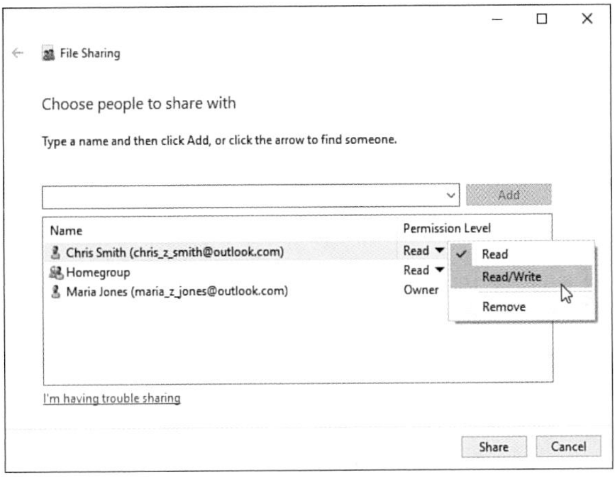

FIGURE 7.16

Use the File Sharing dialog box to share a particular file or folder with specific people and to set their type of access to it.

USING ADVANCED SHARING

As you saw in the preceding section, a homegroup gives you an easy way to set up and manage sharing. But you can also use advanced sharing settings if you need to or if you simply prefer to have full control over sharing.

ENABLING ADVANCED SHARING

First, you need to enable Advanced Sharing by following these steps:

1. Open a File Explorer window.
2. Choose File, Change Folder and Search Options to display the Folder Options dialog box.
3. Click the View tab to display its controls.

4. Near the bottom of the Advanced Settings box, uncheck the Use Sharing Wizard (Recommended) check box.

5. Click OK to close the Folder Options dialog box. Leave the File Explorer window open for now so that you can use it in the next section.

CONFIGURING ADVANCED SHARING FOR A FOLDER OR DRIVE

Now that you've enabled Advanced Sharing, you can use it like this:

1. In a File Explorer window, navigate to the folder or view that contains the folder or drive you want to share.

2. Right-click or long-press the folder or drive to display the shortcut menu, and then click Share With, Advanced Sharing to display the Properties dialog box for the item.

> **TIP** You can also start configuring advanced sharing from the Ribbon. Select the file or folder and then choose Share, Share With, Advanced Sharing.

3. Click the Sharing tab to display its controls (shown on the left in Figure 7.17).

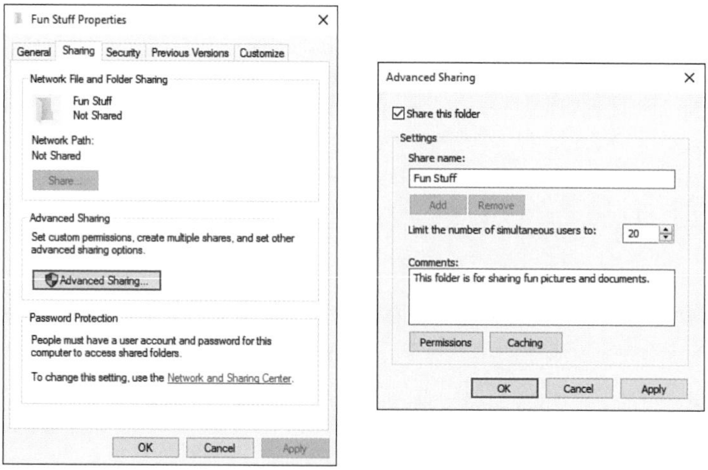

FIGURE 7.17

On the Sharing tab of the Properties dialog box for a folder or drive (left), click the Advanced Sharing button. In the Advanced Sharing dialog box (right), check the Share This Folder check box, edit the share name as needed, and add a comment if necessary.

4. Click Advanced Sharing to display the Advanced Sharing dialog box (shown on the right in Figure 7.17).

5. Check the Share This Folder check box.

6. If necessary, edit the name in the Share Name box. For example, you might add the computer's name (such as Fun Stuff on Maria's PC) so that people can easily see where the folder is located.

7. If necessary, adjust the number in the Limit the Number of Simultaneous Users To box. The default setting is 20.

8. If you want, type a comment in the Comments box to explain what the shared folder is for.

9. Click Permissions to display the Permissions dialog box (see Figure 7.18).

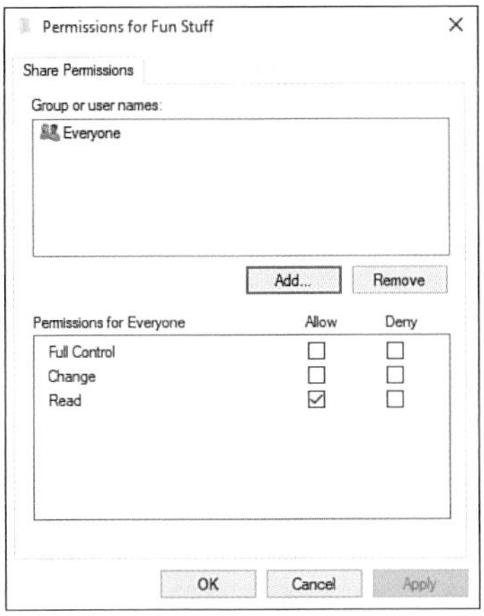

FIGURE 7.18
Use the Permissions dialog box to specify which users and groups can access the shared folder.

10. If the user or group for which you want to set permissions doesn't appear in the Group or User Names box, click Add; otherwise, go to step 14. The Select Users or Groups dialog box appears (see Figure 7.19).

11. In the Enter the Object Names to Select box, type the name or email address of the user you want to add.

12. Click Check Names. Windows verifies the name and displays the object's full name (such as the personal name and email pair shown in the figure) with the full name underlined.

13. Click OK. The user name appears in the Group or User Names box in the Permissions dialog box.

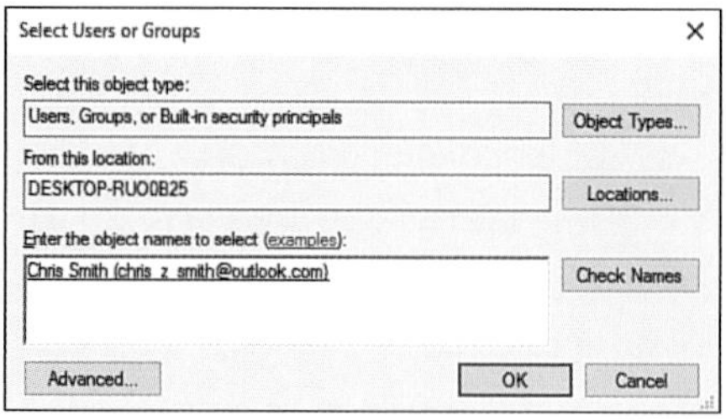

FIGURE 7.19

In the Select Users or Groups dialog box, enter the name of the user or group you want to add.

14. In the Group or User Names box, click the user or group for which you want to set permissions.

15. In the Permissions box, check the Read check box in the Allow column to enable the user or group to view the folder and its contents.

16. In the Permissions box, check the Change check box in the Allow column if you want to enable the user or group to change the folder and its contents.

> **! CAUTION** The Change permission enables someone to create new items, change existing items, or delete existing items. Grant this permission only if you are sure you want the user or group to be able to take these actions.

17. When you finish setting permissions, click OK to close the Permissions dialog box.

> **! CAUTION** The Full Control permission enables someone to take any action with the folder, including setting permissions for other users and groups. Normally, you would not want to grant Full Control for a folder that you own.

18. Click OK to close the Advanced Sharing dialog box.

19. Click OK to close the Properties dialog box for the folder or drive.

HIDING A DRIVE FROM OTHER USERS

If you share your computer with others, you might want to prevent them from seeing a particular drive—for example, so that they don't fill it up with their files.

You can do this by removing the drive letter. This is not secure, but it can be effective if you're dealing with people who aren't computer savvy.

To remove the drive letter, right-click or long-press the Start button, and then click Disk Management on the shortcut menu.

Right-click or long-press the drive and then click Change Drive Letter and Paths to display the Change Drive Letter and Paths dialog box. With the drive letter selected (as it is by default), click Remove, and then click Yes in the Disk Management dialog box that opens. Windows removes the drive letter, and the drive disappears from File Explorer windows.

IN THIS CHAPTER

- Configuring your computer for better performance
- Optimizing and defragmenting the hard drive
- Getting rid of useless apps and extending runtime on the battery

OPTIMIZING YOUR COMPUTER'S PERFORMANCE

This chapter details steps you can take to improve your computer's performance. You may be able to add memory to give your computer more headroom. You can definitely turn off unnecessary visual effects, which tend to sap performance.

You can change the size of the paging file, which Windows uses for virtual memory; control Data Execution Prevention; turn off the Superfetch and Prefetch features; and stop any Windows services that you don't need. You can defragment and optimize your computer's hard drive manually or configure Windows to defragment and optimize it automatically on a schedule.

At the end of the chapter, we'll also dig into ways to extend your computer's runtime on its battery and look at other actions you can take to improve performance when playing games.

ADDING MEMORY IF YOU CAN

Generally speaking, having more memory (random access memory, or RAM) enables a computer to run better. So if your computer doesn't already contain as much RAM as it can, you may be able to boost performance by adding memory.

UNDERSTANDING WINDOWS 10'S MEMORY REQUIREMENTS

As you know, Windows 10 comes in two versions: a 32-bit version and a 64-bit version. The 32-bit version requires a minimum of 1 gigabyte (GB) of RAM. The 64-bit version requires a minimum of 2GB.

These amounts are the absolute minimum needed to install and run Windows. With these amounts of RAM, performance tends to be disappointing, and if you run more than a handful of apps, lags will occur when you're switching among apps.

Consider 2GB as a practical minimum for 32-bit Windows. If your computer can take 4GB, go for that instead. Windows won't actually be able to use the full 4GB of RAM, because 4GB is the limit of the addressable memory area in 32-bit operating systems, and the computer's video RAM and other memory components take up some of the addressable area. But Windows will use as much of the RAM as possible.

Consider 4GB as a practical minimum for 64-bit Windows. If your computer can go to 8GB, 16GB, or more, you will get much better performance.

TIP   To see how much memory your computer has, right-click or long-press the Start button and click System on the shortcut menu. In the System window that opens, look at the Installed Memory (RAM) readout in the System section.

If you need to find out which memory modules your computer contains, you can use a tool such as CPU-Z (free from www.cpuid.com). After downloading and installing CPU-Z, run the app, and then click the SPD tab. In the Memory Slot Selection area, click the drop-down menu and choose the slot you want to inspect. You can then look at the Module Size readout to see the size (such as "1024 MBytes," which is 1GB) and the Max Bandwidth readout to see the type and speed, such as "PC2-5300 (333 MHz)." Figure 8.1 shows an example from an aging computer.

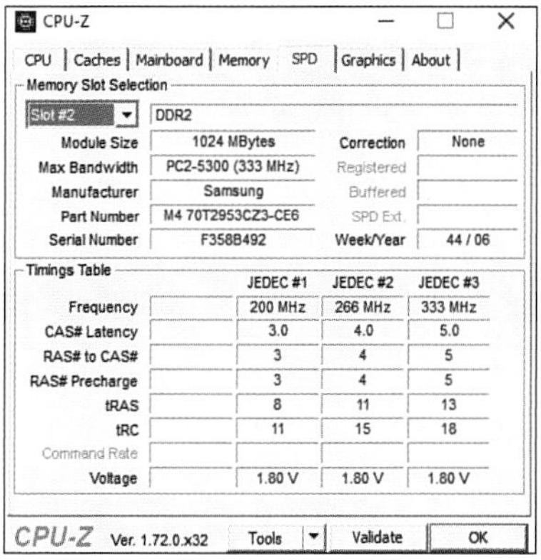

FIGURE 8.1

Use the controls on the SPD tab of the free CPU-Z app to learn the details of the memory modules your computer contains.

Armed with this information, you can start exploring your options for adding memory. But you might also want to use a memory manufacturer's scanner tool to probe your computer's memory and see what upgrades the manufacturer offers. For example, Micron Technology, Inc.'s Crucial division (www.crucial.com) provides a memory scanner that displays information about your computer including the memory modules it contains, the maximum memory it can contain, and available memory modules with which you can upgrade. Such scanners can be an easy way to find upgrades, but it's wise to compare the prices with other sites before you buy.

The other main factor in deciding whether to upgrade your computer's RAM is how difficult the operation actually is. Most tablets and many laptops are designed to be opened only by trained technicians, often with specialized tools. By contrast, most desktops and some laptops are designed to be user-upgradable with only a screwdriver and modest amounts of gumption.

> **TIP** To find instructions on opening your computer and installing RAM, look at the computer manufacturer's website, repair sites such as iFixit (www.ifixit.com), and YouTube.

After installing RAM, open the System window and verify that the Installed Memory (RAM) readout shows the correct amount.

> **☑ TIP**   If you're planning to buy a new computer, max out its RAM when you buy it. This is almost always the best time to add RAM, and you will seldom regret adding it. If the computer you're considering has only a small amount of RAM and can't take more, look for a better model.

TURNING OFF EYE CANDY TO BOOST PERFORMANCE

Windows includes many graphical effects to make the user interface look more attractive. Generally speaking, the more graphical effects your computer has to run, the more effort it has to put in—and the more it may slow down. So if your computer is crawling rather than flying, you might want to turn off some or all of these effects to stop them from sapping its performance.

Follow these steps to turn off graphical effects:

1. Right-click or long-press the Start button, and then click System on the shortcut menu. The System window opens.

2. In the left column, click Advanced System Settings to display the Advanced tab of the System Properties dialog box (see Figure 8.2).

3. Click Settings in the Performance box to display the Performance Options dialog box. This dialog box has three tabs, as you can see in Figure 8.3: the Visual Effects tab, which is usually displayed first; the Advanced tab; and the Data Execution Prevention tab.

4. In the top section of the Visual Effects tab, you'll normally find that the Let Windows Choose What's Best for My Computer option button is selected. If this is the case, and all the check boxes in the list box are selected, Windows considers your computer powerful enough to handle all the visual effects.

> **✎ NOTE**   You can select the Adjust for Best Appearance option button to check all the check boxes in the list box at once. You can click the Adjust for Best Performance option button to uncheck all the check boxes.

FIGURE 8.2
Click Settings in the Performance box on the Advanced tab of the System Properties dialog box.

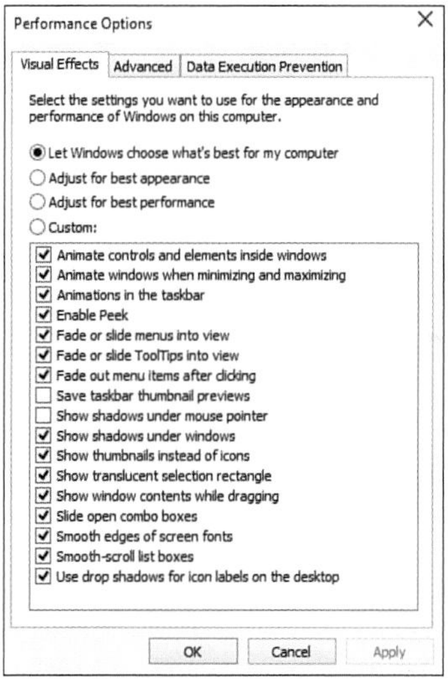

FIGURE 8.3
You can turn off some or all eye candy on the Visual Effects tab of the Performance Options dialog box.

5. To improve performance, either select the Adjust for Best Performance option button (which unchecks all the check boxes) or select the Custom option button and then check or uncheck the check boxes as needed. Table 8.1 explains the visual effects.

6. After making changes, you can click Apply to apply them without closing the Performance Options dialog box. For example, you may want to test the settings you've chosen.

7. When you're satisfied with your choices, click OK to close the Performance Options dialog box.

8. Click OK to close the System Properties dialog box.

Table 8.1   Visual Effects in the Performance Options Dialog Box

Visual Effect	This Setting Controls
Animate Controls and Elements Inside Windows	Various effects including the motions of Start menu tiles and the pulsing color on the default button in an open dialog box
Animate Windows When Minimizing and Maximizing	Whether windows and the Start menu show animations or simply snap into place
Animations in the Taskbar	Whether taskbar thumbnail previews slide or fade into view
Enable Peek	Whether the Peek feature hides open windows while you Alt+Tab through them
Fade or Slide Menus into View	Whether menus fade and slide or simply snap open
Fade or Slide ToolTips into View	Whether ToolTips fade and slide or simply snap into view
Fade Out Menu Items After Clicking	Whether menu items fade after you click them
Save Taskbar Thumbnail Previews	Whether Windows caches the thumbnail previews, enabling it to show them more quickly, or generates them afresh each time
Show Shadows Under Mouse Pointer	Whether shadows appear under the mouse pointer
Show Shadows Under Windows	Whether shadows appear under open windows
Show Thumbnails Instead of Icons	Whether File Explorer windows in Icon view show thumbnails of file contents (such as miniatures of photos) or just generic icons
Show Translucent Selection Rectangle	Whether, when you drag on the desktop, Windows displays a translucent selection rectangle or a plain dotted rectangle
Show Windows Contents While Dragging	Whether, when you drag a window, its contents appear, or just the window's frame appears
Slide Open Combo Boxes	Whether combo boxes slide open smoothly or just snap open

Visual Effect	This Setting Controls
Smooth Edges of Screen Fonts	Whether Windows uses anti-aliasing to make the edges of fonts look smoother or just leaves them rough
Smooth-Scroll List Boxes	Whether list boxes scroll smoothly or in jerks
Use Drop Shadows for Icon Labels on the Desktop	Whether icon labels on the desktop show drop shadows

TIP If you need to increase performance without sacrificing too much in the way of looks, select the Adjust for Best Performance option button (unchecking all the check boxes), but then select the Enable Peek check box, the Show Thumbnails Instead of Icons check box, and the Smooth Edges of Screen Fonts check box.

CONFIGURING THE PAGING FILE

The paging file is a file that Windows uses as virtual memory to supplement RAM. When Windows runs low on RAM, it moves some data from RAM to the paging file so as to free up the RAM. Windows tries to identify data in RAM that you and your apps aren't currently using, because retrieving data from the paging file is much slower than retrieving data from RAM. When Windows gets this right, there's little or no performance hit to your running apps; but when you request data stored in the paging file rather than in RAM, you may notice a lag.

NOTE Virtual memory normally chugs along in the background without advertising itself. If your computer's performance is adequate or better, you can simply leave Windows to manage virtual memory. But if Windows starts displaying messages warning you that virtual memory is low, you'll know you need to increase the size of the paging file.

Windows automatically sets the size and location of the paging file, but you may be able to improve performance by configuring it manually. There are three main parameters you can set:

■ **Minimum size.** Windows automatically sets the minimum size to the same as the amount of RAM in your computer. So if your computer has 4GB of RAM, the minimum paging file size is 4096MB.

- **Maximum size.** Windows automatically sets the maximum size to three times the amount of RAM. So if your computer has 4GB of RAM, the maximum page file size is 12,288MB.
- **Location.** Windows automatically puts the paging file on your computer's boot drive. This is mostly because many computers have only one drive, so the boot drive is the only option. If your computer has multiple drives, you can move the paging file to another drive. You can also set a separate paging file for each drive if you want.

> ☑ **TIP**   If your computer has multiple physical drives, put the paging file on a drive separate from the boot drive. Windows uses the boot drive a lot for system files, so you may be able to improve performance by moving the paging file to a different drive.

> ❗ **CAUTION**   If your computer has a single physical drive divided into two (or more) logical drives, don't bother moving the paging file from the boot drive to another drive. Because both logical drives are using the same physical drive, moving the paging file won't improve performance enough to be worthwhile.

You can also turn off the paging file altogether. In theory, this might be a good idea if your computer contains so much RAM that it will never need virtual memory. But in practice, turning off the paging file isn't wise. First, some apps are incredibly greedy for RAM, some by design and others through inept memory management, so Windows may end up needing virtual memory. And second, some apps assume that virtual memory will be available and will throw errors if it is not.

> 📝 **NOTE**   The normal reason for configuring the paging file is to improve performance. But if your device is severely short of storage, you may need to reduce the size of the paging file to make more space for other files. This is effective, but you should treat it as a short-term measure. As soon as you can, free up some more space on the drive so that you can restore the paging file to its normal size.

Follow these steps to configure the paging file:

1. Right-click or long-press the Start button, and then click System on the shortcut menu. The System window opens.

2. In the left column, click Advanced System Settings to display the Advanced tab of the System Properties dialog box.

3. Click Settings in the Performance box to display the Performance Options dialog box.

4. Click the Advanced tab to display its contents (see Figure 8.4).

FIGURE 8.4

On the Advanced tab of the Performance Options dialog box, make sure the Programs option button is selected. Then click the Change button in the Virtual Memory box.

5. In the Processor Scheduling box at the top, make sure the Programs option button is selected instead of the Background Services option button (which is for servers).

6. Click the Change button to display the Virtual Memory dialog box (see Figure 8.5).

7. Uncheck the Automatically Manage Paging File Size for All Drives check box if you want to take control of the paging file manually. When you do this, the other controls in the dialog box become available.

8. In the Paging File Size for Each Drive box, click the drive you want to affect. Normally, you'll want to start with the C: drive.

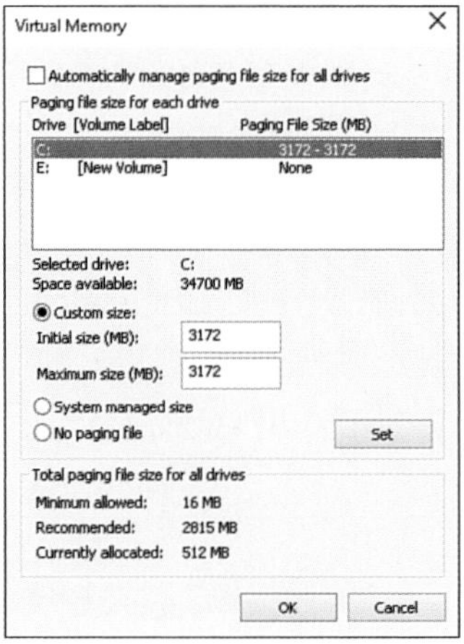

FIGURE 8.5

In the Virtual Memory dialog box, uncheck the Automatically Manage Paging File Size for All Drives check box to enable the other controls.

9. Select the Custom Size option button.

10. Type the starting size in megabytes in the Initial Size box. For example, enter 2048 to make the paging file's initial size 2GB.

11. Type the largest size in megabytes in the Maximum Size box. For example, enter 3072 to make the paging file's largest size 3GB.

> **TIP** Some Windows experts recommend setting the initial size and maximum size to the same figure to fix the size of the paging file. Doing this ensures that Windows doesn't waste time resizing the paging file, which may involve writing parts of it to far-flung sectors on a hard disk.

> **NOTE** When you need to change back from using a custom size (or using no paging file) to having Windows manage the paging file for you, select the System Managed Size option button.

12. Click Set. The size appears in the Paging File Size column of the Paging File Size for Each Drive box.

13. If necessary, repeat steps 8 through 12 to set the size of paging files for other hard drives or SSDs in your computer.

14. Click OK to close the Virtual Memory dialog box.

15. If the System Properties dialog box appears, telling you that you need to restart your computer to make the changes take effect, click OK.

16. Click OK to close the Performance Options dialog box.

17. Click OK to close the System Properties dialog box.

18. If the System Properties dialog box appeared in step 15, restart Windows now.

> **NOTE** Windows needs to restart if you decrease the size of the paging file or move it to another drive, but not if you increase its size.

CONTROLLING DATA EXECUTION PREVENTION

Windows includes a feature called Data Execution Prevention (DEP) that attempts to prevent viruses and malware from running. DEP works by blocking programs from executing code in system memory locations that are reserved for Windows and authorized apps.

DEP is turned on by default for what Windows calls "essential Windows programs and services." Normally, you're pretty safe leaving this default setting. But if you want to crank up the level of protection, you can turn on DEP for all apps and services except for those you specify. Doing this may result in DEP blocking a bona fide app or service you need to run. If this happens, you add the app or service to the list of exceptions.

Follow these steps to configure DEP:

1. Right-click or long-press the Start button, and then click System on the shortcut menu. The System window opens.

2. In the left column, click Advanced System Settings to display the Advanced tab of the System Properties dialog box.

3. Click Settings in the Performance box to display the Performance Options dialog box.

4. Click the Data Execution Prevention tab to display its contents (see Figure 8.6).

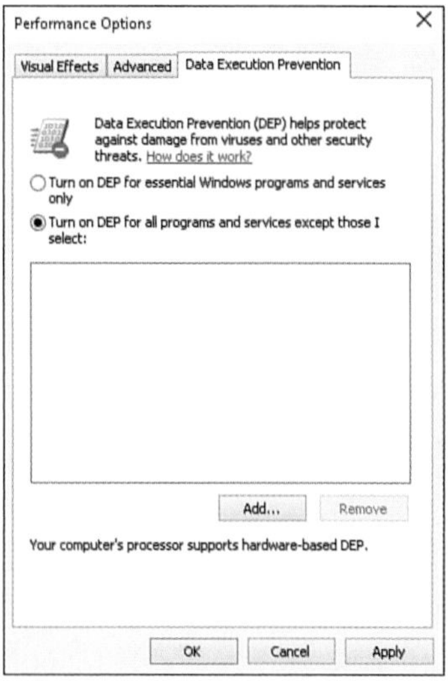

FIGURE 8.6

On the Data Execution Prevention tab of the Performance Options dialog box, you can specify any apps or services you want to exempt from DEP blocking.

5. Select the Turn On DEP for All Programs and Services Except Those I Select option button instead of the Turn On DEP for Essential Windows Programs and Services Only option button (the default setting).

6. If you need to create an exception for an app or a service, click the Add button, navigate to and select the app or service in the resulting Open dialog box, and then click the Open button. Windows adds the app or service to the list box, from where you can subsequently remove it by using the Remove button if necessary.

7. Click OK to close the Performance Options dialog box.

8. If the System Properties dialog box appears, telling you that you need to restart your computer to make the changes take effect, click OK.

9. Click OK to close the System Properties dialog box.

10. If the System Properties dialog box appeared in step 8, restart Windows now.

STOPPING UNNECESSARY SERVICES

Under the hood, Windows runs many services, system processes that perform particular actions. For example, the Computer Browser service keeps a list of the computers on the network to which your computer is connected, and the

DHCP Client service registers and updates IP addresses and DNS records for your computer.

Many services (including those two) are essential to Windows, so stopping them may cause problems. But there are other services that you may not need and that you can turn off to improve your computer's performance. Table 8.2 lists services that you may want to disable.

> **NOTE** Some of the services listed in Table 8.2 may not be running. For example, the Fax service is typically set to Manual startup because most people send few faxes these days.

Table 8.2   Windows Services You May Want to Disable

Service Name	What It Does	Safe to Disable If
BitLocker Drive Encryption Service	Enables the BitLocker encryption feature	You don't use BitLocker
Bluetooth Support Service	Enables Bluetooth communications	You don't use Bluetooth
Certificate Propagation	Copies digital certificates from smart cards into the active user's certificate store on the computer	You don't use smart cards
Encrypting File System (EFS)	Enables you to encrypt and decrypt files on drives formatted with the NTFS file system	You don't use encryption
Fax	Enables you to send and receive faxes	You don't send faxes
Microsoft iSCSI Initiator Service	Manages Internet SCSI (iSCSI) sessions, connecting to remote data storage	You don't use iSCSI
Netlogon	Establishes a secure connection between your computer and the domain controller in a Windows Server–based network	Your computer doesn't connect to a work network
Offline Files	Enables you to store copies of files located on network drives on your computer for when it has no Internet connection	You don't use Offline Files
Print Spooler	Sends print jobs to a printer or the print-to-PDF service	You don't use a printer or print-to-PDF

Table 8.2   Continued

Service Name	What It Does	Safe to Disable If
Remote Desktop Configuration	Enables configuring the Remote Desktop feature	You don't use Remote Desktop
Remote Desktop Services	Enables accessing the computer via Remote Desktop	You don't use Remote Desktop
Remote Desktop Services UserMode Port Redirector	Redirects ports for Remote Desktop Services	You don't use Remote Desktop
Remote Registry	Enables editing the Registry from another computer	You don't need remote Registry editing
Secondary Logon	Enables you to use alternative credentials, such as when accessing a network resource	You don't need to use alternative credentials
Smart Card	Controls access to smart cards your computer uses	You don't use smart cards with your computer
Smart Card Device Enumeration Service	Manages smart card readers connected to your computer	You don't use smart cards with your computer
Smart Card Removal Policy	Enables you to configure the computer to lock when a smart card is removed	You don't use smart cards with your computer
Touch Keyboard and Handwriting Panel Service	Enables input via the Touch Keyboard and the Handwriting Panel	You don't use the Touch Keyboard or handwriting input
Windows Connect Now – Config Registrar	Enables your computer to connect to a wireless network via the Wi-Fi Protected Setup (WPS) feature	You don't use WPS to connect to wireless networks
Windows Defender	Protects your computer against malevolent software (malware)	You use a third-party security product instead
Windows Defender Network Inspection Service	Protects against attacks on known security holes in network protocols	You use a third-party security product instead
Windows Firewall	Protects your computer from attacks across the network	You use a third-party firewall or security product that includes a firewall

Follow these steps to stop a service:

1. Right-click or long-press the Start button to open the shortcut menu.

2. Click Computer Management to open a Computer Management window. This window shows the console tree on the left, enabling you to navigate among the different items you can manage, and the current console in the main part of the window.

3. In the console tree, double-click Services and Applications (or click the arrow to its left) to expand the Services and Applications category if it is collapsed. (If you can already see Services and WMI Control under Services and Applications, the category is already expanded.)

4. In the console tree, click Services to display the Services console in the main part of the window (see Figure 8.7).

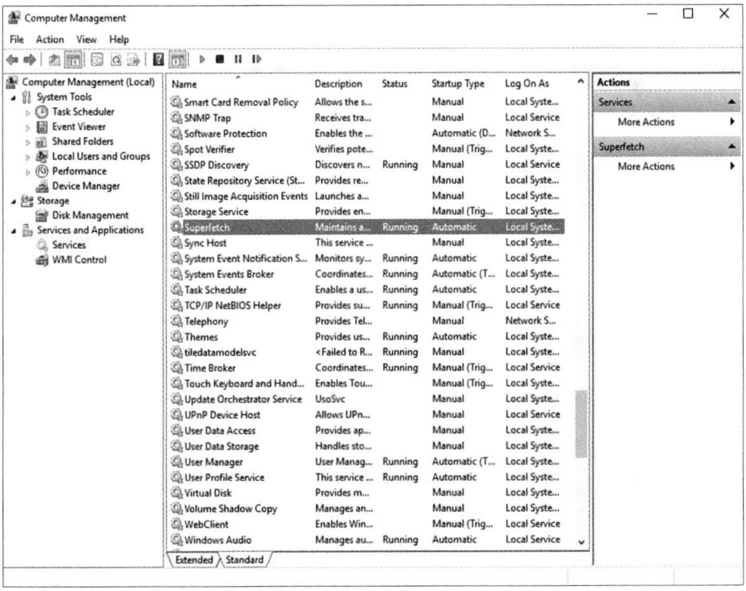

FIGURE 8.7

In the Computer Management window, expand the Services and Applications category in the left pane and then click Services to display the Services console.

> **TIP** If you're working in a small window, as in the screens shown here, make sure the Standard tab is selected in the lower-left corner of the Services console rather than the Extended tab. The Extended tab includes a column on the left of the Services console that shows the name of the selected service, links for stopping and restarting the service, and a description of what it does. This column is handy when you have plenty of space, but if you don't, it prevents some of the other columns from appearing in the window, making it harder to see what you're doing. You can also click Show/Hide Console Tree, the fourth button from the left on the toolbar, to hide the console tree to give yourself more space.

5. Double-click the service you want to stop. This example uses Superfetch, which you may want to stop on a computer that has a solid-state device rather than a rotating hard drive. The Properties dialog box for the service opens—in this case, the Superfetch Properties dialog box (see Figure 8.8).

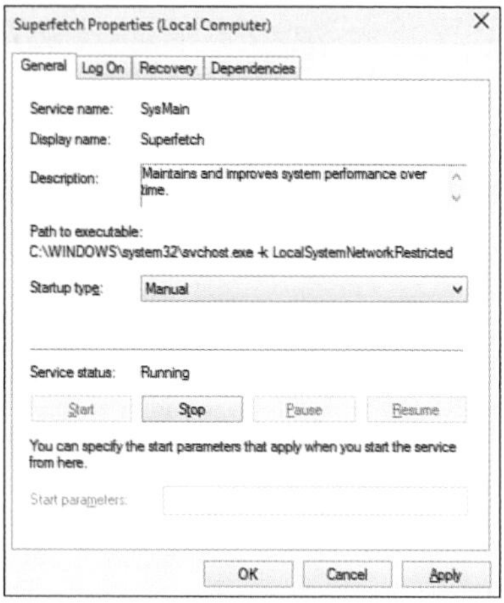

FIGURE 8.8
In the Properties dialog box for the service you're stopping, set the Startup Type to Disabled and click the Stop button.

6. Click the Startup Type drop-down menu and then click Disabled to prevent Windows from running the service automatically in the future. Most services have the Automatic startup type or the Automatic (Delayed Start) startup type, which allows Windows to start them when it thinks they're needed.

7. Click the Stop button to stop the service. Windows displays a progress dialog box briefly while it stops the service.

8. Click OK to close the Properties dialog box for the service.

9. Stop any other services by repeating steps 5–8.

10. Close the Computer Management window by clicking the Close (×) button, pressing Alt+F4, or choosing File, Exit.

TURNING OFF SUPERFETCH AND PREFETCH

Windows includes features called Superfetch and Prefetch that try to make your computer more responsive by anticipating the apps you will run and loading those apps into memory. Superfetch and Prefetch are usually helpful if your computer has a regular hard drive, the kind that contains spinning platters. If your computer has a solid-state device (SSD) rather than a hard drive, however, Superfetch and Prefetch not only may deliver no improvement but also may contribute to wearing out the SSD by writing extra data to it unnecessarily. (SSDs have a limited number of read and write operations.)

Windows tries to analyze your computer's storage to determine whether it will benefit from Superfetch and Prefetch. If your computer has an SSD, or multiple SSDs, or it mixes SSDs and hard drives, you should check whether Superfetch and Prefetch are running. If they are, you may want to try disabling them to see whether doing so changes your computer's performance.

TURNING OFF SUPERFETCH

Superfetch is a service, so to turn it off, you use the Services window as explained in the section "Stopping Unnecessary Services," earlier in this chapter: Open the Services window and double-click the Superfetch service; set the service's Startup type to Disabled, and click the Stop button; and then click the OK button.

TURNING OFF PREFETCH

To turn off Prefetch, you use the Registry Editor. Follow these steps:

1. Right-click or long-press the Start button to open the shortcut menu.

> **! CAUTION** Before making changes using Registry Editor, you should back up the Registry. See the section "Making Advanced Changes by Editing the Registry" in Chapter 14 for more information.

2. Click Run to display the Run dialog box.

3. Type **regedit** and press Enter or click OK to open Registry Editor. If the User Account Control dialog box opens, verifying that you want to run Registry Editor, click Yes.

4. Navigate to this location: `HKEY_LOCAL_MACHINE\SYSTEM\CurrentControlSet\Control\Session Manager\Memory Management\PrefetchParameters`. The easiest way to do this is by double-clicking each folder in turn in the left pane—double-click `HKEY_LOCAL_MACHINE`, double-click `SYSTEM`, double-click `CurrentControlSet`, and so on—and then click `PrefetchParameters` when you reach the `Memory Management` folder. Alternatively, you can click the triangular arrow to the left of each folder to expand it. The right pane shows the keys in the folder (see Figure 8.9).

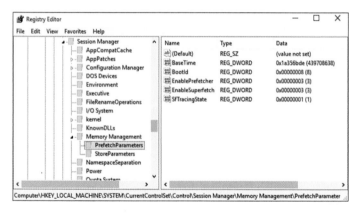

FIGURE 8.9

To turn off Prefetch, navigate to the `PrefetchParameters` folder in Registry Editor.

5. In the right pane, double-click `EnablePrefetcher` to open the Edit DWORD dialog box (see Figure 8.10).

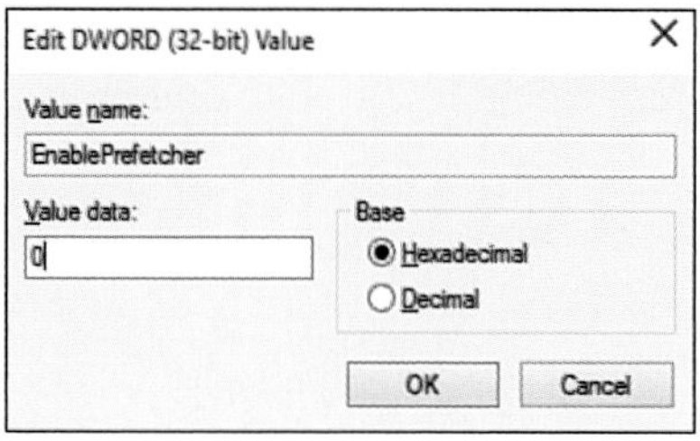

FIGURE 8.10

In the Edit DWORD dialog box, type the value you want to use for EnablePrefetcher.

6. In the Value Data box, type the appropriate value (see Table 8.3).

7. Click the OK button to close the Edit DWORD dialog box.

8. Close Registry Editor unless you need to make further changes in it.

Table 8.3   `EnablePrefetcher` Values for Controlling Prefetch

Value	Effect
0	Disable Prefetch
1	Enable Prefetch for apps but not for boot files
2	Enable Prefetch for boot files but not for apps
3	Enable Prefetch for both apps and boot files

REDUCING THE NUMBER OF STARTUP ITEMS

You might well have noticed that the more software you install on your computer, the more slowly it tends to run. Often, this is because software you install configures itself to run automatically when Windows starts.

Running software automatically can be helpful, especially for software that enables Windows to communicate with hardware devices you sometimes connect to your computer. But running too much software automatically at startup can slow down your computer. So it's a good idea to check which items are running at startup and remove any that you don't need to run.

To see which items are running automatically at startup, you can use the Startup tab in Task Manager. Follow these steps:

1. Right-click or long-press Start to display the shortcut menu.

> **TIP** You can also open Task Manager by right-clicking or long-pressing open space or the clock on the taskbar and then clicking Task Manager on the shortcut menu.

2. Click Task Manager to open Task Manager.

> **NOTE** If Task Manager opens as a small window, click More Details to expand it.

3. Click the Startup tab to display its contents (see Figure 8.11).

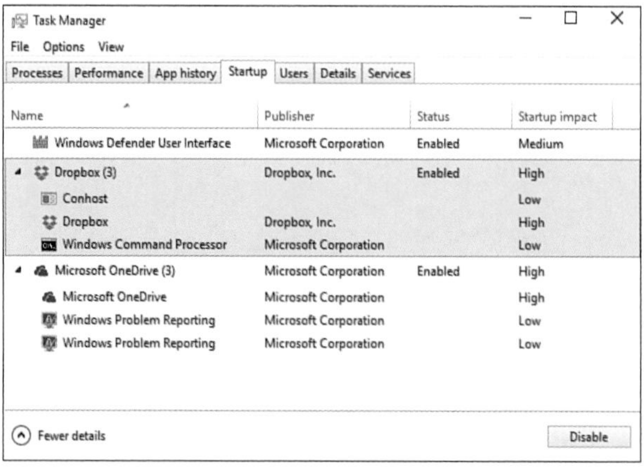

FIGURE 8.11

Use the Startup tab in Task Manager to see which items are running at startup and their startup impact. You can disable an item if necessary.

> **TIP** If you're not sure what a startup item is, right-click or long-press it in the list on the Startup tab and then click Search Online on the shortcut menu to look up what it is and does.

4. If necessary, click the right-pointing arrow to the left of an item that shows a number after its name—such as Dropbox (3) in this example—to display the individual items it is running.

5. To disable an item, click it, and then click Disable.

> **TIP** If you want to dig deeper into your computer's startup items, try the AutoRuns for Windows app. You can download this free from the Microsoft website. Go to www.microsoft.com; search for "AutoRuns for Windows"; and then download it, extract the files, and double-click the file named AutoRuns. The AutoRuns app rounds up all the items that are running automatically and presents them on tabs such as Logon, Explorer, Scheduled Tasks, Services, and Drivers, enabling you to see exactly what's running (and, if necessary, stop any item).

OPTIMIZING AND DEFRAGMENTING YOUR COMPUTER'S HARD DRIVE

Another way to improve performance is to optimize and defragment your computer's hard drive. Fragmentation occurs when the operating system saves files to sectors located in different parts of the disk rather than sectors next to each other. This means that the drive's read head has to travel farther to retrieve the various parts of the file, which takes longer. Defragmenting the drive rewrites sectors to put related information in adjacent or nearby sectors as much as possible.

> **! CAUTION** Only hard drives with spinning platters need defragmenting. Don't defragment an SSD—doing so won't help performance but will gradually wear out the SSD.

As well as defragmenting the drive, Windows can optimize it by putting frequently needed files in quickly accessible locations.

> **TIP** Some computer security and maintenance suites include defragmentation features that disable Windows' built-in defragmentation tools. If you use such a suite, check whether it includes defragmentation.

Windows can optimize drives automatically on a schedule. You might want to adjust the schedule to suit your needs. You might also want to optimize and defragment a drive right now to try to cure performance problems.

CHECKING FREE SPACE AND OPENING THE OPTIMIZE DRIVES WINDOW

Follow these steps to check the amount of free space on a drive and to open the Optimize Drives window:

1. Open a File Explorer window. For example, click the File Explorer button on the Taskbar, or choose Start, File Explorer.

2. Click This PC in the Navigation pane to display the computer's contents.

3. In the Devices and Drives list, right-click or long-press the hard drive—normally called Local Disk (C:)—to display the shortcut menu.

4. Click Properties to display the Properties dialog box for the drive. The General tab appears at the front (see Figure 8.12).

FIGURE 8.12

On the General tab of the Properties dialog box for your computer's hard drive, make sure the drive has plenty of free space.

5. Look at the readout in the middle to make sure that the drive has plenty of free space. If less than 20% of the drive is free, you might want to free up some space before defragmenting the drive. One way to free up space is by using the Disk Cleanup tool, which you can run by clicking Disk Cleanup on the General tab.

> **TIP** The defragmenter can rearrange files more efficiently if your hard drive has plenty of space free.

6. Click the Tools tab to display its contents (see Figure 8.13).

7. Click Optimize to open the Optimize Drives window (see Figure 8.14).

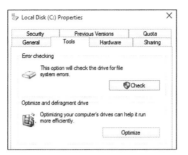

FIGURE 8.13
Click Optimize on the Tools tab of the Properties dialog box for your computer's hard drive.

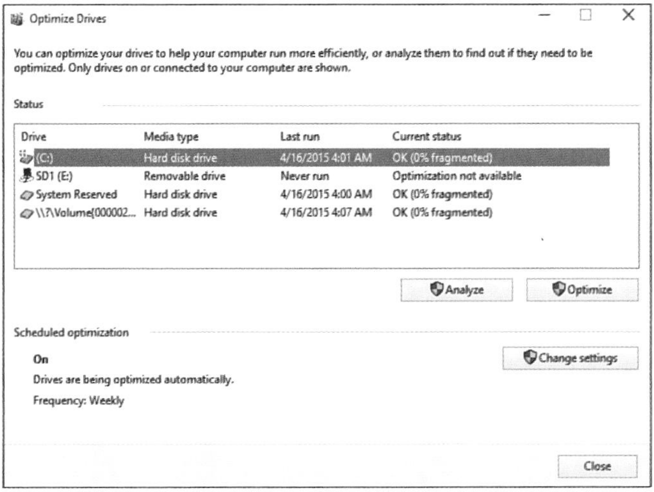

FIGURE 8.14
From the Optimize Drives window, you can analyze a drive, optimize a drive, or change settings for scheduled optimization.

ANALYZING AND OPTIMIZING A DRIVE

After opening the Optimize Drives window, you can analyze a drive by clicking Analyze or optimize a drive by clicking Optimize. Analyzing the drive simply gives you a readout showing the amount of fragmentation on the drive, so normally you'll want to click Optimize, which makes Optimize Drives analyze the drive and then optimize it.

In the old days, the Drive Defragmenter tool, which was the predecessor of Optimize Drives, used to display a highly colorful screen showing which blocks of data it was relocating and where. These days, Optimize Drives simply displays a readout in the Current Status column saying what it is doing: analyzing the drive, performing the first pass, performing the second pass, and so on.

When optimization is complete for the drive you chose, you can optimize another hard drive if your computer has another, or simply click Close to close the Optimize Drives window.

NOTE If the Current Status readout shows that the drive is still fragmented, click Optimize again to run optimization once more. Depending on the state of the drive, you may not be able to get it down to 0% fragmentation.

CHOOSING SETTINGS FOR SCHEDULED OPTIMIZATION

From the Optimize Drives window, you can also choose which drives to optimize automatically and how frequently to optimize them. To do so, follow these steps:

1. Click Change Settings in the Optimize Drives window to display the Optimize Drives dialog box (see Figure 8.15).

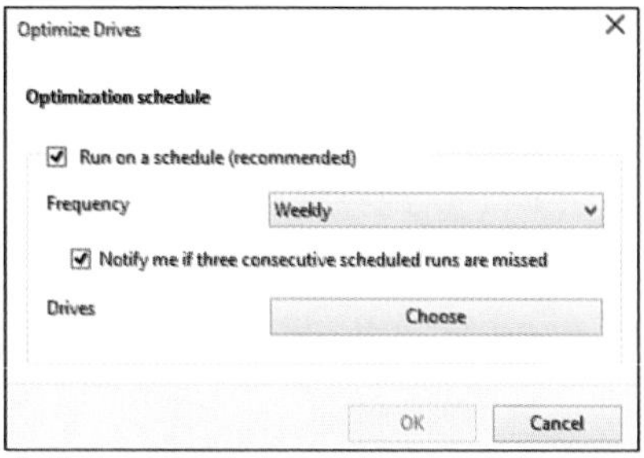

FIGURE 8.15

In this Optimize Drives dialog box, set up the schedule on which to optimize your computer's drives.

2. Check the Run on a Schedule (Recommended) check box if you want to schedule optimization. This is normally a good idea. (If you uncheck this check box, go to step 9, because you can't choose any other settings.)

3. Click the Frequency drop-down menu and choose the frequency: Daily, Weekly, or Monthly. Weekly is the default setting and usually works pretty well.

4. Check the Notify Me If Three Consecutive Scheduled Runs Are Missed check box if you want to receive a notification if Windows repeatedly misses the scheduled optimization. (This might happen because you turn off your computer at night.)

5. Click the Choose button to display another Optimize Drives dialog box (see Figure 8.16). This one shows the drives that Windows can optimize automatically.

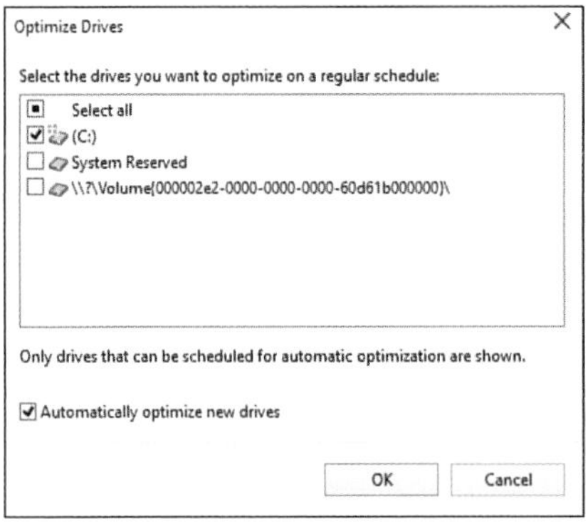

FIGURE 8.16
In this Optimize Drives dialog box, choose which drives to optimize automatically.

6. Check the check box for each drive you want to optimize automatically. Uncheck each other drive's check box.

7. Check the Automatically Optimize New Drives check box if you want Windows to automatically optimize new drives you connect to your computer.

8. Click OK to close this Optimize Drives dialog box and return to the Optimize Drives dialog box for the schedule.

9. Click OK to close the other Optimize Drives dialog box.

10. Click Close to close the Optimize Drives window.

GETTING RID OF USELESS APPS

To keep your computer running well, spend a few minutes getting rid of any useless apps installed on it. Many computer manufacturers include extra apps on

PCs, ostensibly to provide extra functionality but more usually because they get paid for including them; and you may well be tempted to install free apps or trial versions of apps in order to get things done or simply have fun. In either case, your computer may well contain a bunch of apps that you don't use and—worse—that are taking up disk space and sapping performance.

> **NOTE** Windows gives you two tools for removing apps: Apps & Features in the Settings app, which you use for apps from the Windows Store; and Programs and Features in Control Panel, which you use for apps from other sources. This section shows you how to use Programs and Features. See Chapter 9, "Installing, Running, and Managing Apps," for coverage of Apps & Features.

Follow these steps to remove apps you don't need:

1. Right-click or long-press the Start button to display the shortcut menu.

2. Click Programs and Features to display the Programs and Features screen in Control Panel (see Figure 8.17).

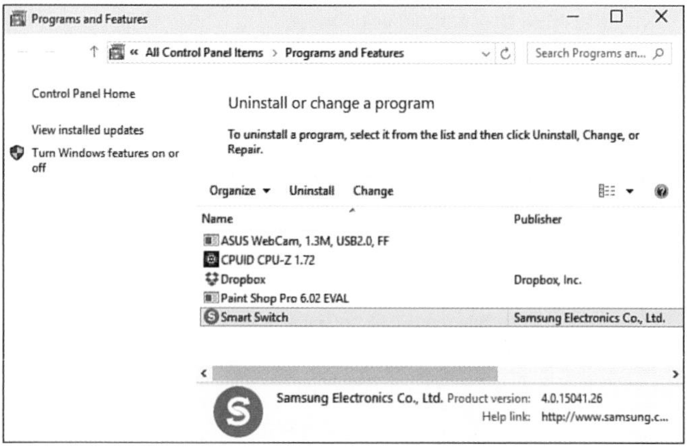

FIGURE 8.17

On the Programs and Features screen in Control Panel, click the app you want to remove, and then click Uninstall.

3. Click the app you want to uninstall.

4. Click Uninstall.

5. In the confirmation dialog box, choose any options available, and then click the button to proceed. For example, in the Smart Switch – InstallShield

Wizard dialog box shown in Figure 8.18, you can select or uncheck the Delete Temporary Save File check box before you click the Yes button to proceed.

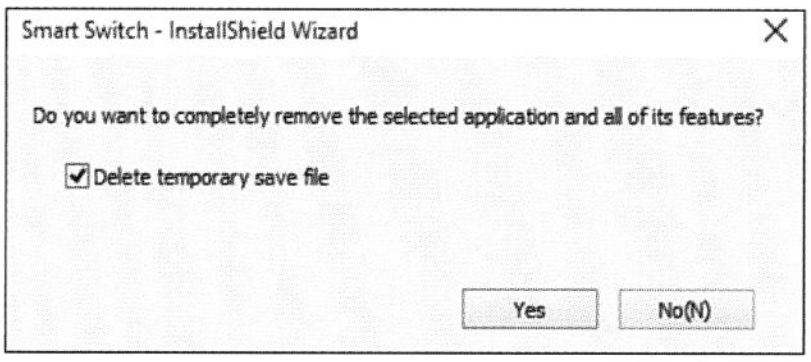

Smart Switch - InstallShield Wizard   ✕

Do you want to completely remove the selected application and all of its features?

☑ Delete temporary save file

Yes   No(N)

FIGURE 8.18

In the confirmation dialog box, choose any options, and then click the button for proceeding, such as the Yes button here.

EXTENDING RUNTIME ON THE BATTERY

If your computer is a laptop or a tablet, you likely want to get the maximum possible runtime on the battery at least sometimes. To maximize runtime, you need to reduce power consumption to an acceptable minimum. What that means depends on the computer, what you're doing with it, and how many features you're prepared to sacrifice for the sake of power.

To reduce the amount of power your computer consumes, you should turn on Battery Saver and set a sensible power plan, use Airplane mode or turn off Wi-Fi and Bluetooth individually when possible, and avoid using power-hungry apps. The following subsections have the details.

SETTING A SENSIBLE POWER PLAN

To configure your computer's power use, you'll probably want to use both the Settings app and Control Panel. Follow these steps:

1. Click Start and then click Settings to open the Settings app.
2. Click System to display the System screen.
3. Click Battery Saver in the left column to display the Battery Saver controls.
4. In the Battery Saver area, set the Battery Saver Is Currently switch to On to turn on Battery Saver.
5. Look at the text below the switch, which shows the power-remaining percentage below which Battery Saver will turn on automatically. If necessary, change the level by clicking Battery Saver Settings and dragging the slider on the Battery Saver Settings screen; then click the Back arrow to return to the System screen.

6. In the left column, click Power & Sleep to display the Power & Sleep controls (see Figure 8.19).

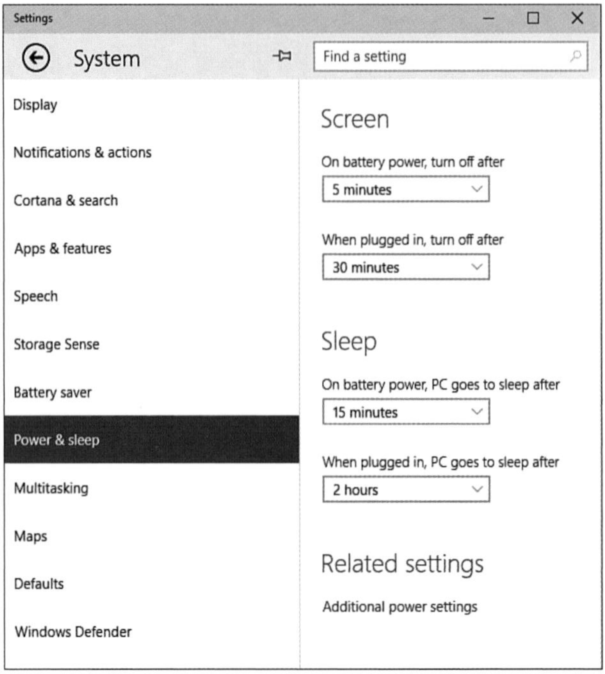

FIGURE 8.19

Use the Power & Sleep controls on the System screen to set short screen-off and sleep settings when your PC is running on the battery.

7. In the Screen area, open the On Battery Power, Turn Off After drop-down menu and choose a short time, such as 1 Minute or 2 Minutes.

8. In the Sleep area, open the On Battery Power, PC Goes to Sleep After drop-down menu and set a short time, such as 3 Minutes or 5 Minutes.

> **NOTE** The sleep timeout cannot be shorter than the screen-off timeout. If you set the sleep timeout shorter than the screen-off timeout, Windows adjusts the screen-off timeout to match the sleep timeout.

9. In the Related Settings area, click Additional Power Settings. The Power Options screen in Control Panel appears, showing the Choose or Customize a Power Plan pane (see Figure 8.20).

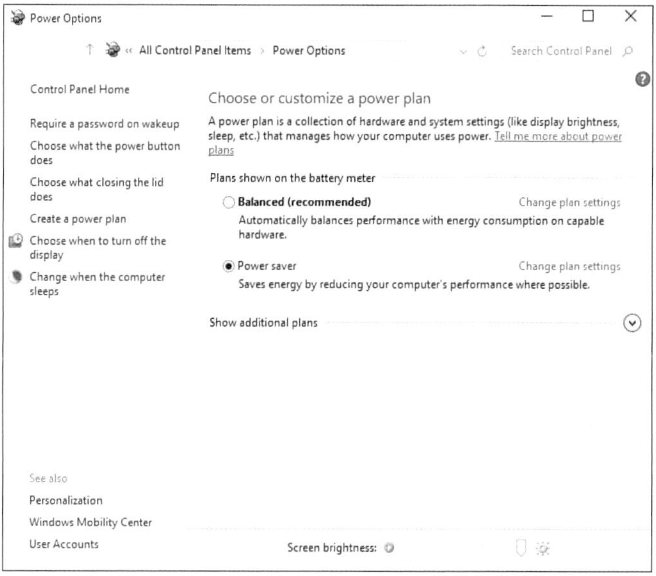

FIGURE 8.20

In the Choose or Customize a Power Plan pane in the Power Options screen in Control Panel, you can choose the Power Saver plan and customize its settings.

10. In the Plans Shown on the Battery Meter area, click the Power Saver option button, if it is available. The options shown here might vary depending on your computer system.

11. Click Change Plan Settings on the Power Saver line to display the Edit Plan Settings screen (see Figure 8.21).

12. If necessary, open the Turn Off the Display drop-down menu in the On Battery column and choose a shorter time.

13. If necessary, open the Put the Computer to Sleep drop-down menu in the On Battery column and choose a shorter time for this too.

14. Drag the Adjust Plan Brightness slider in the On Battery column as far to the left as you can bear.

15. Click Save Changes to save the changes you've made.

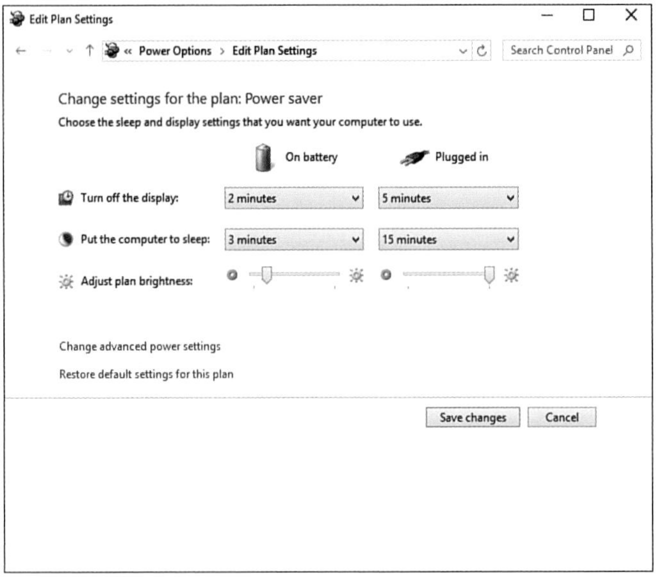

FIGURE 8.21

On the Edit Plan Settings screen, customize the Turn Off the Display setting, the Put the Computer to Sleep setting, and the Adjust Plan Brightness setting in the On Battery column.

SAVING MORE POWER BY CHANGING ADVANCED POWER SETTINGS

From the Edit Plan Settings screen, you can click Change Advanced Power Settings to display the Advanced Settings tab of the Power Options dialog box. Here, you can configure various other settings to save power and secure your computer. This sidebar explains the settings you'll typically benefit most from changing, leaving you to explore the other settings on your own.

In the Power Saver category at the top, expand the Require a Password on Wakeup item. You can then set Yes or No as needed for On Battery and for Plugged In. Requiring a password on wakeup helps keep your computer secure.

In the Hard Disk category, you can configure the Maximum Power Level setting and the Turn Off Hard Disk After setting. For example, you might choose a Maximum Power Level of 20% for On Battery and a Turn Off Hard Disk After setting of 5 Minutes for On Battery to save power.

In the Wireless Adapter Settings category, expand the Power Saving Mode item and make sure On Battery is set to Maximum Power Saving. For Plugged In, you'll normally want one of the other settings—Maximum Performance, Low Power Saving, or Medium Power Saving.

In the Sleep category, the Sleep After setting is the setting you've already set—either the On Battery Power, PC Goes to Sleep After setting in Settings or the Put the Computer to Sleep setting in Control Panel. The Allow Hybrid Sleep setting enables you to choose whether your computer uses hybrid sleep. Hybrid sleep is mostly designed for desktop computers to protect you against losing work if the power goes out; you wouldn't normally want to use it on a mobile computer unless it's a laptop that you always run from an outlet because the battery is dead or missing. The Hibernate After setting enables you to decide how quickly to put your computer into hibernation; hibernation saves battery power but means that it takes longer to wake your computer and start using it after it has sunk into a coma. The Allow Wake Timers setting enables you to control whether timed events can wake the computer from sleep; normally, you'd want to set this to Disable for On Battery.

In the Battery category, set up what happens when the battery runs low. Windows lets you configure three levels: first, the Low Battery Level, at which point you'd normally receive a warning; second, the Reserve Battery Level, at which point Windows displays an alert telling you that it is switching to Reserve Power mode and prompts you to connect the computer to power; and third, the Critical Battery Level, at which point Windows would normally put the computer to sleep, make it hibernate, or make it shut down.

First, expand the Critical Battery Action setting and choose the appropriate action—Sleep, Hibernate, or Shut Down—for On Battery. Then expand the Critical Battery Level and change the battery percentage for On Battery if necessary. The default is 5%, but if you trust your battery, you could go a little lower. If you choose Sleep rather than Hibernate or Shut Down, use a higher level, because your computer still consumes some power while asleep.

After choosing what happens when the battery hits the critical level, choose what to do at the low level. Expand the Low Battery Level setting and set the percentage; you'll normally want it at least 5% higher than the Critical Battery Level. Then expand the Low Battery Notification setting and make sure both On Battery and Plugged In are set to On—you don't want to turn off the notification unless you set the Low Battery Action to Sleep, Hibernate, or Shut Down. Normally, you're better off setting the Low Battery Action to Do Nothing, taking action yourself when you receive the notification, or having the Critical Battery Action take action for you if you're not present.

Last, expand the Reserve Battery Level setting and set the percentage you want to use. The default setting is 7%. You'll normally want to keep the Reserve Battery Level setting below the Low Battery Level but above the Critical Battery Level.

USING AIRPLANE MODE AND TURNING OFF WI-FI OR BLUETOOTH

Your computer's capability to stay in touch wirelessly is great when you need it, but when you want to work offline, you can save power by turning off wireless hardware. You can either use Airplane mode, cutting off all wireless communications, or turn off Wi-Fi and Bluetooth separately.

You can control Airplane mode, Wi-Fi, and Bluetooth easily from the Settings app:

- **Airplane mode and Wi-Fi.** Click Start, Settings, Network & Internet, and then click Airplane Mode. You can then either set the Airplane Mode switch to On or set the Wi-Fi switch to Off.
- **Bluetooth.** Click Start, Settings, Devices, Bluetooth, and then set the Bluetooth switch to Off.

AVOIDING POWER-HUNGRY APPS

If you're trying to conserve battery power so that you can get more work done, avoid running power-hungry apps that aren't part of your work. Videos and games tend to be the worst offenders here, especially any that involve using a disc in an optical drive, but regular apps can chew through power as well. If you find that your laptop or tablet tends to run hot while playing a particular highly demanding game or running a complex app, you've likely identified a battery hog.

CHOOSING SETTINGS FOR PLAYING GAMES

If you use your computer for playing demanding games, you'll likely want to work your way through this chapter configuring your computer for performance. All the items in the chapter can help improve game performance—apart from extending runtime on the battery, which tends to detract from performance.

But if you've already added memory, turned off eye candy and unnecessary services, stripped your startup items to a lean and hungry group, junked any useless apps, configured the paging file, and optimized and defragmented the hard drive, what else can you do to improve performance?

Here are seven things you can do to improve performance:

- Close other apps. While you're playing the game, you don't need to have your email app, productivity app, music app, and other apps running. You certainly don't want your BitTorrent client taking processor power and hogging your Internet connection. You don't need Skype unless you're using it to talk to other people in the game.

- Disconnect any peripherals you don't need for the game.
- On a laptop or tablet, set the power settings for performance rather than for battery life. Run the device on the charger rather than on the battery. Get a laptop cooler if necessary.
- If your laptop has both integrated graphics and dedicated graphics, such as NVIDIA Optimus, make sure it's using the dedicated graphics for anything demanding. Or use dedicated graphics for anything if you can take the hit to battery life.
- Update your drivers to the latest versions.

> ✓ **TIP** If your computer has NVIDIA graphics, you can use NVIDIA's GeForce Experience to keep your graphics drivers updated automatically and to apply optimal settings for games.

- Disable hibernation.
- Make sure your computer's drive has plenty of free space. You can free up space by running Disk Cleanup.

And here are three performance-enhancers to avoid:

- **Beta drivers.** Beta (prerelease) drivers may provide extra features or promise better performance, but you risk making your computer unstable. Unless this is a dedicated gaming machine, beta drivers are not a sensible choice.
- **Registry cleaners.** Some Registry cleaners can be helpful because they remove unnecessary information from the Registry. Others can cause disaster. So if you must use one, research it carefully, and back up the Registry before using it. See the section "Making Advanced Changes by Editing the Registry" in Chapter 14 for instructions on backing up the Registry.
- **Game boosters.** Game boosters promise to make games run faster by restricting background tasks and making more resources available to the game. As of this writing, most game boosters seem not to be effective. Here, too, do some in-depth research before trying a game booster.

IN THIS CHAPTER

- Getting apps from the Windows Store and other sources
- Managing your apps and removing unwanted apps
- Choosing your default apps for opening files

9

INSTALLING, RUNNING, AND MANAGING APPS

To get almost anything done in Windows, you must use an app. Windows comes with enough apps to cover basic needs, from editing text files and viewing photos to playing music, but you will probably want to add other apps to create and manipulate the files with which you work and play.

This chapter covers how to install apps, manage them, and remove apps you don't need. You also learn how to choose your default apps for opening files.

GETTING THE APPS YOU NEED

Windows comes with various apps built in, and whoever sold or provided your computer may have added others. But most likely you will need to add apps, from either the Windows Store or other sources, such as the apps you already have on disc or as distribution files.

CHOOSING WHERE WINDOWS INSTALLS APPS BY DEFAULT

The Storage feature enables you to control where Windows installs apps by default. Choose Start, Settings, System to display the System window, click Storage to display the Storage pane, and then choose the appropriate location in the New Apps Will Save To drop-down menu. See Chapter 6, "Sorting Out Your Files, Folders, and Storage," for detailed coverage of Storage.

GETTING APPS FROM THE STORE

Windows 10 comes set to use the Windows Store as its primary source of apps. The Windows Store is a Microsoft service that offers both free apps and "paid apps"— apps for which you must pay—along with games, music, and multimedia files.

NOTE Getting apps from the Store has a couple of benefits. First, although it's not yet comprehensive, the Store is a good place to find a wide selection of apps, because Microsoft is encouraging developers to sell their apps through the Store. Second, the apps in the Store are checked for quality and are guaranteed not to contain malicious code.

NOTE You can install apps you get from the Windows Store on multiple devices. As of this writing, you can install an app on up to 10 devices.

LAUNCHING THE STORE APP AND BROWSING THE APPS

To see which apps are available in the Store, launch the Store app from the taskbar or from the Start menu. The Start menu usually contains a tile for the Store app, but if you don't find one, you can launch the app from the All Apps list.

At first, the Store window usually displays the Store home screen, which includes some apps, some games, and other content. Click Apps on the toolbar to display the Apps screen, which lets you focus on apps (see Figure 9.1).

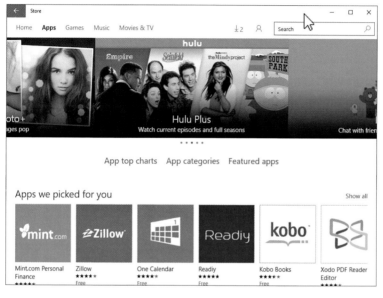

FIGURE 9.1

Click Apps on the toolbar in the Store window to browse or search apps on the Windows Store.

From here, you can locate apps in any of these ways:

- **Browse by lists.** The Apps screen contains various lists, such as Apps We Picked for You, Top Free Apps, Top Paid Apps, and Best-Rated Apps. You can click the Show All link on any of these lists to display the whole list.

- **Browse by App Top Charts, App Categories, or Featured Apps.** Click App Top Charts, App Categories, or Featured Apps near the top of the screen.

- **Search for apps.** Click in the Search box in the upper-right corner of the screen and type your search terms.

After you've found an app you want to learn more about, click it to display its screen (see Figure 9.2). You can then read the app's description; if necessary, click the More link near the end of the description to expand the description. Beyond the description, you can look at screenshots of the app, view ratings and read reviews, and see a full list of the app's features.

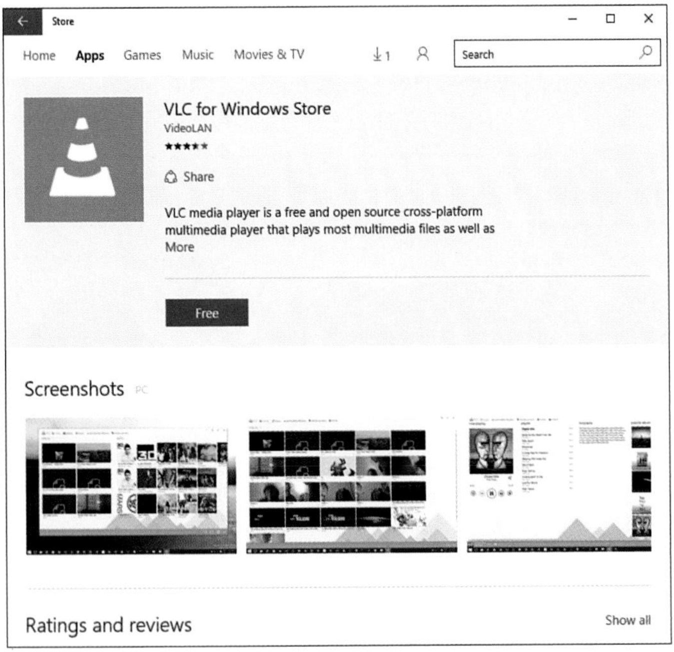

FIGURE 9.2
On the app's screen in the Store app, read the description, browse the screenshots, and dig into the ratings and reviews to learn more about the app.

HAVING TROUBLE FINDING OR INSTALLING THE APP YOU WANT?

Sometimes you may not be able to find a particular app in the Store even though you know the app exists. One possibility is that the publisher has stopped selling the app, but you can usually determine quickly whether this is the case by searching other software sellers online. More likely, the publisher has not released the app in your country or region; this sometimes happens because the app requires modifications or different permissions to be sold in other countries or regions.

If you can find an app on the Windows Store but you can't install that app, try restarting your computer. Sometimes updates that Windows has installed can block you from installing apps from the Windows Store until you restart Windows.

If restarting your computer doesn't enable you to install the app, it's possible your computer's hardware doesn't meet the app's system requirements. Look at the Details section of the app's page in the Store and check the specifics.

If your computer's hardware seems to muster up, there's one more move you can try. This is clearing your computer's cache for the Windows Store, because the cache might contain corrupted data that's blocking you from installing an app. To clear the cache, click the Start button, type **wsreset.exe**, and then press Enter. Running this command launches the Store app, so you can then try the installation again.

INSTALLING AN APP FROM THE STORE

If you decide to get the app, click the Free button or the price button. If it's a free app, the Store app starts downloading it. If it's a paid app, the Store app may prompt you to enter your PIN or password. The Store app then displays the Buy App dialog box, in which you choose your means of payment.

NOTE You can pay for apps either by using a means of payment you've set up in your Microsoft account, such as the credit card that suffers for your Xbox habit, or by redeeming a code. To redeem a code, click the Account icon on the toolbar and then click Redeem a Code on the drop-down menu. The Store app causes your default browser, such as Microsoft Edge, to display the Redeem Your Code or Gift Card screen in your Microsoft account. You can then enter the number of the code or gift card and click Redeem to redeem it.

The Store app then downloads the app, showing a progress readout with a Pause button (the standard Pause icon, two vertical lines) and a Stop button (the × button).

TIP While the Store app is downloading the app, you can click the Pause button to pause the download. You might need to do this if the app is large and the download is taking more time than you have. You can then restart the download by clicking the Restart button (the clockwise curling arrow) that replaces the Pause button.

When the download finishes, the Store app installs the app. You can then open the app in either of these ways:

- **Click the Open button on the app's page in the Store app.** This is handy if you still have the app's page displayed.
- **Click the app's icon on the Start menu.** The app appears on the Recently Added list. If you've removed the Recently Added list from the Start menu, click All Apps and then navigate to the app's icon.

When the app opens, you can perform any setup needed. For example, many apps have configurable options you can set, whereas other apps require you to set up an online account for accessing or storing data.

USING THE MY LIBRARY FEATURE

The My Library screen in the Store app gives you quick access to the apps, games, music, and other items you've acquired or purchased from the Windows Store. To access the My Library feature, click the Account icon on the toolbar and then click My Library.

The download arrows on the right side of the buttons on the My Library screen (see Figure 9.3) indicate the apps you haven't yet installed on this computer. You can click the download arrow to start downloading the app, or click elsewhere on the button to display the app's screen, where you can refresh your memory of the app and decide whether to install it.

KEEPING YOUR WINDOWS STORE APPS UPDATED

To get the best performance out of your apps, and to minimize security problems, it's a good idea to install updates to the apps soon after they become available. The Store app checks for updates periodically, but you can also check for updates manually whenever you want.

NOTE The Store app may be set to install updates automatically.

CAUTION App updates sometimes cause problems on some computers, so unless an app has a problem already that you urgently need to solve, it's usually a good idea to wait a few days after an app update becomes available and let other people try it first. If all seems well, you can update the app; if there's an explosion of complaints, you'll likely want to wait until the app's developer fixes the problem before you update the app on your computer.

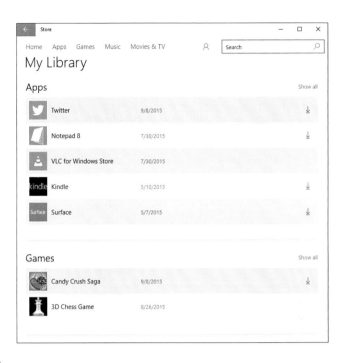

FIGURE 9.3

On the My Library screen in the Store app, click the download arrow on the right of an app's button to start installing that app.

To see which updates are available, click the Downloads icon to the left of the Account icon on the toolbar in the Store app. This icon appears when the Store app has identified an available update or download. If the Downloads icon doesn't appear, click the Account icon to open the drop-down menu, and then click Downloads. Either way, the Downloads and Installs screen appears, and you can click the Check for Updates button to force the Store app to check for new updates.

After you can see what's available, you can click an item on the Downloads and Installs screen to download and install it.

CHOOSING SETTINGS FOR THE STORE APP

You can configure three settings to control how the Store app behaves. To reach the settings, click the Account icon on the toolbar in the Store app and then click Settings on the drop-down menu. You can then set these settings:

■ **Update Apps Automatically.** Set this switch to On to allow the Store app to download and install updates automatically. Set this switch to Off if you want to handle updates manually—for example, to protect yourself against the occasional poorly programmed update.

- **Show Products on Tile.** Set this switch to On if you want the Store tile on the Start menu to show products.

- **Only Update the Tile When I'm on Wi-Fi.** If you set the Show Products on Tile switch to On, set this switch to On to allow the Store app to update the information on the tile only when your computer is using a Wi-Fi connection rather than a cellular connection.

Stay on the Settings screen for the next section.

REMOVING A DEVICE FROM YOUR WINDOWS STORE ACCOUNT

As mentioned earlier, you can install apps you download from the Windows Store on multiple devices—10 devices as of this writing.

If you run into your device limit, you can remove a device from your Windows Store account. Removing the device prevents any apps you've installed on it from the Windows Store from working anymore.

In the Account section of the Settings screen, click Manage Your Devices to display the Devices with Apps and Games You Downloaded from the Store screen (see Figure 9.4) in your Microsoft account in your default browser, such as Microsoft Edge.

The browser displays the Remove screen for the device, such as the Remove Your Laptop screen shown in Figure 9.5. Check the I'm Ready to Remove This Device check box, and then click the Remove button.

Now that you've removed this device, you can add another device to your Windows Store account by logging in to Windows on the device.

GETTING AND INSTALLING APPS FROM OTHER SOURCES

Although Microsoft has set up Windows to use the Windows Store as its primary source of apps, you can freely install apps from other sources as well. For example, you can buy apps from online stores or brick-and-mortar stores and then install them, either from physical discs or from distribution files. And you can install any apps that you already have on discs or in files.

STARTING AN INSTALLATION FROM AN OPTICAL DISC

To install an app from an optical disc, such as a CD or DVD, insert the disc in an optical drive connected to your computer.

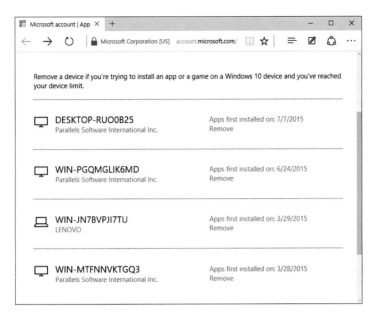

FIGURE 9.4

In your Microsoft account, click the Remove button for the device you want to remove from your Windows Store account.

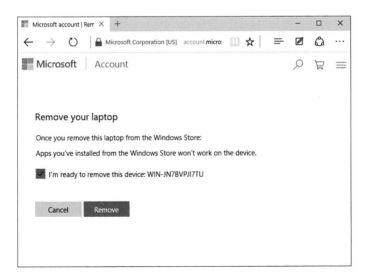

FIGURE 9.5

On the Remove screen, check the I'm Ready to Remove This Device check box, and then click the Remove button.

Windows usually assesses the contents of the disc and displays a pop-up balloon above the notification area prompting you to tap to choose what happens with the drive. Tap the balloon to display the Choose What to Do with This Disc dialog box (see Figure 9.6).

FIGURE 9.6

In the Choose What to Do with This Disc dialog box, click the Run button to run the installer or click Open Folder to View Files if you want to examine the disc's contents.

If you want to go ahead and run the installer, click the Run item, which usually shows an app name such as SETUP.EXE or INSTALL.EXE. Otherwise, click the Open Folder to View Files item to open a File Explorer window showing the disc's contents so that you can decide whether to install the app.

STARTING AN INSTALLATION FROM A DISTRIBUTION FILE

If you have downloaded an app from a source other than the Windows Store, you'll have a distribution file containing the app. The distribution file will normally be either an executable file or a zip file:

- **Executable file.** Double-click the file to start the installation.
- **Zip file.** Double-click the file to display its contents in a File Explorer window, and then choose Extract, Extract All to launch the Extract Compressed (Zipped) Folders wizard (see Figure 9.7). If you want to use a different destination folder than that shown in the Files Will Be Extracted to This Folder box, click the Browse button and choose the folder. Check the Show Extracted Files When Complete check box, and then click the Extract button. In the File Explorer window that opens, double-click the executable file, such as SETUP.EXE, to launch the installation.

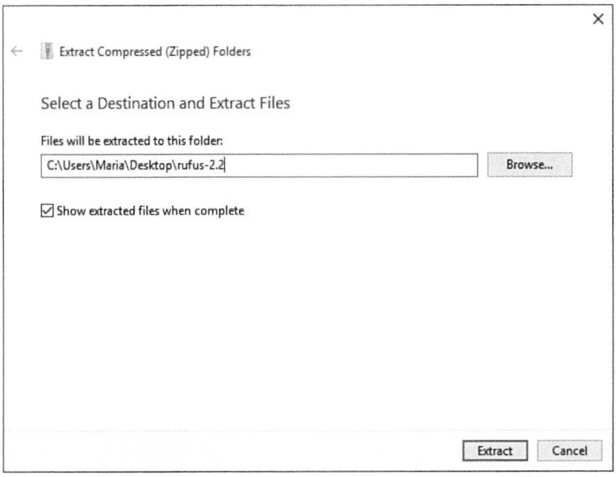

×

← Extract Compressed (Zipped) Folders

Select a Destination and Extract Files

Files will be extracted to this folder:

C:\Users\Maria\Desktop\rufus-2.2   [Browse...]

☑ Show extracted files when complete

[Extract] [Cancel]

FIGURE 9.7

On the Select a Destination and Extract Files screen of the Extract Compressed (Zipped) Folders Wizard, choose the destination folder and click the Extract button.

Depending on the app you're installing, Windows may display a User Account Control dialog box (see Figure 9.8) to confirm that you want to install the app (as opposed to malevolent software having launched the installation). Verify the program name and the publisher, and then click the Yes button to proceed.

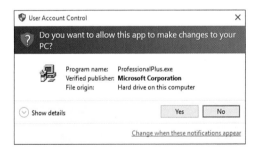

FIGURE 9.8

If Windows displays the User Account Control dialog box, make sure the program name and publisher are correct before clicking the Yes button.

CHOOSING SETTINGS FOR THE APP YOU'RE INSTALLING

After launch, the installer usually prompts you to accept the end-user license agreement for the app. After you have done this, the app may prompt you to enter your product key or other identifying information.

YOU MIGHT WANT TO AVOID ACTIVATING THE APP IMMEDIATELY

Some apps require activation before you can use them fully. Activation often ties the app to the computer on which you have installed it, making it difficult or impossible to transfer the app to another computer.

If you use multiple computers, you might want to be able to try the app on each of them to see which computer it's most useful for. In this case, make sure you disable any option for automatic activation during setup. The app will prompt you to activate it periodically afterward, so there is no risk you will forget.

After you've negotiated the formalities, the installer may display settings you can configure for the app, as in the example shown in Figure 9.9. Choose settings to suit your needs, and then click the Install button or other button to complete the installation.

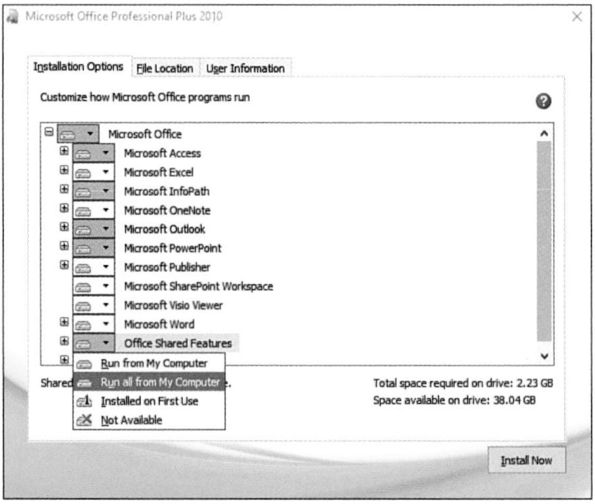

FIGURE 9.9
If the installer displays an options screen, choose the settings that will suit you best.

! CAUTION Many installers automatically create a shortcut on the desktop for the app. Unless you like having your desktop full of app shortcuts and find them a more convenient way to launch apps than the Start menu or the taskbar, uncheck the check box for creating a shortcut during installation.

After the installation finishes, you can launch the app from the Start menu.

MAKING OLDER APPS RUN WITH COMPATIBILITY MODE

Any new apps you buy should be optimized for Windows 10, and any recent apps for Windows 7, Windows 8, or Windows 8.1. But apps designed for older versions of Windows may not work unless you choose suitable settings in Compatibility mode.

> **NOTE** You can use Compatibility mode to install an app if the installer crashes when run normally.

If you know that the app requires Compatibility mode, you can set it to run with Compatibility mode from the start. But more likely you'll try running the app normally, see a crash message such as that shown in Figure 9.10, and then apply Compatibility mode to get the app working.

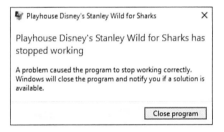

FIGURE 9.10
If an app crashes when you run it normally, try applying Compatibility mode.

> **NOTE** Windows may prompt you to use Compatibility mode for an app. If not, try Compatibility mode yourself anyway. Search online using the app's name and "Compatibility mode" to find recommended settings.

Here's how to choose settings in Compatibility mode:

1. Open a File Explorer window to the folder that contains the app file. The easiest way to do this is to click Start, right-click or long-press the app in the Recently Added list or the Apps list, and then click Open File Location on the shortcut menu.

2. In the File Explorer window, right-click or long-press the app file to display the shortcut menu.

3. Click Properties to display the Properties dialog box.

4. Click the Compatibility tab to display its controls. Figure 9.11 shows the Compatibility tab of the Properties dialog box with settings chosen.

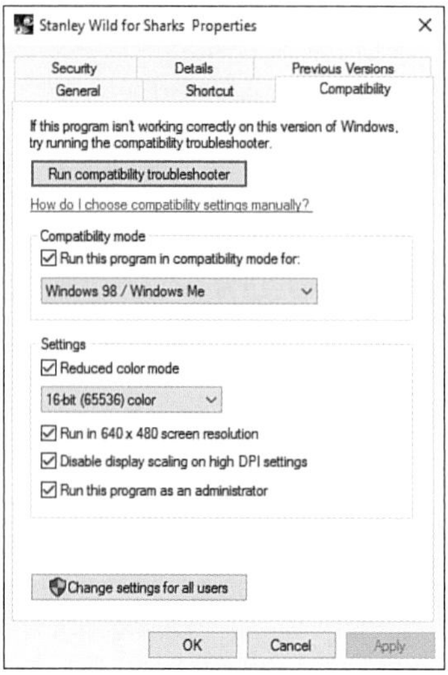

FIGURE 9.11

You can configure Compatibility mode for an app on the Compatibility tab of the Properties dialog box for the app's file.

CONFIGURING COMPATIBILITY MODE AUTOMATICALLY

The Program Compatibility Troubleshooter feature can configure Compatibility mode automatically for some apps. This feature is well worth trying, because it can save you time and effort. To launch the Program Compatibility Troubleshooter, click the Run Compatibility Troubleshooter button near the top of the Compatibility tab in the Properties dialog box or click Troubleshoot Compatibility on the shortcut menu for the app's file in a File Explorer window.

If the Program Compatibility Troubleshooter's efforts fail, configure Compatibility mode settings manually as explained in the main text.

5. In the Compatibility Mode box, check the Run This Program in Compatibility Mode For check box, and then choose the appropriate version of Windows in the drop-down menu.

✓ TIP To determine which version of Windows to use for Compatibility mode, look at the app's packaging (if you still have it) or on the Web. If the app is designed for several versions of Windows, try using the latest version for Compatibility mode. For example, if an app is designed for Windows 98, Windows Me, and Windows XP, try choosing Windows XP in the Compatibility Mode drop-down menu.

✎ NOTE Checking the Run This Program in Compatibility Mode For check box and choosing the right operating system version in the drop-down menu may be all you need to do to get the app running. For other apps, you may need to choose settings in the Settings box. You can click Apply at any point to apply the settings you've chosen so far without closing the Properties dialog box. You can then try starting the app. If it works correctly, you're all set; if it doesn't, go back to the Properties dialog box and try other settings.

6. If necessary, go to the Settings box and check the Reduced Color Mode check box. Then open the drop-down menu and select the color mode: 8-Bit (256) Color, or 16-Bit (65536) Color.

7. Also if necessary, check the Run in 640 × 480 Screen Resolution check box. You may need this for some older games designed to run on obsolete hardware.

8. Also if necessary, check the Disable Display Scaling on High DPI Settings check box. Normally, you'd want to check this check box if the app uses a large-scale font that appears distorted in Windows 10.

9. Also if necessary, check the Run This Program as an Administrator check box.

! CAUTION Check the Run This Program as an Administrator check box only if you've found a specific and convincing recommendation to do so. This setting may be needed for apps designed for Windows 95, Windows 98, or Windows Me, which used a different programming model than apps designed for Windows

NT and the versions of Windows based on it (Windows 2000, Windows XP, Windows Vista, Windows 7, Windows 8 and 8.1, and Windows 10).

Running a program as an administrator enables it to take a wider range of actions on your computer than running the program normally does. It may enable the app to destabilize Windows or to access files you wouldn't want it to access.

NOTE You can click the Change Settings for All Users button to apply the compatibility settings for all users. If the app won't run normally, and you have the administrator permissions required to make this change, doing so is normally a good idea.

10. When you finish making changes in the Properties dialog box, click OK to close it.

KEEPING YOUR NON-WINDOWS STORE APPS UPDATED

As you'd expect, apps from sources other than the Windows Store don't benefit from the Store's ability to coordinate updates. Each app (or each suite of apps) handles updates on its own.

Apps use different mechanisms for updates. Some have a command for updating, such as Help, Check for Updates, that you can run at any point to see whether updates are available. Some apps come configured to check for updates automatically; look in the app's options (usually Tools, Options) to see whether you can configure the frequency of checking to suit you.

Some suites of apps have an automatic-update tool that handles checking for all the apps in the suite centrally. Such a tool may automatically run the first time you run one of the apps in the suite, enabling you to set up checking for updates. If not, look in the suite's folder on the Start menu to see whether the suite has such a tool, launch it manually, and dig into the options it offers.

MANAGING THE APPS YOU'RE RUNNING

You already know the essential moves for managing apps—how to launch an app, how to switch from one app to another, how to resize and position app windows, and how to close an app. In this section, we'll examine how to use the Windows Task Manager tool to deal with apps that stop responding and to identify apps that are either hogging resources or otherwise causing performance problems on your computer.

CLOSING AN APP THAT STOPS RESPONDING

If an app stops responding to input from the keyboard, mouse, or touchscreen, you will need to close the app. Usually, you can do this by using Task Manager.

OPENING TASK MANAGER

Open Task Manager in one of these ways:

- **Open Task Manager using the mouse or touchscreen.** Right-click or long-press Start, and then click Task Manager on the shortcut menu.

> **TIP** You can also right-click or long-press open space on the taskbar (if you can find any) or right-click or long-press in the notification area and then click Task Manager on the shortcut menu.

- **Open Task Manager using the keyboard.** Press Ctrl+Alt+Delete to display the screen that contains the Lock, Switch User, Sign Out, and Task Manager commands. Press the down arrow key to select Task Manager, and then press Enter. (Alternatively, click Task Manager.)

CLOSING AN APP WITH TASK MANAGER

Task Manager usually opens in its Fewer Details mode, which shows only the list of running apps (see Figure 9.12). If you know which app is causing problems, you can close it by clicking it in the list of apps and then clicking End Task. Windows doesn't confirm closing the app.

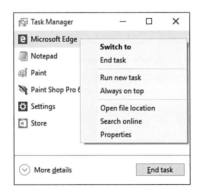

FIGURE 9.12

In its Fewer Details mode, Task Manager shows only the list of running apps. You can close an app by clicking it and then clicking End Task.

GOING FURTHER WITH OTHER ACTIONS IN TASK MANAGER

For more actions to take with the app, right-click or long-press its entry in the list. The shortcut menu (see Figure 9.13) offers the following commands:

- **Switch To.** Click this command to make the app active.

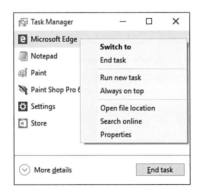

FIGURE 9.13

The shortcut menu for an app in Task Manager enables you to switch to a running app, close the app, or find out information about the app.

> **☑ TIP** If you lose an app and can't locate its window in the Windows inter-
> face, open Task Manager. You can then double-click the app (or right-click or long-
> press it and click Switch To on the shortcut menu) to make the app active.

- **End Task.** Click this command to close the app.
- **Run New Task.** Click this command to open the Create New Task dialog box (see Figure 9.14), which you can use to open an app. Type the app's name in the Open box; or click the drop-down arrow and choose a recent app you've run this way; or click Browse, navigate to and select the app in the Browse dialog box that opens, and then click the Open button. You can check the Create This Task with Administrative Privileges check box if you need to run the task as an administrator rather than as a standard user. Click the OK button to run the app.

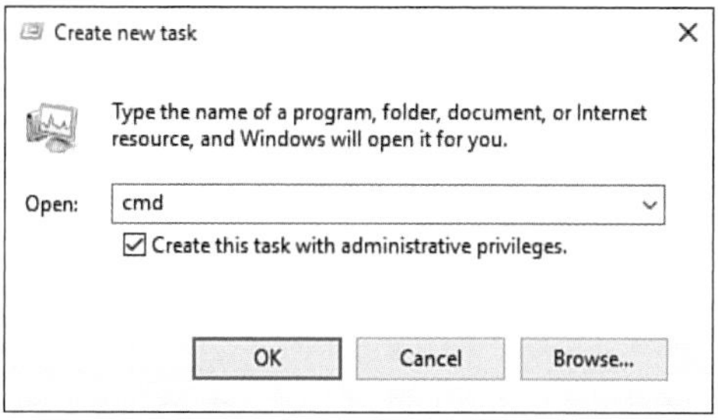

FIGURE 9.14
Use the Create New Task dialog box to open an app from Task Manager.

> **☑ TIP** Opening an app via the Create New Task dialog box can be helpful
> when the Windows interface isn't responding correctly but you can access Task
> Manager. For example, you might open a command-prompt window so that you
> can give commands.

- **Always on Top.** Click this command to keep the Task Manager window on top of all the other windows. Keeping Task Manager on top can be useful when you're troubleshooting problems.
- **Open File Location.** Click this command to open a File Explorer window showing the folder that contains the app or system process you've selected.

■ **Search Online.** Click this command to search online for the name of the app or system process you've selected. You might want to search to find out what a particular app or process does.

■ **Properties.** Click this command to display the Properties dialog box for the app or system process you've selected. The Properties dialog box enables you to view detailed information about the app or process. The Previous Versions tab contains details of any previous version of the app and gives you a way to restore a version if necessary.

> ☑ **TIP**   Most of the information in the Properties dialog box isn't usually directly useful for troubleshooting—but you may need to find out the file version of the app if it keeps crashing or otherwise causing grief. To find this out, look at the File version readout on the Details tab of the Properties dialog box.

EXAMINING APPS AND PROCESSES IN TASK MANAGER

If you want to see the details of the apps you're running, and see information about the background processes that Windows is running on your behalf, click More Details in the lower-left corner of the Task Manager window to switch Task Manager to More Details view. This view has seven tabs, as you can see in Figure 9.15, which shows the Processes tab, the tab that appears first:

■ **Processes.** This tab shows the apps you're running (in the Apps list) and the background processes that Windows is running (in the Background Processes list). You can right-click or long-press a column heading to choose which columns of information you want to display.

> ☑ **TIP**   To sort the processes, click the column heading by which you want to sort. You can reverse the sort order by clicking the column heading again. For example, if you want to see which apps are using the most processor cycles, click the CPU column heading. Task Manager normally gives you a descending sort for this column, but if you get an ascending sort, click the column heading again to switch to a descending sort.

■ **Performance.** This tab enables you to get an overview of your computer's performance. We'll look at the Performance tab in the section "Identifying Performance Problems in Task Manager," later in this chapter.

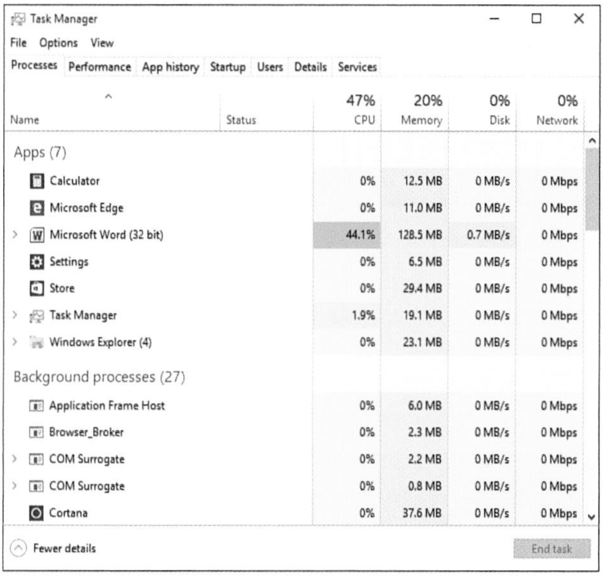

FIGURE 9.15
Use the Processes tab in More Details view in Task Manager to see detailed information on the apps you're running and the background processes Windows is running.

■ **App History.** This tab lets you see the demands that your apps have been putting on your computer. We'll look at the App History tab in the section "Identifying Resource Hogs in Task Manager," later in this chapter.

■ **Startup.** This tab allows you to see which apps and tools your computer is set to launch at startup, together with their approximate startup impact (High, Medium, or Low).

> **NOTE** See the section "Reducing the Number of Startup Items" in Chapter 8 for coverage of the Startup tab.

■ **Users.** This tab enables you to see which users are logged in to the computer, which apps they're running and which processes Windows is running for them, and what impact they're having on the system. See the section "Seeing Which Other Users Are Logged In and Which Apps They're Running," later in this chapter, for details.

- **Details.** This tab lists the apps and processes running on the computer. See the section "Viewing the Details of the Apps and Services Running," later in this chapter, for more information.
- **Services.** This tab lists the services on the computer and shows their current status, such as Running or Stopped. See the section "Viewing the Current Status of Services," later in this chapter, for details.

> **TIP** In More Details view, you can choose Options, Always on Top to keep Task Manager on top of other windows.

IDENTIFYING PERFORMANCE PROBLEMS IN TASK MANAGER

You can use the Performance tab of the More Details view in Task Manager to identify performance problems your computer is suffering. For example, you can see whether the CPU is running at full throttle, whether all the memory is in use, and how hard the disks and the network connection are working.

Click the Performance tab to display its contents (see Figure 9.16), go to the left pane, and then click the component for which you want to view performance information. For example, click CPU to see a graph of the CPU's performance.

IDENTIFYING RESOURCE HOGS IN TASK MANAGER

The More Details view in Task Manager also enables you to identify resource hogs. Click the App History tab to display its contents (see Figure 9.17), and then click the column heading of the column by which you want to sort. For example, click the CPU Time column heading to see which apps have used the most processor time.

> **TIP** You can right-click or long-press a column heading on the App History tab to change the columns displayed. For example, you may want to display the Downloads column or the Uploads column to see which apps have been transferring the most data across your computer's Internet connection.

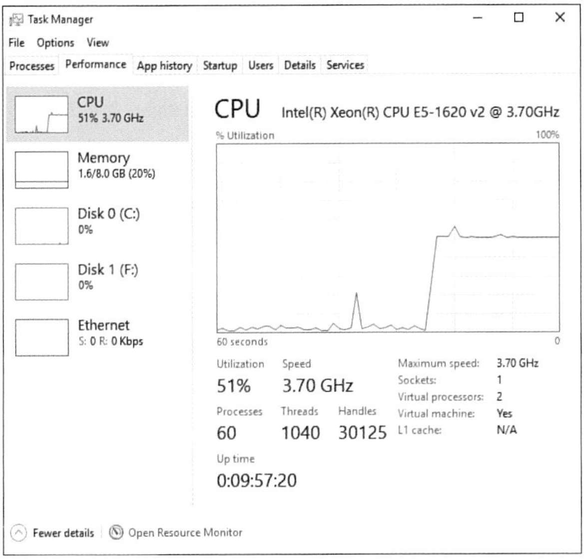

FIGURE 9.16
On the Performance tab in Task Manager, click the component in the left column whose performance you want to view in the right pane.

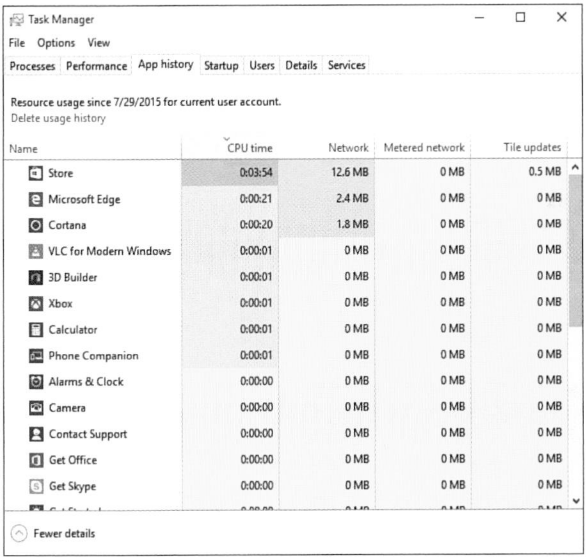

FIGURE 9.17
Use the App History tab of Task Manager to see which apps have been using the most CPU time, network bandwidth, or Internet data transfer.

SEEING WHICH OTHER USERS ARE LOGGED IN AND WHICH APPS THEY'RE RUNNING

The Users tab of the More Details view in Task Manager enables you to see which users are logged in to the computer. Double-click a user's entry in the list to display the full list of apps and services the user is running (see Figure 9.18). If necessary, you can right-click or long-press an app or a service and click End Task on the shortcut menu to end it.

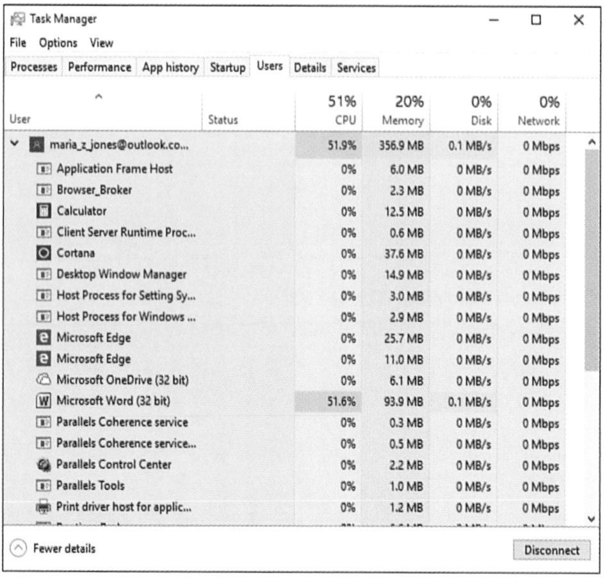

FIGURE 9.18

On the Users tab, you can see not only which users are logged in to your computer but also which processes they are running.

> **TIP**   You can disconnect another user's session by right-clicking or long-pressing the user's name on the Users tab and then clicking Disconnect in the shortcut menu. You must be an administrator to disconnect another user like this—and you should remember that the user may lose unsaved data when you disconnect him.

VIEWING THE DETAILS OF THE APPS AND SERVICES RUNNING

The Details tab of the More Details view in Task Manager (see Figure 9.19) enables you to see the status of each app or service running on the computer. You can right-click or long-press an item to display the shortcut menu, which includes the following commands:

■ **End Task.** Click this item to end the current task.

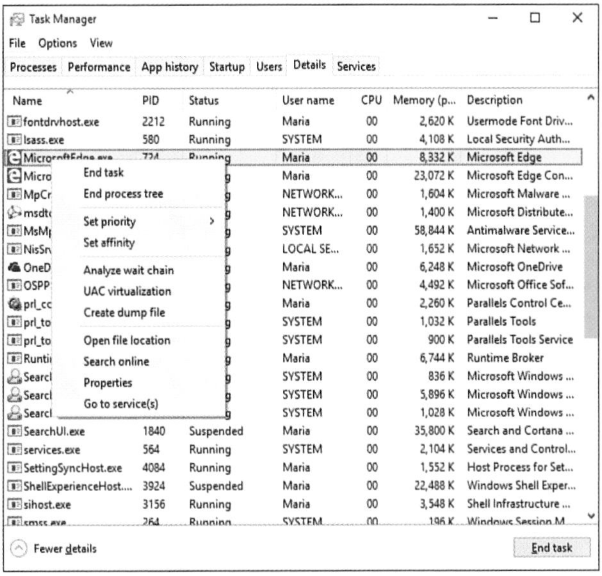

FIGURE 9.19

On the Details tab in Task Manager, you can view the status of each app or service. You can also end a task or a process tree if necessary.

■ **End Process Tree.** Click this item to end the selected process and any other processes it has created, either directly or indirectly.

■ **Set Priority.** Click this item to display the Set Priority submenu, on which you can click the priority to assign to the process: Realtime, High, Above Normal, Normal, Below Normal, or Low.

> **! CAUTION** Use the End Task command and End Process Tree command on the Details tab in Task Manager only when absolutely necessary. You should also avoid using the Set Priority command, because Windows automatically assigns suitable priority levels to all system processes.

■ **Go to Service(s).** Click this item to display the corresponding service on the Services tab in Task Manager.

VIEWING THE CURRENT STATUS OF SERVICES

The Services tab of the More Details view in Task Manager (see Figure 9.20) enables you to see the current status of all the services on your computer. From the Services tab, you can take the following actions:

■ **Start, stop, or restart a service.** Right-click or long-press the service, and then click the Start command, the Stop command, or the Restart command on the shortcut menu.

FIGURE 9.20
Use the Services tab in Task Manager to examine the status of a service, stop it, or restart it.

■ **Go to the details for a running service.** Right-click or long-press the service, and then click Go to Details to display the service's entry on the Details pane in Task Manager.

■ **Open the Services console.** Either click Open Services at the bottom of the window or right-click or long-press a service and then click Open Services on the shortcut menu.

■ **Look up a service online.** Right-click or long-press the service and then click Search Online on the shortcut menu. You might want to look up a service online to find out what it does and establish whether you can safely stop it.

REMOVING UNWANTED APPS

If your computer contains any apps that you neither need nor want, take a few minutes to get rid of them. Windows enables you to remove apps easily using the Apps & Features screen in the Settings app.

Here's how to remove an app:

1. Choose Start, Settings to open the Settings window.

2. Click System to display the System screen.

3. Click Apps & Features in the left pane to display the Apps & Features pane (see Figure 9.21).

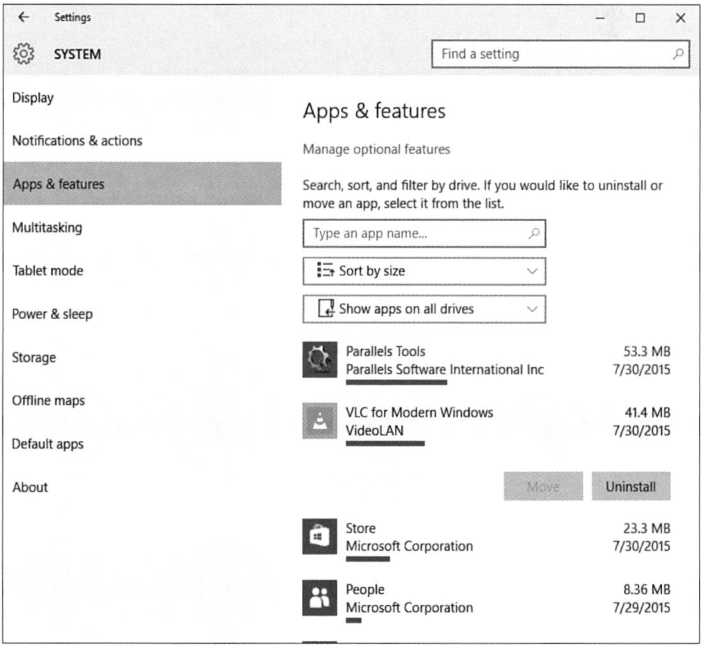

FIGURE 9.21

In the Apps & Features pane on the System screen in the Settings app, click the app you want to remove, and then click Uninstall.

4. Optionally, click the Sort drop-down menu, and then click the means of sorting you want to use: Sort by Size, Sort by Name, or Sort by Install Date.

5. Optionally, click the Show Apps drop-down menu, and then click Show Apps on All Drives, This PC, or a particular drive, as needed.

6. Either scroll to locate the app, or click in the Type an App Name box and start typing the app's name to locate it quickly.

7. Click the app to select it. The Move button and the Uninstall button appear. Some apps display a Modify button instead of a Move button.

8. Click Uninstall. Windows displays a confirmation message box.

9. Click Uninstall in the message box as well. Windows then removes the app.

REMOVING AN APP USING CONTROL PANEL

You can also remove an app using Control Panel. This works only for apps you have installed from sources other than the Windows Store. To do so, right-click or long-press Start and then click Control Panel. In the Control Panel window, click Uninstall a Program under the Programs heading. On the Uninstall or Change a Program screen, you can click the app you want to remove, and then click Uninstall. Follow the prompts to uninstall the app.

SETTING THE DEFAULT APPS YOU NEED

To make sure that files open in the apps you want to use, you can set default apps. A default app is the app that opens automatically when you open a particular type of file—for example, by double-clicking the file in a File Explorer window.

UNDERSTANDING HOW DEFAULT APPS WORK

As you know, each filename includes a file extension, the part of the name after the final period. For example, if you create and save a document in Microsoft Word, it has a name such as My Document.docx, in which .docx is the file extension. Most apps automatically include a suitable file extension for each file you create; in this case, Microsoft Word adds the .docx to the name automatically unless you specify another file extension. Similarly, if you create a text file in the Notepad accessory app, Notepad assigns the .txt file extension by default.

Windows uses the file extension to identify the file type of each file, so it's important not to change file extensions capriciously. When you open a file, Windows checks the file extension and automatically uses the app that's registered as the default app for that file type. So when you double-click a file with a .docx file extension in a File Explorer window, Windows opens that file extension's default app, which is normally Word.

OPENING THE DEFAULT APPS PANE IN THE SETTINGS APP

To set your default apps, first display the Default Apps pane in the Settings app like this:

1. Choose Start, Settings to open the Settings window.

2. Click System to display the System screen.

3. Click Default Apps in the left column to display the Default Apps pane (see Figure 9.22).

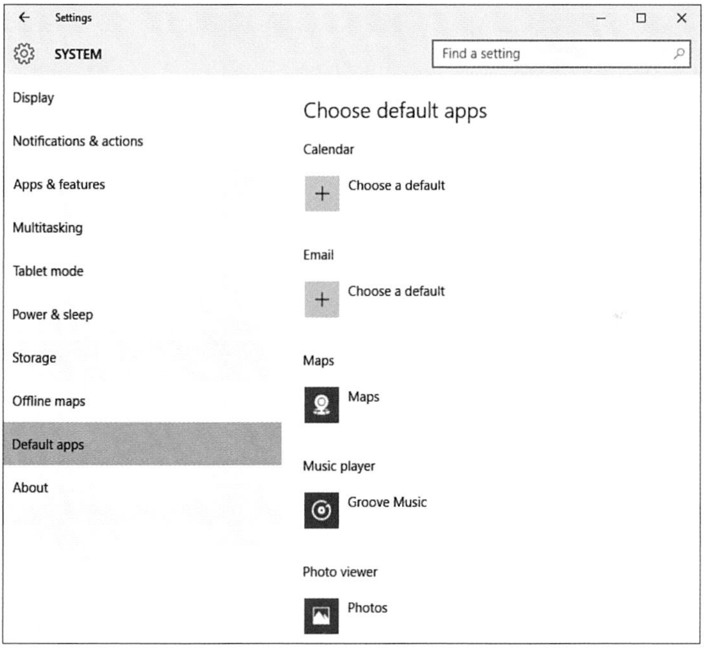

FIGURE 9.22

You can set default apps by clicking the buttons in the Choose Default Apps area in the Default Apps pane in the Settings app.

CHOOSING YOUR DEFAULT APPS

Now look at the Choose Default Apps list and see which you need to change. If any of the items shows the Choose a Default message, click the + button to display the Choose an App pop-up menu. This menu contains a button for any app on your computer that can perform this role and the Look for an App in the Store button, which you can click to launch the Store app and search for a suitable app.

Similarly, you can click one of the current default apps to see which alternatives are available on your system or in the Store.

CHOOSING DEFAULT APPS BY FILE TYPES OR BY PROTOCOLS

The Settings app also enables you to choose default apps by file types or by protocols. As an example of the former, you could set a text editor or a word processing app as the default app for the .txt (Text Document) file type. As an example of the latter, you could set your favorite browser as the default app for the HTTP (URL:HyperText Transfer Protocol) protocol.

To choose default apps by file types, click Choose Default Apps by File Type toward the bottom of the Default Apps pane. On the Choose Default Apps by File Type screen that appears, scroll down to the file type for which you want to set the default app. You can then click the existing app or the Choose a Default button to display the Choose an App pop-up menu, and then click the app you want to use for that file type.

To choose default apps by protocols, click Choose Default Apps by Protocol toward the bottom of the Default Apps pane. On the Choose Default Apps by Protocol screen, navigate to the protocol for which you want to set the default app. You can then click the existing app or the Choose a Default button to display the Choose an App pop-up menu, and then click the app you want to use for that protocol.

CHOOSING DEFAULT APPS BY APPS

Windows also enables you to choose default apps by selecting an app and then choosing the file types and protocols for which you want it to be the default. To do this, open the Set Default Programs screen in Control Panel in one of these ways:

■ **From the Settings app.** Choose Set Defaults by App at the bottom of the Default Apps pane in the Settings app.

■ **From the Start menu.** Right-click or long-press Start, click Control Panel, click Programs, and then click Set Your Default Programs.

On the Set Default Programs screen (see Figure 9.23), click the app in the Programs list on the left. You can then click Set This Program as Default to set the app as the default app for all the file types and protocols it can handle, or click Choose Defaults for This Program to choose just those file types and protocols you want.

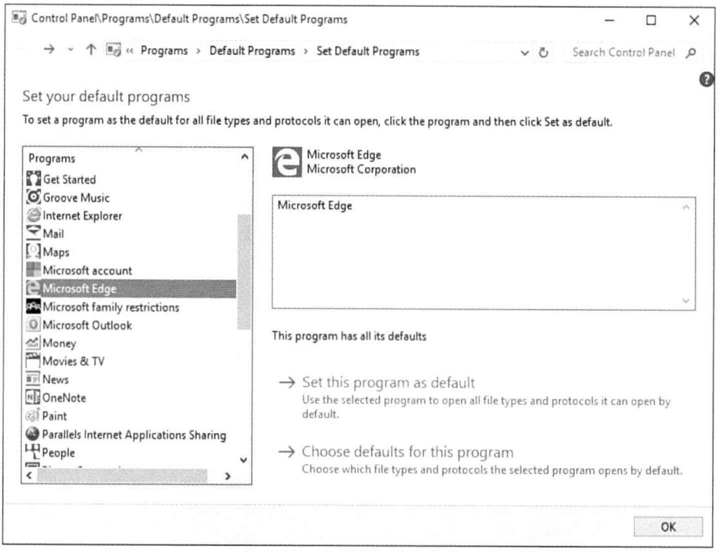

FIGURE 9.23

On the Set Default Programs screen in Control Panel, select the app you want to affect. You can then click Set This Program as Default to use the program for all its file types and protocols or click Choose Defaults for This Program to choose individual file types and protocols.

If you click Choose Defaults for This Program, Control Panel displays the Set Program Associations screen (see Figure 9.24). Check the appropriate check boxes in the Extensions list and in the Protocols list, and then click the Save button to save the changes.

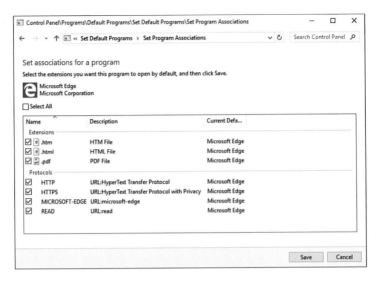

FIGURE 9.24

On the Set Program Associations screen in Control Panel, check the boxes for the file extensions and protocols for which you want this app to be the default app, and then click the Save button.

OPENING A FILE IN A NON-DEFAULT APP AND CHANGING THE DEFAULT APP

Default apps are handy, but you'll likely sometimes want to open a file in a different app than the default app. To do so, follow these steps:

1. Open a File Explorer window to the folder that contains the file you want to open. (If the file is on the desktop, you can work directly there—no need to open a File Explorer window.)

2. Right-click or long-press the file to display the shortcut menu.

3. Click Open With to display the Open With submenu (see Figure 9.25).

4. If the app you want to use appears on the Open With submenu, click it.

If the Open With submenu doesn't show the app you want to use, click Choose Another App to display the How Do You Want to Open This File? dialog box (see Figure 9.26). From here, you can take three actions:

■ **Click Look for an App in the Store.** Click this button and then click OK to launch the Store app and search for apps that can handle the file extension of the file you clicked.

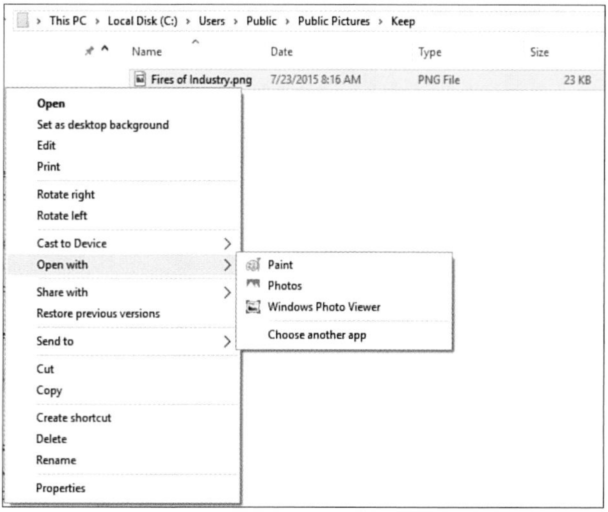

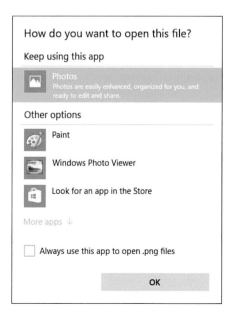

FIGURE 9.25

Use the Open With submenu on the shortcut menu to open a file in an app other than the default app.

FIGURE 9.26

In the How Do You Want to Open This File? dialog box, choose the app you want to use. You can check the Always Use This App to Open Files check box to change the default app.

■ **Click More Apps to display other possible apps.** Click this button to display any more apps that Windows thinks can handle this file type but that Windows isn't displaying on the Open With submenu. If one of the apps is the one you want, click it and then click OK to open the file in it.

!CAUTION If you open the file in one of the apps listed under More Apps, Windows adds that app to the Open With submenu. This is fine if you've chosen the right app, but it can be a problem if you've picked the wrong app.

Some of the apps on the More Apps list may be wild guesses. For example, on the computer shown in these screens, Windows suggests Notepad and WordPad as apps that can open a PNG image file. Both Notepad and WordPad *can* open a PNG file—but each opens it as if it were text, displaying a lengthy document of gibberish characters.

If you choose the wrong app, you can remove it as explained in the nearby sidebar "Remove an App from the Open With Submenu."

■ **Change the default app.** If you want to change the default app for the file type, click the app in the list, check the Always Use This App to Open Files check box, and then click OK.

NOTE Changing the default app as explained here removes the corresponding default app in the Default Apps pane in the Settings app. For example, if you use this technique to change the default app for PNG files from the Photos app to the Paint app, Windows removes Photos from the Photo Viewer setting on the Default Apps list. But Windows doesn't make Paint the default app for Photo Viewer.

REMOVE AN APP FROM THE OPEN WITH SUBMENU

If you put the wrong app on the Open With submenu, you can remove it by using Registry Editor. See the section "Making Advanced Changes by Editing the Registry" in Chapter 14 for details.

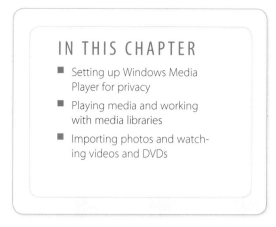

IN THIS CHAPTER

- Setting up Windows Media Player for privacy
- Playing media and working with media libraries
- Importing photos and watching videos and DVDs

10

ENJOYING MUSIC, PHOTOS, AND VIDEOS

Windows 10 includes apps to help you enjoy music, photos, and videos on your computer—and share them with others. In this chapter, we'll look at how to set up Windows Media Player without compromising your privacy, how you can put your existing music on your computer, and how to watch videos and DVDs. We'll also explore the Groove Music app and the Groove music service.

UNDERSTANDING WINDOWS MEDIA PLAYER AND GROOVE MUSIC

Windows comes with two main apps that you can use for playing music:

- **Windows Media Player.** Windows Media Player is the main music tool for Windows. Windows Media Player enables you to rip songs from your CDs, organize your songs into a music library, and play back music or burn

it to CD. Windows Media Player also enables you to organize and view your photos and your video files.

■ **Groove Music.** Groove Music is an app that connects to Microsoft's Groove online service. Groove Music can also play your music both from your computer and from your account on Microsoft's OneDrive storage service.

We'll look at Windows Media Player in detail and then quickly go over the key features of Groove Music.

USING WINDOWS MEDIA PLAYER

Windows Media Player enables you to manage your music, photos, and videos in a single app. This section covers the most widely useful features of Windows Media Player and those that cause the most problems—starting with the configuration choices you must make before you can use Windows Media Player at all.

To get started, choose Start, All Apps, Windows Media Player to launch Windows Media Player.

SETTING UP WINDOWS MEDIA PLAYER TO PROTECT YOUR PRIVACY

The first time you run Windows Media Player, you have to go through its setup routine. The Welcome to Windows Media Player screen appears (see Figure 10.1), offering you the choice between the Recommended Settings option button and the Custom Settings option button.

> **NOTE** If you have already set up Windows Media Player, you can change the privacy settings by choosing Organize, Options and then working on the Privacy tab in the Options dialog box.

If you select the Recommended Settings option button, you simply need to click the Finish button to finish setting up Windows Media Player. But usually you'll do better to select the Custom Settings option button and click the Next button (the Next button replaces the Finish button when you select the Custom Settings option button) so that you can choose settings that suit you.

In the Select Privacy Options dialog box that appears (see Figure 10.2), you can configure the following settings:

- **Display Media Information from the Internet.** Uncheck this check box unless you want Windows Media Player to attempt to retrieve information from the Internet for every song you play and every video you watch. Retrieving this information gives Microsoft or its business partners not only the details of the media you play but also your identifying information.

FIGURE 10.1

In the Welcome to Windows Media Player dialog box, select the Custom Settings option button if you want to reduce the amount of personally identifiable information you share with Microsoft and its business partners.

! CAUTION If you check the Display Media Information from the Internet check box, Windows Media Player may display ads containing offers for the song or video you're playing or for related items.

NOTE If you want to read the privacy statements for Windows Media Player and for Microsoft's WindowsMedia.com site (which provides Internet radio stations), click the Privacy Statement tab of the Select Privacy Options dialog box, and then click the upper View Statement button (for Windows Media Player) or the lower View Statement button (for WindowsMedia.com). You can also read the Windows Media Player privacy statement online by clicking the Read the Privacy Statement Online link on the Privacy tab of the Options dialog box for Windows Media Player.

FIGURE 10.2

Choose settings on the Privacy Options tab of the Select Privacy Options dialog box. Click the Privacy Statement tab if you want to read the privacy statement.

- **Update Music Files by Retrieving Media Information from the Internet.** Check this check box if you want Windows Media Player to download tag information about music files you import (rip) from CD or add directly to your media library. This option is usually helpful, because otherwise you must type in the tag information for CDs manually.

- **Download Usage Rights Automatically When I Play or Sync a File.** Check this check box if you want Windows Media Player to automatically download a usage rights license when you try to play a song or a video that has restricted usage permissions.

> **TIP** Uncheck the Download Usage Rights Automatically When I Play or Sync a File check box. Windows Media Player then prompts you to download usage rights when you try to play a file that needs them. You can then decide whether to download the usage rights, simply not play the file, or perhaps get rid of the file.

- **Send Unique Player ID to Content Providers.** Check this check box only if you want Windows Media Player to send a number that uniquely identifies your Windows account and your computer to Microsoft and its partners when Windows Media Player retrieves information from them.

> **⚠ CAUTION** The Send Unique Player ID to Content Providers feature is highly intrusive. Normally, you would want to make sure this check box is unchecked.

- **I Want to Help Make Microsoft Software and Services Even Better by Sending Player Usage Data to Microsoft.** Check this check box if you want Windows Media Player to share details of how you use the app to Microsoft. This information uniquely identifies your Windows account and your computer.

> **⚠ CAUTION** The "I Want to Help…" option is neatly phrased to encourage you to share information with Microsoft, but bear in mind that doing so intrudes fairly heavily on your privacy.

- **Store and Display a List of Recently/Frequently Played.** In this area, check or uncheck the Music check box, the Pictures check box, the Video check box, and the Playlists check box, as needed. You might want to try checking these check boxes and seeing whether you find the list of recently played and frequently played items useful; if the list isn't useful to you, open the Options dialog box, click the Privacy tab, and then turn off this tracking.

After making your choices in the Select Privacy Options dialog box, click the Next button to display the Select the Default Music and Video Player dialog box (see Figure 10.3). Here, you can choose whether to make Windows Media Player the default player for all the music and video file types it can handle or whether to choose specific file types for Windows Media Player.

If you want to use Windows Media Player for all the file types, select the Make Windows Media Player the Default Music and Video Player option button, and then click the Finish button. Windows Media Player then opens.

If you want to use other media players as well, select the Choose the File Types That Windows Media Player Will Play option button, and then click the Finish button. Windows then displays a dialog box telling you to choose Settings, System, Default Apps to change your default apps; click the OK button to dismiss the dialog box. You'll then see the Windows Media Player window.

FIGURE 10.3

In the Select the Default Music and Video Player dialog box, choose whether to use Windows Media Player for all the music and video file types it can handle or only for those you specify.

> **NOTE** See the section "Setting the Default Apps You Need" in Chapter 9 for instructions on setting default apps. The subsection called "Choosing Default Apps by Apps" explains the procedure you would use to set the file types for which you want to use Windows Media Player as the default player.

NAVIGATING WINDOWS MEDIA PLAYER

After you've finished the initial setup routine, the Windows Media Player window appears (see Figure 10.4). Most likely, you'll find this easy to navigate. These are the main features:

- **Path bar.** This bar shows your current location, such as Library > Music > Artist > Angelfish. As in a File Explorer window, you can click an earlier item in the path to return to it; for example, here you can click Artist to display the Artist screen, click Music to display the Music library, or click Library to display the Library folder.

- **Organize button.** This button gives you access to the main menu, which includes commands for managing libraries, changing the layout, and opening the Options dialog box.

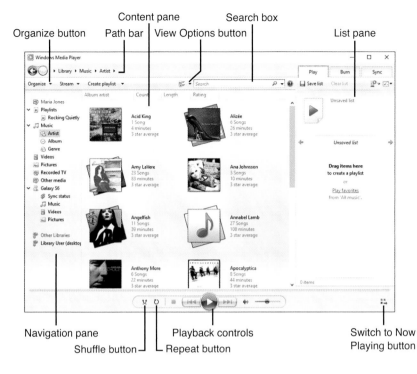

FIGURE 10.4

Windows Media Player has a straightforward interface.

- **View Options button.** This button enables you to choose the view to use for the Content pane. For example, with the Music library selected, you can choose between Expanded Tile view (which shows CD covers with brief details and the track list) and Details view (which shows a more straightforward list of tracks).

- **Navigation pane.** This pane enables you to navigate among libraries and through their contents. Your own library appears at the top of the pane, with the Playlists category, the Music category, the Videos category, and the Pictures category below it. You can click an item to display its contents in the Content pane.

TIP You can customize the Navigation pane to contain the items you want. For example, you can add columns such as Year or Composer for music items, Genre or Rating for videos, and Tags or Date Taken for photos. Choose Organize, Customize Navigation Pane to open the Customize Navigation Pane dialog box, check the box for each column you want to show, and then click the OK button.

- **Content pane.** This pane shows the contents of the item you have selected in the Navigation pane.
- **List pane.** This pane displays the current list for playing, burning, or syncing, depending on whether the Play tab, the Burn tab, or the Sync tab is displayed.

NOTE You can toggle the display of the List pane by choosing Organize, Layout, Show List (either placing a check mark next to the Show List item or removing the existing check mark). You can also hide the List pane by clicking the List Options button (the button with the check mark icon and a drop-down arrow, on the right side of the bar across the top of the List pane) and then clicking Hide List on the drop-down menu.

- **Search box.** Click here and type your search terms to search the current selection.
- **Shuffle button.** Click this button to play the items in a random order.
- **Repeat button.** Click this button to turn repeating on or off.
- **Playback controls.** Use these controls to manage playback as usual.
- **Switch to Now Playing button.** Click this button to switch to Now Playing view, which provides a compact interface to enable you to focus on other apps while enjoying music. The left screen in Figure 10.5 shows Now Playing view as it first appears; the right screen shows the controls that appear when you move the mouse pointer over the Now Playing window.

ADDING YOUR MUSIC TO WINDOWS MEDIA PLAYER

Before you can listen to your music in Windows Media Player, you must add your music to your Music library. Windows Media Player automatically loads all the files in your Music library, but you can also import files from other locations if needed.

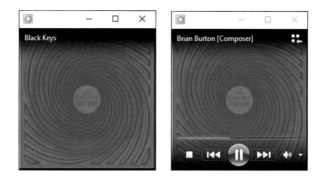

FIGURE 10.5

You can switch Windows Media Player to Now Playing view (left) when you want to focus on other apps. When you need the playback controls, move the mouse pointer over the Now Playing window (right).

WHERE IS YOUR MUSIC LIBRARY?

Your Music library is normally stored in the Music folder within your account, which itself is stored in the Users folder on your computer's system drive. For example, if your account is named Maria and your computer's system drive is drive C:, your Music library would be stored in the C:\Users\Maria\Music folder.

If you use OneDrive, the local OneDrive folder is usually stored in your account's folder, with the OneDrive Music folder inside it. So continuing the preceding example, your OneDrive Music folder would be stored in the C:\Users\Maria\OneDrive\Music folder.

If you have set up a OneDrive account on your computer, the Music library includes the OneDrive Music folder as well. So any songs you have stored in your OneDrive Music folder appear in Windows Media Player.

ADDING YOUR EXISTING MUSIC FILES TO WINDOWS MEDIA PLAYER

The normal way to add music files to Windows Media Player is to place those files in your Music library. You can place the files in the library in two ways:

- **Add the files to a folder in the Music library.** The most straightforward way is to put the files in a folder that already belongs to the Music library. For example, because your Music library is stored in the \Music\ folder in your user account, any subfolder you create in the \Music\ folder also becomes part of your Music library.

■ **Add the files' folder to the Music library.** You can also add other folders to the Music library using the technique you'll learn in a moment. This technique is useful for folders you can't easily place within the `\Music\` folder—for example, folders on an external drive connected to your computer.

To add a folder to the Music library, follow these steps in Windows Media Player:

1. Choose Organize, Manage Libraries, Music to open the Music Library Locations dialog box (see Figure 10.6).

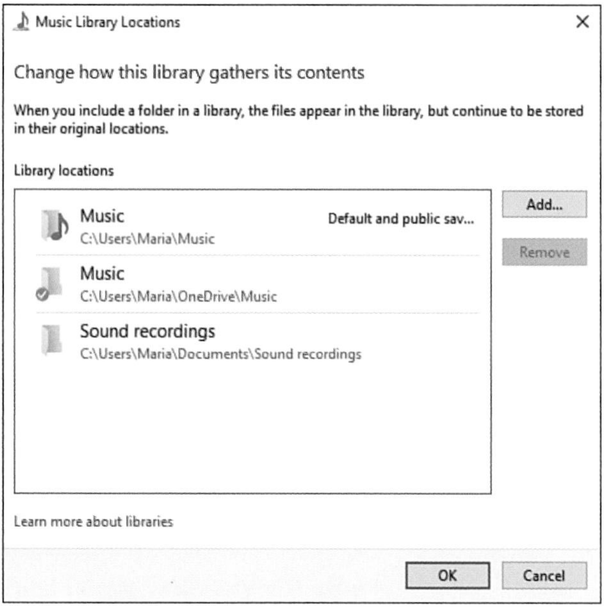

FIGURE 10.6
Click the Add button in the Music Library Locations dialog box to add a folder to your Music library.

2. Click the Add button to open the Include Folder in Music dialog box.
3. Navigate to the folder that contains the folder you want to add, and then click the folder.
4. Click the Include Folder button. Windows Media Player closes the Include Folder in Music dialog box, and the folder appears in the Music Library Locations dialog box.

> **NOTE** You can also use the Music Library Locations dialog box to remove folders from your Music Library. Just click the folder in the Library Locations list box and then click the Remove button.

5. Click the OK button to close the Music Library Locations dialog box.

> **TIP** You can also add music files that are stored in folders that are not included in your Music library. To do so, open a File Explorer window to the folder that contains the files, select the files, and then drag them to the Windows Media Player window. (You can also drag files from the desktop to the Windows Media Player window.) This technique is sometimes useful for adding stray files, but in general, you may find it better to keep your music files in the folders you include in your Music library.

CHOOSING WHICH MUSIC FORMAT TO USE FOR RIPPING FROM CD

You can choose among eight audio file formats for your music in Windows Media Player. It's important to make the right choice so that you get the audio quality you need, file sizes that are acceptable, and music that will play on all the devices you want to use.

Of the eight formats in which Windows Media Player can create audio files, the first four formats are from Microsoft and are close relations to each other:

■ **Windows Media Audio.** This is Microsoft's standard format for compressed audio. It uses lossy audio compression (see the nearby tip) to produce files that have good sound quality but only moderate file size.

> **TIP** Most audio formats use either lossless compression or lossy compression to reduce the amount of space needed for an audio file. *Lossless compression* retains the full audio quality, whereas *lossy compression* loses some of the details—preferably the details that the human ear would normally miss anyway because they're masked by other sounds. Lossy compression is adjustable, so you can choose the quality, but typically it can compress audio far more than lossless compression.

- **Windows Media Audio Pro.** This sounds like a professional version of Windows Media Audio, but it's actually designed to create smaller files for devices with less storage.
- **Windows Media Audio (Variable Bit Rate).** This is the same as the Windows Media Audio format except that it uses a variable bit rate (see the nearby note) instead of a constant bit rate.

> **NOTE** Audio encoders use several settings to determine the quality and—indirectly—the file size. The key setting is the *bit rate*, which is the number of bits (individual pieces) of data per second. The bit rate can be either constant or variable. Variable bit rate (VBR) gives better quality than constant bit rate (CBR) at the same bit rate because it can use the bits more intelligently to store the data.

- **Windows Media Audio Lossless.** If there were a professional version of Windows Media Audio, this would be it. The lossless compression gives full audio quality, but the file size is correspondingly large.

The four remaining audio formats are more or less industry standards:

- **MP3.** Technically, MP3 stands for "MPEG-1 Audio Layer III" or "MPEG-2 Audio Layer III," where "MPEG" stands for "Moving Pictures Expert Group." Most people simply use the abbreviation. MP3 is a lossy audio format that sounds okay for music at bit rates of 128Kbps and pretty good at higher bit rates, such as 256Kbps or 320Kbps.
- **WAV (Lossless).** Waveform Audio File Format (WAVE or WAV, after the three-letter file extension) is an uncompressed audio format. This means it delivers full-quality audio, but because the file sizes are huge, you would normally want to use a different lossless format instead.

> **! CAUTION** Apart from the file size, the WAV format has another disadvantage: It doesn't have containers for the tag information in which the other formats store the artist, album, song name, and so on. This means that the only way to identify WAV files is by their filenames.

- **ALAC (Lossless).** Apple Lossless Audio Coding, also known as Apple Lossless Encoding, is a lossless compressed audio format developed by Apple. Like other lossless audio formats, ALAC gives full quality at the cost of a large file size.

> **☑ TIP** As you might expect, Apple's hardware and software products all support ALAC. So if you use an iPhone, an iPad, or an iPod, ALAC is a fine choice—provided that you're prepared to sacrifice quantity of music for quality of music. Even the iPod shuffle, which has space for only around four hours' worth of ALAC files, can play back ALAC.

■ **FLAC.** Free Lossless Audio Codec (FLAC) is a lossless compression format. FLAC delivers full-quality sound, but its files are large.

> **✎ NOTE** FLAC is an open-source format, which means that anyone can use it without paying licensing fees. By contrast, MP3 and the Windows Media Audio formats are proprietary and require the payment of licensing fees. Usually, the manufacturers of the devices pay these fees, so you, as the user of a device, don't need to pay.

CONFIGURING WINDOWS MEDIA PLAYER TO RIP CDS

Before you use Windows Media Player to rip audio files from your CDs, take a minute to choose suitable settings. Follow these steps:

1. In Windows Media Player, choose Organize, Options to display the Options dialog box.

2. Click the Rip Music tab to display its contents (shown on the left in Figure 10.7).

3. Look at the folder shown in the Rip Music to This Location box. Normally, the folder will be the `Music` folder in your user account. If you want to change the location, click the Change button to open the Browse for Folder dialog box, navigate to and select the appropriate folder, and then click the OK button.

4. Click the File Name button to display the File Name Options dialog box (shown on the right in Figure 10.7). Use its controls to specify how you want Windows Media Player to name the ripped files, and then click OK to close it.

5. In the Rip Settings area, open the Format drop-down menu and choose the format you want: Windows Media Audio, Windows Media Audio Pro, Windows Media Audio (Variable Bit Rate), Windows Media Audio Lossless,

MP3, WAV (Lossless), ALAC (Lossless), or FLAC (Lossless). Look back to the preceding section, "Choosing Which Music Format to Use for Ripping from CD," for details on these formats and advice about which to use.

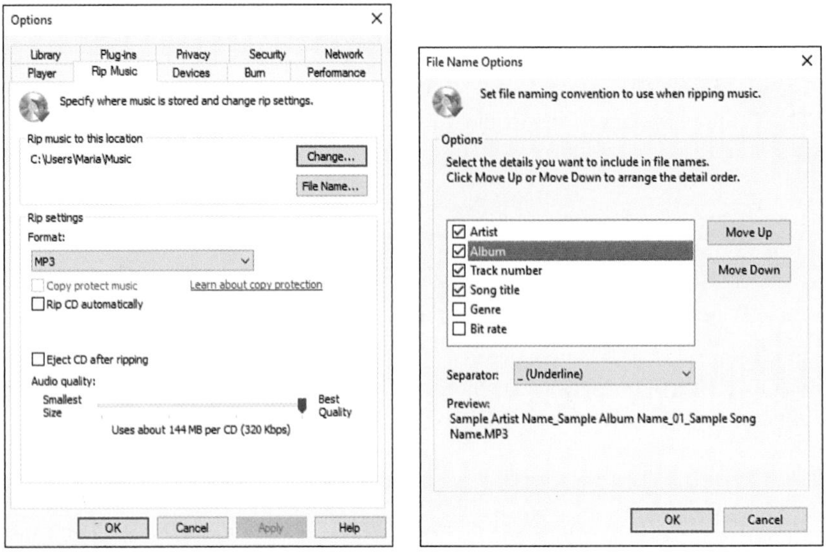

FIGURE 10.7

Choose settings on the Rip Music tab of the Options dialog box (left) before you rip your CDs with Windows Media Player. Use the File Name Options dialog box (right) to tell Windows Media Player how to name the song files.

NOTE For any of the Windows Media Audio formats, you can check the Copy Protect Music check box if you need to prevent yourself from inadvertently sharing the music files with other people without having authorization to do so. Checking this check box makes Windows Media Player apply digital-rights management (DRM) to the files you rip. The other four formats, such as MP3 and FLAC, do not support DRM, so this check box is unavailable when you select one of these formats.

6. Check the Rip CD Automatically check box if you want Windows Media Player to rip each audio CD automatically when you insert it.

> **✓ TIP** The Rip CD Automatically feature can be useful for building your music library quickly, but it prevents you from verifying that the CD's information is correct before ripping the files. If you want to verify the CD's information (for example, to fix any incorrect song names), uncheck this check box.

7. Check the Eject CD After Ripping check box if you want Windows Media Player to make your CD drive eject the CD when it finishes the ripping.

> **! CAUTION** Check the Eject CD After Ripping check box only if your computer's optical drive always has enough space to open safely. On a laptop, it's best to uncheck this check box in case the optical drive may sometimes be obstructed.

8. Drag the Audio Quality slider along the Smallest Size–Best Quality axis to the point that suits you best.

> **✓ TIP** If time permits, try ripping the same set of songs at different audio qualities, listen to them using your normal listening device (such as headphones), and see which quality you prefer.

9. Click the OK button to apply your changes and close the Options dialog box.

RIPPING CDS WITH WINDOWS MEDIA PLAYER

After you've configured Windows Media Player with suitable settings for ripping CDs, you can insert a CD and rip music files from it.

Click the entry for the optical drive in the Navigation pane on the left of the Windows Media Player window to display the CD's tracks (see Figure 10.8). Windows Media Player automatically checks the check box for each track by default. You can uncheck the check box for any track you don't want to rip, or uncheck the check box in the Album column heading to uncheck all the check boxes if you want to check just a few.

FIGURE 10.8

Insert a CD, choose which songs to rip in Windows Media Player, and then click the Rip CD button on the toolbar to start ripping.

TIP   You can adjust your ripping settings by using the Rip Settings drop-down menu on the Windows Media Player toolbar after selecting an audio CD in the Navigation pane. (If you don't see the Rip Settings drop-down menu, click the arrows to the right of the Rip CD button.) Use the Format submenu to change the format, or use the Audio Quality to change the bit rate within that format. Click Rip CD Automatically, placing a check mark next to this item, to turn on automatic ripping as soon as you insert the CD. Click Eject CD After Ripping, placing a check mark next to this item, to eject the CD automatically after ripping.

After choosing the songs you want to rip, click the Rip CD button on the toolbar to start ripping.

HAVING TROUBLE POWERING AN EXTERNAL USB DRIVE?

If your computer's USB port doesn't deliver enough power for an external optical drive, here are five solutions to try.

First, if your computer is a laptop or a tablet, try connecting it to power. Doing so may increase the amount of power the USB port delivers.

Second, if your computer has multiple USB ports, try another port. Depending on the computer, some ports may deliver more power than others.

Third—again for a computer with multiple USB ports—try using a Y cable, one that has two USB connectors at the end that connects to the computer. Two ports may deliver enough power when one doesn't. If your optical drive didn't come with a Y cable, you'll need to get one.

Fourth, connect a powered USB hub to your computer, and connect the optical drive to the hub. Read the hub's documentation to find out whether some ports deliver more power than others.

Fifth, connect a powered USB hub *and* use a Y cable.

PLAYING MUSIC WITH WINDOWS MEDIA PLAYER

After you've added your music to your Music library, playing music is easy: Navigate to the music you want to play, by using the Navigation pane and the Content pane, and then double-click a song to set it playing. You can then control playback using the controls at the bottom of the Windows Media Player window.

To play songs in your preferred order, you can create playlists. To create a playlist, follow these steps:

1. Click the Play tab to display its controls. (If the List pane was hidden, clicking the Play tab displays it.)

2. If the Play tab already contains songs, click the Clear List button at the top of the List pane (unless you want to keep the songs).

3. Drag songs from the Content pane to the List pane.

4. Drag songs up and down the List pane to get them into the order you want.

5. Click the Save List button, type the name for the list in the text box that appears, and then press Enter or click elsewhere.

Windows Media Player adds the playlist to the Playlists list in the Navigation pane, and you can play it from there.

SYNCING MUSIC WITH YOUR PHONE OR TABLET

If your phone or tablet comes with an app for syncing media and other content from a PC, you'll normally do best to use that app for adding music to the device. For example, if you have an iPhone, you'll normally want to use Apple's iTunes app to sync music. iTunes is free, and you can download the latest version from the Apple website (www.apple.com/itunes/download). Similarly, Samsung provides an app called Smart Switch (www.samsung.com/smartswitch) for syncing content to its latest phones and tablets and an app called Kies (go to www.samsung.com and search for Kies) for older phones and tablets.

If your device's manufacturer doesn't offer such an app, you can use Windows Media Player to sync music to your device. Connect the device to your computer, turn it on (or wake it if it's dozing), and unlock it if it's locked. Open Windows Media Player and wait for it to identify the device.

After Windows Media Player has recognized the device, you can click the Sync tab to display the Sync pane and set up the list of files you want to sync to the device (see Figure 10.9). Drag files from the Content pane to the List pane as usual, and then drag them into the order you want. When the list is ready for syncing, click the Start Sync button on the toolbar at the top of the List pane to start the sync.

FIGURE 10.9
After connecting your phone or tablet to your computer, you can set up the list of files to sync on the Sync tab. Click the Start Sync button to start the sync running.

SQUEEZING MORE MUSIC AND VIDEO ONTO YOUR PHONE OR TABLET

To pack more music and video files on your phone or tablet, you can select a maximum quality level for music or a maximum quality level for videos and TV shows.

To do so, connect the device; choose Organize, Options to display the Options dialog box; and then click the Devices tab to display its controls. In the Devices box, double-click the device (or, if you prefer, click the device and then click the Properties button) to display the Properties dialog box for the device.

Click the Quality tab to display its controls. Then, in the Music box, click the Select Maximum Quality Level option button and drag the slider to the appropriate position on the Smallest Size—Best Quality axis. Next, go to the Videos and TV Shows box, click the Select Maximum Quality Level option button there too, and drag this box's slider to the appropriate position. Click the OK button to close the Properties dialog box, and then click the OK button to close the Options dialog box.

IMPORTING PHOTOS AND VIDEOS USING WINDOWS MEDIA PLAYER

After Windows Media Player has established a connection to your phone or tablet, you can use Windows Media Player to import photos and videos from the device into your Pictures library and your Videos library. Follow these steps to import pictures; the process for videos is similar but (as you'd expect) involves the Videos collection instead of the Pictures collection:

1. Connect your device to your computer.
2. Open Windows Media Player if it's not already open; if it is open, make it active.
3. In the Navigation pane, double-click the entry for your device to display its contents.
4. Click the Picture item under your device. The Content pane displays thumbnails, tiles, or details of the pictures on the device, depending on the view you are using. (To change the view, click the View Options button to the left of the Search box and then click Icon, Tile, or Details on the menu.)
5. Click the Sync tab of the List pane to display its controls.
6. Drag the appropriate pictures to the Sync List area on the Sync tab.
7. Click the Copy to Device button on the toolbar at the top of the List pane. Windows Media Player copies the pictures to your Pictures library.

SHARING MEDIA LIBRARIES

Windows Media Player enables you to share your media libraries with other people on your network, such as your family members. Similarly, you can connect to the media libraries that other people share.

SHARING YOUR MEDIA LIBRARY

To share your media library with other people on your network, you need to turn on media streaming. You do this by working on the Advanced Sharing Settings screen in Control Center. Follow these steps:

1. Right-click or long-press the Network icon in the notification area to display the shortcut menu.

NOTE You can also open the Network and Sharing Center screen by right-clicking or long-pressing Start, clicking Control Panel, clicking Network and Internet, and then clicking Network and Sharing Center.

2. Click Open Network and Sharing Center to open a Control Panel window showing the Network and Sharing Center screen.

3. In the left column, click the Change Advanced Sharing Settings link to display the Advanced Sharing Settings screen.

4. Click the All Networks heading to expand its contents (see Figure 10.10).

5. Click the Choose Media Streaming Options link to display the Media Streaming Options screen (see Figure 10.11).

6. Click the Turn On Media Streaming button. The Media Streaming Options screen displays the Choose Media Streaming Options for Computers and Devices controls (see Figure 10.12).

7. In the Name Your Media Library box, type the name under which you want your media library to appear on the network. You might want to use your name for easy identification, or you might prefer a brief description of the types of content you're sharing.

NOTE Make sure the Show Devices On drop-down list is set to Local Network rather than All Networks if you're choosing settings for your local network.

TIP By default, your computer shares all its media. If you want to change the default sharing settings, click the Choose Default Settings link and work in the Default Media Streaming Settings dialog box. Apart from its name, this dialog box is the same as the Customize Media Streaming Settings dialog box, which you'll meet shortly.

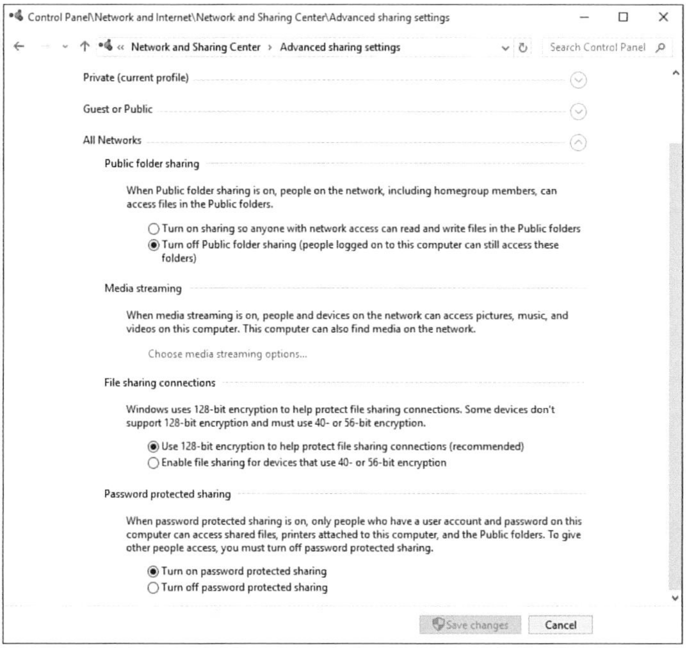

FIGURE 10.10
On the Advanced Sharing Settings screen, expand the All Networks section, and then click the Choose Media Streaming Options link.

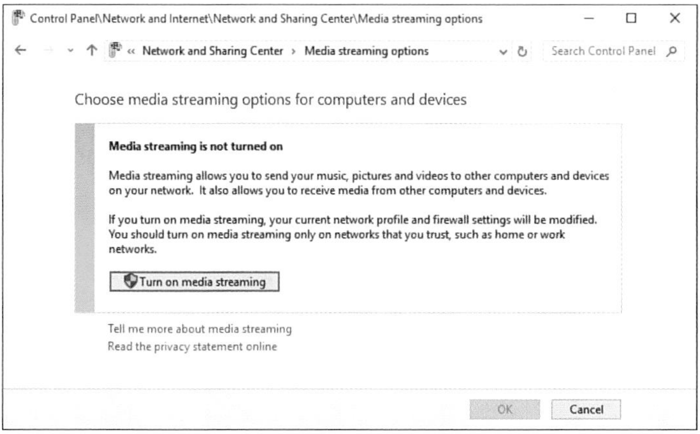

FIGURE 10.11
On the Media Streaming Options screen, click the Turn On Media Streaming button.

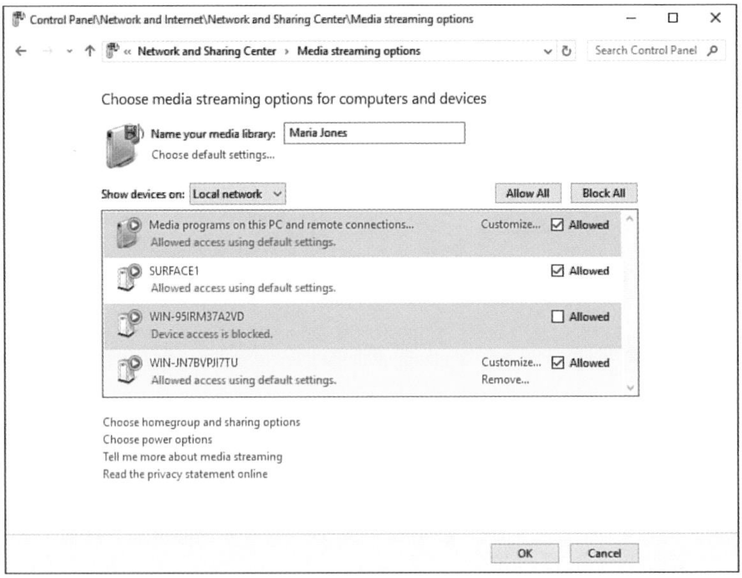

FIGURE 10.12

Use the Choose Media Streaming Options for Computers and Devices controls to specify which devices may access your media library.

8. In the large list box, choose which devices may access your content. You can click the Allow All button to check the check box for each device, or click the Block All button to block all of them; or you can check or uncheck each individual computer's Allowed check box as needed.

9. If you need to customize the content available to a particular device, click it (or hold the mouse pointer over it) and then click the Customize link that appears. In the Customize Media Streaming Settings dialog box that opens (see Figure 10.13), uncheck the Use Default Settings check box, and then use the other controls to specify which content to share. When you finish, click the OK button to close the Customize Media Streaming Settings dialog box.

10. Click the OK button to finish working on the Media Streaming Options screen.

11. Click the Close button (the × button at the right end of the title bar) to close the Advanced Sharing Settings window.

Other computers on the network can now access the media you're sharing—provided that media streaming is enabled on them.

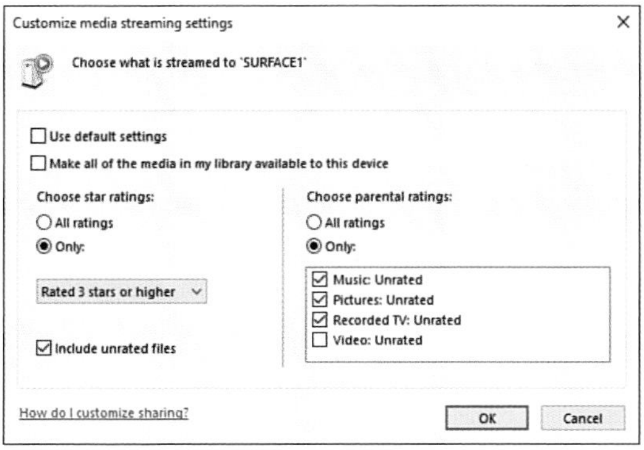

FIGURE 10.13

Use the controls in the Customize Media Streaming Settings dialog box to specify which content a particular device can access.

USING SHARED MEDIA LIBRARIES

After you enable media streaming, you can connect to and use the media libraries that other computers are sharing on your network.

To connect to a shared library, simply double-click its name in the Other Libraries section of the Navigation pane in Windows Media Player. You can then click the collection you want to browse (such as Music), and then explore and play its content.

SHARING MEDIA FILES VIA NETWORK ATTACHED STORAGE

Sharing your media via Windows Media Player works well provided that the sharing computers are always connected to the network and always powered on when people want to enjoy the media files. But if the computers involved are laptops or tablets, or if they're desktops that you don't want to leave running all the time, you may want to look at the alternative, which is to share your files via a network attached storage (NAS) device. This device is essentially a minimalist computer with plenty of storage, usually spinning hard drives rather than solid-state devices (which cost much more for the same capacity).

Many types of NAS devices are available to suit different needs and pockets. Some come with custom setup software, but most enable you to configure them via a web browser.

One quick warning: Take a few minutes to configure the security settings on your NAS device. Many NAS devices allow you to access your content remotely via the Internet. This can be a great feature, but you must secure it with a strong password or passcode so that would-be intruders cannot access it too.

Out of the box, some NAS devices may be accessible from the Internet without any security. Unless you're certain you need Internet access, it's much safer to disable it, allowing only devices on your local network to connect to the NAS device.

EXPLORING THE GROOVE MUSIC APP AND THE GROOVE SERVICE

Groove Music is an app included with most versions of Windows 10. Groove Music enables you to play music in three ways:

- **Stream music from the Groove service.** Groove is a streaming music service run by Microsoft. You can play any of a wide range of music genres by streaming it across the Internet, but you must sign up for a subscription to Groove. You can get a 30-day trial to see whether Groove suits you.
- **Play music stored on your computer.** If you have added music files to your computer, you can use Groove to play them.
- **Play music you've stored on OneDrive.** You can upload your music files to your storage on OneDrive to make the files available to any of your devices anytime those devices have an Internet connection.

> **NOTE** The Groove streaming service started off as Zune Music, and then changed to Xbox Music before becoming Groove.

GETTING STARTED WITH GROOVE MUSIC

To get started with Groove Music, launch the app by clicking Start and then clicking the Groove Music tile. If there's no Groove Music tile, choose Start, All Apps, Groove Music.

The first time you launch Groove Music, the app displays the Welcome to Groove screen (see Figure 10.14). From here, you can click three buttons:

- **Go to Collection.** Click this button to go to the music you've added to Groove. Likely enough, there'll be no music at first, but you can fix this. See the section "Adding Music to Your Groove Music Collection," later in this chapter, for details.

FIGURE 10.14

From the Welcome to Groove screen, you can access your local music collection, sign up for a Groove Music Pass, or upload your music to OneDrive.

- **Get a Groove Music Pass.** Click this button to launch the Store app, which displays the Groove Music Pass screen. Click the Start a Free Trial button to begin the process of signing up for a free 30-day trial subscription. You then sign in with your Microsoft account and choose the payment method you want to impoverish after the free trial ends.

> **! CAUTION** The same caution applies to Groove as to any free trial that requires you to provide a payment method: When signing up, make a note in your calendar to review your subscription before the end of the trial period, and cancel in good time if you don't want to start paying.

> **NOTE** If you're considering signing up for Groove, you may want to
> investigate other online music services, such as Spotify (www.spotify.com) or
> Apple Music (www.apple.com/music). Some services, such as Spotify, offer free,
> ad-supported levels as well as subscription plans.

■ **Get Started.** Click this button to open a Microsoft Edge window to the
Groove area in OneDrive so that you can upload songs from your computer
to OneDrive. Click the Add Songs to OneDrive button to display the `Music`
folder. You can then drag music files from a File Explorer window to the
Microsoft Edge window to add the files to OneDrive.

ADDING MUSIC TO YOUR GROOVE MUSIC COLLECTION

To add your existing music to your Groove Music collection, click the Go to
Collection button. Groove Music automatically searches through the folders in your
Music library and displays the screen shown in Figure 10.15.

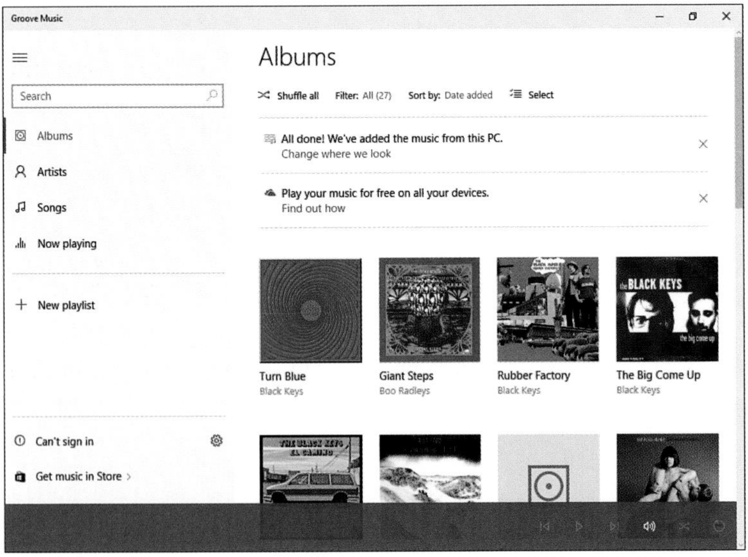

FIGURE 10.15
On the Music screen, you can click the Change Where We Look link to change the folders included
in your Music library.

If you need to add other folders, follow these steps:

1. Click the Change Where We Look link to display the Build Your Collection from Your Local Music Files dialog box (see Figure 10.16).

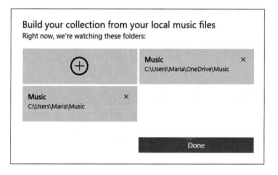

Build your collection from your local music files
Right now, we're watching these folders:

⊕

Music   ×
C:\Users\Maria\OneDrive\Music

Music   ×
C:\Users\Maria\Music

Done

FIGURE 10.16

In the Build Your Collection from Your Local Music Files dialog box, click the Add (+) button to add a folder to your Music library.

2. Click the Add (+) button to display the Select Folder dialog box.
3. Navigate to the folder you want to add, and then click it.
4. Click the Add This Folder to Music button to add the folder to your Music library.

> **NOTE** To remove a folder from your Music library, click its Delete (×) button in the Build Your Collection from Your Local Music Files dialog box, and then click the Remove Folder button in the Remove This Folder? dialog box that opens.

5. Click the Done button to close the Build Your Collection from Your Local Music Files dialog box.

> **NOTE** Groove Music doesn't include a feature for ripping songs from CD. Instead, use Windows Media Player to rip CDs, as explained in the section "Ripping CDs with Windows Media Player," earlier in this chapter.

PLAYING MUSIC WITH GROOVE MUSIC

After you've added all your music files to Groove Music, you can easily play the music.

In the Navigation pane, click the Albums button, the Artists button, or the Songs button to change to the view by which you want to browse. You can then double-click an artist or an album to display the available tracks, and double-click a track to start it playing. After that, you can use the controls at the bottom of the Groove Music window (see Figure 10.17) to control playback.

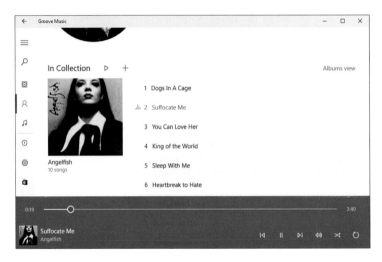

FIGURE 10.17

After starting a song playing, use the controls at the bottom of the Groove Music window to control playback.

CREATING PLAYLISTS IN GROOVE MUSIC

Groove Music enables you to create playlists to play back songs in your preferred order. Follow these steps to start a playlist:

1. Navigate to the first song you want to include.

2. Right-click or long-press the song to display the shortcut menu.

3. Click or highlight Add To on the shortcut menu, and then click New Playlist on the Add To submenu. The Name This Playlist dialog box opens.

4. Type the name for the new playlist.

5. Click the Save button.

Now that you've created the playlist, it appears on the Add To submenu, so you can easily add another song to it by right-clicking or long-pressing the song, clicking or highlighting Add To on the shortcut menu, and then clicking the playlist's name.

To play the playlist, click its name in the Navigation pane, and then double-click the song you want to start playing.

> **TIP** If you have playlists in iTunes, you can import them into Groove Music. To do so, click the Settings button (the gear icon) in the Navigation pane, and then click the Import iTunes Playlists link in the Settings pane.

WATCHING VIDEOS AND DVDS

You can use Windows Media Player to watch videos: Simply click the Videos collection in the Navigation pane, locate the video you want to play, and then double-click it to start it playing.

Windows Media Player doesn't play DVDs—in fact, Windows 10 doesn't include an app for playing DVDs. Given that fewer and fewer computers now have a built-in optical drive, this is arguably fair enough, but the main reason Windows lacks a DVD-playing app is more likely the cost of licensing one.

Microsoft's solution for playing DVDs is the app called Windows DVD Player, which costs $14.99 from the Microsoft Store. At this writing, Windows DVD Player provides only minimal features, so you may prefer to look elsewhere.

> **NOTE** If you upgrade to Windows 10 from a version of Windows that includes Windows Media Center, you should get DVD Player free as part of the upgrade. Check to see if it's available for your version of Windows—or if Microsoft is offering it for free, as it sometimes does.

Generally speaking, you're better off using the third-party app called VLC for playing back DVDs—and perhaps other video files, because VLC can play back an impressively wide range of formats. You can download VLC free from the VideoLAN Organization website (http://www.videolan.org).

CONNECTING YOUR COMPUTER TO YOUR TV

If you have a large-screen TV, you likely want to connect your computer to your TV so that you can watch your movies and DVDs on it. Windows 10 makes this easy as long as you have the right type of cable, so check the inputs on the TV and the outputs on your computer and then dig in the box where you keep your cables and converters.

If you have a choice of connection types, HDMI is usually the best bet, because it carries both a high-definition video signal and the accompanying audio. For other connection types, such as DVI or VGA, you will need to run a separate audio cable to carry the audio from the computer to the TV.

When you connect your computer to your TV, Windows automatically detects your TV as a display. You can configure the TV as explained in the section "Sorting Out Your Displays" in Chapter 4.

IN THIS CHAPTER

- Navigating Microsoft Edge like a pro
- Controlling Microsoft Edge with keyboard shortcuts
- Configuring Microsoft Edge for comfort and security

BROWSING THE INTERNET SAFELY

Windows 10 comes with a new browser, Microsoft Edge, with which Microsoft is gradually replacing Internet Explorer. Windows 10 still includes Internet Explorer, and you can use it if you need it—for example, for websites that require Internet Explorer.

Microsoft Edge features a stripped-down interface but includes plenty of features for a full browsing experience, including favorites, Reading List, Reading mode, and the ability to annotate web pages.

NAVIGATING MICROSOFT EDGE LIKE A PRO

If you've used other web browsers, you'll have no problem coming to grips with the essentials of browsing with Microsoft Edge. The new browser has a streamlined interface (see Figure 11.1) with easy-to-find controls, most of which work in the same way as those on other browsers.

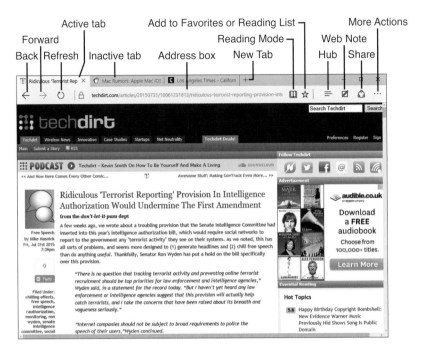

Active tab   Add to Favorites or Reading List ⌐   More Actions

Forward   Reading Mode ⌐   Web Note

Back | Refresh | Inactive tab   Address box   New Tab   Hub | Share

FIGURE 11.1

Microsoft Edge has a streamlined interface with easy-to-use controls.

The More Actions menu (see Figure 11.2), which you display by clicking the More Actions button (the three dots, …) at the right end of the toolbar, contains the following commands:

■ **New Window.** Click this item to open a new Microsoft Edge window (as opposed to a new tab in the same window). If your hands are on the keyboard, it's quicker to press Ctrl+N.

■ **New InPrivate Window.** Click this item to open a new Microsoft Edge window for InPrivate browsing. InPrivate browsing enables you to browse without saving data such as the pages you visit, temporary files used to display those pages, and cookies from the websites, beyond the end of your InPrivate browsing session.

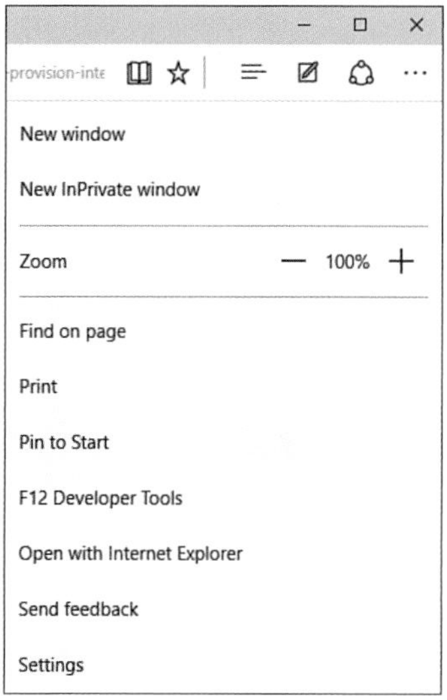

FIGURE 11.2

The Microsoft Edge More Actions menu contains only a few commands.

! CAUTION InPrivate browsing enables you to make sure the details of browsing sessions are not stored on your computer, but it doesn't confer anonymity on the Internet. As usual, your Internet service provider can determine—and may log—the pages you visit, and government agencies may be able to access any information the Internet service provider has logged.

■ **Zoom.** Click the – button to zoom out by a 25% increment or the + button to zoom in by 25%.

✓ TIP You can zoom more quickly with keyboard shortcuts. Press Ctrl+– to zoom out by 25% or Ctrl++ to zoom in by 25%, or press Ctrl+0 to zoom to 100%. For full-screen and restore, use the standard Windows keyboard shortcuts—press Windows Key+up arrow to switch to full screen and Windows Key+down arrow to restore the window.

■ **Find on Page.** Click Find on Page to display the Find on Page controls, which enable you to search for specific text on the page. You can also press Ctrl+F to display the Find on Page controls.

- **Print.** Click Print, or press the Ctrl+P keyboard shortcut, to display the Print dialog box.

- **Pin to Start.** Click this item to pin the current page to the Start menu to give you instant access to it.

- **F12 Developer Tools.** Click this item to open the Developer Tools window, which you can use for troubleshooting web page layout and script issues.

- **Open with Internet Explorer.** Click this command to open the current page in Internet Explorer.

- **Send Feedback.** Click this item to display the Feedback & Reporting pane, which enables you to send Microsoft feedback about Microsoft Edge. For example, you can report problems with a particular website, report problems with Microsoft Edge itself, or suggest features you'd like to see Microsoft add to the browser.

- **Settings.** Click Settings to open the Settings pane, which enables you to configure Microsoft Edge. See the section "Configuring Microsoft Edge for Comfort and Security," later in this chapter, for information on choosing settings.

VIEWING PAGES

As with most browsers, you can click the Address box and then type or paste in the address—the Uniform Resource Locator, or URL—of the web page you want to view. But in most cases, you're better off getting to the page in other ways, such as by clicking a link on a page you're already viewing, clicking a link in another app, or searching for what you want and then clicking a link on the page of results that the search engine produces.

> ✅ **TIP** From the keyboard, press Ctrl+L to select the current contents of the Address box. Alternatively, press F4 to select the current contents of the Address box and open the drop-down menu showing the pages you've viewed recently.

To make a page easier to view, you can zoom in and out, either by using the Zoom buttons on the More Actions menu or by using the keyboard: Press Ctrl++ to zoom in by 25% increments or press Ctrl+– to zoom out by 25% increments.

> **TIP** If your computer has a touchscreen, you can also zoom in by placing two fingers (or finger and thumb) together on the screen and then pinching apart, or zoom out by placing two digits apart on the screen and then pinching them together.

WORKING WITH TABS AND WINDOWS

As with most browsers, Microsoft Edge enables you to browse using multiple tabs within a window. Tabs are great when you're looking at separate pages that you don't need to compare with each other.

When you do need to compare two web pages with each other, you're better off using multiple windows than multiple tabs. You can then position the windows so that you can see both—for example, by snapping one window left and the other right—and compare them directly.

And you can open multiple tabs in each window if you need to—for example, when you're shopping for multiple products.

These are the moves you need to know for working with tabs and windows:

- **Open a linked page in the same tab.** Click the link. If you're navigating with the keyboard, press Tab (to move forward) or Shift+Tab (to move back) until the link is selected, and then press Enter.

- **Open a linked page in a new tab.** Either right-click the link and then click Open in New Tab on the shortcut menu, or simply Ctrl+click the link.

- **Open a new tab.** Click the New Tab button (the + button) on the tab bar or press Ctrl+T.

- **Refresh all open tabs.** Right-click a tab and then click Refresh All Tabs on the shortcut menu.

- **Rearrange your tabs.** Click a tab and drag it to where you want it.

- **Duplicate a tab.** Right-click the tab and then click Duplicate Tab. Microsoft Edge puts the duplicate tab immediately after the original tab.

> **TIP** Duplicating a tab is useful when you want to keep your current page open but also go browsing to pages linked to it. You can also duplicate a tab by pressing Ctrl+K.

- **Move a tab to a new window.** Right-click the tab and then click Move to New Window on the shortcut menu. You can also drag the tab out of the current window and onto the desktop to create a new window containing the tab.
- **Open a new window.** Press Ctrl+N.
- **Close a tab you don't need.** Click × to close the tab. You can also press Ctrl+W to close the active tab.

> **TIP** You can close multiple tabs at once in two ways. If there's just one tab you want to keep, right-click that tab, and then click Close Other Tabs on the shortcut menu. If you want to close all the tabs to the right of a particular tab, right-click that tab, and then click Close Tabs to the Right on the shortcut menu.

BROWSING FAST WITH PAGE PREDICTION

The Page Prediction feature enables you to quickly display the next page in a website by swiping across the screen or by clicking a Next button (a > arrow) that appears on the right side of the page. Similarly, you can go back by clicking the Previous button (a < arrow) on the left side of the screen. Page Prediction works only with pages designed for the feature, but you'll find quite a lot of those on the web these days.

> **TIP** If Page Prediction isn't working, you may need to enable it. Click the More Actions button, click Settings, and then click View Advanced Settings to display the Advanced Settings pane. You can then set the "Use Page Prediction to Speed Up Browsing, Improve Reading, and Make My Overall Experience Better" switch to On.

> **! CAUTION** Enabling the Page Prediction feature makes Microsoft Edge share your browsing history with Microsoft to help Microsoft improve Page Prediction.

COPYING TEXT WITH CARET BROWSING

The Caret Browsing feature enables you to select text on a web page by using the keyboard. Press F7 to toggle Caret Browsing on. Microsoft Edge displays a cursor in the text. Press the arrow keys to move the cursor to where you want to start your selection. You can then hold down Shift while you press the arrow keys to select the text you want.

After you select the text, press Ctrl+C to copy it to the Clipboard so you can paste it elsewhere. You can also copy the text by right-clicking the selection and then clicking Copy on the shortcut menu.

When you finish using Caret Browsing, press F7 to toggle it off again.

REMOVING DISTRACTIONS WITH READING MODE

When you want to focus on the text of the web page you're reading, switch to Reading mode. Reading mode hides everything except the main story, helping you avoid distractions such as ads, items at the top of the page, and items in sidebars.

To toggle Reading mode on or off, click the Reading Mode icon—the open book—at the right end of the Address box, or simply press Ctrl+Shift+R.

BROWSING THE SMART WAY WITH FAVORITES

When you find a web page you want to be able to visit again easily, create a favorite for it. Here's what to do:

1. With the page active, click Add to Favorites or Reading List on the toolbar to open the Add to Favorites or Reading List pop-up panel (see Figure 11.3).

2. Click Favorites at the top if Reading List is selected.

3. In the Name box, edit the default name as needed, or simply type a descriptive name that will enable you to identify the page easily. The default name is the title of the web page.

4. Click the Create In drop-down menu and then click the folder in which you want to store the favorite. You can create a new folder by clicking Create New Folder.

5. Click Add to add the favorite.

> **☑ TIP**   If you'll want to go to the favorite frequently, create it on the Favorites bar. You can access the favorite without opening the Hub panel.

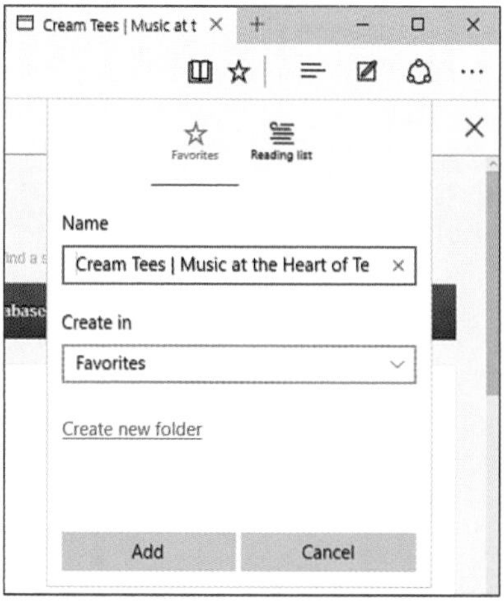

FIGURE 11.3

Use the Add to Favorites or Reading List pop-up panel to create a favorite for a page you want to visit again.

After you've created the favorite, you can go back to it quickly:

1. Click Hub on the toolbar to display the Hub panel, which contains the Favorites, Reading List, History, and Downloads tabs.

2. Click Favorites (the star icon) to display the Favorites list, unless it's displayed already.

3. If the favorite is in a folder, click that folder to display its contents.

4. Click the favorite to display the web page.

RETURNING TO PAGES YOU VIEWED EARLIER

Microsoft Edge keeps a list of all the pages you visit. This list is called your history, and you can use it to return to a page you visited before but for which you didn't create a favorite.

To access your history, click Hub on the toolbar to display the Hub panel, which contains four tabs: Favorites, Reading List, History, and Downloads. Click History (the clock icon with an arrow going counterclockwise) to display the History list. You can then click the page you want to view.

DELETING UNWANTED HISTORY ITEMS

Microsoft Edge makes it easy to delete history items you don't want to keep: You simply click the × button to the right of an item to remove it.

To remove a single item, move the mouse pointer over it, and then click the × button that appears. To remove a section of history, such as Last Hour or Today, click the × that appears to its right. Or click Clear All History at the top of the History tab to clear all your history.

For instructions on clearing other browsing data, see the section "Clearing Your Browsing Data," later in this chapter.

CATCHING UP WITH YOUR READING LIST

Microsoft Edge has a Reading List feature that makes it easy to line up web pages for reading later.

TIP Reading List saves the page in its current state, so when you return to it, the page is the same. By contrast, when you display a favorite, Microsoft Edge downloads the latest version of the page.

Here's how to add the current page to Reading List:

1. Click the Add to Favorites or Reading List button (the star icon) at the right end of the Address box to display the Add to Favorites or Reading List pop-up panel.

2. Click the Reading List tab to display its contents.

3. Optionally, click in the Name box and change the name of the page. The default name is the title of the web page, which might be long and might contain information you don't need. You can click the × button at the right end of the Name box to delete the current name, and then type a descriptive name.

4. Click Add. Microsoft Edge adds the page to your reading list.

When you want to read something on Reading List, follow these steps:

1. Click Hub on the toolbar to display the Hub panel.

2. Click Reading List (the icon showing a stack of papers) to display Reading List, unless it's displayed already.

3. Click the page you want to view.

> **NOTE** To remove a page from Reading List, right-click or long-press it, and then click Remove on the drop-down menu.

ANNOTATING WEB PAGES WITH WEB NOTE

The Web Note feature in Microsoft Edge enables you to annotate a web page you're viewing. You can then save the marked-up version on your computer or share it with someone else.

To use Web Note, browse to the page you want to annotate, and then click the Web Note button (the pen-on-paper icon) on the toolbar. The Web Note toolbar appears (see Figure 11.4), allowing you to take the following actions:

- **Choose the pen color and size.** Click Pen to activate the pen. A triangle appears in the lower-right corner of the button. Click Pen again to display the pop-up panel, and then click the color you want. To change the size, click Pen once more to open the pop-up panel again, and then click the size you need.

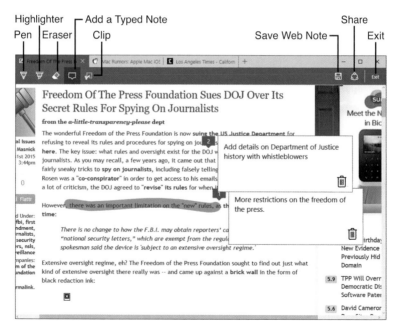

FIGURE 11.4

The Web Note toolbar provides easy-to-use tools for making notes, saving them, and sharing them.

- **Choose the highlighter color and shape.** Click Highlighter to activate the highlighter. A triangle appears in the lower-right corner of the button. Click Highlighter again to display the pop-up panel, and then click the highlight color you want. To change the highlighter shape, click Highlighter again to open the pop-up panel, and then click the shape.

- **Erase what you've drawn.** Click Eraser to activate the eraser. A triangle appears in the lower-right corner of the button. Click Eraser again to display the pop-up panel, and then click Clear All Ink.

- **Type in some text.** Click Add a Typed Note to activate the Typed Note feature, and then click with the crosshair pointer that appears on the point in text where you want to attach the note. Microsoft Edge opens a box in which you can type the text.

> **NOTE** To get rid of a typed note, click the Delete icon (the trash icon) inside it.

- **Clip part of the page.** When you want to clip part of a page as a picture, click Clip to activate clipping mode. You can then drag to select the part of the page you want to clip; when you finish, the Copied! button appears, letting you know that Microsoft Edge has copied the material. You can then paste the clipping into pretty much any app that accepts pictures. For example, you might paste the clipping into OneNote and then add text to it.

- **Save your notes.** To save your notes, click Save Web Note (the disk icon) at the right end of the Web Note toolbar. In the Add To panel that appears, click OneNote, Favorites, or Reading List, as needed. For OneNote, open the Choose a Section drop-down menu and choose the section in which to store the note, and then click Send. For Favorites, change the name in the Name box if you want, select the folder in the Create In drop-down menu, and then click Add. For Reading List, change the name in the Name box as needed, and then click Add.

- **Share your notes.** Click Share at the right end of the Web Note toolbar to display the Share pane, and then click the means of sharing you want to use.

- **Stop using Web Note.** Click Exit at the right end of the Web Note toolbar.

CONTROLLING MICROSOFT EDGE WITH KEYBOARD SHORTCUTS

You can use the keyboard shortcuts explained in Table 11.1 to control Microsoft Edge.

Table 11.1   Keyboard Shortcuts for Microsoft Edge

Keyboard Shortcut	What It Does
Essential Moves	
Tab	Select the next item on the page.
Shift+Tab	Select the previous item on the page.
Enter	Click the item you've selected using Tab or Shift+Tab.
Left arrow	Scroll left.
Right arrow	Scroll right.
Up arrow	Scroll up.
Down arrow	Scroll down.
Home	Scroll up to the start of the page.
End	Scroll down to the end of the page.
Ctrl+Shift+B	Toggle the display of the Favorites bar.
Ctrl+F	Open the Find on Page controls.
Ctrl+G	Open the Reading List.
Ctrl+H	Open the History panel.
Ctrl+I	Open the Favorites panel.
Ctrl+J	Open the Downloads panel.
Ctrl+L	Select the contents of the Address bar.
Ctrl+Shift+R	Toggle Reading mode on or off.
F7	Toggle Caret Browsing on or off. (You learn how to make the most of Caret Browsing later in this chapter.)
Working with Pages	
Ctrl+R	Refresh the current page.
F5	Refresh the current page.
Alt+left arrow	Go back to the previous page in the same tab.
Alt+right arrow	Go forward to the page from which you have gone back in the same tab.
Backspace	Go back to the previous page in the same tab.
Ctrl++	Zoom in by 25% increments.

Keyboard Shortcut	What It Does
Ctrl+–	Zoom out by 25% increments.
Ctrl+0	Zoom to 100%.
Ctrl+P	Display the Print dialog box.
Working with Tabs	
Ctrl+1	Switch to the first tab.
Ctrl+2 to Ctrl+8	Switch to the tab identified by the number, if that tab is open.
Ctrl+9	Switch to the last tab, no matter how many tabs are open.
Ctrl+T	Open a new tab.
Ctrl+W	Close the current tab.
Ctrl+Shift+T	Reopen the tab you just closed.
Ctrl+Tab	Switch to the next tab.
Ctrl+Shift+Tab	Switch to the previous tab.
Ctrl+K	Open a new tab to the same address as the current tab.
Working with Windows	
Ctrl+N	Open a new window.
Alt+F4	Close the active window.

CONFIGURING MICROSOFT EDGE FOR COMFORT AND SECURITY

It's a good idea to spend a few minutes configuring Microsoft Edge to make it work the way you prefer. Click the More Actions button to open the More Actions menu, and then click Settings to open the Settings pane. The left screen in Figure 11.5 shows the upper part of the Settings pane, and the right screen shows the lower part.

CONFIGURING GENERAL SETTINGS

At the top of the Settings pane, you can configure settings to control Microsoft Edge's appearance, startup behavior, and searching:

- **Choose a Theme.** Open this drop-down menu and choose Light or Dark to control the overall look of Microsoft Edge.

- **Show the Favorites Bar.** Set this switch to On if you want the Favorites bar to appear all the time. The Favorites bar is useful, especially if you customize it, but you may want to hide it if your computer has a small screen.

SETTINGS	SETTINGS
Choose a theme	Clear browsing data
Light	Choose what to clear
Show the favorites bar	Reading
● Off	Reading view style
	Default
Import favorites from another browser	Reading view font size
Open with	Medium
● Start page	
○ New tab page	Advanced settings
○ Previous pages	View advanced settings
○ A specific page or pages	
	About this app
Open new tabs with	Microsoft Edge 20.10240.16384.0
Top sites	© 2015 Microsoft
	Terms of use
Clear browsing data	Privacy statement
Choose what to clear	
Reading	
Reading view style	

FIGURE 11.5

Use the Settings pane to configure Microsoft Edge to work your way.

TIP You can toggle the display of the Favorites bar by pressing Ctrl+Shift+B.

- **Import Favorites from Another Browser.** Click this link to import favorites from another web browser, such as Internet Explorer.

- **Open With.** In this area, choose what you want Microsoft Edge to display when you open the browser for a new session. Select the Start Page option button to use the Microsoft Edge start page. Select the New Tab Page option button to open the new tab page. Select the Previous Pages option button to have Microsoft Edge open the last set of tabs you had open. If you prefer a particular page, click the A Specific Page or Pages option button, click the drop-down menu, and then click the option you want. To use a page that isn't listed, click Custom, and then enter the address in the text box that appears. You can then click the + button and add another page if you want.

! CAUTION The Previous Pages setting can be great for resuming your browsing where you left off, but you might find that it opens pages you didn't want to see again—or pages you don't want nearby people to see.

TIP You can also make Microsoft Edge start with a blank page. To do so, click the New Tab Page option button, open the Open New Tabs With drop-down menu, and click A Blank Page.

- **Open New Tabs With.** Open this drop-down menu and click Top Sites and Suggested Content, Top Sites, or A Blank Page, as needed.
- **Clear Browsing Data.** Click the Choose What to Clear button to choose which browsing data to clear. We'll go over this in the section "Clearing Your Browsing Data," later in this chapter.
- **Reading View Style.** Open this drop-down menu and click Default, Light, Medium, or Dark to specify the color scheme you want to use for Reading view. The Default color is beige, which is easier on the eyes than white.
- **Reading View Font Size.** Open this drop-down menu and click Small, Medium, Large, or Extra Large to select the font size you find most comfortable for reading.

CONFIGURING ESSENTIAL ADVANCED SETTINGS

When you finish choosing settings in the Settings pane, click the View Advanced Settings button to display the Advanced Settings pane. The left screen in Figure 11.6 shows the upper part of the Advanced Settings pane, and the right screen shows the lower part.

These are the settings you can configure in the upper part of the Advanced Settings pane:

- **Show the Home Button.** Set this switch to On to display the Home button to the right of the Refresh button. After setting this switch to On, you can enter the address for the Home page in the text box and click Save.
- **Block Pop-Ups.** Set this switch to On if you want to block pop-up windows. These are the windows that open automatically on websites that are keen to show you things you don't want to see.

■ **Use Adobe Flash Player.** Set this switch to On if you want Microsoft Edge to use Adobe Flash Player. Flash is a technology that many websites use as of this writing, so you need to set this switch to On to experience such websites fully.

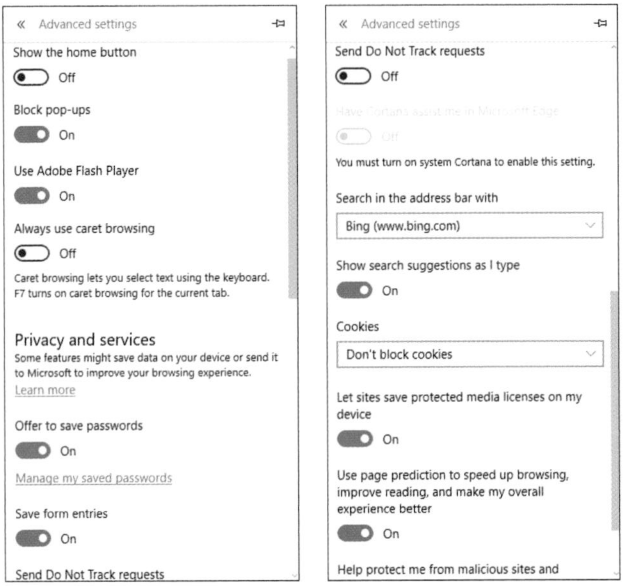

FIGURE 11.6

The Advanced Settings pane includes settings for blocking pop-ups, saving passwords and form entries, and controlling search suggestions and cookies.

> **! CAUTION** Flash Player has suffered many security problems in the past. If you set the Use Adobe Flash Player switch to On, you should keep Flash Player up to date. Flash Player normally notifies you when an update is available.

■ **Always Use Caret Browsing.** Set this switch to On if you want to use the Caret Browsing feature in every window and tab. If you set the switch to Off, you can press F7 to enable Caret Browsing in the active tab when you need it.

CONFIGURING PRIVACY AND SERVICES SETTINGS

In the Privacy and Services section of the Advanced Settings pane, you can configure the following settings:

- **Offer to Save Passwords.** Set this switch to On if you want Microsoft Edge to offer to save passwords you enter on websites. You can click the Manage My Saved Passwords link to display the Manage Passwords pane, in which you can delete passwords as needed.

- **Save Form Entries.** Set this switch to On if you want Microsoft Edge to save items you enter in web forms. For example, by storing your address information, Microsoft Edge can enter it for you in subsequent web forms, saving you time and typos.

- **Send Do Not Track Requests.** Set this switch to On to have Microsoft Edge send Do Not Track requests to websites you visit.

> **!CAUTION** As the name says, Do Not Track requests are only requests. Many websites do not honor Do Not Track requests, so don't rely on their having any effect.

- **Have Cortana Assist Me in Microsoft Edge.** Set this switch to On if you want to use the Cortana assistant in Microsoft Edge.

- **Search in the Address Bar With.** Open this drop-down menu and choose the search provider you want to use for search terms you type in the address bar. You can click the <Add new> item to add a new provider.

- **Show Search Suggestions as I Type.** Set this switch to On to have Microsoft Edge send what you type in the Address box to Microsoft's servers so that they can return search suggestions. This feature can help you find what you're looking for, but it increases the amount of information you are giving Microsoft.

- **Cookies.** Open this drop-down menu and click Don't Block Cookies, Block Only Third Party Cookies, or Block All Cookies, as needed. Block Only Third Party Cookies is the best choice for general browsing.

> **! CAUTION** Choosing the Block All Cookies setting in the Cookies drop-down menu might seem a good idea—but it prevents many websites from working correctly. Normally, it's best to block third-party cookies and allow cookies from the sites you visit.

■ **Let Sites Save Protected Media Licenses on My Device.** Set this switch to On if you will play protected media files, such as movies or TV shows. Letting sites save the licenses for these files on your device enables you to play back protected files even when your computer doesn't have an Internet connection.

■ **Use Page Prediction to Speed Up Browsing, Improve Reading, and Make My Overall Experience Better.** Set this switch to On if you want Microsoft Edge to try to predict the next page you will want to load from the current page and to automatically download the next page so that the Page Prediction feature works.

> **! CAUTION** Page Prediction can speed up your browsing, but you should bear two concerns in mind. First, Page Prediction may cause your computer to download (but not display) some pages that you wouldn't choose to view; this may make it look to your ISP, or any agency getting data from your ISP, as though you viewed those pages. Second, Page Prediction can increase your data usage substantially, which can be a concern if you're browsing via a cellular connection or some other metered plan.

■ **Help Protect Me from Malicious Sites and Downloads with SmartScreen Filter.** Set this switch to On to enable the SmartScreen Filter feature. When you try to download an app, SmartScreen Filter checks with Microsoft's servers to see whether the app is considered dangerous; if so, SmartScreen Filter prevents Microsoft Edge from downloading it. SmartScreen Filter also tries to protect your computer against "drive-by downloads," which is when a website you visit attempts to install software on your computer without your knowledge or permission.

> **NOTE** These are some of the settings you can configure when setting up Windows in the first place if you click Customize Settings rather than Use Express Settings on the Set Up for You, So You Can Get Going Fast screen in Windows Setup.

> **! CAUTION** The services in the Privacy and Services section of the Advanced Settings pane can help speed up your browsing, get you more relevant results, and protect your computer against malevolent sites. But be clear that, simply in order to work, these services require Microsoft Edge to share with Microsoft your browsing history and the keystrokes you type in the app. If you see this sharing as a threat to your privacy, disable these features.

CLEARING YOUR BROWSING DATA

As you browse, Microsoft Edge stores a large amount of data about the pages you visit and the files you download. Websites also place small files called *cookies* on your computer to help them track your movements on their sites and to implement features such as shopping carts and tailored product recommendations.

When you want to get rid of some—or all—of the stored data, click the Choose What to Clear button under the Clear Browsing Data heading in the Settings pane. The Clear Browsing Data pane appears showing its regular list of items (see the left screen in Figure 11.7). You can then check the check box for each item you want to delete:

- **Browsing History.** Check this box to delete all your history. This is an easy way of getting rid of potentially embarrassing history items, but it also prevents you from using history to return to pages you found interesting but didn't make favorites.

- **Cookies and Saved Website Data.** Check this check box to delete all the cookies and website data that sites have stored on your computer.

> **! CAUTION** After deleting cookies and website data, you may need to log in manually to accounts that you could log in to automatically using cookies. You may also have to reset your preferences for websites.

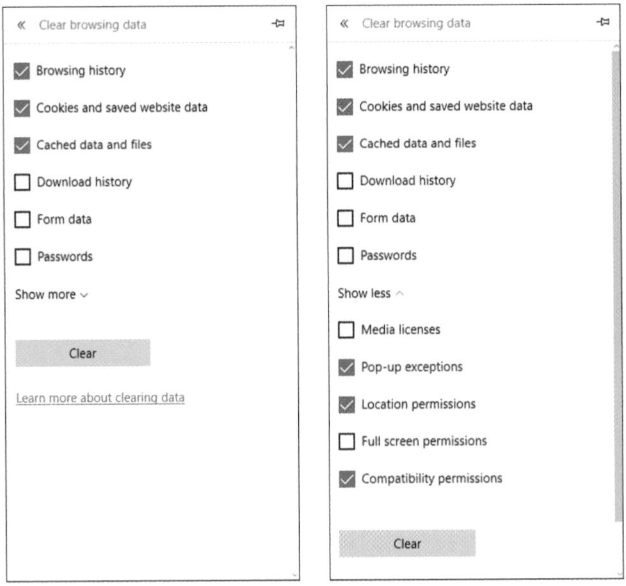

FIGURE 11.7

The Clear Browsing Data pane enables you to delete your browsing history, cookies, temporary Internet files, and more. Click the Show More link (left) to display the full list of items you can clear (right).

- **Cached Data and Files.** Check this check box to delete the temporary files that Microsoft Edge has stored on your computer to help it display web pages quickly. If you delete these files, Microsoft Edge may take longer to visit sites you visit frequently, because it has to download all the images for each page instead of being able to pull unchanged images from its cache on your computer.

- **Download History.** Check this check box to delete the list of the files you have downloaded. The files themselves stay in your computer's file system until you delete them.

- **Form Data.** Check this check box to delete any form data, such as your name and address, that Microsoft Edge has saved to help you fill in web forms more quickly and accurately.

- **Passwords.** Check this check box to delete any passwords you've allowed Microsoft Edge to save.

When you've made your choices, you can click Clear to implement them. But you can also click the Show More link to display the other items you can clear:

- **Media Licenses.** Check this check box to clear media licenses you have installed on your computer.

- **Pop-Up Exceptions.** Check this check box to clear the list of sites that you have allowed to display pop-up windows in Microsoft Edge.

- **Location Permissions.** Check this check box to clear any permissions you have granted to websites to track your location in Microsoft Edge.

- **Full Screen Permissions.** Check this check box to clear any permissions you have granted for websites to switch to full screen.

- **Compatibility Permissions.** Check this check box to clear any permissions you have granted for websites to use compatibility features.

After checking the appropriate check boxes, click the Clear button to clear the data.

When you finish choosing settings, click the More Actions button to close the Settings pane. You can also click anywhere in the Microsoft Edge window outside the Settings pane.

IN THIS CHAPTER

- Setting up your email accounts
- Communicating via email
- Communicating via Skype

12

COMMUNICATING VIA EMAIL AND SKYPE

Windows 10 comes with strong features for communicating via email and via text, audio, and video across the Internet. In this chapter, we start out by looking at how to set up your email accounts in the Mail app and how to use Mail to send, receive, and manage email messages. We then move on to installing and setting up Skype, configuring the most important of its many settings, and using it to communicate with your contacts across the Internet.

COMMUNICATING VIA EMAIL

Windows includes the Mail app for sending, receiving, and managing email. In this section, we'll look at how to set up your email accounts in Mail, how to navigate the app's interface, and how to configure your email accounts and the Mail app itself.

SETTING UP YOUR EMAIL ACCOUNTS

To start working with email, add your email accounts to the Mail app.

WHICH EMAIL ACCOUNT TYPES CAN YOU USE IN THE MAIL APP?

The Mail app can check a wide range of account types. As you'd likely expect, Mail can handle Outlook.com accounts—which include accounts from Live.com, Hotmail, and MSN, as well as Outlook.com itself—and Exchange accounts, which include Exchange Server accounts and Office 365 accounts.

Mail can also check Google accounts, such as Gmail and Google Apps accounts; Yahoo! Mail accounts; accounts on Apple's iCloud service; and accounts that use the standard POP3 and IMAP mail protocols.

If you used a Microsoft account to set up your Windows account, that account will already be set up in the Mail app. You can then add your other email accounts to Mail.

Launch Mail by clicking Start and then clicking Mail. Mail usually appears as a live tile on the Start menu; if not, you can find it in the All Apps list.

The first time you launch Mail, the app displays the Welcome screen. Click Get Started to display the Accounts screen (see Figure 12.1), which shows the accounts you have already set up.

If the list shows all the email accounts you need to use in Mail, you can click the Ready to Go button to start working with Mail; skip ahead to the next section, "Navigating in the Mail App." But if you have other email accounts, click the Add Account button instead and continue with this section.

When you click Add Account, Mail displays the Choose an Account dialog box (see Figure 12.2). Click the appropriate account type, and then follow the steps in the corresponding subsection that follows.

Mail makes setting up email accounts as straightforward as possible—but the variety of account types and the occasional balkiness of mail servers means you have to stay on your toes. The following subsections tell you what you need to know to set up the various account types.

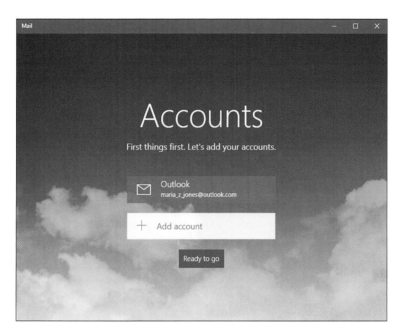

FIGURE 12.1

The Accounts screen shows the accounts you have set up so far in Mail. Click the Add Account button to add another account.

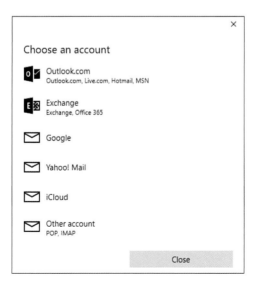

FIGURE 12.2

In the Choose an Account dialog box, click the type of account you want to set up.

SETTING UP AN OUTLOOK.COM ACCOUNT

If your email account is on Outlook.com, Live.com, Hotmail, or MSN, set it up using the Outlook.com account type. Follow these steps:

1. In the Choose an Account dialog box, click the Outlook.com button. The Add Your Microsoft Account dialog box opens (see Figure 12.3).

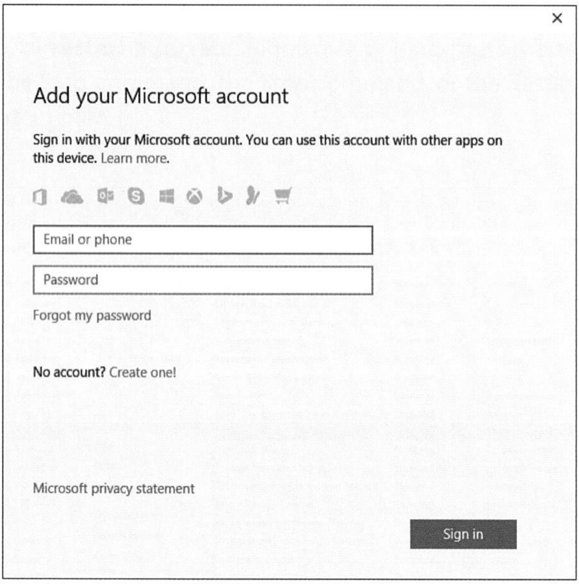

FIGURE 12.3

In the Add Your Microsoft Account dialog box, enter your email address or phone number, type your password, and click the Sign In button.

2. Type your email address or your phone number in the Email or Phone box.

3. Type your password in the Password box.

4. Click Sign In. Mail verifies the account information and then displays the All Done! dialog box to tell you that your account was set up successfully.

5. Click Done. Your account appears in the Accounts screen.

Click the Ready to Go button if you want to start using Mail now, or click the Add Account button if you need to add another account now.

SETTING UP AN EXCHANGE ACCOUNT

Exchange Server systems tend to be complex, so you may run into some complications when setting up an Exchange account in Mail.

The account can be either a regular Exchange account, such as you might have for your workplace, logging in to an Exchange Server system; or an Office 365 account, which you might have either as a personal account or as a work account. (Office 365 uses Exchange Server for mail behind the scenes.)

After you click the Exchange button in the Choose an Account dialog box, the Exchange dialog box (see Figure 12.4) prompts you only for your email address instead of asking for your email address and password. When you click the Next button, Mail looks up your account and tries to determine what other information you need to provide for it to set up the account.

> **NOTE** The information needed to set up an Exchange account varies depending on the account type and the configuration of the Exchange Server system.

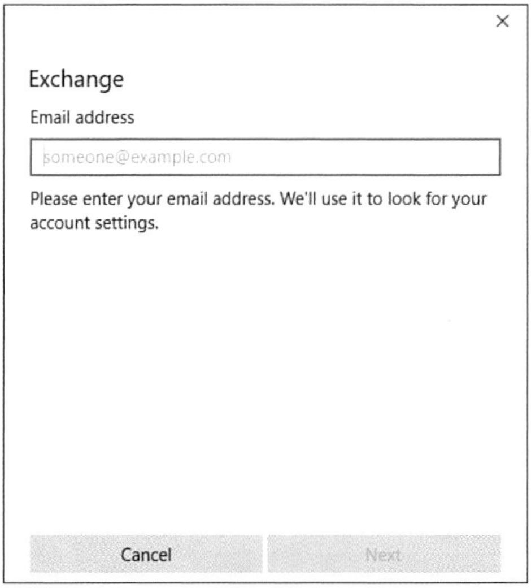

FIGURE 12.4

In the Exchange dialog box, type your email address and then click the Next button. Mail then works out which account details you need to provide.

Next, Mail normally prompts you for your password. After you provide the password and click the Next button, Mail displays the Heads Up dialog box (see Figure 12.5). This dialog box warns you that "your organization might collect information about you" and that it might "install or remove apps, change settings or disable features, delete content, or reset your device."

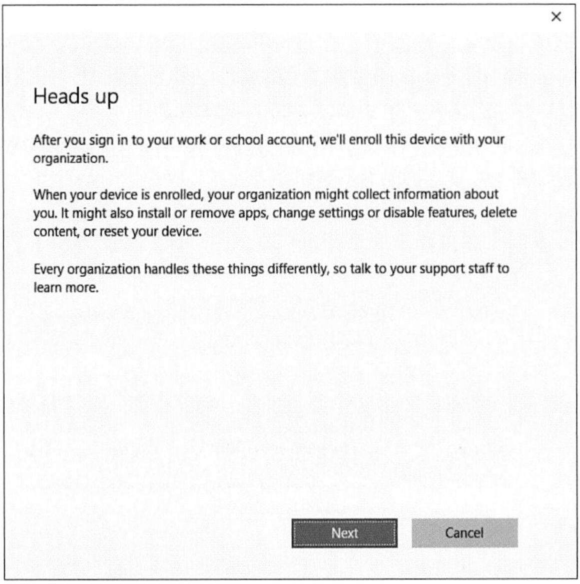

FIGURE 12.5

When you see the Heads Up dialog box, read the warning carefully, and make sure you understand its implications before you click the Next button.

> **! CAUTION** It's vital you understand the implications of the Heads Up warning before you finish setting up the Exchange account. Connecting your computer to an Exchange system enables the Exchange administrator to make changes remotely to your computer. The administrator's powers include removing apps you need, disabling features you rely on, deleting files you've created, and even wiping out all the content on your computer by resetting it.
>
> Under normal circumstances, an administrator would take drastic actions with your computer only if the computer belongs to the company or organization and it goes missing. But if you set up an Exchange account on your personal computer, the administrator has the same powers over it. So you would be well advised to ensure your backup system is working, and to use it regularly.

Assuming you bite the bullet and click the Next button in the Heads Up dialog box, Mail tries to set up the Exchange account. Often this works (as it should do), but sometimes it doesn't. Mail may prompt you to check your information and try again; if this happens, make sure you've entered the email address and the password correctly, and then click Sign-in again.

If Mail displays the Something Went Wrong dialog box shown in Figure 12.6 when you're trying to set up an Exchange account, you can click the Try Again button to try again with the same information. This sometimes works if the problem is that the server was too busy to respond to Mail's request. But in most cases the appearance of this Something Went Wrong dialog box indicates that you need to enter more information in order for Mail to be able to set up the account.

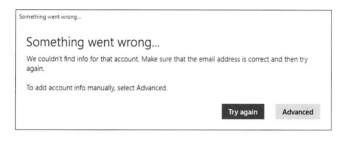

Something went wrong...

Something went wrong...

We couldn't find info for that account. Make sure that the email address is correct and then try again.

To add account info manually, select Advanced.

Try again   Advanced

FIGURE 12.6

If the Something Went Wrong dialog box appears when you're setting up an Exchange account, you usually need to click the Advanced button and provide more information.

To enter this information, click the Advanced button in the Something Went Wrong dialog box. The Exchange dialog box then appears again, but with many more fields for you to fill in (see Figure 12.7). These are the fields:

- **Email Address.** This is the email address you entered in the first place. You shouldn't need to change it.

- **Password.** This is the password you entered already. You shouldn't need to change this either.

- **User Name.** Type in your user name for the Exchange Server system. Ask the system's administrator for your user name if you're not sure what it is. The user name may or may not be the same as your email address.

> **TIP** For some systems, you may need to enter in the User Name box the domain followed by a backslash and your full email address. For example, if your email address is john@surrealmacs.com, you would enter **surrealmacs.com\john@surrealmacs.com**. This looks awkward, especially if it's too long to fit in the User Name text box, but it is correct and it does work.

- **Domain.** The domain is an area in the Exchange Server system. Ask your administrator whether you need to enter a domain and (if so) which domain.

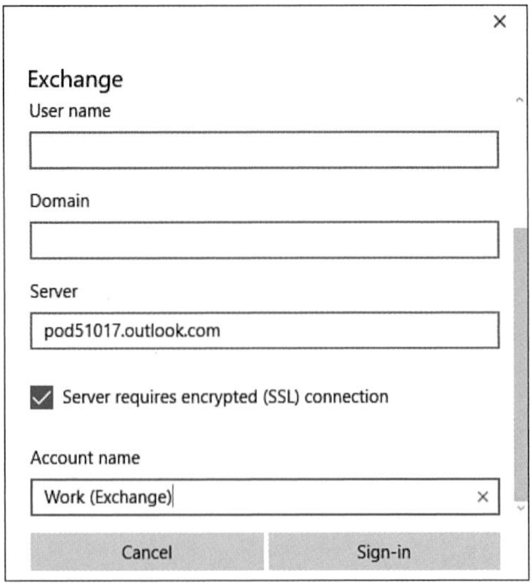

FIGURE 12.7

For some Exchange accounts, you may need to enter further details, such as the full user name, the Exchange domain, and the Exchange server hostname or IP address.

> **NOTE** Using the right domain can be crucial to getting your Exchange Server account to work. Exchange Server systems tend to be complex, and it is hard to guess the domain name. What's especially awkward is that you may not need to enter a domain name at all, but usually only the administrator can tell you whether to enter it.

- **Server.** Type the host name (such as server1.surrealmacs.com) or the IP address (such as 217.44.81.100) in this box.
- **Server Requires Encrypted (SSL) Connection.** Usually, you'll need to check this check box in order to connect to the Exchange system.
- **Account Name.** Type the descriptive name you want to assign to the Exchange account.

After you've entered all this information correctly, click the Sign-in button. When Mail is able to set up the account, it displays the All Done! dialog box; click Done to return to the Accounts screen, where you can set up another account if necessary.

SETTING UP A GOOGLE ACCOUNT

Setting up a Google account in the Mail app is usually straightforward. When you click Google in the Choose an Account dialog box, Mail displays the Connecting to a Service dialog box (see Figure 12.8).

FIGURE 12.8
In the Connecting to a Service dialog box, type the email address for your Google account, and then click the Next button.

Click in the Enter Your Email box, type your email address into it, and then click the Next button. The Connecting to a Service dialog box then prompts you for the authentication information needed. Normally, you just need to type your password in the Password box, and then click the Sign In button.

The Connecting to a Service dialog box then displays a list of what Mail and Windows are asking to do (see Figure 12.9):

- **View and Manage Your Mail.** You're allowing Mail to view your email, delete messages and send messages, delete labels, and so on.
- **Know Who You Are on Google.** You're allowing Mail to associate you with your public Google profile.
- **View Your Email Address.** You're allowing Mail to view your email address.
- **Manage Your Calendars.** You're allowing Mail to view your calendars in Google Calendar and make changes to them.

■ **Manage Your Contacts.** You're allowing Mail to view your contacts in Google Contacts and make changes to them.

FIGURE 12.9

In this Connecting to a Service dialog box, review the permissions you're granting to Mail and Windows, and then click the Allow button.

All of this is pretty straightforward. You can click an Information button (the i icon) to display a More Info dialog box that shows some more information about the item.

If you're happy to assign Mail and Windows these permissions, click the Allow button (if not, click the Deny button). Mail sets up the Google account and displays the All Done! dialog box, and you can click the Done button to return to the Accounts screen.

SETTING UP A YAHOO! MAIL ACCOUNT OR AN ICLOUD ACCOUNT

Setting up a Yahoo! Mail account or an iCloud account usually presents no problems.

Click the Yahoo! Mail button in the Choose an Account dialog box to display the Yahoo! Mail dialog box, or click the iCloud button to display the iCloud dialog box.

After you enter your email address and password and click the Sign-in button, Mail checks that the credentials are valid. Mail then displays the Your Name dialog box, in which you enter your name the way you want it to appear on messages you send.

SETTING UP A POP3 ACCOUNT OR AN IMAP ACCOUNT

When setting up a POP3 account or an IMAP account, you usually need to provide the names of the mail servers to use. Click the Other Account button in the Choose an Account dialog box, enter your email address and password in the Other Account dialog box that opens, and then click the Sign-in button.

UNDERSTANDING POP3, IMAP, SMTP, AND EXCHANGE

POP3, IMAP, SMTP, and Exchange are four technologies widely used for mail servers. POP3 and IMAP are protocols that email clients (such as the Mail app on your computer) use to communicate with incoming mail servers—the servers from which you receive your messages. SMTP is a protocol used for many outgoing mail servers—the servers that send your messages for you. Exchange is Microsoft's Exchange Server technology for email, scheduling, and calendars.

POP is the acronym for Post Office Protocol, and POP3 is version 3 of Post Office Protocol. IMAP is the acronym for Internet Mail Access Protocol, a newer protocol than POP3. SMTP is the abbreviation for Simple Mail Transfer Protocol, a protocol for sending mail.

The main difference between POP3 and IMAP is that POP3 is mostly designed to download your messages to your email client, removing them from the server, whereas IMAP is designed to enable you to view and manage your messages on the server without downloading them to your email client.

The advantage of IMAP is that, with your messages on the server, you can view and manage them from multiple devices. So if you view a message on your computer, the message is marked as having been read on your other computers and devices as well. And if you delete a message on (say) your tablet, it disappears from your computer's mailbox too.

Your email provider will tell you which account type—POP3, IMAP, or Exchange—to specify when setting up your account. If your email provider gives you the choice between POP3 and IMAP, you'll normally want to choose IMAP in Mail on your computer so that you can access your messages on other computers and devices as well.

Mail then tries to look up the email account. If it cannot locate the account, it displays the Other Account dialog box again, prompting you to check the email address. Click the Try Again button.

After another failure or two, Mail displays the Advanced button in place of the Try Again button. Click the Advanced button to display the Internet Email Account dialog box (see Figure 12.10), in which you enter the following details:

- **Account Name.** Type the descriptive name you want to see for the account in Mail.

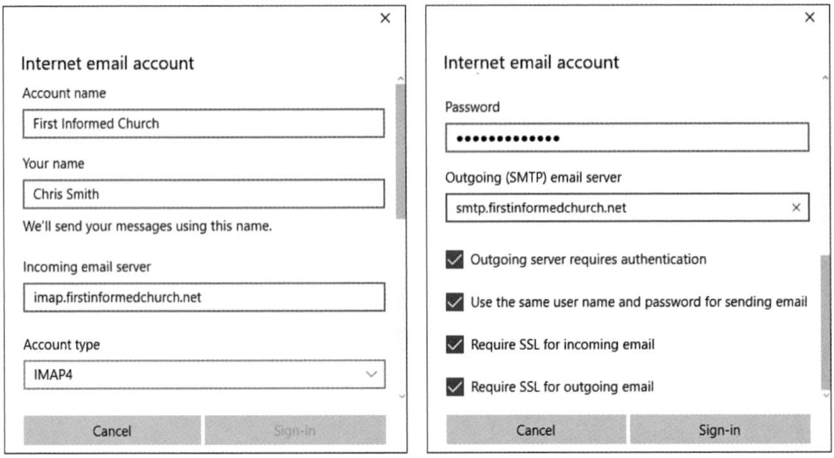

FIGURE 12.10
Enter the details of your POP3 account or IMAP account in the Internet Email Account dialog box.

- **Your Name.** Type your name the way you want it to appear on messages you send.
- **Incoming Email Server.** Type the address of the incoming mail server, such as pop3.surrealmacs.com or imap.firstinformedchurch.net.
- **Account Type.** Open this drop-down menu and choose POP3 or IMAP4, depending on your account type.
- **User Name.** Type your email address in this box.
- **Password.** Enter your password for the email account. Mail carries over the password you entered in the Other Account dialog box, so you shouldn't need to enter it again.
- **Outgoing (SMTP) Email Server.** Type the address of the outgoing mail server, such as smtp.surrealmacs.com or imap.firstinformedchurch.net.

■ **Outgoing Server Requires Authentication.** Check this check box to use authentication for the outgoing server.

> ⌐✎ **NOTE**   Most outgoing mail servers require authentication. This security measure helps prevent people from sending junk email messages (spam).

■ **Use the Same User Name and Password for Sending Email.** If you check the Outgoing Server Requires Authentication check box, check this check box if your email provider's system requires you to use the same user name for sending email as for receiving it. If you need to use a different user name or password, uncheck this check box, and then enter the user name and password in the boxes in the Outgoing Server Login Info area, which appears when you uncheck the check box.

■ **Require SSL for Incoming Email.** Check this check box to use Secure Sockets Layer (SSL) encryption for receiving incoming email. You'll almost always need to do this.

■ **Require SSL for Outgoing Email.** Check this check box to use SSL encryption for outgoing email. Most email systems require you to use SSL.

After entering all this information, click the Sign-in button. After you've gotten everything right, the All Done! dialog box opens, and you can click the Done button to return to the Accounts screen.

CLOSING THE ACCOUNTS SCREEN

When you finish adding your email accounts to Mail, click the Ready to Go button in the Accounts screen. The Mail window then appears, and you can start working with email.

NAVIGATING IN THE MAIL APP

The Mail app has an easy-to-navigate interface. The following list explains its main components, which are labeled in Figure 12.11.

■ **Expand/Collapse.** Click this button to expand or collapse the sidebar.

■ **New Mail.** Click this button to start a new message.

■ **Search.** Click this box, type your search terms, and press Enter.

■ **Sync This View.** Click this button to sync the folder you're viewing.

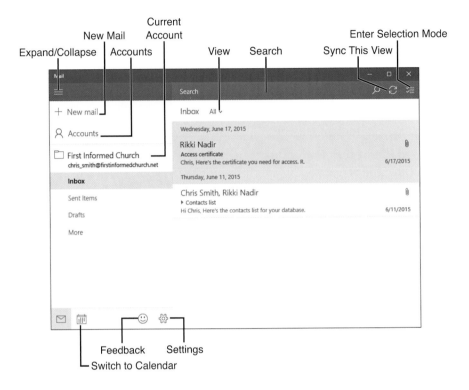

FIGURE 12.11
Mail's interface is easy to navigate.

- **Enter Selection Mode.** Click this button to switch to Selection Mode, which displays a check box to the left of each message so that you can easily select the messages you want to work with.
- **View.** Click this drop-down menu and then click All, Unread, or Flagged to control which messages the view displays.
- **Accounts.** Click this button to display the Accounts pane (see Figure 12.12), in which you can click the account you want to display.

> **TIP** If you need instant access to an account, right-click or long-press it in either the Accounts pane or the left pane, and then click Pin to Start on the shortcut menu.

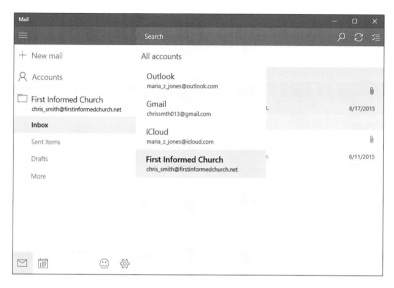

FIGURE 12.12
Click the Accounts button to display the Accounts pane when you want to switch from one email account to another.

- **Current Account.** Click this button to display the folders in the account you're currently working with. You can then click the folder you want to view.
- **Switch to Calendar.** Click this button to switch to the Calendar window. The Calendar window has a corresponding Switch to Mail button that you can click to switch back to the Mail window.
- **Feedback.** Click this button to send Microsoft feedback about Mail.
- **Settings.** Click this button to display the Settings pane. We'll dig into the settings later in this chapter.

READING MESSAGES

After you've navigated to the account and mailbox you want to view, you see the messages the mailbox contains. As you can see in Figure 12.13, each message has a preview that shows the sender's name, the message title, and the first part of the message—as much as will fit on a single line in the preview. You can move the mouse pointer over a message to display three action icons—Archive, Delete, and Flag—in the upper-right corner of a message preview, as in the first message in the figure.

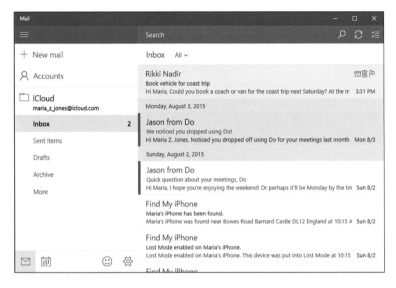

FIGURE 12.13
You can click a message to open it, or simply manage the message directly in the mailbox.

The following list explains the actions you can take with a message from the mailbox. Depending on the account type you're using, only some of the actions may be available.

- **Archive the message.** Move the mouse pointer over the message, and then click the Archive icon in the upper-right corner.

> **TIP** If you enable swipe actions, as discussed in the section "Choosing Options for Mail," later in this chapter, you can swipe left or right to take actions on the message. (You get to choose one action for swiping left and one action for swiping right.)

- **Delete the message.** Move the mouse pointer over the message, and then click the Delete icon in the upper-right corner. Alternatively, right-click or long-press the message, and then click Delete on the shortcut menu.

- **Set a flag on the message.** Move the mouse pointer over the message, and then click the Flag icon in the upper-right corner. Alternatively, right-click or long-press the message, and then click Set Flag on the shortcut menu.

- **Mark the message as read or unread.** Right-click or long-press the message, and then click the Mark as Unread item or the Mark as Read item on the shortcut menu. (If you've read the message, the Mark as Unread item appears on the shortcut menu; if you haven't read the message, the Mark as Read item appears.)

- **Move the message to a folder.** Right-click or long-press the message, click Move on the shortcut menu, and then click the appropriate folder in the Move To panel that appears in the middle of the Mail window.

> **TIP** You can also move a message to a folder by clicking the message and dragging it to the left. When the Move To panel appears, drag the message to the appropriate folder and then drop it there.

DEALING WITH THE MAKE MY PC MORE SECURE DIALOG BOX

If the Make My PC More Secure dialog box (see Figure 12.14) opens, you'll know that the Exchange account you've set up in Mail isn't fully configured yet. Click the Enforce These Policies button if you want to go ahead and grant the Exchange system the rights it needs in order to administer your computer.

> **NOTE** If you decide you don't want the Exchange system to administer your computer after all, you'll need to remove the Exchange account from Mail. Click the Cancel button to close the Make My PC More Secure dialog box, and then follow the instructions in the section "Removing an Email Account from Mail," later in this chapter.

FIGURE 12.14

The Make My PC More Secure dialog box opens if you have set up an Exchange account but not granted the Exchange system the rights to administer your computer.

CONFIGURING YOUR EMAIL ACCOUNTS AND THE MAIL APP

To make Mail work your way, you can configure its many settings. Your options include choosing sync settings for an account, setting a background picture, customizing the view so you can read your messages easily, and choosing settings for the Mail app as a whole.

OPENING AN ACCOUNT TO CHANGE SETTINGS

To start configuring your email accounts, open the account you want to affect. Follow these steps:

1. Click the Settings button in the Mail window to display the Settings pane.
2. Click Accounts at the top of the Settings pane to display the Accounts pane.
3. Click the account to open the dialog box for configuring it.

> **TIP** To go straight to the Settings dialog box for an account, right-click or long-press that account in either the Accounts pane or the left pane, and then click Account Settings on the shortcut menu.

CHOOSING SYNC SETTINGS

Click the Change Mailbox Sync Settings button in the Account Settings pane for an account to display the Sync Settings dialog box for the account (see Figure 12.15). You can then configure these settings:

■ **Download New Content.** Open this drop-down menu and choose the frequency for downloading new content: As Items Arrive, Based on My Usage, Every 15 Minutes, Every 30 Minutes, Hourly, or Daily. Your account may offer different options.

WHAT FREQUENCY SHOULD YOU CHOOSE FOR DOWNLOADING NEW CONTENT?

How frequently you should download new content depends on the email account and how you use it. For example, for your primary email account, you'll likely want to choose either the As Items Arrive setting or the Every 15 Minutes setting. For a secondary account you keep for social media, the Daily setting might be more suitable.

You may want to try the Based on My Usage setting for an account you use only occasionally. But in general, choosing a specific interval—even if it is Daily—is clearer for most accounts.

The As Items Arrive setting is great for making sure you get your important messages as soon as possible, but you may find that it chews through battery life on tablets and laptop computers. If you need to dial down the frequency, console yourself with the thought that productivity gurus mostly recommend checking email less frequently so as not to become distracted from the tasks you should be prioritizing.

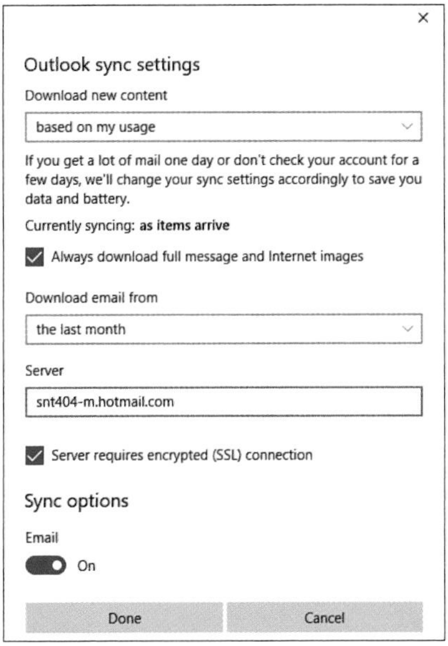

FIGURE 12.15

In the Sync Settings pane for an email account, you can choose how frequently to download new messages, whether to download full messages and images, and how much email to download.

- **Always Download Full Message and Internet Images.** Check this check box if you want to download the full content of each message, including any attachments, and any images stored on the Internet.

> **! CAUTION** Checking the Always Download Full Message and Internet Images check box can increase your data usage, which may be a concern on metered connections. But it also has another problem: A sender can include in a message a link to an image on the Internet in order to find out whether and when you receive the message. The sender can receive this information when Mail retrieves the image from the Internet server.
>
> If you uncheck the Always Download Full Message and Internet Images check box, you can look at the content of messages and decide which images to retrieve.

- **Download Email From.** Open this drop-down menu and choose the period of time you want to sync: The Last 3 Days, The Last 7 Days, The Last 2 Weeks, The Last Month, or Any Time. Your account may offer different options.

> **NOTE** Only you know how many days' worth of email you need to sync for any particular account—but keep in mind that the more email you sync, the longer syncing will take, and the more data Mail will need to transfer across your Internet connection. Both are more of a concern for a laptop or tablet computer you use on a metered Internet connection than for a desktop you use on an all-you-can-eat connection.

- **Server.** You can enter a different server in this box if necessary. Normally, you won't need to change the server.

> **NOTE** To choose server settings for some account types, you need to click Advanced Mailbox Settings.

- **Server Requires Encrypted (SSL) Connection.** Check this check box if the server requires you to use SSL to secure the connection, as most servers do.
- **Sync Options area.** Set the Email switch and each other switch to On if you want to sync the item. The switches in this area depend on the email account and its capabilities; for some accounts, the Email switch may be the only switch.

When you finish working in the Sync Settings dialog box, click the Done button to close it. Mail returns you to the Account Settings dialog box for the account, where you need to click Save to save the changes you've made.

REMOVING AN EMAIL ACCOUNT FROM MAIL

Follow these steps to remove an email account from Mail:

1. In the Mail app, click the Settings button to display the Settings panel.
2. Click Accounts to display the Accounts pane.
3. Click the account you want to remove. The Account Settings dialog box for the account opens.
4. Click Delete Account. The Delete This Account? dialog box opens, warning you that deleting the account will remove all the account's content—as you would likely expect.
5. Click Delete. Mail removes the account and displays the Accounts pane again.

NOTE You can't remove the email account associated with your Windows account from Mail.

SETTING A BACKGROUND PICTURE

You can change the background picture for Mail by clicking the Background Picture button in the Settings pane, clicking Browse in the Background Picture pane, and then using the Open dialog box to select the picture you want to use.

CUSTOMIZING THE VIEW FOR EASY READING

To customize the view in Mail for easy reading of your messages, click the Reading button in the Settings pane. You can then configure the following settings in the Reading pane:

- **Auto-Open Next Item.** Set this switch to On if you want Mail to automatically open the next item when you finish dealing with the current item—for example, by filing it or by deleting it. Auto-opening the next item is usually helpful for working through your messages.

- **Mark Item as Read.** In this area, select the appropriate option button to specify when Mail should mark a message as having been read. Your options are the When Selection Changes option button, the Don't Automatically Mark Item as Read option button, and the When Viewed in the Reading Pane option button. If you select the When Viewed in the Reading Pane option button, enter the number of seconds to wait in the Seconds to Wait box.

■ **Caret Browsing.** In this area, set the Use the Caret to Navigate the Reading Pane switch to On if you want to be able to use the arrow keys to move through your mailboxes.

When you finish choosing settings in the Reading pane, click the Back (<) button to return to the Settings pane. Or you can simply click in the main part of the Mail window to close the Reading pane (and the Settings pane) and get back to your messages.

CHOOSING OPTIONS FOR MAIL

To choose options for Mail, click the Options button in the Settings pane to display the Options pane. The left and right screens in Figure 12.16 show the Options pane, in which you can configure the following settings:

■ **Account.** Open this drop-down menu at the top of the pane and then click the account for which you want to configure options.

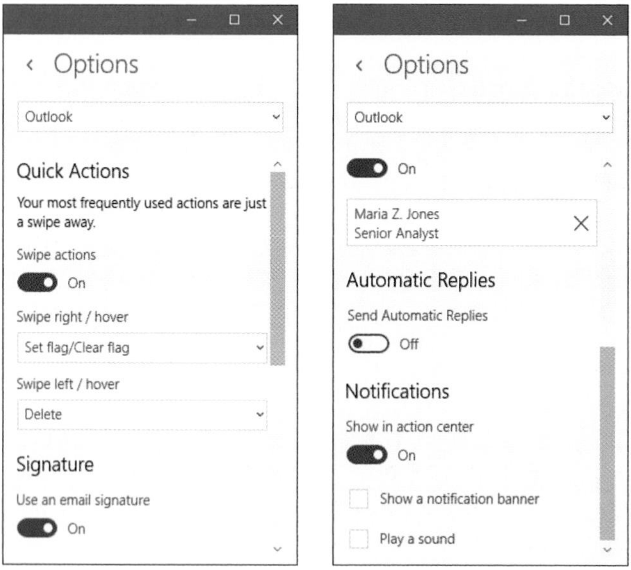

FIGURE 12.16

Choose the account you want to configure in the drop-down menu at the top of the Options pane. You can then configure settings in the Quick Actions, Signature, Automatic Replies, and Notifications areas.

■ **Swipe Actions.** Set this switch to On if you want to be able to use swipe actions in your mailboxes.

■ **Swipe Right/Hover.** If you set the Swipe Actions switch to On, you can open this drop-down menu and choose the action you want to take by swiping right on a touchscreen or hovering the mouse pointer over a regular screen. Your choices are Set Flag/Clear Flag, Mark as Read/Unread, Delete, and Move.

■ **Swipe Left/Hover.** If you set the Swipe Actions switch to On, you can open this drop-down menu and choose the action you want to take by swiping left on a touchscreen or hovering the mouse pointer over a regular screen. As with Swipe Right/Hover, your choices are Set Flag/Clear Flag, Mark as Read/Unread, Delete, and Move.

■ **Use an Email Signature.** Set this switch to On if you want Mail to automatically enter your signature text at the end of each message you create or forward. Type the text in the box that appears; press Enter to create multiple lines.

■ **Send Automatic Replies.** Set this switch to On when you want Mail to reply automatically to incoming messages. This feature is useful for out-of-office messages or vacation messages. Type your message in the box that appears. Normally, you'll want to check the Send Replies Only to My Contacts check box to limit the number of automatic responses.

■ **Show in Action Center.** Set this switch to On if you want messages sent to this account to appear in Action Center. If you need to keep right on top of messages sent to this account, check the Show a Notification Banner check box, the Play a Sound check box, or both.

When you finish choosing options for one account, you can go back to the top of the pane and choose another account for which to set options. When you're done in the Options pane, click the Back (<) button to return to the Settings pane, or click the main part of the Mail window to return to your messages.

CONFIGURING TRUST CENTER

Mail and the Office apps can connect to Microsoft's online services to get what Microsoft calls "locally relevant content"—information related to your current location that may be relevant to the way you use the apps.

To choose whether Mail and the Office apps fetch this locally relevant content for you, click the Trust Center button in the Settings pane to display the Trust Center pane. You can then set the Enable Locally Relevant Content switch to On or Off, as needed.

COMMUNICATING VIA SKYPE

Skype is a communications service that enables you to do the following:

- **Chat via text.** You can chat via text with multiple people. You can run multiple chats at once.

- **Share files.** You can share files with other people, either while chatting or separately.

- **Make voice calls.** You can make calls either to other computers running Skype or to the regular telephone system. You can talk either to a single person or to multiple people in a conference call.

- **Make video calls.** You can make video calls to other computers. As with voice, a video call can be either with one other person or with multiple people.

GETTING THE SKYPE APP

First, see whether Skype is installed on your computer. Windows doesn't include Skype itself, but it does include the Get Skype app, a Windows Store app that enables you to download the Skype installer if Skype isn't installed.

NOTE The Get Skype app doesn't download Skype from the Windows Store—it just helps you download the Skype installer. So unlike with a Windows Store app, which handles the installation automatically for you, you have to run the Skype installer.

Click Start, type **skype** in the Search box, and see which search results you get. If the Skype for Desktop result appears, your computer has Skype installed and you're in business; click this result to launch the Skype app. If just the Get Skype result appears, click it to launch the Get Skype app, and then click the Download Skype button to download the Skype installer.

Installing Skype is mostly straightforward. Here's what you need to know:

- **Running the installer.** When your browser finishes downloading the Skype installer, click the Run button to launch the installer.

> **NOTE** If clicking Run in Microsoft Edge crashes the browser and fails to fully launch the Skype installer, open a File Explorer window to your `Downloads` folder and double-click the `SkypeSetup.exe` file.

- **Choose whether to install Skype Click to Call.** Click to Call scans open documents and web pages and identifies phone numbers that Skype should be able to call, some free but most using Skype credit. If you don't want to use this feature, uncheck the Install Skype Click to Call check box on the Skype Click to Call page.

- **Sign in to Skype.** On the Sign In screen (see Figure 12.17), choose how to sign in. You have three options: Click Skype Name to sign in with your existing Skype account; click Microsoft Account to sign in with your existing Microsoft account, such as an Outlook.com account, a Hotmail account, an Xbox Live account, or a Windows Live account; or click Sign In with Facebook to log in using Facebook so that you can use your Facebook account with Skype.

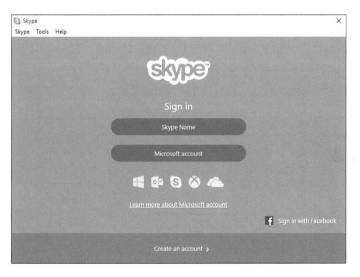

FIGURE 12.17

On the Sign In screen, click Skype Name or Microsoft Account to choose how to sign in to Skype. If you need a new account, click Create an Account.

> **NOTE** You can click Create an Account to open the Create an Account or Sign In page on the Skype website in your default browser. Here, you have three choices: You can create a standalone Skype account; you can create a Skype account linked to your existing Microsoft account; or you can create a Skype account linked to your existing Facebook account.

COMPLETING THE INITIAL SETUP ROUTINE

The first time you run Skype, the app runs you through a brief setup routine to make sure that everything is working and add a profile picture to your account. When the Setting Up Skype screen appears (see Figure 12.18), check that your speakers or headphones, microphone, and video are working:

■ **Speakers or headphones.** Make sure the drop-down menu in the Speakers area shows the right speakers or headphones. Then click the Test Sound button and verify that the sound comes through loud (enough) and clear.

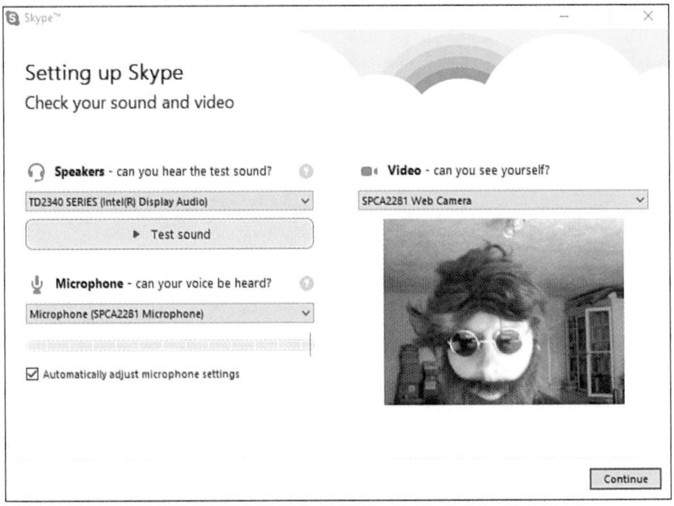

FIGURE 12.18

On the Setting Up Skype screen, make sure that your speakers, microphone, and video are working, and then click the Continue button.

■ **Microphone.** Make sure the drop-down menu in the Microphone area shows the microphone you want to use. Then verify that the level indicator shows green bars to about halfway across when you speak at a normal volume.

Check the Automatically Adjust Microphone Settings check box if you want Skype to be able to adjust the volume to compensate for changes.

> **TIP** The Automatically Adjust Microphone Settings option usually works well for quiet and moderately noisy environments. But if you're making calls in a boiler factory, you'll probably need to control the microphone sensitivity manually.

- **Video.** Check that the drop-down menu in the Video area shows the webcam or other video input you want to use for Skype. Then look at the preview and adjust the camera—or reposition yourself—as needed.

Click the Continue button to move along. The Setting Up Skype: Add a Profile Picture screen appears. You can either click the Continue button and follow the prompts to add a profile picture, either by taking it on your webcam or by selecting an existing photo on your computer; or click the Add Later button if you need to fix your hair, your face, or other aspects of reality before immortalizing yourself online.

> **TIP** You can change your profile picture at any time by choosing Skype, Profile, Change Your Picture and then working on the Set Your Profile Picture screen. This screen gives you access to your previous profile pictures, enabling you to swap quickly among them. So you can give yourself a different look—professional, casual, suave—for different calls, as needed.

NAVIGATING THE SKYPE SCREEN

When you finish the initial setup routine, the Skype window appears (see Figure 12.19). Skype has an easy-to-use interface, in which these are the main features:

- **Menu bar.** The menu bar gives you access to the Skype menus, as usual.
- **Your account and status.** This button shows your name, profile picture, and status. You can change your status by moving the mouse pointer over the status icon (such as the green circle with the white check mark shown here), clicking the drop-down menu that appears, and then clicking the status in the drop-down menu.

FIGURE 12.19
Skype has an easy-to-use interface.

- **Search.** Click this button to search by name or keyword.
- **Home.** Click this button to display the Home screen.
- **Call Phones.** Click this button to display the Call Phones screen, which enables you to make voice calls to landline phones or cellular phones.
- **Contacts.** Click this tab to display the Contacts list, which shows your contacts and their status.
- **Recent.** Click this tab to display the Recent list, which shows your recent conversations.

Skype has seven menus, positioned at the top of the screen as normal:

- **Skype menu.** This menu includes commands for changing your online status, editing your profile, changing privacy settings, accessing your account, buying Skype Credit, changing your password, signing out of the service, and closing the app.
- **Contacts menu.** This menu includes commands for adding contacts and creating groups; managing your contact lists; sorting and hiding contacts; and backing up contacts, restoring them, and managing your blocked contacts.
- **Conversation menu.** This menu contains commands for starting and managing conversations, such as sending an instant message, a video message, or an SMS message to a contact; adding people to a conversation,

or blocking people; and leaving a conversation. You can also search your conversations by keywords and view old messages.

- **Call menu.** This menu includes commands for starting a voice call or video call, and for answering an incoming call; changing audio and video settings; sharing screens; and taking actions such as putting a call on hold, muting your microphone, and hanging up.
- **View menu.** This menu includes commands for switching among views; displaying your profile; and moving to split window view, which enables you to view separate conversations simultaneously by using multiple windows.
- **Tools menu.** This menu contains commands for changing the language, setting up Skype Wi-Fi, and displaying the Options dialog box, which you use for configuring Skype (see the next section).
- **Help menu.** This menu contains commands for getting help for Skype.

COMMUNICATING VIA SKYPE

After you've set up Skype, communicating with your contacts is straightforward. On the Contacts tab (see Figure 12.20), click the contact with whom you want to communicate, and then choose the means of communication:

- **Call.** Click this button to place an audio call.
- **Video Call.** Click this button to place a video call.
- **Send Contacts and Media.** Click this button to send a photo, a file, a video message, or contact information.
- **Text.** Click in this box and type the text you want to send. Press Enter to send it.
- **Insert Emoticon.** Click this button to display the Emoticon panel. You can then click an emoticon to insert it in the Text box. Type any text needed and press Enter to send the message.
- **Add People.** Click this button to add other people to the conversation or call to the contact.

Skype places the call or sends the text or file. It then displays controls for managing the call or conversation.

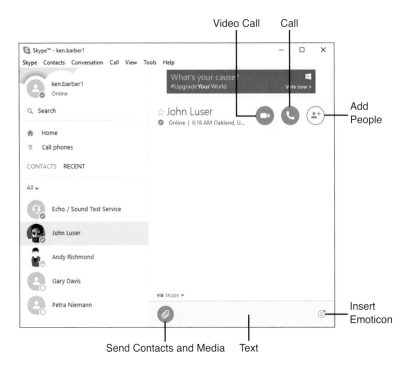

FIGURE 12.20
To communicate with a contact, click the contact, and then click the appropriate button.

CONFIGURING SKYPE TO WORK YOUR WAY

Skype has a ton of settings, and you should plan to go through them before you use the app extensively, because changing some of the settings is essential to avoiding nuisance calls and protecting your privacy.

The following subsections take you through the most important settings, making sure you know which settings are available and what your options are. I'll leave you to investigate some of the less vital settings on your own—but please do investigate them, for two reasons. First, you may disagree with my assessment of what's important. Second, Skype may have changed or added settings.

OPENING THE OPTIONS DIALOG BOX

To get started configuring Skype, choose Tools, Options to display the Options dialog box. As you can see in Figure 12.21, the sidebar on the left side of the Options dialog box contains six category buttons. These are the mid-gray buttons: General, Privacy, Notifications, Calls, IM & SMS, and Advanced. Each of these category buttons contains two or more subcategories. For example, the General category (which is expanded in Figure 12.21) contains five subcategories: General Settings, Audio Settings, Sounds, Video Settings, and Skype WiFi.

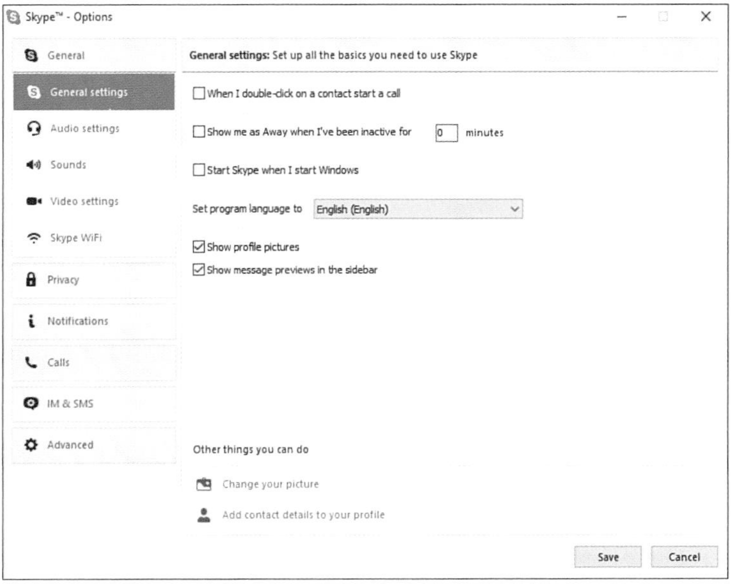

FIGURE 12.21

To configure Skype, work in the Options dialog box.

CHOOSING OPTIONS ON THE GENERAL SETTINGS SCREEN

Start by clicking the General category in the sidebar and then clicking the General Settings subcategory. Here, you should set the following settings:

- **When I Double-Click on a Contact Start a Call.** Check this check box if you want to be able to start a call by double-clicking a contact.

- **Show Me as Away When I've Been Inactive for *N* Minutes.** Check this check box if you want Skype to change your status to Away after the number of minutes you specify of inactivity.

- **Start Skype When I Start Windows.** Check this check box if you want to launch Skype automatically each time you sign in to Windows. This setting is handy if you use Skype all the time, or even frequently.

- **Show Profile Pictures.** Check this check box if you want to see profile pictures. They're usually helpful, but you run into the occasional eyesore.

■ **Show Message Previews in the Sidebar.** Check this check box if you want Skype to display message previews in the sidebar. Previews are usually helpful for seeing what's going on.

CHOOSING OPTIONS ON THE AUDIO SETTINGS SCREEN

The Audio Settings screen enables you to configure your microphone, speakers, and ringing. These settings are all straightforward.

You can click the Show Advanced Options button to display the Advanced Options screen, which lets you specify the order in which to use your microphones and speakers or headphones. For example, if you use a headset sometimes and your laptop's built-in microphone the rest of the time, you'd drag the entry for the headset's microphone above the entry for the laptop's microphone in the Microphone list.

CHOOSING OPTIONS ON THE SOUNDS SCREEN

The Sounds screen enables you to choose which events Skype plays sounds for and which sounds it plays for those events.

In the Select Which Events Play a Sound box, work your way through the list of events—Ringtone, Dial Tone, Busy Signal, and so on. Check the check box for each event for which you want a sound to play. With the event still selected, go to the Choose Which Sound to Play drop-down menu and select the ringtone you want.

You can click the Import Sounds button to import your own sound files to the My Custom Sounds box. You can then use these sounds for events.

CHOOSING OPTIONS ON THE VIDEO SETTINGS SCREEN

The Video Settings screen has two settings you'll likely want to set:

■ **Webcam Settings.** Click this button to display the Video Capture Filter Properties dialog box, in which you can adjust the picture your webcam is producing. For example, if the picture looks like twilight in a coal sack, you could turn up the Brightness setting and play with the Backlight Comp setting.

■ **Automatically Receive Video and Share Screens With.** In this area, select the Anyone option button, the People in My Contact List Only option button (the default), or the No One button, as needed.

CHOOSING OPTIONS ON THE SKYPE WIFI SCREEN

On the Skype WiFi screen, check the Enable Skype WiFi check box if you want to allow your computer to use Skype WiFi. Skype WiFi lets you use your Skype credit to pay for the use of public Wi-Fi hotspots, so it can be handy for a laptop or tablet you carry with you.

CHOOSING OPTIONS ON THE PRIVACY SETTINGS SCREEN

Click the Privacy button in the sidebar to display the Privacy category, and then click the Privacy Settings button to display the Privacy Settings screen. Here, you can configure the following settings:

- **Allow Calls From.** In this area, select the Anyone option button or the People in My Contact List Only option button, as needed.
- **Automatically Receive Video and Share Screens With.** In this area, select the Anyone option button, the People in My Contact List Only option button (the default), or the No One button, as needed.

> **NOTE** The Automatically Receive Video and Share Screens With setting appears on both the Privacy Settings screen and the Video Settings screen.

- **Allow IMs From.** In this area, first select the Anyone option button or the People in My Contact List Only option button, as appropriate. Then open the Keep History For drop-down menu and choose the length of time: No History, 2 Weeks, 1 Month, 3 Months, or Forever.

> **! CAUTION** Keep your IM history forever only if you must—for example, for legal reasons. You can clear your IM history at any point by clicking the Clear History button in the Allow IMs From area of the Privacy Settings screen.

- **Accept Skype Browser Cookies.** Check this check box if you are prepared to allow Skype to store cookies (small text files) on your computer to track your preferences. You can click the Clear Skype Cookies button to get rid of all the Skype cookies at any point.
- **Allow Microsoft Targeted Ads, Including Use of Skype Profile Age and Gender.** Uncheck this check box unless you want to allow Microsoft to use some of your Skype information to try to serve you targeted ads.

WORKING ON THE BLOCKED CONTACTS SCREEN

The Blocked Contacts screen in the Privacy category of Skype options enables you to manage your list of blocked contacts. The controls here are straightforward:

- **Block a contact.** When you want to prevent a contact from contacting you via Skype, open the drop-down menu and click the contact's name. Then click the Block This Person button. Skype adds the contact's name to the Blocked People box.

- **Unblock a contact.** When you're ready to bring a contact back in from the cold, click the contact in the Blocked People box, and then click the Unblock This Person button.

CHOOSING OPTIONS ON THE NOTIFICATION SETTINGS SCREEN

Click the Notifications button in the sidebar to display the Notifications category, and then click the Notification Settings button to display the Notification Settings screen (see Figure 12.22). Here, you can configure the following settings:

- **Display a Notification in the Windows Tray When Someone....** In this area, check the check boxes for the events for which you want notifications and uncheck the check boxes for those you don't need brought to your attention. The events are Comes Online, Goes Offline, Starts an IM with Me, Sends Me a Video Message, Sends Me a File, Requests My Contact Details, Leaves Me a Voice Message, Has a Birthday, and Sends Me Contacts.

- **Display a Notification in the Windows Tray When Skype....** In this area, check the Sends Me a Message check box if you want to receive a notification when Skype sends you a message.

- **Do Not Show Notifications When.** In this area, you can check the Recording a Video Message or Sharing Screens check box if you want to suppress notifications when you're recording or sharing.

> **NOTE** The Sounds screen in the Notifications category of the Options dialog box contains the same controls and fulfills the same purpose as the Sounds screen in the General category. Look back to the section "Choosing Options on the Sounds Screen," earlier in this chapter, for coverage of sounds.

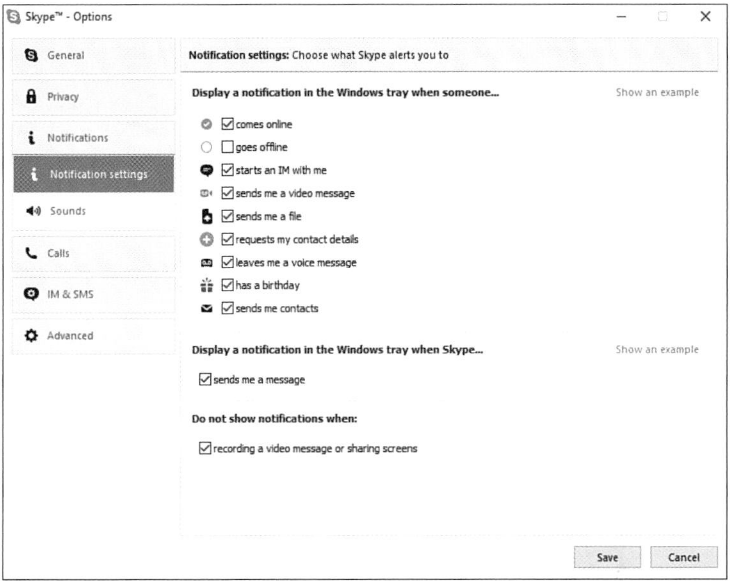

FIGURE 12.22

On the Notification Settings screen, specify which notifications you want by checking and unchecking the check boxes.

CHOOSING OPTIONS ON THE CALL SETTINGS SCREEN

Click the Calls button in the sidebar to display the Calls category, and then click the Call Settings button to display the Call Settings screen.

On the Basic Options part of this screen (which appears at first), select the Allow Anyone to Call Me option button or the Only Allow People in My Contact List to Call Me option button, as appropriate.

Then click the Show Advanced Options button to display the Advanced Options part of the screen, which contains these settings you'll probably want to set:

■ **Show Call Controls When Skype Is in the Background.** Check this check box if you want the Skype controls to be visible when an app other than Skype is in the foreground. This option is helpful, especially if you use Skype extensively.

■ **Answer Incoming Calls Automatically.** Check this check box if you want Skype to pick up incoming calls automatically. After checking this check box, you can check the Start My Video Automatically When I Am in a Call check box if you want Skype to start your video automatically as well.

> **! CAUTION** Enable the Answer Incoming Calls Automatically feature only if you're convinced it'll be helpful. Usually, it's easy enough to pick up calls manually when you're at your computer—and when you're not at your computer, you might not want Skype to pick up calls for you.

■ **For Emergency Calls, My Default Location Is.** Open this drop-down menu and select your location in case you need to place emergency calls using Skype.

SETTING UP CALL FORWARDING

The options on the Call Forwarding screen enable you to forward your Skype calls to a landline phone, a mobile phone, or another Skype account. Click the Call Forwarding Options link to display the controls for setting up call forwarding. You can then check the Forward My Calls To check box, specify the destination in the drop-down menu under it, and set the delay in the Forward Calls if I Do Not Answer Within *N* Seconds box.

> **NOTE** To use call forwarding, you must either buy Skype Credit or pay for a Skype subscription. After using call forwarding, remember to turn it off when you no longer need it.

Click the Add More Phone Numbers link if you want to set up two or three numbers or Skype accounts for call forwarding.

> **! CAUTION** When you set up multiple numbers or Skype accounts for call forwarding, Skype forwards calls to all the numbers or accounts *at the same time*. As of this writing, you can't set up multiple numbers or accounts and then choose which to use at any given point—you can only enable or disable forwarding to all the numbers or accounts at once.

SETTING UP VOICE MESSAGES

The Voice Messages screen contains only the Set Up Voice Messaging link, which you can click to open the Skype website in your default browser, such as Microsoft

Edge. After logging in to your account, you can set the Enable Voice Messaging and Never Miss a Call Again switch to On.

> **TIP** After enabling voice messaging, set up email alerts or SMS alerts for voice messages you receive. These alerts help you avoid missing vital messages by forgetting to check your voice messages.

> **NOTE** The Video Settings screen in the Calls category contains the same controls and has the same effect as the Video Settings screen in the General category. Look back to the section "Choosing Options on the Video Settings Screen," earlier in this chapter, for coverage of these options.

CHOOSING OPTIONS ON THE IM SETTINGS SCREEN

Click the IM & SMS button in the sidebar to display the IM & SMS category, and then click the IM Settings button to display the IM Settings screen.

At first, the IM Settings screen displays only one option, which bashfully hides its name:

■ **Allow IMs From.** Select the Allow Anyone to Send IMs to Me option button or the Only Allow People in My Contact List to Send Me Instant Messages option button, as needed.

Next, click the Show Advanced Options button to display options for choosing how long to keep your IM history, configuring the effects of pressing Enter and Ctrl+V (separately), and choosing where to store files you receive via Skype.

CHOOSING OPTIONS ON THE IM APPEARANCE SCREEN

The IM Appearance screen enables you to configure the way instant messaging appears in Skype. Your options include setting a font and size that you like; choosing whether to display images and other media previews; and choosing whether to display emoticons, advanced text formatting, and timestamps.

> **NOTE** The SMS Settings screen contains links for learning more about sending SMS (basically, text messages to phone numbers) on your computer and for buying Skype Credit to enable you to send SMS to mobile phones.

CHOOSING OPTIONS ON THE ADVANCED SETTINGS SCREEN

Click the Advanced button in the sidebar to display the Advanced category, and then click the Advanced Settings button to display the Advanced Settings screen. Here, you can configure the following settings:

- **Use Skype to Call callto: Links on the Web.** Check this check box if you want to be able to start a Skype call by clicking a web page link that uses the callto: protocol.

- **Use Skype to call tel: Links on the Web.** Check this check box if you want to be able to start a Skype call by clicking a web page link that uses the tel: protocol.

- **Keep Skype in the Taskbar While I'm Signed In.** Check this check box to keep the Skype button visible in the Taskbar all the time you're signed into Skype. Provided you're not desperate for space on the taskbar, having the button there is handy for access to Skype.

- **Show Skype Watermark During Calls.** Uncheck this check box if you want to remove the Skype watermark that appears on video calls.

TURNING OFF AUTOMATIC UPDATES FOR SKYPE

The Automatic Updates screen in the Options dialog box contains only a Turn Off Automatic Updates button. If you have administrator permissions, you can click this button to turn off automatic updating for Skype on your computer. If you don't turn off automatic updating, Skype upgrades itself—without consulting you—when updates are available.

> **CAUTION** Turning off automatic Skype updates on your account turns them off for all users of the computer. There's no in-between setting. Because updates may fix vulnerabilities in Skype that could expose your computer to attack across the Internet, it's normally best to let Skype apply the updates.

CHOOSING OPTIONS ON THE CONNECTION SCREEN

The Connection screen in the Options dialog box enables you to control how Skype connects to the Internet. These are the options on the Connection screen:

- **Use Port *N* for Incoming Connections.** This box shows the port Skype is using for incoming connections. Usually, you should leave the default setting; in some configurations, you can't change it anyway.

- **Use Port 80 and 443 for Additional Incoming Connections.** Check this check box if you want to let Skype use these two ports for extra incoming connections, as needed. This is normally a good idea.

- **Proxy.** In this drop-down menu, choose Automatic Proxy Detection (the default), HTTPS, or SOCKS5, as needed. For HTTPS or SOCKS5, enter the proxy's hostname or IP address in the Host box and the port number in the Port box.

- **Enable Proxy Authentication.** Check this check box if the proxy server requires Skype to authenticate your computer, and then enter the user name in the Username box and the password in the Password box.

- **Enable uPnP.** Check this check box if you want Skype to use the Universal Plug and Play (usually abbreviated to UPnP, although Skype uses uPnP) to detect network settings. This is a good idea for home networks.

- **Allow Direct Connections to Your Contacts Only.** Check this check box if you want to restrict Skype to using direct connections only for people who are in your contacts list. For other connections, Skype establishes the connection through its servers and hides your computer's IP address, which is good for security but means Skype may take longer to set up your calls.

CONFIGURING KEYBOARD SHORTCUTS ON THE HOTKEYS SCREEN

The Hotkeys screen in the Options dialog box (see Figure 12.23) lets you enable or disable keyboard shortcuts as a whole. If you enable keyboard shortcuts, you can choose which ones to use, and you can customize the keyboard shortcuts for different actions.

Check the Enable Keyboard Shortcuts check box at the top, and then check the check box in the Active column for each shortcut you want to use.

To change the keys used for a shortcut, click the shortcut in the list, and then click the Change Selected Shortcut button. In the Set Hotkey For dialog box that opens (see Figure 12.24), check the Shift check box, the Ctrl check box, or the Alt check box as needed; type the key in the box on the right; and then click the OK button.

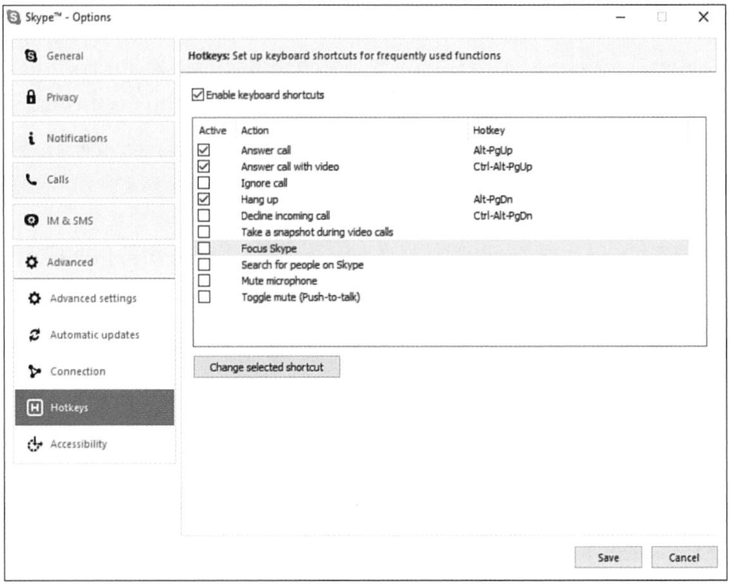

FIGURE 12.23

On the Hotkeys screen in the Options dialog box, check the Enable Keyboard Shortcuts check box, and then choose which keyboard shortcuts to use.

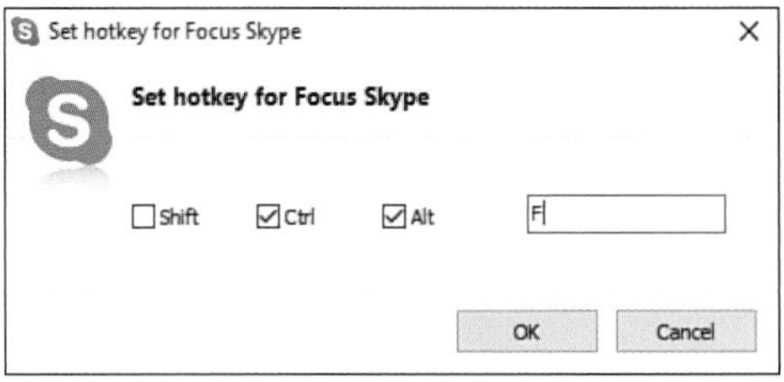

FIGURE 12.24

Use the Set Hotkey For dialog box to create custom keyboard shortcuts for controlling Skype easily.

CHOOSING OPTIONS ON THE ACCESSIBILITY SCREEN

The Accessibility screen in the Options dialog box contains only one setting, the Enable Accessible Mode check box. Check this check box to turn on Accessible Mode, which enables screen reader apps to work in Skype—for example, to read your messages aloud.

SAVING YOUR CONFIGURATION CHANGES

When you finish configuring Skype, click the Save button. Skype saves your changes and closes the Options dialog box.

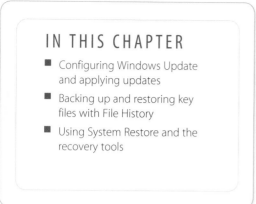

IN THIS CHAPTER

- Configuring Windows Update and applying updates
- Backing up and restoring key files with File History
- Using System Restore and the recovery tools

13

UPDATING AND TROUBLESHOOTING WINDOWS

To keep your computer running at its best and to protect it from online threats, you should apply updates to Windows soon after Microsoft makes them available. Updates may include fixes for existing problems—such as patches that fix newly discovered security threats—or new features. You can configure the Windows Update tool to get updates the way you prefer.

To keep your data and settings safe, you can set up the File History tool to back up your essentials to an external drive. If problems occur, you can recover files from File History.

To protect your computer's system configuration and restore it to the state it was in before problems occurred, you can use the System Restore feature. And when things go seriously wrong, you can use the recovery tools that Windows includes.

MAKING WINDOWS UPDATE WORK YOUR WAY

Most versions of Windows come set to install updates automatically—so if you don't want the updates installed, you should change the settings.

> **NOTE** The Home edition of Windows 10 comes set to download updates automatically. You can't change this setting, but you can choose between having Windows install the updates automatically and having Windows notify you before installing them.

CONFIGURING WINDOWS UPDATE

To check or change your Windows Update settings, display the Windows Update pane in the Settings app. Follow these steps:

1. Choose Start, Settings to open the Settings window.
2. Click Update & Security to display the Update & Security screen. Windows automatically selects the Windows Update item in the left column, so the Windows Update pane appears (see Figure 13.1).

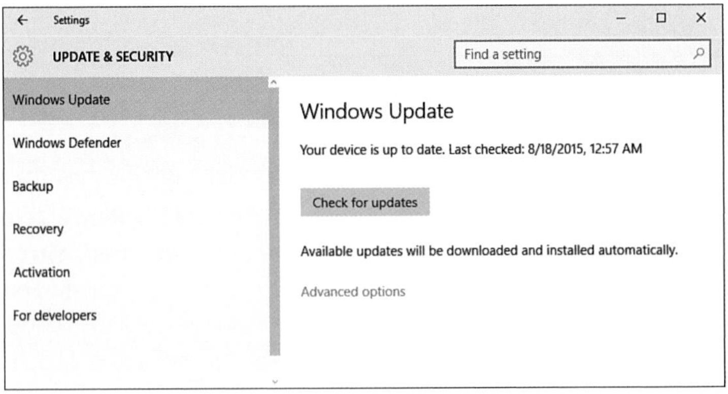

FIGURE 13.1

The Windows Update pane on the Update & Security screen of the Settings app shows any available updates. You can click the Check for Updates button to force a check for any updates released since Windows last checked.

Now look at the readouts in the Windows Update pane:

- **Status.** At the top of the Windows Update pane, you'll see a status summary, such as "Your device is up to date" followed by the date and time Windows last checked for updates, or "Updates are available" followed by a summary of the updates.

- **Available updates.** This readout shows your current setting, such as "Available updates will be downloaded and installed automatically."

If you want to change your settings, click the Advanced Options link at the bottom of the Windows Update pane. In the Advanced Options pane that appears (see Figure 13.2), you can choose the following settings:

- **Choose How Updates Are Installed.** In this drop-down menu, choose Automatic (Recommended) if you want to install updates automatically. Choose Notify to Schedule Restart if you prefer to control when Windows installs the updates.

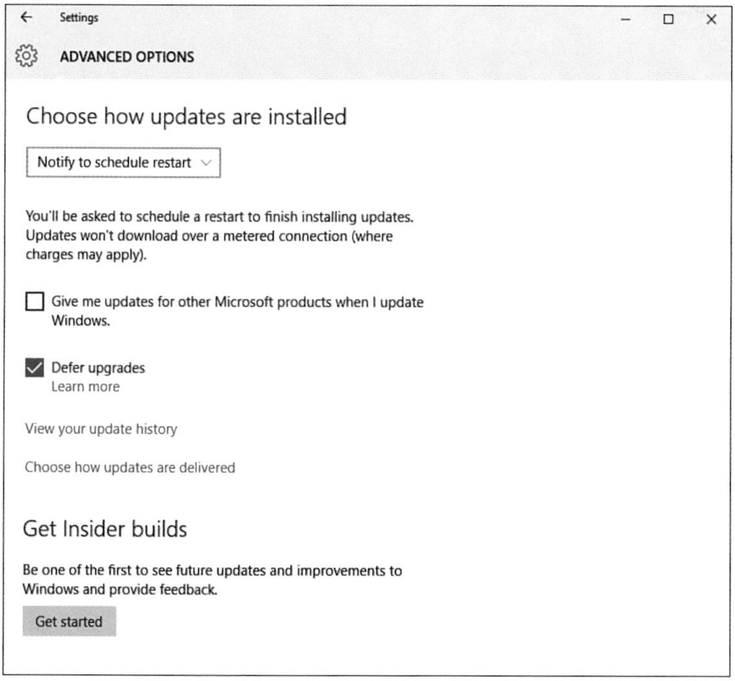

FIGURE 13.2

In the Advanced Options pane, choose how to receive updates for Windows.

WINDOWS 10 TIPS AND TRICKS

NOTE The Defer Upgrades check box doesn't appear in Windows 10 Home Version.

!CAUTION Windows Update tries to avoid downloading updates over a metered Internet connection, such as a 3G connection or an LTE connection on a cellular-capable tablet or laptop. This limitation is eminently sensible but may not always work as intended. If your computer sometimes uses a metered Internet connection (whether cellular or not), you may find it wise to check for updates manually when your computer is safely using a nonmetered connection.

■ **Give Me Updates for Other Microsoft Products When I Update Windows.** Check this check box if you want your computer to download updates for other Microsoft software installed on your computer when it gets updates for Windows.

NOTE When installing updates automatically, Windows tries to select a time that you don't normally use your computer, such as 3:00 a.m. This usually works pretty well, but if you need to have your computer available at all hours of the day and night, you may prefer to install updates only at times that suit you.

■ **Defer Upgrades.** Check this check box if you want to delay the downloading and installation of new features.

NOTE The Defer Upgrades feature applies only to new features. Even if you check the Defer Upgrades check box, Windows still downloads and installs security upgrades.

■ **Get Started.** Click the Get Started button in the Get Insider Builds section if you would like to test future updates and improvements to Windows. Insider builds enable you to see fixes and new features and to provide feedback on them before Microsoft unleashes them on the wider world. Once you've signed up for this program, the Stop Insider Builds button appears in place of the Get Insider Builds button, giving you an escape route.

> **! CAUTION** Don't use Insider builds of Windows on any computer whose contents you value or that you require for day-to-day use.

WHY MIGHT YOU NOT WANT TO INSTALL UPDATES AUTOMATICALLY?

Installing updates as soon as possible can help not only keep your computer running smoothly but also eliminate existing bugs and keep it protected against online threats. So in general, allowing Microsoft to check for and install updates automatically is a great boon—especially if you're more interested in getting things done with your computer than spending time coping and configuring it.

The downside to installing updates automatically is that some updates can sometimes cause problems on some computers. Microsoft works hard to make sure updates work, both for altruistic reasons and because updates causing problems rather than fixing them produces a publicity nightmare for the company. But given the extreme variety of computers that run Windows, it's impossible for Microsoft to check everything.

So if your computer contains data and apps you can't do without, you may prefer to wait a few days after Microsoft releases an update before installing it. If you hear howls of distress from the Twittersphere, social media, or your colleagues, wait until Microsoft releases a fix for any problems the update causes. But if the update installs without fuss—as most updates do—install it on your computer as soon as is convenient, because waiting longer may mean leaving your computer open to any threats against which the update provides protection.

APPLYING AN UPDATE

If you find Windows has scheduled a restart to apply an update, as in Figure 13.3, look at the time and date to make sure they suit you. If so, leave the We'll Schedule a Restart During a Time You Usually Don't Use Your Device option button selected. If not, click the Select a Restart Time option button, set the time in the Time box, and choose the day in the Day drop-down menu.

Alternatively, save any documents that contain unsaved changes, and then click the Restart Now button to apply the updates now.

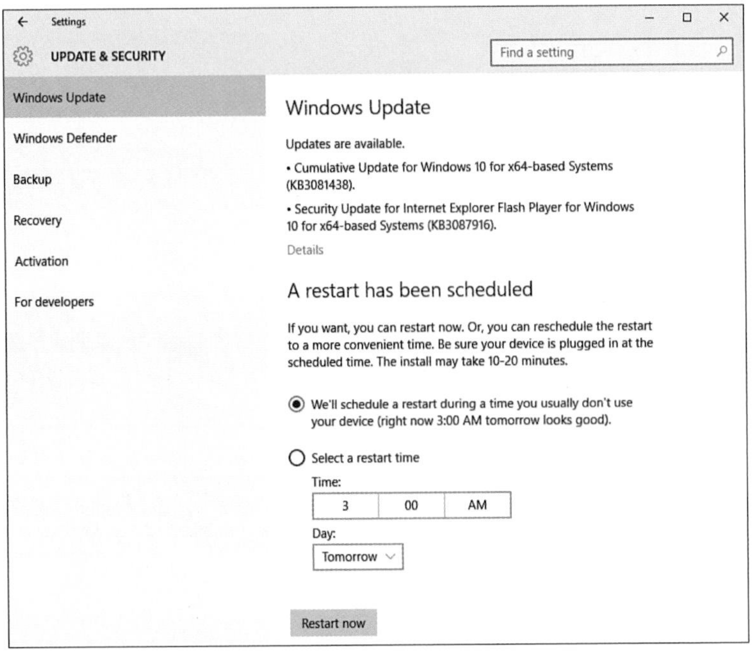

FIGURE 13.3
If Windows has scheduled a restart to apply an update it has downloaded, you can change the time and day or simply click Restart Now to install the updates without waiting.

> **! CAUTION** Interrupting Windows while it's applying updates can prevent your computer from running stably—so don't apply updates just before you have to grab your computer and head for work or for the airport. Instead, look at the length of time that appears in the paragraph of text under the A Restart Has Been Scheduled heading (such as "The install may take 10–20 minutes"), and allow yourself plenty of time beyond that just to be safe.

BACKING UP KEY FILES WITH FILE HISTORY

File History is a powerful feature that enables you to save copies of your files to an external drive or a network share so that you can recover them after disaster strikes. File History tracks files in the folders you specify and automatically backs up any file to which you make changes.

File History is not enabled by default, so you must enable it.

> **NOTE** File History requires an external drive or a network share so that it provides protection even if your computer suffers a serious mishap. If you use an external drive, it is best to dedicate that drive to File History rather than using the drive for other purposes as well. If you are buying a new drive for File History, get one with several terabytes of storage so that you will be able to keep File History for several months.

ENABLING FILE HISTORY

After attaching an external drive or connecting to a network share, follow these steps to enable File History:

1. Choose Start, Settings to open the Settings window.
2. Click Update & Security to display the Update & Security screen.
3. In the left column, click Backup to display the Backup pane (see Figure 13.4).

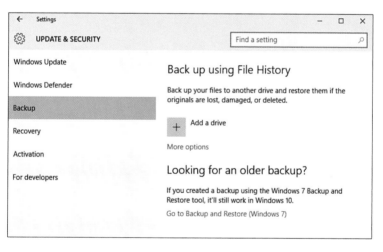

FIGURE 13.4

In the Backup pane in the Settings app, click Add a Drive to add the drive you will use for File History.

4. Click Add a Drive to display the pop-up panel for adding a drive.
5. Click the drive you want to use. The Automatically Back Up My Files switch appears in the Backup pane, set to On (see Figure 13.5).

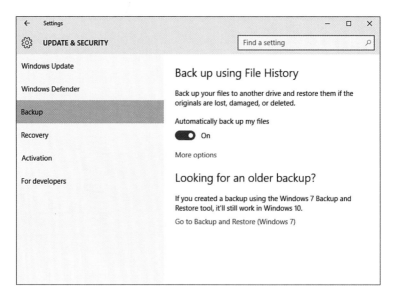

FIGURE 13.5

After you select the drive, the Backup pane displays the Automatically Back Up My Files switch and sets it to On.

6. Click the More Options link to display the Backup Options screen. The left screen in Figure 13.6 shows the top part of the screen, and the right screen shows the bottom part.

7. Open the Back Up My Files drop-down menu and select the backup frequency. Your options run from Every 10 Minutes to Daily; the default is Every Hour, which works well for general use.

8. Open the Keep My Backups drop-down menu and choose how long to keep the backups: Until Space Is Needed; a length of time ranging from 1 Month to 2 Years; or Forever, which is the default.

9. Use the controls in the Back Up These Folders list to specify which folders to back up. You can click the Add a Folder button to add a folder. To remove a folder, click its button, and then click the Remove button that appears.

10. Use the Add a Folder button in the Exclude These Folders list to specify any folders you want to exclude from the backups. For example, you might exclude folders containing music or movies that you have stored elsewhere; this would keep down the size of backups and allow more backups to fit on the backup drive.

11. If you want to back up your files now rather than waiting for the next interval you specified in step 7, click the Back Up Now button near the top of the window.

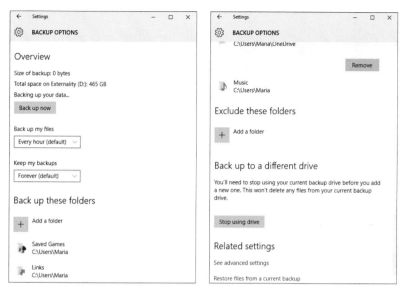

FIGURE 13.6

On the Backup Options screen, you can choose how frequently to back up your files, how long to keep the backups, and which folders to back up.

File History is now set to back up your files.

USING HISTORY TO RESTORE FILES

After enabling File History, you can use it to restore the files you need. To do so, follow these steps:

1. Choose Start, Settings to open the Settings window.
2. Click Update & Security to display the Update & Security screen.
3. In the left column, click Backup to display the Backup pane.
4. Click More Options to display the Backup Options screen.
5. In the Related Settings section at the bottom of the screen, click the Restore Files from a Current Backup link to open the File History window (see Figure 13.7).
6. At the bottom of the window, click the Previous Version button (the left arrow) or the Next Version button (the right arrow) to move to the version you want.

FIGURE 13.7

In the File History window, navigate to the backup you want to use, select the item you want to recover, and then click the green Restore to Original Location button.

> **TIP** You can press Ctrl+left arrow to display the previous version or Ctrl+right arrow to display the next version.

7. Navigate to the folder that contains the item or items you want to recover.
8. Click the item or items.
9. Click the Restore to Original Location button (the green button with the curling arrow) to restore the item.
10. If the Replace or Skip Files dialog box opens, click the Replace the File in the Destination button, the Skip This File button, or the Compare Info for Both Files button, as appropriate.
11. When you finish restoring files, click the Close button (the × button at the right end of the title bar) to close the File History window.

RESOLVING ISSUES IN ACTION CENTER

Windows monitors your computer's system to identify any problems. When it discovers issues you need to deal with, it displays a message in the Action Center pane to let you know. For example, in Figure 13.8, the Security and Maintenance section contains a recommendation to disable three apps that are starting automatically, because such automatic startup may sap performance.

> **NOTE** The Action Center icon in the notification area appears white when you have new notifications and dark when you have none. You can open Action Center by clicking the Action Center icon in the notification area or by swiping in from the right side of a touchscreen.

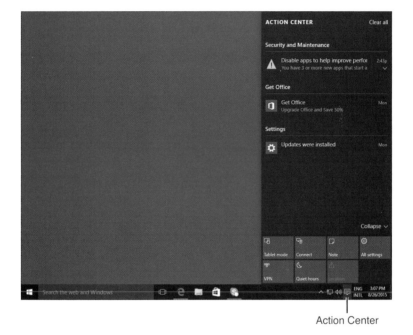

Action Center

FIGURE 13.8

In the Action Center pane, you can click a message such as the Security and Maintenance message shown here to go directly to the Windows tool for dealing with the issue.

Click a message to open or activate the Windows tool that enables you to deal with the issue. For example, if you click the Disable Apps message shown in this example, Windows opens Task Manager and displays the Startup tab (see Figure 13.9) so that you can disable the apps that are set to start automatically.

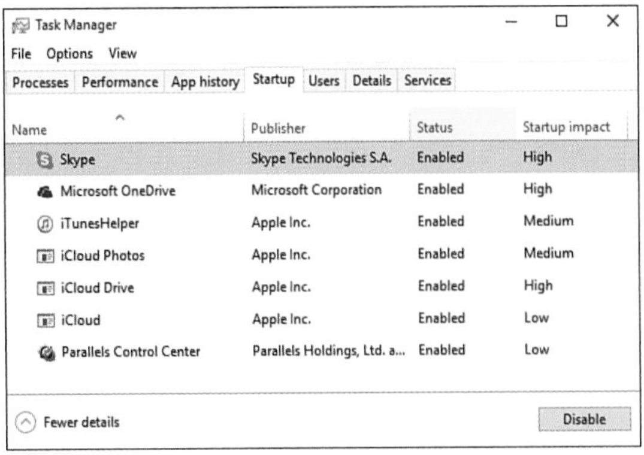

FIGURE 13.9
You can use the Startup tab of Task Manager to disable apps that are set to start automatically.

> **NOTE** See the section "Reducing the Number of Startup Items" in Chapter 8 and the section "Managing the Apps You're Running" in Chapter 9 for detailed coverage of Task Manager.

REVIEWING SECURITY AND MAINTENANCE ISSUES

To check the status of your computer, you can review messages and resolve problems on the Security and Maintenance screen in Control Panel. Follow these steps to open Control Panel and display the Security and Maintenance screen:

1. Right-click or long-press Start to display the shortcut menu.

2. Click Control Panel to open a Control Panel window.

3. Under the System and Security heading, click the Review Your Computer's Status link to display the Security and Maintenance screen (see Figure 13.10).

4. Look at the Review Recent Messages and Resolve Problems section to see whether Windows has identified any issues that need your attention.

5. After dealing with any issues, click the Security heading or the Maintenance heading, depending on which section you want to expand. The section's settings appear. Figure 13.11 shows the Security section expanded.

6. Look through the settings to see whether you need to change any. You can click a Change Settings link (such as the one for Windows SmartScreen in Figure 13.11) to change the settings.

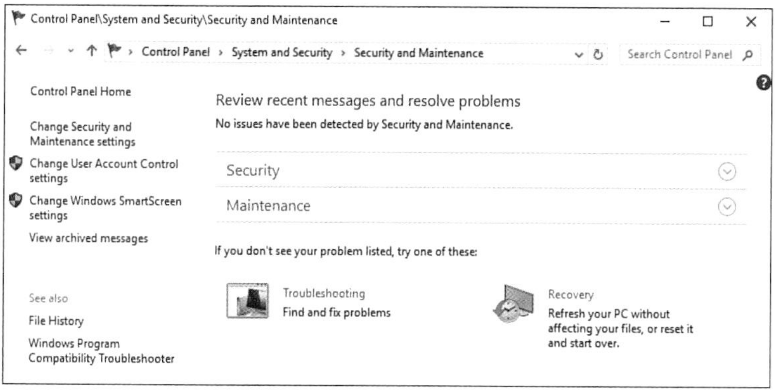

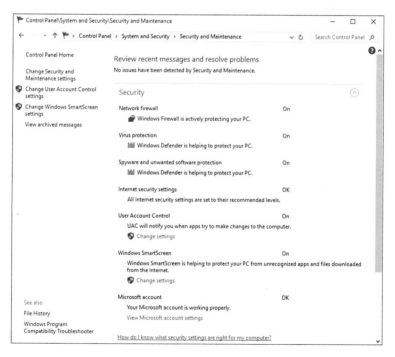

FIGURE 13.10

On the Security and Maintenance screen, see if the Review Recent Messages and Resolve Problems section contains any messages or problems. If not, you can expand the Security section or the Maintenance section to browse the settings.

FIGURE 13.11

Review the Security settings to make sure your computer is protected against viruses, spyware, and other threats.

CREATING AND USING SYSTEM RESTORE POINTS

System Restore enables you to save snapshots of your computer's configuration so that you can restore it to an earlier configuration after a problem occurs. For example, if you install a driver that causes Windows to crash, you may be able to recover by restoring Windows to an earlier configuration.

> **!CAUTION** System Restore protects your Windows configuration and enables you to restore it when things go wrong. System Restore doesn't protect your documents and files at all. So even if you configure System Restore, you must also use File History or another backup tool to protect your documents and files.

CREATING SYSTEM RESTORE POINTS

Windows can create system restore points automatically, but you can also create them manually as needed. If System Restore is not enabled on your computer, you need to enable it.

DISPLAYING THE SYSTEM PROTECTION TAB OF THE SYSTEM PROPERTIES DIALOG BOX

To work with System Restore, first display the System Protection tab of the System Properties dialog box by following these steps:

1. Right-click or long-press Start to display the shortcut menu.

2. Click System to open a Control Panel window to the System window.

> **☑ TIP** You can open the System window from the keyboard by pressing Windows Key+Break.

3. In the left pane, click System Protection to display the System Protection tab of the System Properties dialog box (see Figure 13.12).

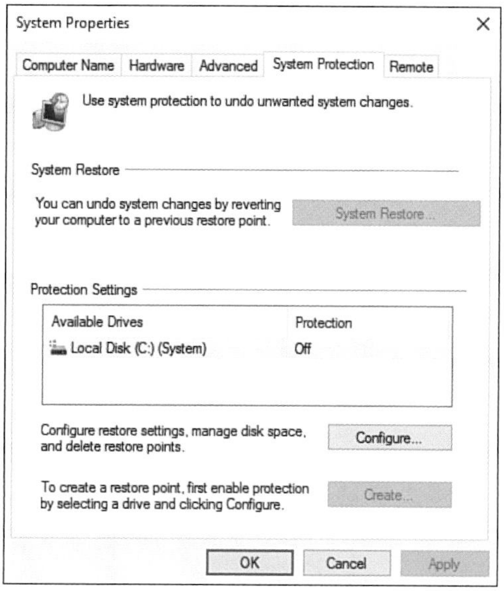

FIGURE 13.12

You can configure System Restore from the System Protection tab of the System Properties dialog box.

CONFIGURING SYSTEM RESTORE TO SUIT YOUR NEEDS

Now that you've displayed the System Protection tab of the System Properties dialog box, you can configure System Restore to meet your needs. Follow these steps:

1. In the Protection Settings box, click the drive you want to affect. For most computers, you'll want to protect the system drive, which is usually the C: drive.

2. Click the Configure button to display the System Protection for Local Disk dialog box for the drive (see Figure 13.13).

3. In the Restore Settings area at the top of the dialog box, select the Turn On System Protection option button instead of the Disable System Protection option button.

4. In the Disk Space Usage area, drag the Max Usage slider to the appropriate point on the scale—for example, 15%.

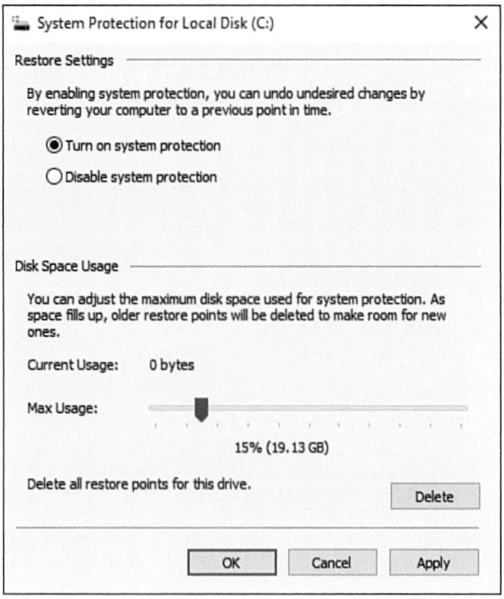

FIGURE 13.13

In the System Protection for Local Disk dialog box, select the Turn On System Protection option button and drag the Max Usage slider to the appropriate point.

> **NOTE** You can click the Delete button in the System Protection for Local Disk dialog box to delete all the restore points that System Restore has created. Normally, you'd do this only if you've run out of space on the drive and you've exhausted all your other options for reclaiming space.

5. Click the OK button to apply your changes and close the System Protection dialog box.

Now that you've set up System Restore, it creates restore points automatically on its own schedule and when you take actions that may destabilize Windows, such as installing unapproved third-party software. You can also create restore points manually as explained in the next section.

CREATING SYSTEM RESTORE POINTS MANUALLY

You can create system restore points manually at any time you want. Normally, you'd create a restore point before taking an action that might cause Windows to become unstable, such as updating the driver software for a device or installing an app from a source other than the Microsoft Store.

To create a restore point manually, follow these steps:

1. Display the System Protection tab of the System Properties dialog box. For example, press Windows Key+Break and then click System Protection in the left pane of the System window.

2. Click the Create button to display the System Protection: Create a Restore Point dialog box (see Figure 13.14).

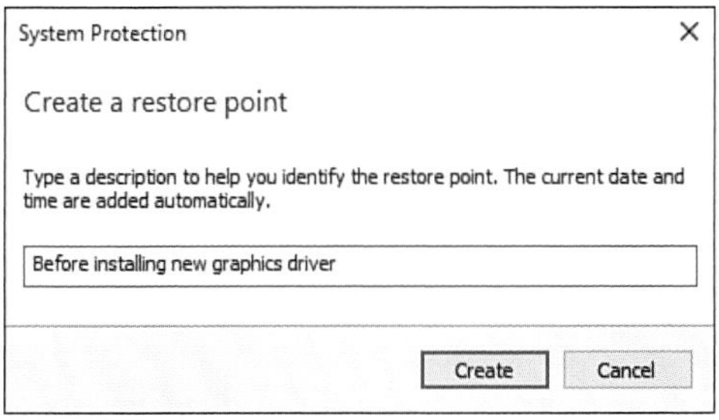

System Protection   ✕

Create a restore point

Type a description to help you identify the restore point. The current date and time are added automatically.

Before installing new graphics driver

[Create]   [Cancel]

FIGURE 13.14

In the System Protection: Create a Restore Point dialog box, type the name or description for the restore point, and then click the Create button.

3. Type a description for the restore point, such as **Before installing new graphics driver**. Windows automatically adds the date and time to the restore point name, so you don't need to include those details.

4. Click the Create button. Windows creates the restore point and then displays a System Protection dialog box saying that it was created successfully.

5. Click the Close button to close the System Protection dialog box.

6. Click the OK button to close the System Properties dialog box.

RESTORING WINDOWS TO A SYSTEM RESTORE POINT

When you need to restore Windows to an earlier configuration, you can use System Restore to go back to a restore point. You can use System Restore in either of two ways, depending on how well (or otherwise) your computer is running:

- **Launch System Restore from the System Properties dialog box.** If Windows is running well enough for you to open the System Properties dialog box, you can launch the System Restore Wizard from there.

- **Launch System Restore from the Advanced Options screen in the recovery tools.** See the section "Using the Advanced Startup Tools," later in this chapter.

Follow these steps to launch the System Restore Wizard when Windows is running normally:

1. Display the System Protection tab of the System Properties dialog box. For example, right-click or long-press Start, click System, and then click System Protection in the left pane of the System window.

2. In the System Restore area, click the System Restore button to launch the System Restore Wizard.

3. On the first screen, click the Next button to display the Restore Your Computer to the State It Was In Before the Selected Event screen of the wizard (see Figure 13.15).

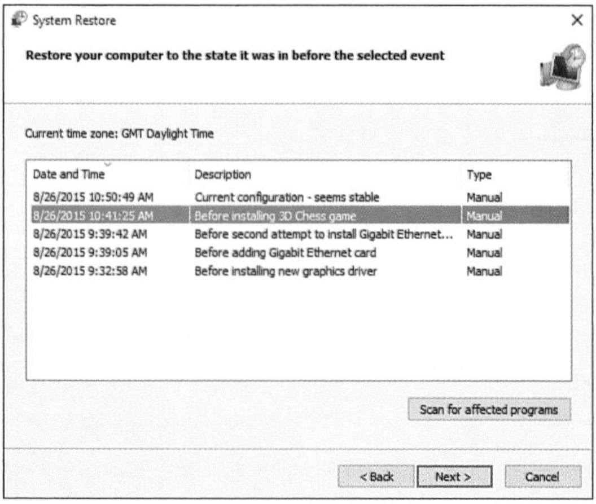

FIGURE 13.15

On the Restore Your Computer to the State It Was In Before the Selected Event screen of the System Restore Wizard, click the restore point you want to use.

4. Click the restore point you want to use.

5. Click the Scan for Affected Programs button to see which apps (if any) will be affected by your restoring Windows to the selected restore point. Windows displays the System Restore dialog box shown in Figure 13.16.

6. Look at the Programs and Drivers That Will Be Deleted list box to see which apps and drivers Windows will remove when restoring your computer to the restore point you chose. If you need these apps and drivers, you will need to reinstall them.

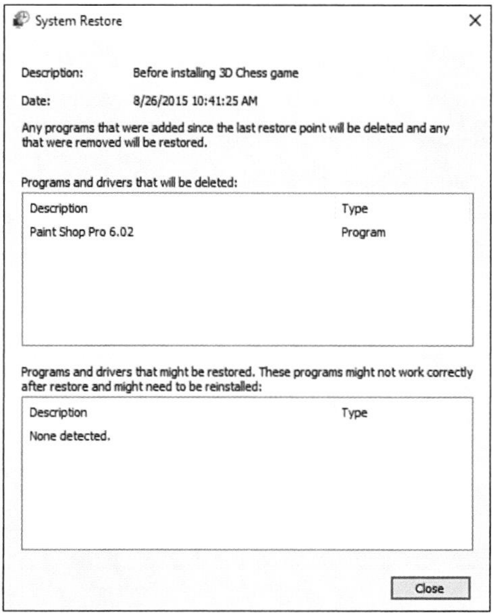

FIGURE 13.16

In this System Restore dialog box, review the Programs and Drivers That Will Be Deleted list box to see which apps and drivers you might need to reinstall after using the restore point.

> **NOTE** One or more of the apps or drivers shown in the Programs and Drivers That Will Be Deleted list box might be the cause of whatever problems have prompted you to use System Restore—so you might not need (or want) to install all of them.

7. Similarly, look at the Programs and Drivers That Might Be Restored list box to see which (if any) apps and drivers you may need to reinstall.

8. Click the Close button to close the System Restore dialog box, returning to the Restore Your Computer to the State It Was In Before the Selected Event screen of the wizard.

> **NOTE** If the System Restore dialog box shows a long list of apps and drivers that you will need to reinstall, you might want to click the Back button in the System Restore Wizard and try a more recent restore point—if there is one.

9. When you've chosen the restore point, click the Next button. The wizard displays the Confirm Your Restore Point screen (see Figure 13.17).

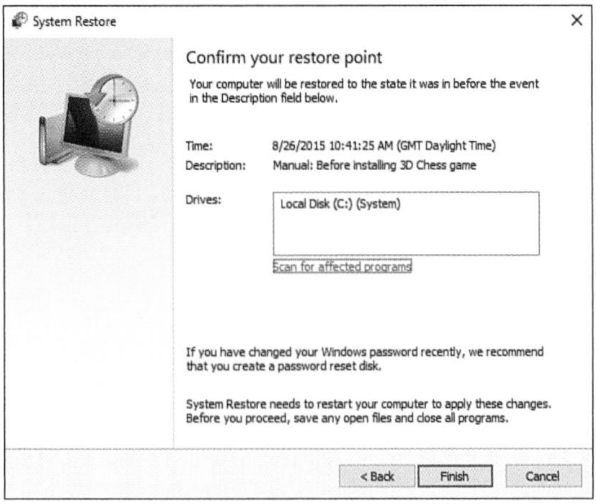

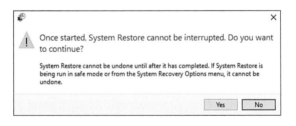

FIGURE 13.17

On the Confirm Your Restore Point screen, verify your choices and then click the Finish button.

10. Look through the details and make sure you've chosen the right restore point.

11. Click the Finish button. The wizard displays a warning dialog box (see Figure 13.18).

FIGURE 13.18

Click the Yes button in this dialog box to proceed with the System Restore operation; click No if you decide not to run System Restore.

12. Click the Yes button. The wizard closes. System Restore then restarts your computer, displaying progress information as it does so (see Figure 13.19).

13. When the lock screen appears, log in as usual. A System Restore dialog box then appears (see Figure 13.20), confirming that the system has been restored to its earlier state.

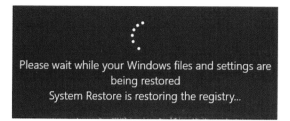

FIGURE 13.19

Wait while System Restore restores the Registry to its previous state.

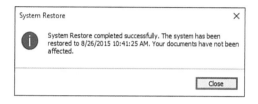

FIGURE 13.20

Windows displays this System Restore dialog box to confirm that it has restored the system to its earlier state.

14. Click the Close button to close the System Restore dialog box. You can then resume using Windows.

UNDOING A SYSTEM RESTORE OPERATION

If restoring the system to a restore point doesn't fix the problems your computer was exhibiting, you can undo the System Restore operation.

> **! CAUTION** If you're going to undo a System Restore operation, you must do so before you make other changes to the system.

To undo the last System Restore operation, follow these steps:

1. Display the System Protection tab of the System Properties dialog box. For example, press Windows Key+Break and then click System Protection in the left pane of the System window.

2. In the System Restore area, click the System Restore button. The System Restore Wizard appears, displaying the Restore System Files and Settings screen (see Figure 13.21).

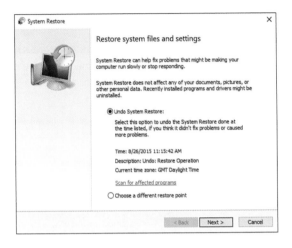

FIGURE 13.21

To undo a System Restore operation, click the Undo System Restore button in this System Restore dialog box.

3. Click the Undo System Restore option button.

> **NOTE** Alternatively, you can select the Choose a Different Restore Point option button and see whether you can get better results from another restore point.

4. Click the Next button. The wizard displays the Confirm Your Restore Point screen.

5. Verify that the Description readout is "Undo: Restore Operation."

6. Click the Finish button. The wizard displays a warning dialog box (shown in Figure 13.18, earlier in this chapter).

7. Click the Yes button, and then wait while System Restore restores your system to the condition it was in before you reverted to the restore point.

SOLVING PROBLEMS WITH THE RECOVERY TOOLS

Windows includes several recovery tools that you can use to solve serious problems that occur on your computer:

- **Reset your PC.** You can reset your PC by reinstalling Windows.

- **Revert to an earlier build of Windows.** If you have updated Windows to a new build that seems to be causing problems, you might be able to go back to the earlier build.

- **Start up from a USB drive or a DVD drive.** If Windows won't run normally, you can start up from another device to troubleshoot problems or to reinstall Windows.

- **Change your PC's firmware settings.** You may sometimes need to change settings in your PC's firmware, the software that runs the PC's hardware.

- **Change Windows startup settings.** If Windows won't start correctly, you may need to adjust startup settings to enable it to start.

- **Repair Windows startup files.** If Windows won't start correctly, you may need to repair the startup files.

- **Restore Windows from a system image.** If Windows becomes corrupted, you may be able to restore it from a file that contains an image of how the system was configured.

This section shows you how to use the recovery tools, starting with how to find them.

> **TIP** The tools discussed here are the standard Windows tools. Your computer may include other recovery tools that you can invoke by giving a particular command at startup. Read your computer's documentation to find out about such tools.

ACCESSING THE RECOVERY TOOLS

Follow these steps to access the recovery tools:

1. Choose Start, Settings to open the Settings window.

2. Click Update & Security to display the Update & Security screen.

3. In the left pane, click Recovery to display the Recovery pane (see Figure 13.22).

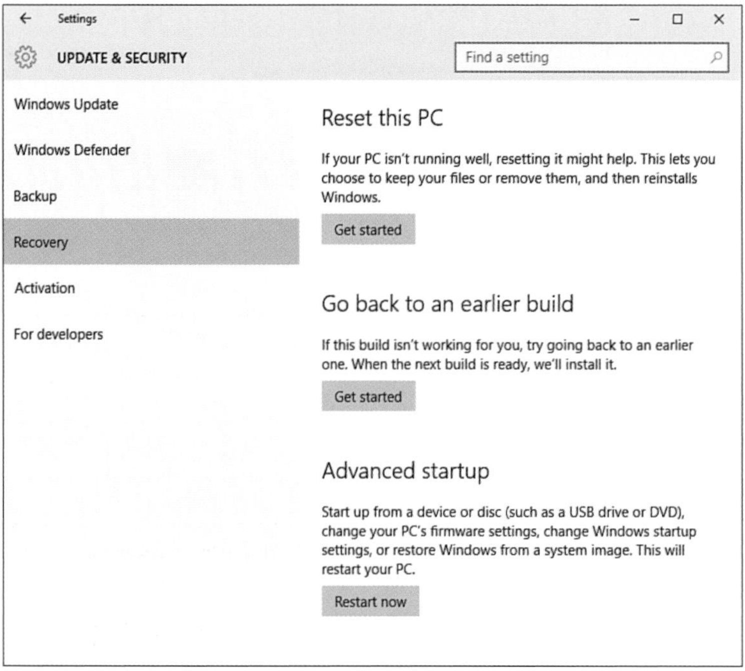

FIGURE 13.22

From the Recovery pane in the Settings app, you can reset your PC, go back to an earlier build of Windows, or perform an advanced startup.

4. Click the button for the tool you want to use. We'll look at the details in the following sections.

RESETTING YOUR PC

The everyday meaning of "resetting" your PC is to restart it (or, in tech terms, to "power-cycle" it). In the recovery tools offered by Windows, resetting has a different meaning: to reinstall Windows, either keeping your files in place or wiping them out.

To reset your PC, follow these steps from the Recovery pane in the Settings app:

1. Click the Get Started button under the Reset This PC heading. The Choose an Option dialog box opens (see Figure 13.23).

2. Click the Keep My Files button if you want to keep your files. Click the Remove Everything button if you've backed up your files and you want to wipe the slate clean.

3. Click the Continue button, and wait while the reinstallation completes.

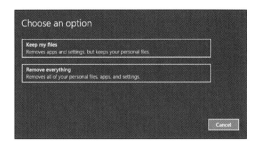

FIGURE 13.23

In the Choose an Option dialog box, choose whether to keep your files when reinstalling Windows or to remove all your files.

GOING BACK TO AN EARLIER BUILD OF WINDOWS

If you've updated Windows to a new build and find that it doesn't work well enough, you can go back to the earlier build. To do so, follow these steps from the Recovery pane in the Settings app:

1. Click the Get Started button under the Go Back to an Earlier Build heading. The Why Are You Going Back? dialog box opens.

> **NOTE**   As you might expect, you can use the Go Back to an Earlier Build feature only if your computer contains an earlier build to which Windows can revert. If you've deleted the Previous Version of Windows files on the System and Reserved screen in the Settings app (for example, to recover precious disk space), you won't be able to go back to that earlier version.

> **CAUTION**   To help avoid your computer running low on storage, Windows 10 may delete the files for your earlier version of Windows 30 days after you install the new version. So if you upgrade and wish you hadn't, revert to the earlier version soon rather than waiting to see if the new version grows on you.

2. Check the check box for each of the preset reasons that apply, such as My Apps or Devices Don't Work on This Build, or check the For Another Reason check box and vent your frustrations in the Tell Us More box.

3. Click the Next button. The What You Need to Know dialog box appears (see Figure 13.24).

FIGURE 13.24
When going back to an earlier build of Windows, read the information in the What You Need to Know dialog box, and then click the Next button.

4. Read the dialog box information and click the Next button if you want to continue. The Don't Get Locked Out dialog box opens, prompting you to make sure you know the password for your earlier version of Windows.

5. Click the Next button. The Thanks for Trying Out This Build dialog box opens.

6. Click the Go Back to Earlier Build button, and then wait while Windows rolls itself back to the previous version.

USING THE ADVANCED STARTUP TOOLS

If you want to use any of the other startup tools, such as starting your computer from a USB drive or changing Windows startup settings, click the Restart Now button under the Advanced Startup heading on the Recovery screen in the Settings app.

Your computer restarts and then displays the Choose an Option screen (see Figure 13.25).

> **! CAUTION** On your computer, the Choose an Option screen, the Troubleshoot screen, and the Advanced Options screen may show different options than those shown here. In case that's not confusing enough, the options shown here may appear on different screens—so move deliberately and keep your wits about you.

Click the Troubleshoot button. The Troubleshoot screen appears (see Figure 13.26).

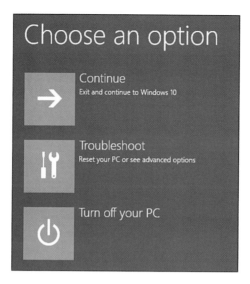

FIGURE 13.25

On the Choose an Option screen, click the Troubleshoot button to access the advanced startup tools.

FIGURE 13.26

On the Troubleshoot screen, click the Advanced Options button to display the Advanced Options screen.

Click the Advanced Options button to display the Advanced Options screen (see Figure 13.27).

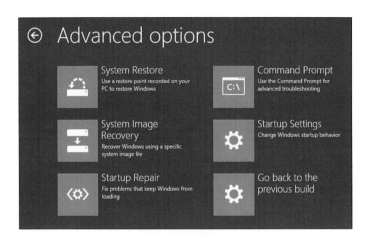

FIGURE 13.27

On the Advanced Options screen, click the button for the advanced startup tool you want to use.

GOING BACK TO AN EARLIER RESTORE POINT WITH SYSTEM RESTORE

To use System Restore to restore your computer's system to an earlier restore point, follow these steps:

1. Click System Restore on the Advanced Options screen to display the System Restore screen.

2. In the Choose an Account to Continue list, click your user account.

3. Type the password for your user account when prompted.

> ✎ **NOTE** The System Restore screen for entering your password shows the keyboard layout that's currently set. You can click the Change Keyboard Layout button to switch to another keyboard layout if necessary.

4. Click the Continue button. The System Restore Wizard launches and displays its first screen.

5. Continue from step 3 in the section "Restoring Windows to a System Restore Point," earlier in this chapter.

RESTORING WINDOWS FROM A SYSTEM IMAGE

If your computer contains a system image that you can use to restore the system, click System Image Recovery on the Advanced Options screen. The Re-Image Your

Computer dialog box opens, presenting a list of the available images. Click the image you want to use, and then follow the prompts to restore Windows from it.

> **NOTE** The Re-Image Your Computer dialog box also enables you to use a system image that's available on the network. To do so, select the Use the Latest Available System Image (Recommended) option button, and then specify the details of the system image.

STARTING UP FROM A USB DRIVE OR A DVD DRIVE

If you have a USB drive or a DVD drive containing a bootable image of Windows, you can use it to repair problems in your computer's system or to reinstall Windows.

To start up from a USB drive or a DVD drive, connect the device before clicking Restart Now. When the Choose an Option screen appears, click the Use a Device button. On the Use a Device screen, click the USB Drive button or the DVD Drive button (as appropriate), and then follow the prompts to start Windows from the device.

> **NOTE** On some computers, the Use a Device button may appear on the Advanced Options screen instead of the Choose an Option screen.

CHANGING WINDOWS STARTUP SETTINGS

To change Windows startup settings, click the Startup Settings button on the Advanced Options screen, and then click the Restart button on the Startup Settings screen that appears.

After Windows restarts, the Startup Settings screen shown in Figure 13.28 appears. Look at the list of options and press the corresponding number key or function key for the option you want to use. For example, press 4 to enable Safe Mode.

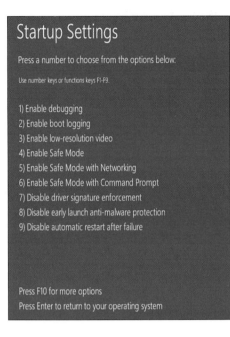

Startup Settings

Press a number to choose from the options below:

Use number keys or functions keys F1-F9.

1) Enable debugging
2) Enable boot logging
3) Enable low-resolution video
4) Enable Safe Mode
5) Enable Safe Mode with Networking
6) Enable Safe Mode with Command Prompt
7) Disable driver signature enforcement
8) Disable early launch anti-malware protection
9) Disable automatic restart after failure

Press F10 for more options
Press Enter to return to your operating system

FIGURE 13.28

On the Startup Settings screen, press the number key or function key for the setting you want to use.

> **TIP**   Safe Mode starts Windows with a limited set of files and drivers and without launching any apps set to run at startup. Safe Mode is especially useful for recovering from misconfigured apps set to run at startup.

REPAIRING WINDOWS STARTUP FILES

To repair Windows startup files, click the Startup Repair button on the Advanced Options screen. Windows then diagnoses problems with the startup files and repairs them automatically.

When the repair is complete, Windows prompts you to restart your computer. Do so.

CHANGING YOUR COMPUTER'S FIRMWARE SETTINGS

To change your computer's firmware settings, follow these steps:

1. On the Advanced Options screen, click the button with a name such as UEFI Firmware Settings (the name varies depending on the hardware).

2. On the screen that appears, click the Restart button. Your computer restarts and displays the screen for configuring the firmware settings.

3. Change the settings as needed.

> **!CAUTION** Before making changes to your computer's firmware settings, make sure you know what you're doing. If you don't have experience with firmware settings, consult an expert, either in person or online.

4. Give the command for committing the changes and restarting your computer.

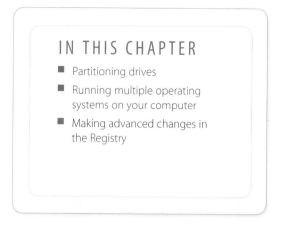

IN THIS CHAPTER

- Partitioning drives
- Running multiple operating systems on your computer
- Making advanced changes in the Registry

14

GOING FURTHER WITH ADVANCED MOVES

In this chapter, you first learn how to split a physical drive into multiple partitions and manage partitions. We then move on to run multiple operating systems on your computer either by dual-booting or by using virtualization technology such as Hyper-V. Finally, we cover how to make changes to the Registry, the vital configuration database of Windows.

WORKING WITH PARTITIONS

Windows enables you to divide a physical hard drive into multiple separate areas called *partitions*. You may want to create multiple partitions so that you can keep your data on a partition separate from your operating system or so that you can install two or more operating systems on your computer.

> **NOTE** A partition is also called a *volume*. You'll find that Windows uses the terms "partition" and "volume" interchangeably to refer to partitions.

EXAMINING THE PARTITIONS ON YOUR COMPUTER'S DRIVE

You can create and edit partitions by using the Disk Management app that comes with Windows. Follow these steps to open Disk Management and see which partitions your computer's drive currently has:

1. Right-click or long-press Start to display the shortcut menu.

2. Click Disk Management to open the Disk Management window (see Figure 14.1).

> **NOTE** To work with partitions, you must be logged in as an administrator.

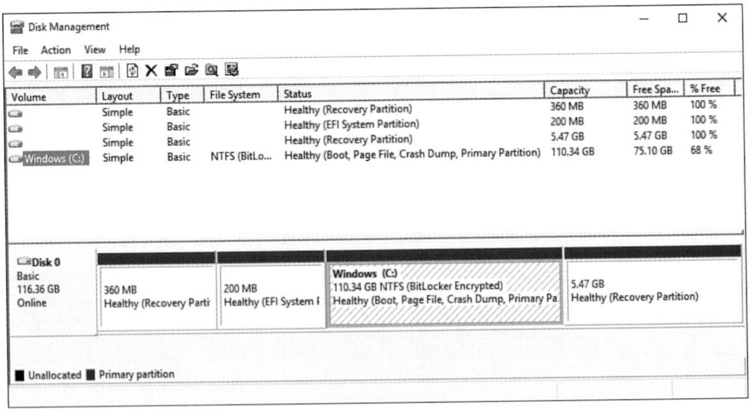

FIGURE 14.1

Open Disk Management to see which partitions your computer currently has and to make changes.

YOUR COMPUTER MAY ALREADY HAVE MULTIPLE PARTITIONS

A typical Windows computer comes with multiple partitions set up on its internal drive. Of these, one partition is the boot partition, which is the partition from which Windows starts and on which Windows and (usually) your apps are installed.

Another partition is the recovery partition, which contains files you can use to repair or reinstall Windows after your system partition comes to grief.

If your computer is built according to the Extensible Firmware Interface (EFI) specification, as many current and recent computers are, it will also have an EFI system partition that's used for initial startup. The EFI system partition is sometimes abbreviated to ESP.

NOTE A normal drive can contain three primary partitions and an extended partition. The extended partition can contain multiple other partitions.

3. Click the partition about which you want to view information.

Here's the information the table at the top of the Disk Management window shows:

- **Volume.** This column shows any label assigned to the volume, such as Windows (C:) for the boot drive.

NOTE The recovery partition and the EFI system partition usually have no label.

- **Layout.** This column shows the volume type. For most consumer-level computers, you'll see the Simple volume type. If you've configured a pool of drives using the Storage feature in the Settings app, as discussed in Chapter 6, "Sorting Out Your Files, Folders, and Storage," you'll see the type you chose: Spanned, Striped, or Mirrored.
- **Type.** This column shows the volume type: Basic for a regular volume, such as most individual computers use, or Dynamic for a volume that's spanned, striped, or mirrored.

■ **File System.** This column shows the file system used for the volume, such as NTFS (BitLocker Encrypted) for a standard Windows installation.

> **NOTE** The File System column shows no file system for the recovery partition and the EFI system partition. This is normal.

■ **Status.** This column shows the volume's status, which includes an overall description (preferably Healthy), its type (such as Boot or System), essential configuration information (such as Page File and Crash Dump), and the partition type (such as Primary Partition).

> **NOTE** In the Status column, Page File indicates that the volume has the paging file stored on it. The paging file provides virtual memory to supplement the computer's physical memory (RAM); see the section "Configuring the Paging File" in Chapter 8 for more information. The Crash Dump status indicates that Windows is configured to dump memory information to the volume following a crash. (In case you're wondering, "dump" there is the correct technical term!)

> **! CAUTION** If you see any status apart from Healthy, you likely need to take action. If the status is Healthy (At Risk), you'll know that Windows can read the volume correctly but it has detected input/output (I/O) errors.

■ **Capacity.** This column shows the volume's capacity. The readouts mix gigabytes (GB) and megabytes (MB), depending on the volume size, so look closely. You might also see terabytes (TB)—if your computer has enough of them.

■ **Free Space.** This column shows how much space is free on the volume—again, using gigabytes or megabytes, depending on the volume size.

■ **% Free.** This column shows the percentage of the volume free.

> **TIP** Look at the % Free column to make sure your boot drive isn't running low on space, because lack of space can degrade performance.

WHAT OTHER STATUSES CAN VOLUMES HAVE?

Ideally, when you look at the Status column in Disk Management, you'll see the Healthy status for each volume. This means that Windows can read the volume correctly and has detected no errors. If you see Healthy (At Risk), Windows can read the volume but has detected I/O errors.

For a dynamic volume, you may see the Initializing status. This means that Windows is getting the volume ready for use. Look again in a while to see whether the status has changed to Healthy.

For a mirrored volume, the Status column shows Resynching when syncing data with the volume's mirrors. (Look back to the section "Creating Pooled Storage with Storage Spaces" in Chapter 6 for details on mirrored volumes and parity volumes.)

For a parity volume, the Status column shows Regenerating while Windows is regenerating data and parity information. You can access the volume normally while regeneration is occurring.

When a volume has failed, you'll see a Failed status. For a basic volume, the straightforward Failed status means that Windows cannot start the volume automatically. The Failed Redundancy status means that one of the physical disks used for the mirrored volume is not online. The Failed Redundancy (At Risk) status means that Windows has detected I/O errors on one of the physical disks used for the mirrored volume and that the data is not protected by redundancy.

Now that you know what partitions your computer's disk has, you can shrink a partition, create a new partition, extend an existing partition, or delete a partition you no longer need. See the following sections for details.

SHRINKING A PARTITION

If you need to create a new partition on your computer's drive, but the current partitions occupy all the space, you can shrink a partition to make space for the newcomer. You can also shrink a partition so as to leave space you may need in the future.

Follow these steps to shrink a partition:

1. In Disk Management, right-click or long-press the partition you want to extend. The shortcut menu appears.

2. Click Shrink Volume. You'll see the Querying Shrink Space dialog box while Disk Management analyzes the partition. Then the Shrink dialog box opens (see Figure 14.2).

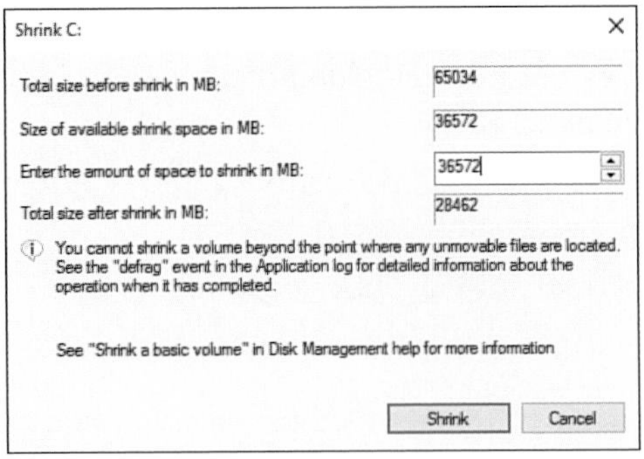

FIGURE 14.2

In the Shrink dialog box, specify the amount of space by which to shrink the partition, and then click the Shrink button.

3. Adjust the value in the Enter the Amount of Space to Shrink in MB box as needed. The Shrink dialog box assumes you want to shrink the drive as far as possible, which is not always the case.

> **! CAUTION**   Don't shrink a drive too far. It's normally best to leave at least several gigabytes free so that you can manipulate files on the drive.

4. Click the Shrink button. Disk Management shrinks the volume by the amount you specified. The Disk Management window shows the volume at its new size, and the amount of space you freed up appears as an Unallocated entry in the diagram in the lower part of the Disk Management window.

CREATING A NEW PARTITION

When you have unallocated space on a partition, you can either create a new partition in it (as discussed here) or extend an existing partition (as discussed in the next section).

> **✓ TIP**   If you're creating a new partition so that you can install another operating system in a dual-boot configuration, you don't have to create it now. Instead, you can create a new partition during the installation.

To create a new partition, follow these steps:

1. In Disk Management, right-click or long-press the Unallocated Space box to display the shortcut menu.

2. Click New Simple Volume to launch the New Simple Volume Wizard, which displays its Welcome screen.

3. Click the Next button to display the Specify Volume Size screen (see Figure 14.3).

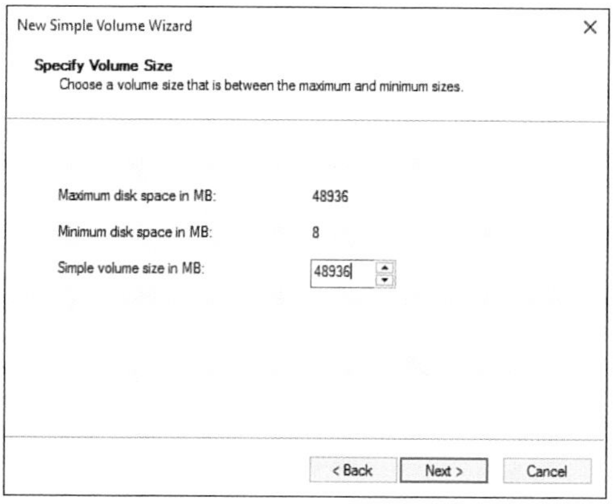

FIGURE 14.3

On the Specify Volume Size screen of the New Simple Volume Wizard, choose how much space to dedicate to the volume.

4. Adjust the value in the Simple Volume Size in MB box as needed. By default, the wizard suggests using all the available space. Often, this is what you'll want to do.

5. Click the Next button. The wizard displays the Assign Drive Letter or Path screen (see Figure 14.4).

6. Select the Assign the Following Drive Letter option button, open the drop-down menu, and choose the letter you want to use for the drive. The wizard suggests the next unused letter after the volumes already in your computer. For example, if your computer has a C: drive on the hard drive and a D: drive that's the optical drive, the wizard suggests E: for the new volume.

NOTE Instead of assigning a drive letter to the new volume, you can mount it in a folder. Doing so is useful if you have multiple volumes but want to have all their contents appear to be on a single drive.

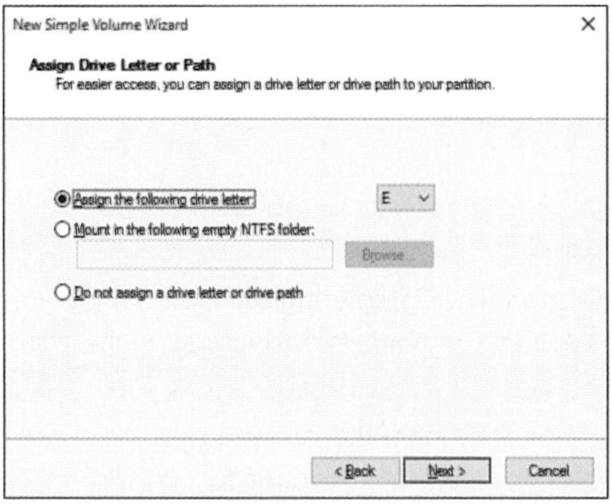

FIGURE 14.4

On the Assign Drive Letter or Path screen of the New Simple Volume Wizard, choose which drive letter to assign to the new volume. Alternatively, you can mount the new volume in a folder.

7. Click the Next button. The wizard displays the Format Partition screen (see Figure 14.5).

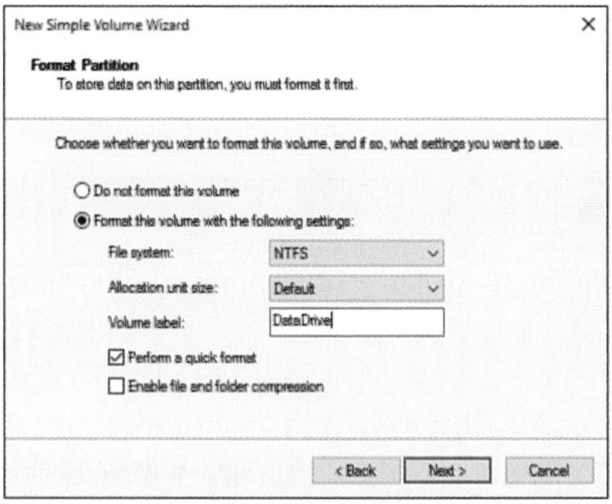

FIGURE 14.5

On the Format Partition screen of the New Simple Volume Wizard, select the Format This Volume with the Following Settings option button, specify the NTFS file system, and enter the volume label.

8. Select the Format This Volume with the Following Settings option button.

9. Make sure that NTFS is selected in the File System drop-down menu.

10. Select Default in the Allocation Unit Size drop-down menu.

11. Type the name for the volume in the Volume Label box.

12. Check the Perform a Quick Format check box if you want Disk Management to perform a quick format rather than a full format. A quick format is usually adequate.

13. Check the Enable File and Folder Compression check box if you want to turn on compression for the volume.

14. Click the Next button. The Completing the New Simple Volume Wizard screen appears, which summarizes the choices you've made.

15. Look through the You Selected the Following Settings box to make sure everything is right. (If not, click the Back button one or more times to go back to where you need to make a change.)

16. Click the Finish button. The wizard creates the partition, and it appears in the Disk Management window.

EXTENDING A PARTITION

If your computer's drive has unused space, either because it was there already or because you have made space by deleting or shrinking a partition, you can extend an existing partition to occupy that space. Extending the partition enables you to "make the drive bigger," which can solve the problem of running out of space on the drive.

Follow these steps to extend a partition:

1. In Disk Management, right-click or long-press the partition you want to extend. The shortcut menu appears.

2. Click Extend Volume to launch the Extend Volume Wizard, which displays its first screen.

3. Click the Next button to display the Select Disks screen (see Figure 14.6).

4. Look at the disk or disks that the wizard has placed in the Selected box. If these are not the disks you want to use, select a disk and click the Remove button to move it back to the Available box. If you need to remove all the disks, click the Remove All button.

5. To add a disk, click it in the Available box and then click the Add button. The wizard adds the disk to the Selected box.

6. Use the spin buttons to adjust the value in the Select the Amount of Space in MB box. The wizard suggests using all the space available, but you can use less if necessary—for example, because you want to leave some space for creating a new partition.

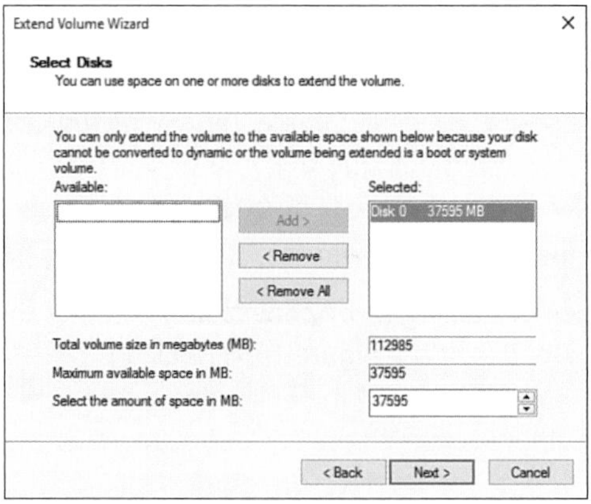

FIGURE 14.6

On the Select Disks screen, add disks as needed from the Available box to the Selected box, and choose the amount of space by which to extend the partition.

7. Click the Next button to display the Completing the Extend Volume Wizard screen, which summarizes the change you're making.

8. Check the details, and then click the Finish button if they're correct. The wizard extends the volume, and the Disk Management window shows the result.

DELETING A PARTITION

If you no longer need a partition, you can delete it. For example, say you have divided your computer's drive so that you can have a boot partition and a data partition, but your boot partition is now running out of space. You can delete the data partition so that you can extend the boot partition into the space the data partition occupied.

> **!CAUTION** Deleting a partition gets rid of all the data the partition contains, so it's vital to move any files you want to keep off the partition before you delete it. Even if you're convinced you don't need the contents of a partition, you might want to back it up in case you find out you were mistaken.
>
> If you delete a partition by accident, you may be able to recover it by using partition-recovery software. Search online using terms such as *Windows 10 recover deleted partition*, and read the reviews of those you find. One tool I've used in the past is Recuva from Piriform Ltd (www.piriform.com/recuva), which includes a free version.

To delete a partition, follow these steps:

1. Right-click or long-press the partition to display the shortcut menu.

2. Click Delete Volume. The Delete Simple Volume dialog box opens, making sure you understand that deleting the volume will erase all the data it contains and recommending that you back up the data first.

3. Click the Yes button if you're certain you want to proceed.

4. If a Disk Management dialog box opens telling you that the drive is encrypted with BitLocker (see Figure 14.7), click the Yes button.

FIGURE 14.7
Disk Management may warn you that the drive is encrypted with BitLocker.

NOTE You cannot delete your computer's boot partition. If you try to do so, you'll find that the Delete Volume command is dimmed and unavailable. Similarly, you cannot delete a recovery partition or an EFI system partition.

CHANGING THE DRIVE LETTER ASSIGNED TO A VOLUME

Here's one other thing you may want to do in Disk Management: Change the drive letter assigned to a volume. To do so, right-click or long-press the volume in Disk Management, and then click Change Drive Letter and Paths on the shortcut menu.

In the Change Drive Letter and Paths For dialog box that opens, click the Change button to display the Change Drive Letter or Path dialog box. Select the Assign the Following Drive Letter option button, choose the letter in the drop-down menu, and then click the OK button.

The Change Drive Letter and Paths dialog box also enables you to mount the volume in a folder as well as having it show up as a drive. To do so, click the Add button to display the Add Drive Letter or Path dialog box. Select the Mount in the Following Empty NTFS Folder option button, click the Browse button and use the resulting dialog box to specify the folder, and then click the OK button.

RUNNING MULTIPLE OPERATING SYSTEMS ON YOUR COMPUTER

If you need to run multiple operating systems on your computer, Windows 10 offers you several alternatives:

- **Dual-boot or multi-boot.** You can install Windows and one or more other operating systems on your computer. You can then boot (start) your computer into the operating system you want to use.

- **Install and run other operating systems with Hyper-V.** If you have the Professional version or the Enterprise version of Windows, you can use the Hyper-V feature to install and run other operating systems on virtual machines.

- **Install and run other operating systems with third-party virtual-machine software.** If your version of Windows doesn't have the Hyper-V feature, you can install third-party virtual-machine software to enable yourself to install and run other operating systems on Windows.

The following sections explain how to use these means of running multiple operating systems.

DUAL-BOOTING OR MULTI-BOOTING WINDOWS WITH ANOTHER OPERATING SYSTEM

If you need to run both Windows and another operating system on the same computer, you can set up the computer to dual-boot the operating systems. If you need three or more operating systems, you can set up the computer to multi-boot. This section focuses on dual booting.

NOTE Unless your computer is a test one that contains no data you value, back up the computer before setting up dual booting on it.

To set up dual booting, your computer must have somewhere to put the new operating system. This can be one of the following:

- **A separate partition on the same drive.** If you've already partitioned your computer's hard drive, as explained earlier in this chapter, you're good to go.
- **Free space on the same drive.** If the drive has enough free space, you can create a new partition while installing the new operating system. (Or you can create a new partition beforehand by using Disk Management and then use that partition.)
- **A separate drive.** If your computer has multiple drives, you can install the new operating system on a separate drive from the existing operating system.

Provided that your computer has a free partition, free space, or a separate drive, launch the operating system you are going to install. How you do this varies depending on the operating system and the media you are using. For example:

- **Optical disc.** If you have the new operating system on an optical disc, insert that disc in the optical drive. Depending on the operating system, you may be able to launch the installer by running an app from within Windows. If not, reboot your computer and start it from the optical drive.

> **NOTE** To start your computer from the optical drive, you may need to press any key (such as the spacebar) when the "Press any key to boot from CD or DVD" message appears briefly.

- **Bootable USB drive.** If you have the new operating system on a bootable USB drive, connect that drive, reboot your computer, and specify the USB drive as the boot drive.

After the installer is running, you must make sure you install the operating system on the correct partition. For example, if you're installing recent versions of Windows, choose the option button called "Custom: Install Windows Only (Advanced)" on the Which Type of Installation Do You Want? screen (see Figure 14.8) instead of the option button called "Upgrade: Install Windows and Keep Files, Settings, and Applications," which will overwrite your current installation of Windows.

Then (still on Windows), select the partition or area of unallocated space on the Where Do You Want to Install Windows? screen (see Figure 14.9). If you select unallocated space, you can either simply click the Next button to use all that space—the installer automatically creates a partition for you—or click the New link to create a new partition that uses only part of that space.

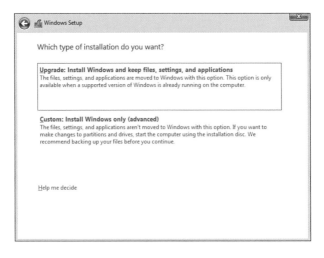

FIGURE 14.8

On the Which Type of Installation Do You Want? screen in Windows Setup, choose the "Custom: Install Windows Only (Advanced)" option button.

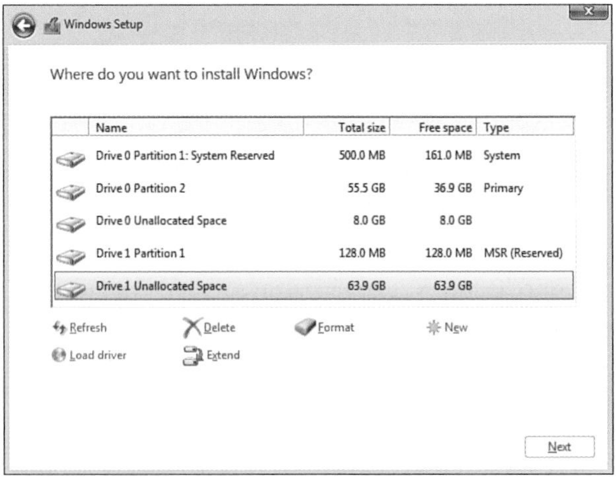

FIGURE 14.9

On the Where Do You Want to Install Windows? screen in Windows Setup, select the correct partition or area of unallocated space.

!CAUTION Picking the wrong partition for the new operating system can overwrite your current operating system—so make sure you get the right partition. If you're dealing with partitions of the same size, or similar sizes, use the Free Space readout to see how much data a partition contains. Checking the free space can help you avoid picking a partition that's already in use.

After choosing where to install the operating system, follow through the remaining steps of the installation. When it finishes, you can start using the new operating system.

INSTALLING AND RUNNING OTHER OPERATING SYSTEMS WITH HYPER-V

The Pro and Enterprise versions of Windows include Hyper-V, a virtualization technology that enables you to run virtual machines on your computer. A virtual machine is essentially a computer implemented in software rather than running directly on actual physical hardware. You can use virtual machines for keeping different tasks separate from each other, for developing and testing software, or for any other purposes you find useful.

ENABLING THE HYPER-V FEATURE

On most computers, you'll need to enable Hyper-V—in other words, make it available—before you can use it.

To enable Hyper V, follow these steps:

1. Save any unsaved data in all the apps you're using. (This is because Windows will need to restart your computer after enabling Hyper-V.)
2. Right-click or long-press Start to display the shortcut menu.
3. Click Programs and Features to open a Control Panel window to the Programs and Features screen.
4. In the left column, click Turn Windows Features On or Off to open the Windows Features dialog box (see Figure 14.10).
5. Check the Hyper-V check box. Doing so checks the check boxes for the two components under it, Hyper-V Management Tools and Hyper-V Platform, and the check boxes for their subcomponents.
6. Click the OK button. The Windows Features dialog box closes, and a larger Windows Features dialog box appears while Windows installs the components.

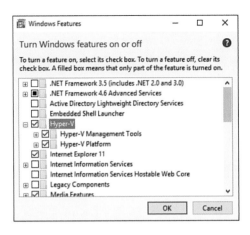

FIGURE 14.10

In the Windows Features dialog box, check the Hyper-V check box and then click the OK button.

7. When the Windows Completed the Requested Changes screen appears, click the Restart Now button.

After Windows restarts, sign back in to Windows.

RUNNING THE HYPER-V MANAGER AND CREATING A VIRTUAL MACHINE

After installing the Hyper-V components, choose Start, All Apps, Windows Administrative Tools, Hyper-V Manager to open the Hyper-V Manager window (see Figure 14.11).

CREATING A VIRTUAL SWITCH

Before you create a virtual machine, you'll probably want to create a virtual switch so that you can connect your virtual machine (or machines) to a network.

To create a virtual switch, follow these steps:

1. In the Actions pane on the right of the Hyper-V Manager window, click Virtual Switch Manager to display the Virtual Switch Manager dialog box. Figure 14.12 shows the top part of this dialog box.

2. In the left pane, if the Virtual Switches heading is collapsed, double-click it to expand it, displaying its contents.

3. Under the Virtual Switches heading, click New Virtual Network Switch to display the Create Virtual Switch pane on the right.

4. In the What Type of Virtual Switch Do You Want to Create? list, click External, Internal, or Private, as needed.

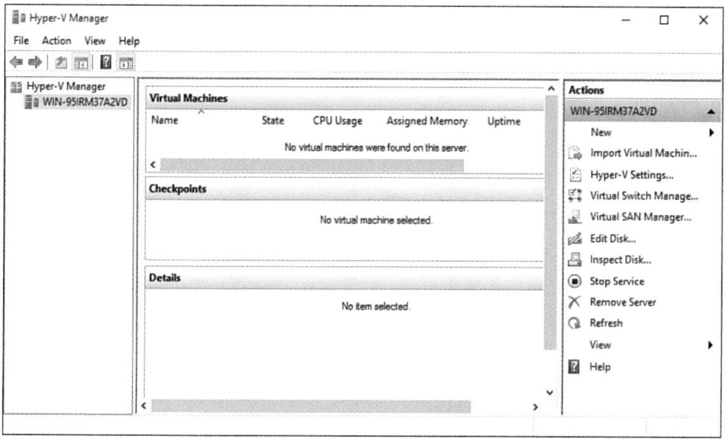

FIGURE 14.11
The Hyper-V Manager window.

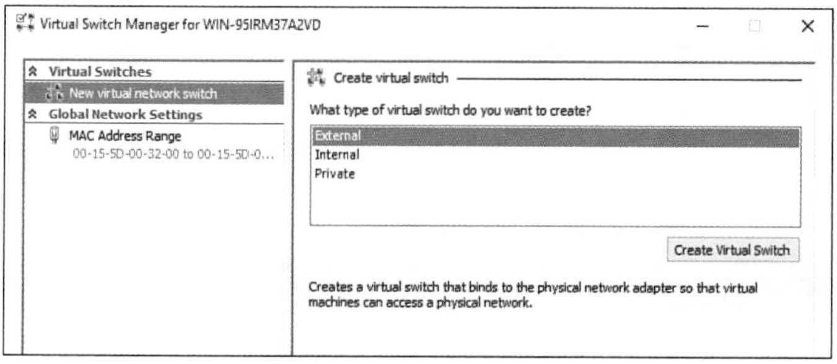

FIGURE 14.12
In the Virtual Switch Manager dialog box, click New Virtual Network Switch, click the switch type (such as External), and then click the Create Virtual Switch button.

> **NOTE**   Create an external switch if you want your virtual machines to be able to connect to your physical network and the Internet. Create an internal switch if you want your virtual machines to be able to communicate only with each other and with the computer on which you're running Hyper-V. Create a private switch if you want your virtual machines to be able to communicate only with each other and not with the computer on which they're running.

5. Click the Create Virtual Switch button. The Virtual Switch Properties pane appears (see Figure 14.13).

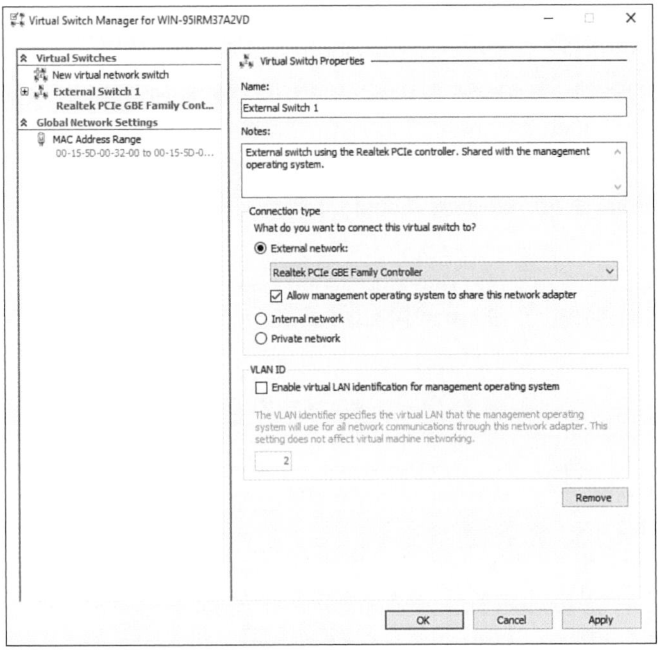

FIGURE 14.13
Specify the details of the new virtual switch in the Virtual Switch Properties pane in the Virtual Switch Manager dialog box.

6. In the Name box, type a descriptive name for the switch. (The default name is New Virtual Switch, which doesn't get you far.)

7. In the Notes box, type any notes needed about the switch.

8. If you're creating an external switch, go to the Connection Type area and make sure the External Network switch option button is selected. Then open the drop-down menu under it and click the network adapter you want the virtual switch to use.

> **NOTE** If your computer has only a single network adapter, Hyper-V Manager should have already selected it in the drop-down menu. But if your computer has two network adapters, such as a wireless network adapter and an Ethernet adapter for wired networks, make sure you select the right one.

9. Also for an external switch only, check the Allow Management Operating System to Share This Network Adapter check box.

10. Click the Apply button to apply your changes. The Apply Networking Changes dialog box opens (see Figure 14.14).

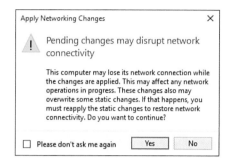

FIGURE 14.14

Click the Yes button in the Apply Networking Changes dialog box.

11. Click the Yes button to apply your changes.

12. Click the OK button to close the Virtual Switch Manager dialog box.

CREATING A VIRTUAL MACHINE

You can then create a new virtual machine by following these steps:

1. From the menu bar, choose Action, New, Virtual Machine to launch the New Virtual Machine Wizard. The wizard displays its Before You Begin screen.

> **NOTE** You can click the Finish button on the Before You Begin screen to create a new virtual machine with default values. But normally it's best to go through the steps of the wizard to configure the virtual machine the way you want it.

2. Click the Next button to display the Specify Name and Location screen of the wizard.

3. In the Name box, type a descriptive name for the virtual machine.

4. Look at the Location box and see where Hyper-V Manager is going to save the virtual machine. If this location isn't suitable, check the Store the Virtual Machine in a Different Location check box, click the Browse button, and select the location.

5. Click the Next button to display the Specify Generation screen of the wizard.

6. Select the Generation 1 option button if you plan to install a 32-bit operating system or you need support for older virtual hardware. Select the Generation 2 option button if you want the latest virtualization features and UEFI-based firmware and you will install a 64-bit operating system.

7. Click the Next button to display the Assign Memory screen of the wizard.

8. In the Startup Memory box, adjust the default amount of memory to suit the needs of the operating system you will install. For example, enter 2048 to use 2048MB (2GB) of memory.

9. Check the Use Dynamic Memory for This Virtual Machine check box if you want Hyper-V Manager to be able to adjust the amount of memory allocated to the virtual machine.

10. Click the Next button to display the Configure Networking screen of the wizard.

11. Open the Connection drop-down menu and choose the virtual switch you created in the previo'us section. If you don't want to connect the virtual machine to a virtual switch, choose Not Connected instead.

12. Click the Next button to display the Connect Virtual Hard Disk screen of the wizard (see Figure 14.15).

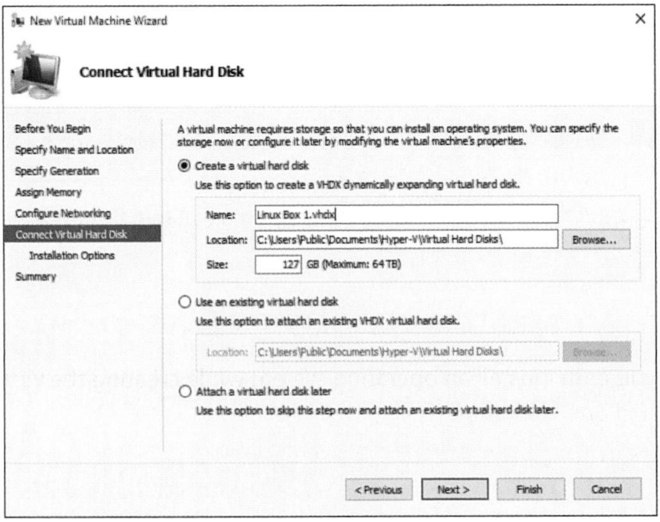

FIGURE 14.15

On the Connect Virtual Hard Disk screen of the New Virtual Machine Wizard, specify the details of the virtual hard disk to connect to the new virtual machine.

13. Select the Create a Virtual Hard Disk option button and adjust the details in the Name box, the Location box, and the Size box, as needed.

> **TIP** If you have an existing virtual hard disk you want to use for the virtual machine, select the Use an Existing Virtual Hard Disk option button, click the Browse button below it and to its right, and use the resulting dialog box to select the file for the virtual hard disk.

14. Click the Next button to display the Installation Options screen of the wizard.

15. If you have a bootable image file containing the operating system you want to install, select the Install an Operating System from a Bootable Image File option button, click the Browse button, and then select the file. Otherwise, select the Install an Operating System Later option button.

> **NOTE** If you have access to an installation server that contains the operating system, select the Install an Operating System from a Network-Based Installation Server option button.

16. Click the Next button to display the Summary screen of the wizard.

17. Make sure the details are correct. If not, click the Previous button one or more times to go back and fix them.

18. Click the Finish button. The wizard closes, and the virtual machine appears in the Hyper-V Manager window.

INSTALLING AN OPERATING SYSTEM ON THE VIRTUAL MACHINE

Assuming you didn't install an operating system while creating the virtual machine, you can install one afterward.

First, you need to connect the image file or the optical drive from which you will install the operating system. This example uses an image file, which is more typical now that many manufacturers are phasing out optical drives.

After that, you need to set the virtual machine to boot from the image file.

Follow these steps to connect an image file and set the virtual machine to boot from it:

1. In the Virtual Machines list in the Hyper-V Manager window, right-click or long-press the virtual machine you want to affect. The shortcut menu opens.

2. Click Settings to open the Settings dialog box for the virtual machine.

3. In the navigation pane on the left, if the Hardware heading is collapsed, double-click the Hardware heading to expand its contents.

4. Below the Hardware heading, click the SCSI Controller item. The SCSI Controller pane appears in the main part of the window.

5. In the Select the Type of Drive You Want to Attach to the Controller list box, click DVD Drive.

6. Click the Add button. A DVD Drive item appears under the SCSI Controller item in the navigation pane, and the DVD Drive pane appears on the right (see Figure 14.16).

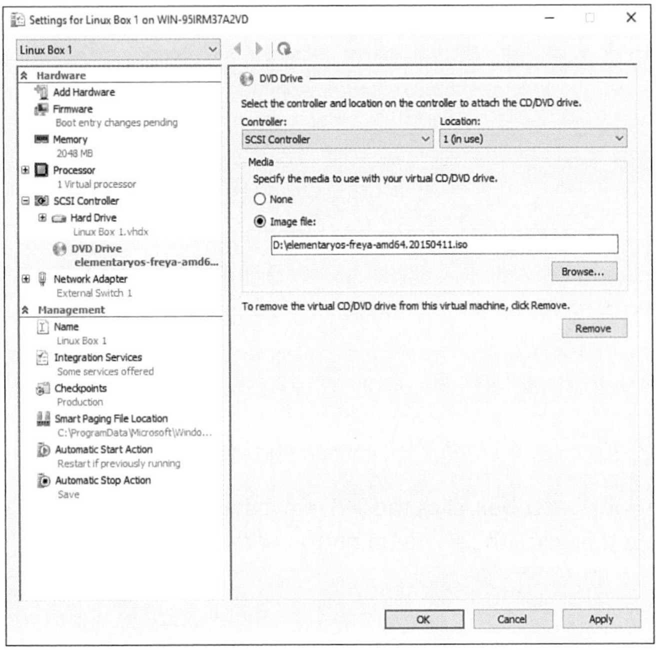

FIGURE 14.16

In the DVD Drive pane, select the Image File option button, click the Browse button, and then locate the image file that contains the operating system.

7. Click the Image File option button.

8. Click the Browse button below the Image File box to display the Open dialog box, navigate to and select the image file, and click the Open button. The file path and filename appear in the Image File text box.

9. Click the Firmware item in the Hardware section of the navigation pane. The Firmware pane appears on the right (see Figure 14.17).

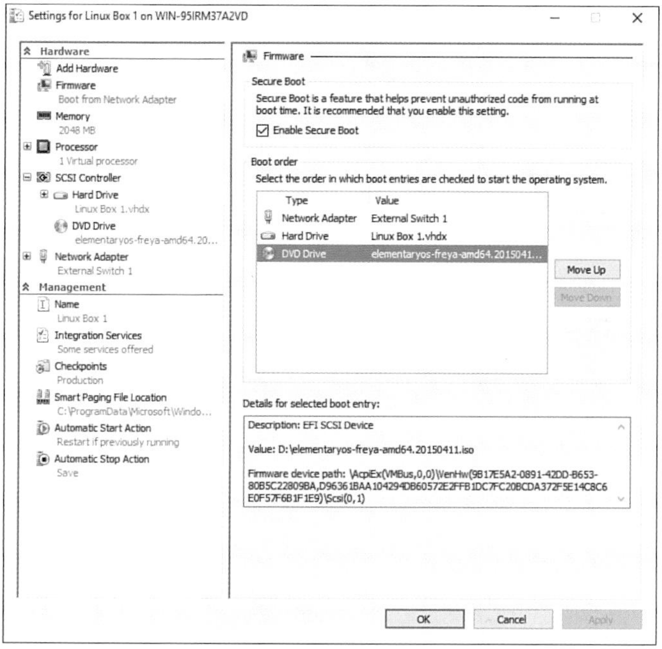

FIGURE 14.17

Use the Firmware pane in the Settings dialog box to move the DVD Drive item up above the Network Adapter item in the Boot Order list.

10. In the Boot Order box, click the DVD Drive item (which represents the image file) and then click the Move Up button to move it up above the Network Adapter item in the list.

11. In the Boot Order box, click the Hard Drive item and then click the Move Up button to move it to the top of the list.

> **TIP** You must rearrange the boot order to prevent the virtual machine from attempting to boot from the network adapter, which it does by default. (This is for installing an operating system from a network installation source.) Put the Hard Drive item at the top of the list so that the virtual machine will boot from it after you have installed the operating system. Put the DVD Drive item next so that the virtual machine will boot from the image file during installation after it finds no operating system on the hard drive.

12. Click the OK button to close the Settings dialog box.

Now that you've connected the image file and set the virtual machine to boot from it, open the virtual machine by double-clicking it in the Virtual Machines box in the Hyper-V Manager window. The virtual machine opens in its own window, and you can start it by clicking the Start button on the toolbar (see Figure 14.18).

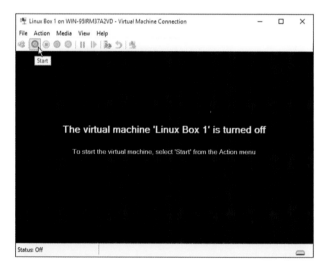

FIGURE 14.18
Click the Start button on the toolbar—or choose Action, Start—to start the virtual machine.

The virtual machine boots using the image file, and you can follow the prompts to complete the installation.

WORKING WITH VIRTUAL MACHINES

After creating your virtual machines and installing operating systems in them, you can run and manage them from the Hyper-V Manager window. These are the main moves you need:

- **Start a virtual machine.** Right-click or long-press the virtual machine in the Virtual Machines list, and then click Start on the shortcut menu.

> **TIP** You can also take most actions for virtual machines by using the toolbar in the virtual machine's own window or the Actions pane on the right side of the Hyper-V Manager window. If the toolbar is not displayed, choose View, Toolbar to display it. To use the Actions pane, click the virtual machine's heading to display the list of actions if the list is collapsed, and then click the appropriate button, such as Start.

- **Save a virtual machine's state.** When you want to stop using a virtual machine for now but don't want to shut it down, save it by clicking the Save button on the toolbar in the virtual machine's window or right-clicking or long-pressing the virtual machine in the Virtual Machines list and then clicking Save on the shortcut menu.

> **NOTE** After saving a virtual machine's state, you can start the virtual machine as usual. The virtual machine wakes up into the saved state.

- **Shut down a virtual machine.** Normally, you shut down a virtual machine's operating system the usual way—for example, in Windows 10, choose Start, Power, Shut Down. But you can also right-click or long-press the virtual machine in the Virtual Machines list and click Shut Down to shut it down.
- **Pause a virtual machine.** Click the Pause button on the toolbar in the virtual machine's window, or right-click or long-press the virtual machine in the Virtual Machines list in the Hyper-V Manager window and then click Pause on the shortcut menu.
- **Change the settings for a virtual machine.** To configure a virtual machine, right-click or long-press it in the Virtual Machines list and then click Settings on the shortcut menu. You can change some settings while the virtual machine is running, but to configure all settings, you must first shut down the virtual machine.
- **Create a checkpoint.** To save a snapshot of the virtual machine's state so that you can return to it later if needed, right-click or long-press the virtual machine in the Virtual Machines list and then click Checkpoint on the shortcut menu.

> **TIP** Create a checkpoint before performing any action that might cause trouble on the virtual machine, such as installing software. If problems occur, you can then revert to the checkpoint to eliminate the problems.

- **Revert to the previous checkpoint.** To revert to the previous checkpoint, right-click or long-press the virtual machine in the Virtual Machines list and then click Revert on the shortcut menu. The Revert Virtual Machine dialog box opens to confirm the change; click the Revert button.
- **Delete a virtual machine.** If you no longer need a virtual machine, right-click or long-press it in the Virtual Machines list and then click Delete on the shortcut menu. The Delete Select Virtual Machines check box opens; click the Delete button.

INSTALLING AND RUNNING OTHER OPERATING SYSTEMS WITH THIRD-PARTY VIRTUAL-MACHINE SOFTWARE

Hyper-V is great—if your version of Windows includes it. But if it doesn't, you can still install and run other operating systems on Windows, but you need to use third-party virtual-machine software instead.

As of this writing, there are two main virtual-machine apps that you can run on Windows 10:

- **VirtualBox.** VirtualBox is a free virtual-machine app available from VirtualBox.org (www.virtualbox.org). VirtualBox is straightforward to use and has plenty of features to get you started.
- **VMware Workstation.** VMware Workstation from VMware Inc. (www.vmware.com/products/workstation) is a full-featured virtualization app. VMWare Workstation costs $249.99 for a license, but there's a 30-day evaluation version that you'll likely want to try first.

MAKING ADVANCED CHANGES BY EDITING THE REGISTRY

The Registry is a database in which Windows stores configuration settings for Windows itself, the apps installed on your computer, and the user accounts set up on it. Windows maintains the Registry automatically, adding and updating settings as needed without your intervention, but you may sometimes need to make changes in the Registry to resolve problems or to make Windows work in specific ways.

! CAUTION Be extremely careful when editing the Registry, because the Registry is essential to keeping Windows running properly, and making the wrong change can make your computer unstable or even prevent Windows from running. Under normal circumstances, you shouldn't need to edit the Registry at all—so make changes only if you're certain that you need to do so.

OPENING REGISTRY EDITOR AND NAVIGATING ITS INTERFACE

To edit the Registry, you use the Registry Editor app. Registry Editor is included with Windows, but it doesn't appear on the Start menu. This is because Microsoft doesn't want most users editing the Registry.

To open Registry Editor, follow these steps:

1. Click Start to open the Start menu.
2. Type **regedit.exe**. A list of search results appears.
3. Click the result called "regedit.exe: Run Command." This result normally appears at the top of the list.

NOTE When you run `regedit.exe`, the User Account Control dialog box may open, asking if you want to allow the app to make changes to your PC. Make sure that the Program Name readout shows Registry Editor and that the Verified Publisher readout shows Microsoft Windows, and then click the Yes button.

Registry Editor opens. As you can see in Figure 14.19, Registry Editor has a straightforward interface:

- **Navigation pane.** This pane appears on the left of the Registry Editor window and contains a collapsible tree showing the settings. The tree's root is your computer, which appears as Computer, and there are five main branches, which we'll examine in a minute. You can expand or collapse any section by double-clicking its heading or by clicking the arrow to its left.
- **Details pane.** This pane appears to the right of the navigation pane and shows the details of the item you've selected in the navigation pane.
- **Status bar.** Appearing at the bottom of the window as usual, the status bar shows the full path to the currently selected item.

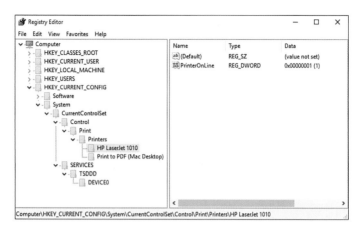

FIGURE 14.19

Registry Editor has a navigation pane on the left, a details pane on the right, and a status bar at the bottom.

> [✎ **NOTE**   This section assumes you're using Registry Editor to edit the Registry on the computer at which you're sitting. But you can also use Registry Editor to edit the Registry on another computer that's connected to the same network. To connect to another computer's Registry, you use the File, Connect Network Registry command; and when you're done, you use the File, Disconnect Network Registry command to disconnect from the other computer.

UNDERSTANDING WHAT'S WHAT IN THE REGISTRY

The Registry contains a vast number of keys, which are the Registry's equivalent of files and folders. Any key can contain one or more items called *value entries*, each of which has a name that's unique within the key, a specific data type, and a value. We'll look at an example in a moment.

The Registry organizes all its keys into five *root keys*, the keys you see in the navigation pane in Figure 14.19. As you can see in Table 14.1, which gives brief details on the root keys, the root key names are mostly long, so each has a three-letter or four-letter abbreviation. So when you see, say, HKCU in online documentation or in this book, you'll know that it stands for HKEY_CURRENT_USER.

Table 14.1   Root Keys in the Registry

Root Key	Abbreviation	Contents
HKEY_CLASSES_ROOT	HKCR	Data about file types and their associations, registered classes.
HKEY_CURRENT_USER	HKCU	Settings for the current user, such as you.
HKEY_LOCAL_MACHINE	HKLM	Data about the computer's hardware and software configuration.
HKEY_USERS	HKU	Data on the user accounts set up on the computer. This key includes a DEFAULT profile for when no user is logged on.
HKEY_CURRENT_CONFIG	HKCC	Data on the hardware configuration using the computer booted for the current session.

> **NOTE** Two of the root keys are actually mirrors of (in lay terms, shortcuts to) keys contained within other root keys. The HKCR root key is a mirror of HKLM\ SOFTWARE\Classes, and the HKCC root key is a mirror of the current key in HKLM\ SYSTEM\CurrentControlSet\Hardware Profiles\.

BACKING UP AND RESTORING THE REGISTRY

Because having the Registry in good shape is critical to Windows running properly and stably, you should back up the Registry before you make any changes to it. You should also know how to restore the Registry from backup in case you make an unfortunate change or the Registry suffers damage from another source.

> **NOTE** Registry backups vary in size but are typically 200MB or more—often much more. You might want to store your Registry backups locally on a flash drive and on an online service.

Follow these steps to back up the Registry:

1. In Registry Editor, choose File, Export to open the Export Registry File dialog box (see Figure 14.20).

2. Using the navigation pane or the Save In drop-down menu, navigate to the folder in which you want to save the Registry backup. For example, you may want to save the backup in a folder that you sync with an online storage site, or you may simply want to save the backup file directly to a flash drive.

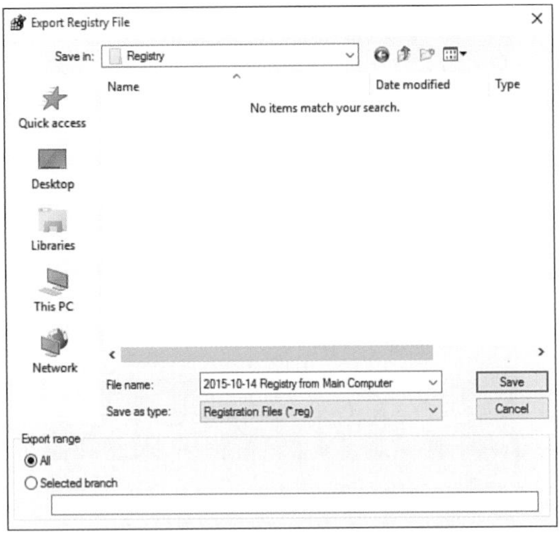

FIGURE 14.20

In the Export Registry File dialog box, select the All option button or the Selected Branch option button, specify the destination folder and filename, and then click the Save button.

3. In the File Name box, enter the filename for the backup file. You may want to include the date and the computer name in the filename so that you'll be able to pick the right backup easily when you need it.

4. Make sure that the Save as Type drop-down menu shows Registration Files (*.reg). This is the default setting, so you shouldn't need to change it.

5. In the Export Range box, make sure the All option button is selected rather than the Selected Branch option button.

> **NOTE** The Selected Branch option button in the Export Range box in the Export Registry File dialog box enables you to back up a single branch of the Registry, such as HKEY_CURRENT_USER. But usually you'll want to back up the entire Registry so that you can restore it in full.

6. Click the Save button. Registry Editor saves the backup to the file. This may take a minute or two.

After you've backed up the Registry, you can restore it from backup easily. Follow these steps:

1. In Registry Editor, choose File, Import to display the Import Registry File dialog box.

2. Navigate to the folder that contains the backup file.

3. Click the backup file.

4. Click Open. You'll see the Import Registry File dialog box as Registry Editor imports the Registry from the file.

AN EXAMPLE: REMOVING AN APP FROM THE OPEN WITH SUBMENU IN FILE EXPLORER

Here's an example of using the Registry. As you saw in Chapter 9, "Installing, Running, and Managing Apps," you can add apps to the Open With submenu that appears on the shortcut menu for a file in File Explorer, enabling you to choose the app with which you want to open the file. But Windows doesn't give you a way to remove apps from the Open With submenu. You may want to remove apps if you add the wrong app by mistake or if the Open With submenu contains apps that can handle the file type but that you never want to use.

Follow these steps to use Registry Editor to remove an app from the Open With submenu in File Explorer:

1. In Registry Editor, double-click the HKEY_CURRENT_USER key in the navigation pane to expand the key's contents.

2. Under HKEY_CURRENT_USER, double-click the SOFTWARE key to expand its contents.

3. Under SOFTWARE, double-click the Microsoft key to expand its contents.

4. Under Microsoft, double-click the Windows key to expand its contents.

5. Under Windows, double-click the CurrentVersion key to expand its contents.

6. Under CurrentVersion, double-click the Explorer key to expand its contents.

7. Under Explorer, double-click the FileExts key to expand its contents.

8. Double-click the file extension you want to affect. This example uses the .png file extension, a widely used picture format.

9. Click the OpenWithList key to display its values in the right pane. You'll see a list of the default app and the other apps that appear on the Open With submenu.

10. Right-click or long-press the entry for the app you want to remove, and then click Delete on the shortcut menu. The Confirm Value Delete dialog box opens (see Figure 14.21), warning you that deleting certain registry values could cause system instability.

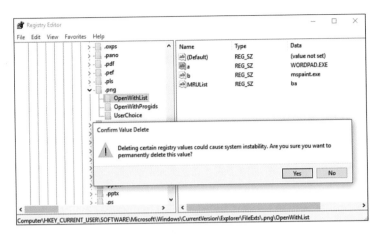

FIGURE 14.21

Click the Yes button in the Confirm Value Delete dialog box to delete the selected value from the Registry.

11. Click the Yes button. Registry Editor deletes the value, and the app disappears from the Open With submenu in File Explorer.

Index

A

Accessibility, Skype, 370
accessing
  files in homegroups, 204
  recovery tools, 395–396
accounts
  changing existing acounts
    to administrator accounts,
    188–189
  connecting local accounts
    to Microsoft accounts,
    182–184
  creating for family
    members, 188
  creating for non-family
    members, 188
  creating for others, 186–189
  domain accounts, 183

  Guest accounts, 187
  local accounts, 182
  Microsoft accounts, 183
  non-administrator
    accounts, 186
  profile pictures, setting, 182
  securing, 184–186
  Skype, creating, 356
  Windows Store, removing
    devices from, 252
Accounts screen, closing, 343
Action Center, 353
  resolving issues, 382–384
Action Center icon, 133
Action Center pane, 383
activating apps, 256
Add a VPN Connection pane, 89

adding
  apps to lock screen, 136–137
  buttons to Quick Access Toolbar, 144–145
  computers to homegroups, 202–203
  existing music files to Windows Media Player, 287–289
  Hibernate command to Power menu, 24
  hidden wireless networks
    via Manually Connect to a Wireless Network Wizard, 67–69
    via Network fly-out, 67
    with Wireless Network Wizard, 67–69
  keyboard layouts, 47
  memory, 212–214
  music
    to Groove Music, 304–305
    to Windows Media Player, 286–295
Add Printers & Scanners pane, 114
addresses
  IP addresses, 76
  IPv4 addresses, 73
  IPv6 addresses, 74
Address toolbar, 128
Add Your Microsoft Account dialog box, 334
adjusting
  folder options, File Explorer, 152
  search options, File Explorer, 152
Adobe Flash Player, 324
Advanced Display Settings pane, 107–110
Advanced Settings
  configuring
    IP settings, 75-78
    Microsoft Edge, 323–324
  Folder Options dialog box, 156–157
  Skype, 368
Advanced Settings pane, 323

Advanced Sharing, 205
  configuring for folders or drives, 206–208
  enabling, 205–206
Advanced Sharing Settings screen, 299
advanced startup tools, 398–400
Advanced tab, Printer Properties dialog box, 117–119
Advanced TCP/IP Settings dialog box, 76
Airplane mode, 71–72, 242
ALAC (Apple Lossless Audio Coding), 290
Always on Top command, Task Manager, 263
annotating web pages with Web Note, 318–319
answering calls in Skype, 365
App History tab, Task Manager (More Details view), 265
Apple Lossless Audio Coding (ALAC), 290
Apply Networking Changes dialog box, 423
apps, 245
  activating, 256
  adding to lock screen, 136–137
  AutoRuns for Windows app, 230
  choosing where to install, 246
  closing with Task Manager, 261–262
  Compatibility mode, 257–260
  default apps, 272
    changing, 278
    choosing, 274–276
    opening Default Apps pane (Settings app), 273
  disabling, 384
  Disk Management app, 406
  downloading, pausing, 249
  getting from Windows Store, 246–247
  installing
    from distribution files, 254–255
    from optical discs, 252–254

from Windows Store, 249–250
settings for, 255–256
opening files in non-default apps, 276
power-hungry apps, avoiding, 242
purchasing, 249
Registry Editor, opening, 431
removing, 271–272
with Control Panel, 272
from Open With submenu, 278
from Open With submenu in File Explorer, 435–436
removing useless apps, 235–237
Skype. See Skype
Task Manager, examining, 264–266
troubleshooting, 248–249
updates, non-Window Store apps, 260
Windows Store
My Library feature, 250
updates, 250–251
Apps and Games, This PC screen, 172
Apps & Features screen, Settings app, 271
archiving messages, Mail app, 346
arranging windows
manually, 57
Snap Assist feature, 56–57
Snap feature, 56–57
with keyboard shortcuts, 58
As Items Arrive setting, 348-349
Assigned Access, 199–200
audio encoders, 290
audio formats, 290
Audio Settings, Skype, 362
Automatically Connect settings, 15
automatic login, 133–135
automatic metrics, 77
automatic replies, sending, 353
Auto-Open Next Item, 351
AutoRuns for Windows app, 230
avoiding power-hungry apps, 242

B

background pictures, Mail app, 351
backing up
files, File History, 378
Registry, 433–434
Backup Options screen, 381
Backup pane, Settings app, 379
Based on My Usage setting, 349
battery life, 241
extending, 237
Battery Saver, 237
behaviors of taskbars, configuring, 126–128
beta drivers, 243
Better Performance option button, 103
biometrics, 184
BitLocker Drive Encryption Service, 223
blank pages, Microsoft Edge, 323
Blocked Contacts, Skype, 364
blocking popups, Microsoft Edge, 323
Bluetooth, turning off, 242
Bluetooth Support Service, 223
boosting performance by turning off eye candy, 214–216
bridging network connections, 82–83
Browser and Protection section, Customize Settings screen, 14
browsers, Microsoft Edge. See Microsoft Edge
browsing
apps, 246–247
favorites, Microsoft Edge, 315–316
InPrivate browsing, Microsoft Edge, 310
web pages, Page Prediction feature, 314
browsing data, clearing (Microsoft Edge), 323, 327–329
browsing history, clearing, 327
buttons
adding to Quick Access Toolbar, 144–145

Close button, 147

Help button, 147

mouse, 34

Open Command Prompt button, 146

Open New Window button, 146

Open Windows PowerShell button, 147

Preview Pane button, 149

Buttons tab, Mouse Properties dialog box, 34

C

CAB files, 161

cached data, clearing, 328

calibrating color on displays, 108

Call Forwarding, Skype, 366

Call menu, Skype, 359

calls

answering in Skype, 365

emergency calls, Skype, 366

Call Settings, Skype, 365–366

Caret Browsing feature, 324, 352

Microsoft Edge, 315–316

categories, choosing for Start menu, 122–123

cellular connections, web browsing, 14

Certificate Propagation, 223

Change permission, 208

changing

default apps, 278

existing acounts to administrator accounts, 188–189

firmware settings, 403

Startup settings, 401–402

channels, wireless networks, 87

check boxes, 160

checking free space, 231–232

checkpoints, virtual machines, 429-430

children, parental controls, 202

Choose What to Do with This Disc dialog box, 254

Choose Which Folders Appear on Start, 123

choosing

default apps, 274–276

drives for custom installation, 7–10

partitions for custom installation, 7–10

sync settings, Mail app, 348–350

Clear Browsing Data pane, 327–328

clearing browsing data, Microsoft Edge, 323, 327–329

ClearType, 108

Click Items as Follows, 154

ClickLock, 34

Clock icon, 132

Close button, 147

closing

Accounts screen, 343

apps with Task Manager, 261–262

desktops, 112

tabs, 314

windows

with command buttons, 55

with keyboard shortcuts, 58

Color Management tab, Printer Properties dialog box, 119

colors

calibrating on displays, 108

Start menu, customizing, 124

command buttons

closing windows, 55

sizing windows, 55–56

command prompt, opening File menu (File Explorer), 146

communicating with Skype, 359–360

Compatibility mode

apps, 257–260

configuring, 258

settings, 257–260

compatibility permissions, clearing, 329

compression, 102

Computer Management window, 225

configuring

advanced settings, Microsoft Edge, 323–324

Compatibility mode, 258

Cortana, 25–27

DEP, 221

displays, 105

external drives, 102–103

general settings, Microsoft Edge, 321–323

IP settings, 72–75

advanced settings, 75–78

keyboards, 43–44

keyboard shortcuts, Hotkeys screen, 369–370

language and keyboard layout, 46–47

libraries, File Explorer, 168–169

mouse, 32–36

network settings, 62

paging file, 217–221

pen and touch input, 42–43

printers, 114–115

privacy and service settings, Microsoft Edge, 325–327

Recycle Bin, 138–139

search options, 161

Skype, 360

Accessibility, 370

Advanced Settings, 368

Audio Settings, 362

Blocked Contacts, 364

Call Forwarding, 366

Call Settings, 365–366

Connections, 369

General Settings, 360–361

IM Appearance, 367

IM Settings, 367

Notification Settings, 364

Options dialog box, 360–361

Privacy Settings, 363

saving changes, 371

Skype WiFi, 363

Sounds screen, 362

turning off automatic updates, 368

Video Settings, 362

Voice Messages, 366–367

System Restore, 387–388

taskbar behaviors, 126–128

Trust Center, 353

typing settings, 44–46

User Account Control, 196–197

Windows 10, 10–12

Windows Media Player to rip CDs, 291–293

Windows Update, 374–376

Confirm Value Delete dialog box, 436

connecting

computers to TVs, 308

displays, 105

to hidden wireless networks, 69

to hotspots, 15

local accounts to Microsoft accounts, 182–184

local printers, 113

network printers, 113–114

to networks, 15

with WPS (Wi-Fi Protected Setup), 66

through proxy servers, 78–81

via VPN, 90–91

wired networks, 62

wireless networks, 63

that broadcast names, 64–66

Connecting to a Service dialog box, 339

connections

Skype, 369

VPN, setting up, 88–90

Connectivity and Error Reporting section, Customize Settings screen, 15

Contacts menu, Skype, 358

Content pane, Windows Media Player, 286

Content view, 151

Control Panel

   apps, removing, 272

   Display screen, 110

   Set Default Programs screen, 275

Conversation menu, Skype, 358

cookies

   clearing, 327

   Microsoft Edge, 325-326

copying text, Microsoft Edge, 315–316

Cortana, 17, 25

   configuring, 25–27

   Microsoft Edge, 325

   searching with, 27

CPU-Z, 212-213

Create an Account for This PC screen, 17–19

custom installation

   choosing drives and partitions for, 7–10

   versus upgrades, 6–7

Customize Media Streaming Settings dialog box, 301

Customize Settings screen, 12

   Browser and Protection section, 14

   Connectivity and Error Reporting section, 15

   Location section, 13–14

   Personalization section, 13

customizing

   File Explorer, 148

     adjusting folder and search options, 152

     layout, 149

     layout of items, 150–151

     Quick Access view, 150

     showing/hiding items, 152

     sorting/grouping items, 151–152

     view options, 155–161

   Start menu, 122–125

     choosing categories of items to display, 122–123

     colors, 124

   taskbar, 125

     moving, 126

     resizing, 126

   taskbars

     adding apps you need most, 128

     choosing which icons appear in notification area, 130–133

     configuring behavior, 126–128

     toolbars, 128–129

   views, Mail app, 351–352

   Windows 10, 13

D

Data Execution Prevention (DEP), controlling, 221–222

Data Execution Prevention tab, Performance Options dialog box, 222

default apps, 272

   changing, 278

   choosing, 274–276

   opening Default Apps pane (Settings app), 273

default gateways, 76

default libraries

   File Explorer, 164

   restoring, 169

default save location, libraries (File Explorer), 167

default settings, 10–12

Defer Upgrades feature, 376

defragmenting, 231-232

Delete command, 137

delete confirmation, 139

deleting

history items, Microsoft Edge, 317

messages, Mail app, 346

partitions, 414

storage spaces, 180

typed notes, Web Note, 319

virtual machines, 430

DEP (Data Execution Prevention), 221

Desktop, This PC screen, 172

desktops

closing, 112

virtual desktops, 111–112

Desktop toolbar, 129

Details pane, 149

Details tab, Task Manager (More Details view), 266, 269

Details view, 151

devices, whitelisting on Wi-Fi networks, 70–71

Device Settings tab, Printer Properties dialog box, 119

Devices screen, Typing pane, 45

DHCP (Dynamic Host Configuration Protocol), 62

disabling

apps, 384

recent app switching, 197–199

services, 223–224

disconnecting

user's sessions, 268

from wired networks, 63

disconnecting from wireless networks, 70

Disk Management app, 406

Disk Management window, 407-408

display adapter properties, 109

Display Color Calibration Wizard, 108-109

displaying

file icons on thumbnails, 156

file size information, 156

full paths, 157

Storage pane, 170

Display pane, opening in Settings app, 105

displays, 104

advanced display settings, 107–110

ClearType, 108

color, calibrating, 108

configuring, 105

connecting, 105

multiple displays, 106-107

orientations, 106

screen refresh rate, 110

settings, 106–107

sizing text, 109

Display screen, Control Panel, 110

Display tab, Tablet PC Settings dialog box, 42

distractions, removing from Reading mode (Microsoft Edge), 315

distribution files, installing apps, 254–255

DNS (domain name system), 62

DNS names, 78

DNS servers, 77

DNS suffixes, 78

Documents, This PC screen, 172

domain accounts, 183

Do Not Track Requests, Microsoft Edge, 325

double-click speed, mouse, 34

Double-Tap Settings dialog box, 41

download history, clearing, 328

downloading

apps, pausing, 249

content, frequency of, 348–349

Downloads, reclaiming space, 174

drive letters
    changing for volumes, 415
    showing, 159
driver software, printers, 113
drives
    choosing for custom installation, 7–10
    external drives, 99
        configuring, 102–103
        ejecting, 104
        formatting, 100–102
    hiding, 209
    mapping to network folders, 91–94
    optimizing, 233–234
        settings for, 234–235
dual-booting Windows with another
    operating system, 416–419
DVD drives, restoring Windows, 401
DVDs
    booting from, 6
    watching, 307
Dynamic Host Configuration Protocol
    (DHCP), 62
dynamic volumes, 409

E

Edit DWORD dialog box, 228
editing Registry, 430-431
EFS (Encrypting File System), 223
ejecting external drives, 104
email, 331
    Mail app. See Mail app
email accounts
    opening, Mail app, 348
    removing, Mail app, 351
    setting up, 332–333
        Exchange accounts, 334–338
        Google accounts, 339–340
        iCloud accounts, 340
        IMAP accounts, 341–343

        Outlook.com accounts, 334
        POP3 accounts, 341–343
        Yahoo! Mail accounts, 340
email signatures, 353
emergency calls, Skype, 366
Emoticon button, 53
empty drives, hiding, 157
End Process Tree command, 269
End Task command, Task Manager,
    263, 269
Every 15 Minutes setting, 348
examining partitions, 406–409
Exchange, 341
Exchange accounts, setting up, 334–338
exclamation points, wireless networks, 64
existing music files, adding to Windows
    Media Player, 287–289
Export Registry File dialog box, 434
express settings, 11
extended partitions, 407
extending
    battery life, 237
    partitions, 413
extensions, hiding, 157
external drives, 99
    configuring, 102–103
    ejecting, 104
    formatting, 100–102
external USB drives, powering, 294–295
Extra Large Icons view, 150
eye candy, turning off to boost perfor-
    mance, 214–216

F

Failed Redundancy status, 409
failed status, volumes, 409
family members, creating accounts for, 188
FAT32 file system, 101

favorites, browsing (Microsoft Edge),
315–316
Favorites bar, 315
Fax service, 223
features of Start menu, 30
File Explorer, 143
  customizing, 148
    *adjusting folder and search
      options, 152*
    layout, 149
    layout of items, 150–151
    Quick Access view, 150
    showing/hiding items, 152
    sorting/grouping items, 151–152
    view options, 155–161
  File menu, 146–147
  finding files/folders, 162–163
  folders, 163
  libraries, 163
    configuring, 168–169
    creating new, 165
    default libraries, 164
    default libraries, restoring, 169
    default save location, 167
    folders, 166–167
    public save location, 167
  mapping network drives, 93
  opening, 144
  Quick Access Toolbar, adding buttons,
    144–145
  removing apps from Open With
    submenu, 435–436
  Ribbon
    navigating, 147–148
    Share tab, 148
    View tab, 148
  search options, configuring, 161

File History, 379
  backing up files, 378
  enabling, 379–381
  restoring files, 381–382
file icons, displaying on thumbnails, 156
file management. *See* File Explorer
File menu, File Explorer, 146–147
files
  accessing in homegroups, 204
  CAB files, 161
  finding, File Explorer, 162–163
  hidden files, 157
  NTFS files, showing in color, 159
  protected operating system files, 159
  reserved files, 171
  restoring, File History, 381–382
  system files, 171
  ZIP, 161
File Sharing dialog box, 205
file size information, displaying, 156
file types, choosing (default apps), 274
finding files/folders, File Explorer, 162–163
firmware settings, changing, 403
flagging messages, Mail app, 346
Flash, 324
Flicks tab, Pen and Touch dialog box, 39-40
folder options, adjusting (File Explorer), 152
Folder Options dialog box, 147, 153
  Advanced Settings box, 156–157
  General tab, 153
  Privacy box, 154
  Search tab, 161
  View tab, 155
folders, 163
  File Explorer, 163
  finding, File Explorer, 162–163
  hidden folders, 157
  libraries, File Explorer, 166–167

folder windows
  launching, 158
  restoring, 159
forgetting wireless networks, 87
formatting external drives, 100–102
form data, clearing, 328
form entries, Microsoft Edge, 325
fragmentation, 231
Free Lossless Audio Code (FLAC), 291
free space, checking, 231–232
free trials, Groove Music, 303
frequency of downloading content, 348–349
Frequent Places, 147
Full Control permission, 208
full paths, displaying, 157
full screen permissions, clearing, 329

G

game boosters, 243
games, settings for, 242–243
general settings, configuring (Microsoft Edge), 321–323
General Settings, Skype, 360–361
General tab
  Folder Options dialog box, 153
  Printer Properties dialog box, 116
Get Going Fast screen, 10–11
Google accounts, setting up, 339–340
graphical effects, turning off, 214–216
Groove Music, 280, 302
  adding music, 304–305
  getting started, 302–304
  playing music, 306
  playlists, creating, 306–307
Groove Music Pass screen, 303
Group By, 151
grouping items, File Explorer, 151–152
Guest accounts, 187

H

handwriting panel, 53
Hard Disk category, 240
hardware
  displays, 104
    advanced display settings, 107–110
    configuring, 105
    connecting, 105
    settings, 106–107
  external drives, 99
    configuring, 102–103
    ejecting, 104
    formatting, 100–102
  printers, 112
    configuring, 114–115
    connecting local printers, 113
    connecting network printers, 113–114
    printer properties, 116–119
  setting preferences, 115
  virtual desktops, 111–112
hardware keyboards, inputting text, 50–51
Hardware tab, Mouse Properties dialog box, 36
HDMI, 308
Heads Up dialog box, 336
Help button, 147
Help menu, Skype, 359
Hibernate command, 24–25
hibernation mode, 22–24
hidden files, 157
hidden folders, 157
hidden wireless networks, 63
  adding via manually connect to Wireless Network Wizard, 67–69
  adding via Network fly-out, 67
  connecting to, 69
Hide Empty Drives feature, 157
Hide Modes That This Monitor Cannot Display, 111

hiding
  drives, 209
  empty drives, 157
  extensions for known file types, 157
  items, File Explorer, 152
  merge conflicts, 157
  protected operating system files, 158
  taskbars, 126
hints, passwords, 19
history items, deleting (Microsoft Edge), 317
HKEY_CLASSES_ROOT, 433
HKEY_CURRENT_CONFIG, 433
HKEY_CURRENT_USER, 433
HKEY_LOCAL_MACHINE, 433
HKEY_USERS, 433
homegroups
  accessing files, 204
  adding computers to, 202–203
  changing items your computer is sharing with, 204–205
  creating, 200–202
  removing computers from, 204
  sharing, 200
Home tab, Ribbon (File Explorer), 147–148
Hotkeys screen, keyboard shortcuts, 369-370
hotspots, connecting to, 15
How to Search box, 161
hybrid sleep, 23
Hyper-V
  creating
    virtual machines, 423–425
    virtual switches, 420–423
  enabling, 419
  installing operating systems on virtual machines, 425
  virtual machines, 428–430
Hyper-V Manager, 420

iCloud accounts, setting up, 340
icons
  Action Center icon, 133
  Clock icon, 132
  Input Indicator icon, 132
  Location indicator icon, 132
  Network icon, 96, 132
  Power icon, 132
  Volume icon, 132
identifying
  performance problems, Task Manager, 266
  resource hogs, Task Manager, 266–267
IMAP, 341
IMAP accounts, setting up, 341–343
IM Appearance, Skype, 367
importing photos/videos, Windows Media Player, 297
improving wireless speed and reliability, 84–87
IM Settings, Skype, 367
InPrivate browsing, 311
  Microsoft Edge, 310
input devices
  mouse, 32
    configuring, 32–36
  touchpads, 32
Input Indicator icon, 132
inputting text
  hardware keyboards, 50–51
  Speech Recognition, 54–55
  touch keyboards, 51–54
installing
  apps
    choosing where to install, 246
    from distribution files, 254–255

from optical discs, 252–254
from Windows Store, 249–250
settings for, 255–256
operating systems on virtual machines, 425–428
Skype, 354–355
updates, 377
Windows 10, 5–6
custom installation, choosing drives and partitions, 7–10
Installing Windows screen, 10-11
interfaces
Registry Editor, 431-432
Skype, navigating, 357
Windows Media Player, 285
Internet Connection Sharing, 94–95
IP addresses, 76
IP settings, configuring, 72–75
advanced settings, 75–78
IPv4 addresses, 73
IPv6 addresses, 74
issues
resolving with Action Center, 382–384
reviewing security and maintenance issues, 384
items
grouping, File Explorer, 151–152
hiding, File Explorer, 152
rearranging on taskbar, 128
removing
from Start menu, 124
from taskbar, 128
showing, File Explorer, 152
sorting, File Explorer, 151–152
iTunes, 295

J

Join a Homegroup Wizard, 203

K

keyboard layouts, adding, 47
keyboards
configuring, 43–44
opening Task Manager, 261
removing, 48
switching languages, 51
touch keyboards, 51–54
keyboard shortcuts
configuring, Hotkeys screen, 369–370
Microsoft Edge, 320–321
resizing, arranging, closing windows, 58

L

language and keyboard layout, configuring, 46–47
Language Options page, 47
languages, switching (keyboards), 51
Large Icons view, 151
Launch Folder Windows in a Separate Process, 158–159
launching
folder windows, 158
Mail app, 332
Store app, 246–247
layout, customizing (File Explorer), 151
LCD panels, native resolution, 107
length of PINs, 184
libraries, 163
File Explorer, 163
configuring, 168–169
creating new, 165
default libraries, 164
default libraries, restoring, 169
default save location, 167
folders, 166–167
public save location, 167
showing, Navigation pane, 160

Libraries folder, 164

Library Locations dialog box, 166

licenses
    media licenses, clearing, 329
    protected media licenses, 326

Links toolbar, 129

List pane, Windows Media Player, 286

List view, 151, 160

Live tiles, 30

local accounts, 182

location, 13
    of operating systems, installing, 419

Location indicator icon, 132

location of
    paging file, 218
    taskbars, 126

Location section, Customize Settings
    screen, 13–14

locking
    computers automatically, 192–193
    computers with startup passwords,
        189–191
    taskbars, 126
    Windows 10, 22

lock screen, 135
    adding apps to, 136–137
    setting pictures or slideshows, 135–136
    turning off, 133

Lock Screen pane, Settings app, 135

login, automatic login, 133–135

lossless compression, 289

lossy compression, 289

M

MAC (Media Access Control), 70

Mail app
    background pictures, 351
    customizing views, 351–352

email accounts. *See also* email accounts
    opening, 348
    removing, 351
    types, 332

email signatures, 353

launching, 332

Make My PC More Secure dialog
    box, 347

messages
    archiving, 346
    deleting, 346
    flagging, 346
    marking, 346
    moving, 347

navigating, 343–345

reading messages, 345–347

sync settings, choosing, 348–350

This PC screen, 172

Trust Center, configuring, 353

Mail apps, options for, 352–353

maintenance issues, reviewing, 384–385

Make It Yours screen, 16–17

Make My PC More Secure dialog box, 347

manually arranging windows, 57

Map Network Drive dialog box, 92

mapping drives to network folders, 91–94

Maps, This PC screen, 172

marking messages, Mail app, 346

Mark Item as Read, 351

maximum quality levels, music, 296

Media Access Control (MAC), 70

media libraries, sharing Windows Media
    Player, 297–301

media licenses, clearing, 329

Media Streaming Options screen, 299

Medium Icons view, 151

Meet Cortana screen, 17–18

memory, adding, 212–214

memory requirements, 212

menus

More Actions menu, 310

Start menu. *See* Start menu

merge conflicts, hiding, 157

messages, Mail app

archiving, 346

deleting, 346

flagging, 346

marking, 346

moving, 347

reading, 345–347

metrics, network adapters, 77

microphones, Speech Recognition, 48

Microsoft accounts, 183

Microsoft Edge, 309

blank pages, 323

browsing data, clearing, 327–329

browsing favorites, 315–316

Caret Browsing feature, 315–316, 324

configuring

advanced settings, 323–324

general settings, 321–323

privacy and service settings, 325–327

cookies, 325-326

copying text, Caret Browsing feature,
315–316

Cortana assistant, 325

deleting history items, 317

Do Not Track requests, 325

InPrivate browsing, 310

keyboard shortcuts, 320–321

More Actions menu, 310

navigating, 309–312

Page Prediction feature, 314, 326

passwords, 325

popups, blocking, 323

protected media licenses, 326

Reading List feature, 317

Reading mode, removing
distractions, 315

returning to page you viewed
earlier, 316

search suggestions, 325

Settings pane, 322

SmartScreen Filter, 326

tabs, 313–314

viewing pages, 312

web pages, annotating with Web Note,
318–319

windows, 313–314

Microsoft iSCSI Initiator Service, 223

Microsoft TCP/IP dialog box, 75

mirrored volumes, 409

mirror space, 175

missing taskbar icons, 130

More Actions menu, Microsoft Edge, 310

More Apps, 278

More Details view, Task Manager, 264–266

Details tab, 269

Services tab, 270

Users tab, 268

mouse, 32

buttons, 34

ClickLock, 34

configuring, 32–36

double-click speed, 34

scrolling, 32–33

mouse clicks, 154

Mouse Properties dialog box, 33

Buttons tab, 34

Hardware tab, 36

Pointer Options tab, 34–36

Pointers tab, 34

Wheel tab, 36

Mouse & Touchpad pane, 32

Mouse section, 32

Touchpad area, 37–38

moving
   messages, Mail app, 347
   taskbar, 126
MP3, 290
multi-booting Windows with other operating systems, 416–419
multiple displays, 106-107
multiple partitions, 407
music
   adding
      to Groove Music, 304–305
      to Windows Media Player, 286–295
   Groove Music. *See* Groove Music
   maximum quality levels, 296
   playing
      with Groove Music, 306
      Windows Media Player, 295
   syncing with phones or tablets, 295
   Windows Media Player. *See* Windows Media Player
Music, This PC screen, 172
Music folder, OneDrive, 287
Music library, adding folders to (Windows Media Player), 287-288
My Library feature, Windows Store, 250

N

NAS (network attached storage), 301
native resolution, 107
navigating
   Mail app, 343–345
   Microsoft Edge, 309–312
   Ribbon, File Explorer, 147–148
   Skype, 357–359
   Windows Media Player, 284–286
Navigation pane, 149, 160
   Windows Media Player, 285-286
Navigation tab, Taskbar and Start Menu Properties, 128

Netlogon, 223
network adapters, metrics, 77
Network and Sharing Center window, 96, 298
network attached storage (NAS), 301
Network Bridge dialog box, 83
network connections, 71
   Airplane mode, 71–72
   bridging, 82–83
   connecting to proxy servers, 79
   prioritizing, 81–82
Network Connections window, 72
Network Discovery, 20-21
network drives, 92
Network fly-out, adding hidden wireless networks, 67
network folders, mapping drives to, 91–94
Network icon, 96, 132
network problems, troubleshooting, 96–98
networks
   connecting to, 15
      with WPS (Wi-Fi Protected Setup), 66
   hidden wireless networks. *See* hidden wireless networks
   SSIDs (service set identifiers), 63
   Wi-Fi networks, whitelisting devices, 70–71
   wired networks
      connecting to, 62
      disconnecting from, 63
   wireless networks
      connecting to, 63
      connecting to wireless network that broadcasts its name, 64–66
      disconnecting from, 70
      forgetting, 87
      passwords, 65
      reconnecting to, 70

network settings, configuring, 62

Networks pane, 20

New Apps Will Save To button, 175

New Simple Volume Wizard, 411-412

New Virtual Machine Wizard, 424

non-administrator accounts, 186

non-default apps, opening files, 276

non-family members, creating accounts for, 188

non-Window Store apps, updates, 260

notes, annotating web pages with Web Note, 319

notification area, taskbars, 127

    choosing which icons appear, 130–133

notifications, 139–141

    configuring how long to display, 141

Notifications & Actions pane

    opening, 140

    Settings app, 131

Notification Settings, Skype, 364-365

Notifications list, configuring settings, 140

NTFS files, showing in color, 159

O

Offline Files, 223

OneDrive

    Music folder, 287

    This PC screen, 172

Open Command Prompt button, 146-147

Open Each Folder in the Same Window, 154

Open File Location command, Task Manager, 263

opening

    command prompt, File menu (File Explorer), 146

    Default Apps pane, 273

    Display pane in Settings app, 105

    email accounts, Mail app, 348

    File Explorer, 144

    files in non-default apps, 276

    Notifications & Actions pane, 140

    Optimize Drives window, 231–232

    Pen and Touch dialog box, 38

    Region & Language pane, 46

    Start menu, 30

    Tablet PC Settings dialog box, 42

    Task Manager, 261

    windows, File menu (File Explorer), 146

    Windows PowerShell, File menu (File Explorer), 147

    Your Family pane, Settings app, 187

Open New Window button, 146

Open Windows PowerShell button, 147

Open With submenu, 277

    removing apps, 278, 435

operating systems

    dual-booting Windows, 416–419

    Hyper-V, enabling, 419

    installing on virtual machines, 425–428

    location of when installing, 419

    running multiple, 416

optical discs, installing apps, 252–254

Optimize Drives dialog box, 234-235

Optimize Drives window, 233

    opening, 231–232

optimizing, 231

    drives, 233–234

        settings for, 234–235

Options dialog box, Skype, 360–361

options for Mail app, 352–353

Organize button, Windows Media Player, 284

orientation of displays, 106

Other, This PC screen, 173

Other Users, This PC screen, 172

Outlook.com accounts, setting up, 334

P

Page Prediction, 14-15

Page Prediction feature, Microsoft Edge, 314, 326

paging file
    configuring, 217–221
    location of, 218

Panes group, layout (File Explorer), 149

parental controls, 202

parental guards, 202

parity space, 176

parity volumes, 409

partitions, 405
    choosing for custom installation, 7–10
    creating new, 410–413
    defined, 8
    deleting, 414
    examining on computer's drive, 406–409
    extended partitions, 407
    extending, 413
    multiple partitions, 407
    shrinking, 409–410

passwords, 184
    clearing, 328
    creating, 19
    hints, 19
    Microsoft Edge, 325
    picture passwords, 184
    startup passwords, 189–191
    wireless networks, 65

Path bar, Windows Media Player, 284

paths, displaying full paths, 157

pausing
    download of apps, 249
    virtual machines, 429

Peek feature, 127

Pen and Touch dialog box
    Flicks tab, 39-40
    opening, 38
    Pen Options tab, 38
    Touch tab, 41

pen and touch input, configuring, 42–43

pen and touch settings, 38–41

Pen Options tab, Pen and Touch dialog box, 38

performance
    apps, removing useless apps, 235–237
    battery life, extending, 237
    boosting by turning off eye candy, 214–216
    configuring external drives, 102–103
    Data Execution Prevention (DEP), controlling, 221–222
    defragmenting, 231
    games, settings for, 242–243
    improving wireless speed and reliability, 84–87
    memory, adding, 212–214
    optimizing drives, 233–234
    paging file, configuring, 217–221
    reducing startup items, 229–230
    stopping unnecessary services, 222–227
    wireless speed, 86

Performance Options dialog box, 215
    Data Execution Prevention tab, 222
    visual effects, 216

performance problems, identifying (Task Manager), 266

Performance tab, Task Manager (More Details view), 264

permissions, 208
    clearing, 329

Permissions dialog box, 207

Personalization and Location settings, 12

Personalization section, Customize Settings screen, 13

phones, syncing music, 295

photos, importing (Windows Media Player), 297

picture passwords, 184

pictures, lock screen, 135–136

Pictures, This PC screen, 172

PIN, 184

plans for power use, 237–240

Playback controls, Windows Media Player, 286

player usage data, sending to Microsoft, 283

playing music
    with Groove Music, 306
    Windows Media Player, 295

playlists, creating in Groove Music, 306–307

Pointer Options tab, Mouse Properties dialog box, 34–36

Pointers tab, Mouse Properties dialog box, 34

POP3, 341–343

pop-up descriptions, showing, 159

pop-up exceptions, clearing, 329

pop-ups, blocking (Microsoft Edge), 323

Ports tab, Printer Properties dialog box, 117

power, saving by changing settings, 240–241

power-hungry apps, avoiding, 242

Power icon, 132

powering external USB drives, 294–295

Power menu, Hibernate command, 24–25

Power Options dialog box, saving changes, 240–241

Power Saver category, 240

power-saving states, sleep and hibernation, 23–24

Power & Sleep controls, 238

power use
    Airplane mode, 242
    setting plans for, 237–240

preferences for printing, 115

Prefetch, turning off, 227–229

preloading, 14

preview handlers, showing Preview pane, 159

Preview pane, showing preview handlers, 159

Preview Pane button, 149

Previous Pages setting, 323

Previous Version of Windows area, reclaiming space, 174

printer properties, 116–119

Printer Properties dialog box, 115
    Advanced tab, 117–119
    Color Management tab, 119
    Device Settings tab, 119
    General tab, 116
    Ports tab, 117
    Security tab, 119
    Sharing tab, 117

printers, 112
    configuring, 114–115
    connecting local printers, 113
    connecting network printers, 113–114
    driver software, 113
    printer properties, 116–119
    setting preferences, 115

print resolution, 115

Print Spooler, 223

prioritizing network connections, 81–82

privacy and service settings, configuring (Microsoft Edge), 325–327

Privacy box, Folder Options dialog box, 154

privacy settings, Windows Media Player, 280–283

Privacy Settings, Skype, 363

problems

network problems, troubleshooting, 96–98

resolving with Action Center, 382–384

processes, Task Manager, 264–266

Processes tab, Task Manager (More Details view), 264

profile pictures, setting for accounts, 182

Program Compatibility Troubleshooter feature, 258

properties

display adapter properties, 109

printer properties, 116–119

Properties command, Task Manager, 264

Properties dialog box, 74, 110, 169

Sharing tab, 206

Tools tab, 233

protected media licenses, 326

protected operating system files, 159

hiding, 158

protocols, choosing (default apps), 274

proxy exceptions, 81

Proxy pane, 80

proxy servers, connecting through, 78–81

public save location, libraries (File Explorer), 167

purchasing apps, 249

Q

quality, maximum quality levels (music), 296

queries, User Account Control, 194–195

Quick Access Toolbar, adding buttons to, 144–145

Quick Access view, customizing (File Explorer), 150

R

RAM (random access memory), 212

reading messages, Mail app, 345–347

Reading List feature, Microsoft Edge, 317

removing pages from, 318

Reading mode, Microsoft Edge (removing distractions), 315

Reading pane, 351

rearranging items on taskbar, 128

recent app switching, disabling, 197–199

reclaiming space, 173–174

Recognition, 49

reconnecting to wireless networks, 70

Recovery pane, Settings app, 396

recovery tools, 395

accessing, 395–396

going back to an earlier build of Windows, 397–398

resetting PCs, 396

Recycle Bin, 124, 137–139

configuring, 138–139

reclaiming space, 174

reducing startup items, 229–230

regedit.exe, 431

Region & Language pane, opening, 46

Registry

backing up, 433–434

editing, 430-431

restoring, 434–435

root keys, 432–433

Registry cleaners, 243

Registry Editor

interfaces, 431-432

opening, 431

removing apps from Open With submenu, 435

Re-Image Your Computer dialog box, 401

Remote Desktop Configuration, 224
Remote Desktop Services, 224
Remote Desktop Services UserMode Port
    Redirector, 224
Remote Registry, 224
Remove screen, 253
removing
    apps, 271–272
        from Open With submenu, 278,
        435-436
        with Control Panel, 272
    computers from homegroups, 204
    devices from Windows Store
        account, 252
    distractions from Reading mode
        (Microsoft Edge), 315
    email accounts, Mail app, 351
    items
        from Start menu, 124
        from taskbar, 128
    keyboards, 48
    pages from Reading List, 318
    Temporary Files, 173–174
    useless apps, 235–237
repairing Windows startup files, 402
Repeat button, Windows Media Player, 286
replies, automatic replies, 353
requirements for memory, 212
reserved files, 171
resetting PCs, recovery tools, 396
resizing
    Start menu, 124
    taskbar, 126
    tiles, 124
    windows
        with command buttons, 55–56
        with keyboard shortcuts, 58
resolution
    native resolution, 107
    print resolution, 115

resolving issues, Action Center, 382–384
resource hogs, identifying (Task Manager),
    266–267
restarting Windows 10, 22
restoring
    computers, going back to earlier restore
        points with System Restore, 400
    default libraries, 169
    files, File History, 381–382
    folder windows, 159
    Registry, 434–435
    Windows
        from system images, 400–401
        to system restore points, 389–392
        from USB drives or DVD drives, 401
reverting to earlier versions of
    Windows, 397
reviewing
    maintenance issues, 384–385
    security and maintenance issues,
        384–385
Ribbon, File Explorer, 147-148
Rip CD Automatically feature, 293
ripping CDs, Windows Media Player,
    291–294
    formats for, 289–291
root keys, Registry, 432–433
Run New Task command, Task
    Manager, 263
running multiple operating systems, 416

S

Safely Remove Hardware and Eject Media
    feature, 103-104
saved website data, clearing, 327
Save Locations list, 174
saving
    controlling where Windows saves items,
        174–175
    notes, Web Note, 319

power by changing settings, 240–241

Skype, configurations, 371

thumbnail previews, 156

virtual machine states, 429

scheduled optimization, choosing settings for, 234–235

scheduling updates, 377

screen-off timeout, 238

screen refresh rate, 110

Screen Saver Settings dialog box, 192

scrolling, mouse, 32–33

SCSI Controller pane, 426

Search box, Windows Media Player, 286

searching with Cortana, 27

Search Online command, Task Manager, 264

search options

adjusting, File Explorer, 152

configuring, 161

search suggestions, Microsoft Edge, 325

Search tab, Folder Options dialog box, 161

Secondary Logon, 224

Secure Sign-In feature, 189, 193–194

securing accounts, 184–186

Securing the Windows Account Database dialog box, 190

security, 189

Assigned Access, 199–200

locking computers with startup passwords, 189–191

recent app switching, 197–199

reviewing issues, 384

Secure Sign-In feature, 193–194

setting computers to lock automatically, 192–193

User Account Control, 194

configuring, 196–197

queries, 194–195

Security and Maintenance screen, 384-385

Security settings, 385

Security tab, Printer Properties dialog box, 119

Select Privacy Options dialog box, 282

Select the Default Music and Video Player dialog box, 284

Select Users or Groups dialog box, 208

sending automatic replies, 353

separator pages, 119

servers, proxy servers (connecting through), 78–81

services

disabling, 223–224

stopping, 225–227

Services console, Standard tab, 226

service set identifiers (SSIDs), 63

Services tab, Task Manager (More Details view), 266, 270

Set Default Programs screen, Control Panel, 75

Set Priority, 269

settings

advanced display settings, 107–110

advanced power settings, 240

As Items Arrive setting, 348-349

Automatically Connect settings, 15

Based on My Usage setting, 349

Compatibility mode, 257–260

default settings, 10–12

displays, 106–107

Every 15 Minutes setting, 348

firmware settings, changing, 403

for games, 242–243

for installing apps, 255–256

Notifications list, 140

pen and touch settings, 38–41

Personalization and Location settings, 12

Previous Pages setting, 323

privacy settings, Windows Media Player, 280

Security settings, 385

Startup settings, 401

Store app, 251–252

sync settings, Mail app, 348–350

for touchpads, 37

Typing settings, 44

Windows Update, 374–376

from virtual machines, 429

Settings app

    Apps & Features screen, 271

    Backup pane, 379

    Default Apps pane, 273

    Lock Screen pane, 135

    Notifications & Actions pane, 131

    opening Display pane, 105

    Recovery pane, 396

    Region & Language pane, 46

    Sign-In options screen, 185

    Windows Update pane, 374

    Your Family pane, 187

Settings pane, 321

    Microsoft Edge, 322

setting up

    email accounts, 332–333

        Exchange accounts, 334–338

        Google accounts, 339–340

        iCloud accounts, 340

        IMAP accounts, 341–343

        Outlook.com accounts, 334

        POP3 accounts, 341–343

        Yahoo! Mail accounts, 340

    Skype, 356–357

    Speech Recognition, 48–50

Set Up a PIN screen, 17

Set Up Assigned Access screen, 199

Set Up Speech Recognition Wizard, 48

Share tab, Ribbon (File Explorer), 148

sharing, 200

    Advanced Sharing, 205

        configuring for folders or drives, 206–208

        enabling, 205–206

    computer's Internet connection, 94–95

    hiding drives, 209

    homegroups, 200

        accessing files, 204

        adding computers to, 202–203

        changing items your computer is sharing with, 204–205

        creating, 200–202

    media libraries, Windows Media Player, 297–301

    notes, Web Note, 319

Sharing tab

    Printer Properties dialog box, 117

    Properties dialog box, 206

Sharing Wizard, 160

shortcut menu, Start menu, 125

Show Below the Ribbon command, 145

showing

    drive letters, 159

    items, File Explorer, 152

    libraries, Navigation pane, 160

    NTFS files in color, 159

    pop-up descriptions, 159

    preview handlers, Preview pane, 159

    status bar, 160

Show Only On commands, 107

shrinking partitions, 409–410

Shuffle button, Windows Media Player, 286

shutting down

    virtual machines, 429

    your computer, 28

signatures (email), 353

signing in/out

    to Skype, 355

    Windows 10, 21

Sign-In options screen, Settings app, 185
simple space, 175
sizing
    Start menu, 31, 124
    text, 109
    tiles, 124
    windows
        with command buttons, 55–56
        with keyboard shortcuts, 58
Skype, 354
    accounts, creating, 356
    communicating via, 359–360
    configuring, 360
        Accessibility, 370
        Advanced Settings, 368
        Audio Settings, 362
        Blocked Contacts, 364
        Call Forwarding, 366
        Call Settings, 365–366
        Connections, 369
        General Settings, 360–361
        IM Appearance, 367
        IM Settings, 367
        Notification Settings, 364
        Options dialog box, 360–361
        Privacy Settings, 363
        saving changes, 371
        Skype WiFi, 363
        Sounds screen, 362
        turning off automatic updates, 368
        Video Settings, 362
        Voice Messages, 366–367
    emergency calls, 366
    getting the app, 354–355
    initial setup, 356–357
    installing, 354–355
    navigating, 357–359
    signing into, 355

Skype menu, 358
Skype WiFi, 363
sleep, 241
sleep mode, 22–24
sleep timeout, 238
slideshows, lock screen, 135–136
Small Icons view, 151
Smart Card, 224
Smart Card Device Enumeration
   Service, 224
Smart Card Removal Policy, 224
SmartScreen Filter, Microsoft Edge, 326
SmartScreen Online Services, 14
Smart Switch, 295
SMTP, 341
Snap Assist feature, arranging windows,
   56–57
Snap feature, arranging windows, 56–57
solid-state-device (SSD), 227
Something Went Wrong dialog box, 337
Sort By, 151
sorting items, File Explorer, 151–152
Sounds screen, Skype, 362
space, reclaiming, 173–174
Speech Recognition
   inputting text, 54–55
   setting up, 48–50
Speech Recognition screen, displaying, 48
speed, wireless speeds, 86
SSD (solid-state-device), 227
SSIDs (service set identifiers), 63, 68
Standard tab, Services console, 226
starting virtual machines, 429
Start menu, 29
   customizing, 122–125
      choosing categories of items to display,
        122–123
      colors, 124

features of, 30

opening, 30

resizing, 124

sizing, 31

startup files, repairing, 402

startup items, reducing, 229–230

Startup Key dialog box, 191

Startup Password dialog box, 190

startup passwords, 189–191

Startup settings, changing, 401–402

Startup Settings screen, 402

Startup tab, Task Manager, 229–230, 384

More Details view, 265

status bar, showing, 160

stopping

services, 225–227

unnecessary services, 222–227

storage

controlling where Windows saves items, 174–175

removing Temporary Files, 173–174

see what's taking up space on your computer, 170–174

Storage pane, opening, 170

storage spaces, 179

changing existing, 180

creating, 176–179

deleting, 180

Storage Spaces feature, 175

Storage pane, displaying, 170

storage spaces, 175–176, 179

changing existing, 180

creating, 176–179

deleting, 180

mirror space, 175

parity space, 176

simple space, 175

Storage Spaces feature, 143, 175

Store app

launching, 246–247

settings for, 251–252

subnet masks, 74

Superfetch, turning off, 227

swipe actions, 352-353

switching

between desktops, 111

between windows, 58–59

languages, keyboards, 51

Switch To command, Task Manager, 262

Switch to Now Playing button, Windows Media Player, 286

syncing music with phones or tablets, 295

sync settings, choosing (Mail app), 348–350

Sync Settings dialog box, 348

Sync Settings pane, 349

System and Reserved, This PC screen, 171

system files, 171

system images, restoring Windows, 400–401

System Properties dialog box, System Protection tab, 386–387

System Protection tab, System Properties dialog box, 386–387

System Restore, 386

configuring, 387–388

going back to an earlier restore point, 400

undoing operations, 393–394

System Restore dialog box, 391

system restore points

creating, 386

manually, 388–389

restoring Windows to, 389–392

T

Tablet PC Settings dialog box, 42
tablets, syncing music, 295
tabs
    closing, 314
    Microsoft Edge, 313–314
Taskbar and Start Menu Properties,
    Navigation tab, 128
taskbars
    configuring behaviors, 126–128
    customizing, 125
        adding apps you need most, 128
        choosing which icons appear in
            notification area, 130–133
        configuring behavior, 126–128
        moving, 126
        resizing, 126
        toolbars, 128–129
    hiding, 126
    location of, 126
    locking, 126
    missing taskbar icons, 130
    moving, 126
    notification area, 127
    resizing, 126
    toolbars, creating new, 129
Task Manager
    Always on Top command, 263
    closing apps, 261–262
    End Task command, 263
    examining apps and processes, 264–266
    identifying resource hogs, 266–267
    More Details view, 264–266
        Details tab, 269
        Services tab, 270
        Users tab, 268
    Open File Location command, 263
    opening, 261

performance problems, identifying, 266
Properties command, 264
Run New Task command, 263
Search Online command, 264
Startup tab, 229-230, 384
Switch To command, 262
Temporary Files
    removing, 173–174
    This PC screen, 173
text
    copying, Microsoft Edge, 315–316
    inputting
        hardware keyboards, 50–51
        Speech Recognition, 54–55
        touch keyboards, 51–54
    sizing, 109
third-party software, virtual machines, 430
This PC screen, 171
    Apps and Games, 172
    Desktop, 172
    Documents, 172
    Mail, 172
    Maps, 172
    Music, 172
    OneDrive, 172
    Other, 173
    Other Users, 172
    Pictures, 172
    System and Reserved, 171
    Temporary Files, 173
    Videos, 172
thumbnails, 156
tile groups, creating, 125
tiles
    sizing, 124
    turning on/off, 125
Tiles view, 151
toggling toolbars, 129

toolbars
  Address toolbar, 128
  creating new, 129
  Desktop toolbar, 129
  Links toolbar, 129
  taskbars, 128–129
  toggling, 129
tools
  advanced startup tools, 398–400
  recovery tools, 395
    accessing, 395–396
    going back to an earlier build of Windows, 397–398
    resetting PCs, 396
Tools menu, Skype, 359
Tools tab, Properties dialog box, 233
Touch Keyboard and Handwriting Panel Service, 224
touch keyboards, inputting text, 51–54
Touchpad area, Mouse & Touchpad pane, 37–38
touchpads, 32
Touch tab, Pen and Touch dialog box, 41
troubleshooting
  apps, 248–249
  missing taskbar icons, 130
  network problems, 96–98
  powering external USB drives, 294–295
Troubleshoot Problems feature, 97–98
Troubleshoot screen, 399
Trust Center, configuring, 353
turning off
  automatic updates, Skype, 368
  Bluetooth, 242
  eye candy to boost performance, 214–216
  lock screen, 133
  Prefetch, 227–229
  Superfetch, 227
  Wi-Fi, 242

turning on/off tiles, 125
TVs, connecting computers to, 308
Typing pane, Devices screen, 45
typing settings, configuring, 44–46

U

undoing System Restore operations, 393–394
unlock methods, 185–186
unnecessary services, stopping, 222–227
updates
  applying, 377
  installing, 377
  non-Window Store apps, 260
  scheduling, 377
  Windows Store, 250–251
  Windows Update, configuring, 374–376
upgrades versus custom installation, 6–7
uPnP, 369
usage rights, 282
USB 2.0, 100
USB 3.0, 100
USB drives
  booting Windows 10, 6
  restoring Windows, 401
useless apps, removing, 235–237
User Account Control, 194
  configuring, 196–197
  queries, 194–195
User Account Control Settings dialog box, 196
user accounts
  changing existing acounts to administrator accounts, 188–189
  connecting local accounts to Microsoft accounts, 182–184
  creating for others, 186–189
  profile pictures, setting, 182
  securing, 184–186

User Accounts dialog box, 134
user's sessions, disconnecting, 268
Users tab, Task Manager (More Details view), 265, 268

V

value entries, 432
videos, 307
Videos, This PC screen, 172
Video Settings, Skype, 362
viewing web pages in Microsoft Edge, 312
View menu, Skype, 359
view options, File Explorer, 155-161
View Options button, Windows Media Player, 285
views, customizing (Mail app), 351–352
View tab
    Folder Options dialog box, 155
    Ribbon, File Explorer, 148
VirtualBox, 430
virtual desktops, 111–112
virtual machines, 419
    checkpoints, 429-430
    creating with Hyper-V, 423–425
    deleting, 430
    Hyper-V, 428–430
    installing, operating systems, 425–428
    pausing, 429
    settings, changing, 429
    shutting down, 429
    starting, 429
    third-party software, 430
virtual machine states, saving, 429
Virtual Memory dialog box, 220
virtual private networking (VPN), 88
    connecting via, 90–91
    setting up connections, 88–90
virtual switches, creating with Hyper-V, 420–423

Virtual Switch Manager dialog box, 421-422
Virtual Switch Properties pane, 421
visual effects, Performance Options dialog box, 216
VLC, 307
VMware Workstation, 430
Voice Messages, Skype, 366–367
Volume icon, 132
volumes
    changing driver letters, 415
    dynamic volumes, 409
    failed status, 409
    mirrored volumes, 409
    parity volumes, 409
VPN (virtual private networking), 88
    connecting via, 90–91
    setting up connections, 88–90

W

watching DVDs and videos, 307
WAV (Waveform Audio File Format), 290
web browsing, cellular connections, 14
Web Note, annotating web pages, 318–319
Web Note toolbar, 318
web pages
    annotating with Web Note, Microsoft Edge, 318–319
    returning to page you viewed earlier, Microsoft Edge, 316
    viewing in Microsoft Edge, 312
Welcome to Groove screen, 303
Welcome to Windows Media Player dialog box, 281
Wheel tab, Mouse Properties dialog box, 36
whitelisting devices on Wi-Fi networks, 70–71
Who Owns This PC? screen, 15–16
Wi-Fi, turning off, 242

Wi-Fi analyzer app, 87
Wi-Fi networks, whitelisting devices, 70–71
Wi-Fi Protected Setup (WPS), 66
Wi-Fi Sense, 15, 88
Wi-Fi Status dialog box, 85
windows
  arranging
    with keyboard shortcuts, 58
    manually, 57
    Snap Assist feature, 56–57
    Snap feature, 56–57
  closing
    with command buttons, 55
    with keyboard shortcuts, 58
  Microsoft Edge, 313–314
  Network and Sharing Center window, 96
  Network Connections window, 72
  opening File menu (File Explorer), 146
  resizing
    with command buttons, 55–56
    with keyboard shortcuts, 58
  switching between, 58–59
Windows
  dual-booting with other operating
    systems, 416–419
  restoring
    from system images, 400–401
    to system restore points, 389–392
    from USB drives or DVD drives, 401
  reverting to earlier versions, 397
  startup files, repairing, 402
  Startup settings, changing, 401–402
Windows 10
  configuring, 10–12
  customizing, 13
  installing, 5–6
    custom installation, choosing drives
    and partitions, 7–10

locking, 22
restarting, 22
signing in/out, 21
upgrades versus custom installation,
  6–7
Windows Connect Now, 224
Windows Defender, 224
Windows Defender Network Inspection
  Service, 224
Windows DVD Player, 307
Windows Firewall, 224
Windows Hello, 184
Windows Internet Naming System
  (WINS), 76
Windows Media Audio, 289
Windows Media Audio Lossless, 290
Windows Media Audio Pro, 290
Windows Media Audio (Variable Bit
  Rate), 290
Windows Media Player, 279
  adding
    existing music files, 287–289
    music, 286–295
  configuring to rip CDs, 291–293
  Content pane, 286
  importing photos/videos, 297
  interfaces, 285
  List pane, 286
  media libraries, sharing, 297–301
  Music library, 287
  navigating, 284–286
  Navigation pane, 285-286
  Organize button, 284
  Path bar, 284
  Playback controls, 286
  playing music, 295
  privacy settings, 280–283
  Repeat button, 286
  ripping music from CDs, 293-294
    formats for, 289–291

Search box, 286

sharing media files via network attached storage, 301

Shuffle button, 286

Switch to Now Playing button, 286

syncing music with phones and tablets, 295–296

View Options button, 285

Windows PowerShell, opening File menu (File Explorer), 147

Windows Security dialog box, 93

Windows services, 223–224

Windows Setup, 10

Windows Store, 246

  accounts, removing devices from, 252

  getting apps, 246–247

  installing apps from, 249–250

  My Library feature, 250

  Store app. *See* Store app

  updates, 250–251

Windows Update, configuring, 374–376

Windows Update pane, 374

WINS (Windows Internet Naming System), 76

wired networks

  connecting to, 62

  disconnecting from, 63

wireless devices, Airplane mode, 71

Wireless Network Properties dialog box, 86

wireless networks

  channels, 87

  connecting to, 63-66

  disconnecting from, 70

  exclamation points, 64

  forgetting, 87

  passwords, 65

  reconnecting to, 70

Wireless Network Wizard, adding hidden wireless networks, 67–69

wireless speed

  improving, 84–87

  performance, 86

wizards

  Display Color Calibration Wizard, 108-109

  Join a Homegroup Wizard, 203

  New Simple Volume Wizard, 411-412

  New Virtual Machine Wizard, 424

  Set Up Speech Recognition Wizard, 48

  Sharing Wizard, 160

  Wireless Network Wizard, 67–69

WPS (Wi-Fi Protected Setup), 66

write caching, 102

X

Xbox Music. *See* Groove Music

Y

Yahoo! Mail accounts, setting up, 340

Your Family pane, Settings app, 187

Z

ZIP, 161

Zip files, installing apps, 254

Zune Music. *See* Groove Music

REGISTER THIS PRODUCT
SAVE 35%*
ON YOUR NEXT PURCHASE!

🖥 How to Register Your Product

- Go to quepublishing.com/register
- Sign in or create an account
- Enter the 10- or 13-digit ISBN that appears on the back cover of your product

🔓 Benefits of Registering

- Ability to download product updates
- Access to bonus chapters and workshop files
- A 35% coupon to be used on your next purchase – valid for 30 days
    To obtain your coupon, click on "Manage Codes" in the right column of your Account page
- Receive special offers on new editions and related Que products

Please note that the benefits for registering may vary by product. Benefits will be listed on your Account page under Registered Products.

We value and respect your privacy. Your email address will not be sold to any third party company.

* 35% discount code presented after product registration is valid on most print books, eBooks, and full-course videos sold on QuePublishing.com. Discount may not be combined with any other offer and is not redeemable for cash. Discount code expires after 30 days from the time of product registration. Offer subject to change.

quepublishing.com